VOLKSWAGEN TRANSPORTER

OWNER'S HANDBOOK
of Maintenance and Repair

COVERS ALL TRUCKS AND STATION WAGONS

1950-1979

By

David Vincent

and Prior Technical Editors

of Clymer Publications

We would like to thank Lee Price of Century Motor Sales, Alhambra, California, and Asher Lee of Aero Volkswagen, Inc., Inglewood, California, for their assistance in the preparation of this book.

I0264288

LOOK FOR THIS SIGN
WHEN NEEDING SERVICE

Published by

FLOYD CLYMER PUBLICATIONS
*World's Largest Publisher of Books Relating to Automobiles,
Motorcycles, Motor Racing, and Americana*
222 N. VIRGIL AVE., LOS ANGELES, CALIF. 90004

INTRODUCTION

The book you now hold in your hand, while unchanged from the original edition, was printed using the latest state of the art digital technology. If this is your first exposure to digital publishing, we hope that you are pleased with the results. Many more titles of interest to the classic automobile and motorcycle enthusiast, collector and restorer are available via our website at **www.VelocePress.com**.

TRADEMARKS

We recognize that some words, model names and designations, for example, mentioned herein are the property of the trademark holder. We use them for identification purposes only. This is not an official publication.

INFORMATION ON THE USE OF THIS PUBLICATION

This manual is a "must have" for owners interested in performing their own maintenance. It includes detailed repair and service data and comprehensive step-by-step instructions and illustrations on dismantling, overhauling, and re-assembly. Certain assemblies require the use of expensive special tools and although repair information may be included it is recommended that these repairs be performed by factory authorized service centers.

In today's information age we are constantly subject to changes in common practice, new technology, availability of improved materials and increased awareness of chemical toxicity. As such, it is advised that the user consult with an experienced professional prior to undertaking any procedure described herein. While every care has been taken to ensure correctness of information, it is obviously not possible to guarantee complete freedom from errors or omissions or to accept liability arising from such errors or omissions. Therefore, any individual that uses the information contained within, or elects to perform or participate in do-it-yourself repairs or modifications acknowledges that there is a risk factor involved and that the publisher or its associates cannot be held responsible for personal injury or property damage resulting from the use of the information or the outcome of such procedures.

It is important that the reader recognizes that any instructions may refer to either the right-hand or left-hand sides of the vehicle or the components and that the directions are followed carefully. One final word of advice, this publication is intended to be used as a reference guide, and when in doubt the reader should consult with a qualified technician.

CONTENTS

IDENTIFICATION	4
ENGINE FOREWORD	5
ENGINE REMOVAL-REFITTING	6
EARLY 1200 ENGINE	10
LATER 1200 ENGINE	46
1500 REPAIR SUPPLEMENT	69
LATER 1500 CHANGES	76
1600 REPAIR SUPLEMENT	84
FUEL SYSTEM	92
CARBURETORS	104
EXHAUST EMISSION CONTROL SYSTEM	127
IGNITION SYSTEM	140
ELECTRICAL SYSTEM	168
FUSES	186
WIRING DIAGRAMS	220
CLUTCH	226
TRANSMISSION-REAR AXLE	232
REAR SUSPENSION	258
DOUBLE JOINT REAR AXLE	262
FRONT AXLE	286
STEERING	301
BRAKE SYSTEM	310
WHEELS AND TIRES	336
HEATER AND CONTROLS	343
VENTILATION	349
BODY	353
CLEANING	367
EMERGENCY PROCEDURES	369
COLD WEATHER OPERATION	372
LUBRICATION	374
SPECIFICATIONS	384

Identification

Three standard identifications are used on the Transporter. The **Identification Plate** is located in the cab on the right-hand side of the ventilator air duct on models manufactured prior to 1968. On later models the plate is between the passenger's seat and the passenger's door on the partition behind the cab seats. The 9-digit number after the words "Fahrgest Nr." is the **Chassis Number.** This describes the model number, model year, and serial number.

<pre>
          22   8   000376
         / | \
       Model Year Serial Number
</pre>

The chassis number is also stamped on the right-hand engine cover plate. This number should be referred to whenever renewing parts other than strictly engine parts. Part changes are often made during the production run rather than with the beginning of a new model year, and Volkswagen dealership parts men and mechanics often need to know the exact chassis number to supply the correct part or information.

The **Engine Number** is stamped on the generator support flange and can be seen from the rear of the vehicle. When ordering replacement parts for the Transporter engine alone, be sure to give this number.

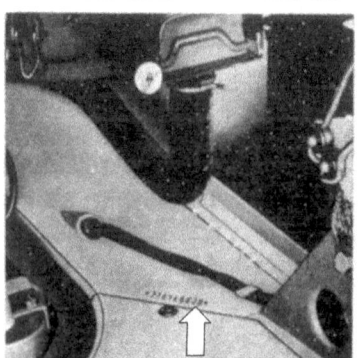

ENGINE FOREWORD

Through the years the Volkswagen Transporter has been powered by the same type of four cylinder, flat opposed, air cooled engine that has been so well proven in the Volkswagen passenger cars. Many of the changes which were later incorporated into the passenger car engines were first built into the VW Transporter, making its features often several years 'ahead' of these vehicles. The full line of engines, carburetors, and ignition systems have been included in this book, making it a complete reference for the first Transporter vehicles brought into the U.S. up to the present.

Since the engine removal and refitting procedure has remained similar over the years, this procedure is given only once at the beginning of this chapter. Those differences (such as the choke cable) not applicable to the particular engine being serviced should be ignored.

When ordering replacement parts for the Transporter engine, be sure to note the engine number stamped near the generator mounting to prevent the purchase of wrong parts. Volkswagens may look the same, but hardly any part of the original vehicle could be used on the latest vehicle.

Beginning in May, 1959 (Chassis No. 469 446), a more powerful engine was installed in the Transporter line. Coincident with this engine change was the introduction of the four speed transmission, fully synchronized in all forward speeds. These engines are covered under the EARLY 1200 ENGINE heading of this chapter.

The engine change in August, 1960 (No. 5 000 001), raised the power from 36 S.A.E. (30 German D.I.N. rating) to 40 S.A.E. (34 German D.I.N. rating) b.h.p. and introduced the automatic choke carburetor. This engine is covered in the section entitled LATER 1200 ENGINE. When the 1200 cc engine was superseded by the 1500 cc engine in August, 1962 (No. 6 375 945), a new carburetor was introduced, helping to improve the performance once again. The changes on this engine are covered in the 1500 REPAIR SUPPLEMENT, and further in-production changes are outlined in the LATER 1500 CHANGES supplement (pointing up the necessity of using the engine or chassis numbers when ordering the respective repair parts).

With the introduction of the 1600 cc (M 157) engine in August, 1967 (No. H O 183 373), power was upped to 57 b.h.p. (S.A.E. rating). These engine changes are covered in the 1600 REPAIR SUPPLEMENT. Later changes were incorporated in the ignition and fuel systems with the introducing of the "smog devices", covered under the EXHAUST EMISSION CONTROL SYSTEM (following the FUEL SYSTEM chapter), and the IGNITION SYSTEM.

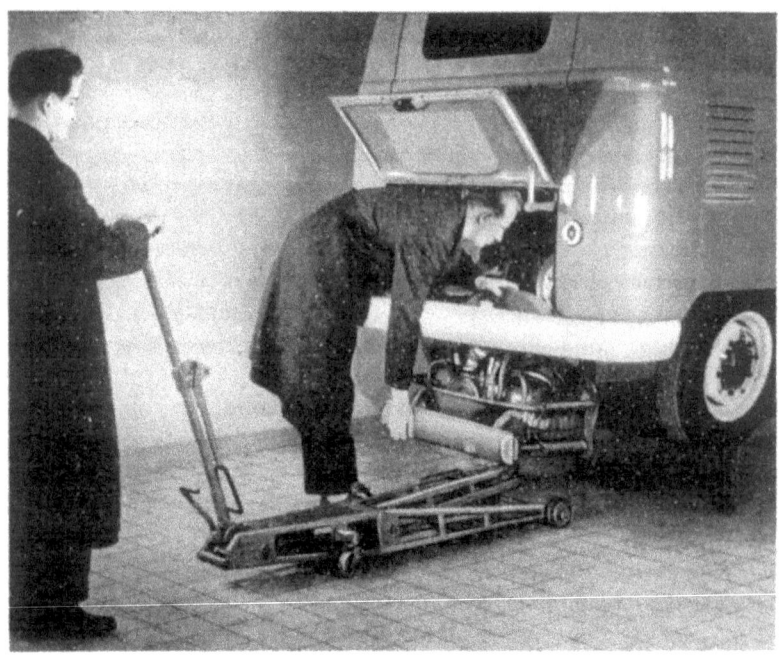

Engine Removal-Refitting

The design of the VW engine and its mounting allows it to be removed as a unit for attention in a very short time and it is most convenient to carry out repairs with it so removed. VW shops are equipped with special tools for handling the engine but a floor jack and car stands can be used. The following steps are taken in the removal:

With the rear end of the transporter jacked up to a height of approximately two feet (bumper to floor);

1. Disconnect battery ground strap.
2. Turn fuel cock to "off".
3. Remove air cleaner, rear apron and sound-neutralizing pipe and tail pipe together.
4. Disconnect wires from generator, coil and oil pressure warning light switch.
5. Disconnect choke and accelerator cables at carburetor.
6. Disconnect both heating control cables and loosen flexible heater pipe at engine.
7. Disconnect fuel hose.
8. Unscrew two lower engine mounting nuts.
9. Withdraw choke control cable and sleeve from fan housing and remove front engine cover plate. Withdraw accelerator cable.

10. Place floor jack under engine.
11. Remove two upper engine mounting nuts (bolts must be kept from turning by assistant).
12. Raise jack slightly to take weight of engine, rock it to break seal at transmission and withdraw rearward until clutch release plate clears drive shaft.
13. Lower engine with jack and withdraw rearward.

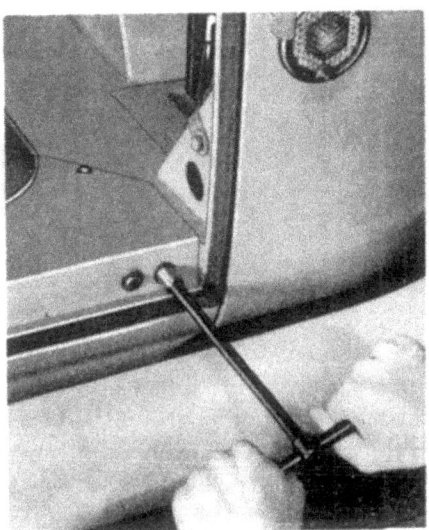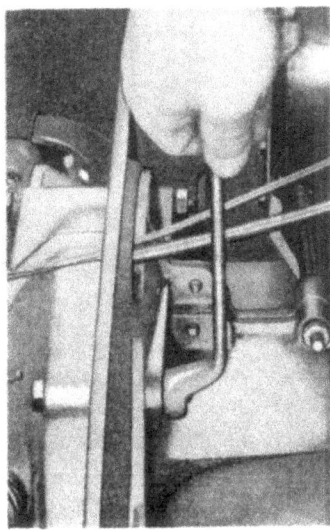

To refit the engine, the reverse of the above procedure is carried out with the following details noted:

1. Check the main drive shaft for run-out. Eccentricity must not exceed .0008 of an inch. Be sure the splines are in good condition and the driven plate slides freely without undue radial clearance.
2. Check the clutch disc contact surface on the flywheel. If there are surface cracks and grooves, have the flywheel remachined or replace it.
3. Check the clutch pressure plate. If it is warped or grooved, have it remachined, reground or, if necessary, replace it. A common cause of clutch chattering is an uneven contact pattern on a pressure plate.
4. Examine the rest of the assembly, and replace as necessary if the pins are loose, the cover is warped or cracked, the release plate is worn (where the levers make contact), or the levers are warped, cracked or worn.
5. If necessary for competition use, have the clutch assembly, flywheel, crankshaft, connecting rods and pistons balanced as an assembly by a specialist shop.

6. Check the clutch lining for wear, cracks, oiliness or burns. Make sure the rivets are tight and the spring leaves are not cracked. Maximum permissible wear from the total lining thickness is .090 of an inch (2.3 mm). Maximum permissible run-out is .03 of an inch (0.8 mm). Straighten if necessary.
7. Check the clutch operating shaft in the transmission case for looseness. If necessary, replace bushings and coat shaft with lithium grease. Be sure lock screw goes into hole in the bushing.
8. Make sure the release bearing is not dirty inside or noisy. DO NOT wash it in any solvent or other liquid, just wipe it with a clean cloth. Replacement is the only service procedure.
9. If so manufactured, lightly sand the plastic coating of the release bearing with medium coarse emery cloth and coat the sanded surface with MoS^2 grease.
10. Use lithium grease to lightly coat the contact points between fork and bearing, then fit the retaining clips properly, making sure the bent end engages behind the arm of the fork.
11. Lubricate the starter shaft bushing, starter drive gear, and flywheel ring gear.
12. Lubricate the needle bearing for the gland nut with a small amount of universal grease, then lubricate the felt ring with engine oil. Wipe away any excess oil and also wipe any excess grease off the drive shaft splines since the clutch disc could be contaminated.
13. Use a small, clean brush or a clean cloth to coat the working surfaces of the splines with MoS^2 powder.

 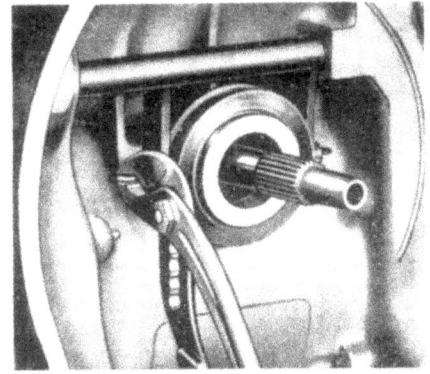

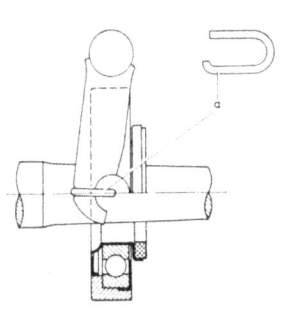 

14. Center the clutch disc with a short section of drive shaft or Special Tool VW 219, then install the pressure plate so the balance markings match. Tighten the bolts evenly and diagonally to a torque of 18 ft. lb. (2.5 mkg).
15. The installed clutch should be checked with a straightedge and a depth gauge. The distance between the clutch release plate and the flywheel should be 1.06 - 1.18 of an inch (26.7 — 30.0 mm) and release plate run-out 0.02 of an inch (0.6 mm) maximum. If not, remove the pressure plate and adjust.
16. Clean the transmission and engine mating flanges.
17. When replacing, be careful not to damage the pilot needle bearing or bushing, clutch release bearing or drive shaft. To facilitate the mating of the splines, engage a gear in transmission and rotate the engine with the fan belt. Avoid jamming the choke control cable sleeve. Insert the lower mounting studs first, tighten the upper nuts lightly, then secure the lower nuts, followed by tightening the upper bolts home.
18. Adjust the choke (if so equipped), accelerator, and clutch cables.

EARLY 1200 ENGINE
1192 cc models prior to August, 1960

1-Crankshaft
2-Flywheel
3-Distributor drive gear
4-Connecting rod
5-Piston
6-Cylinder
7-Cylinderhead
8-Camshaft
9-Push rod
10-Rocker arm
11-Rocker arm shaft
12-Valve
13-Valve spring
14-Oil strainer
15-Oil cooler
16-Oil pump
17-Thermostat
18-Fan
19-Fan housing
20-Throttle ring
21-Generator
22-Air cleaner
23-Carburetor
24-Fuel pump

ENGINE—The Volkswagen Transporter is powered by the same type of four cylinder, aircooled, flat opposed engine that has been so well proven in the VW Sedans. The power unit is attached to the rubber-mounted transmission/differential case with four bolts, the whole being positioned at the rear of the vehicle. The cast light alloy crankcase consists of two halves which are bolted together. Since the halves are machined together, replacements should only be made in pairs.

CYLINDERS—The cast cylinder barrels are spigoted into the crankcase and are interchangeable, together with the corresponding piston. Cylinders are adequately provided with cooling fins.

CYLINDERHEAD—Each pair of cylinders has one detachable light alloy cylinderhead. It is liberally finned and provided with shrunk-in valve seat inserts. Spark plugs are screwed into threaded steel inserts. The cylinderheads are mounted on the cylinders without a gasket, but copper asbestos rings are placed between the flanges of cylinder and cylinderhead.

OVERHEAD VALVES—The overhead valves are situated parallel in the cylinderhead and are operated through a pushrod and rockerarm mechanism. The geardriven camshaft which has only four lobes is carried in three bearings integral with the crankcase. The camshaft gear is of light metal or fiber (most VW's exported to the U.S. have the fiber gears). Exhaust valves are plated with chrome-nickel steel.

CRANKSHAFT—The crankshaft is a short and sturdy forging which has hardened journal surfaces. It is carried in four precision light-alloy bearing shells. Number 2 main bearing is of the split type (made in halves). Crankshaft end thrust is taken by No. 1 bearing (at the front next to the flywheel.)

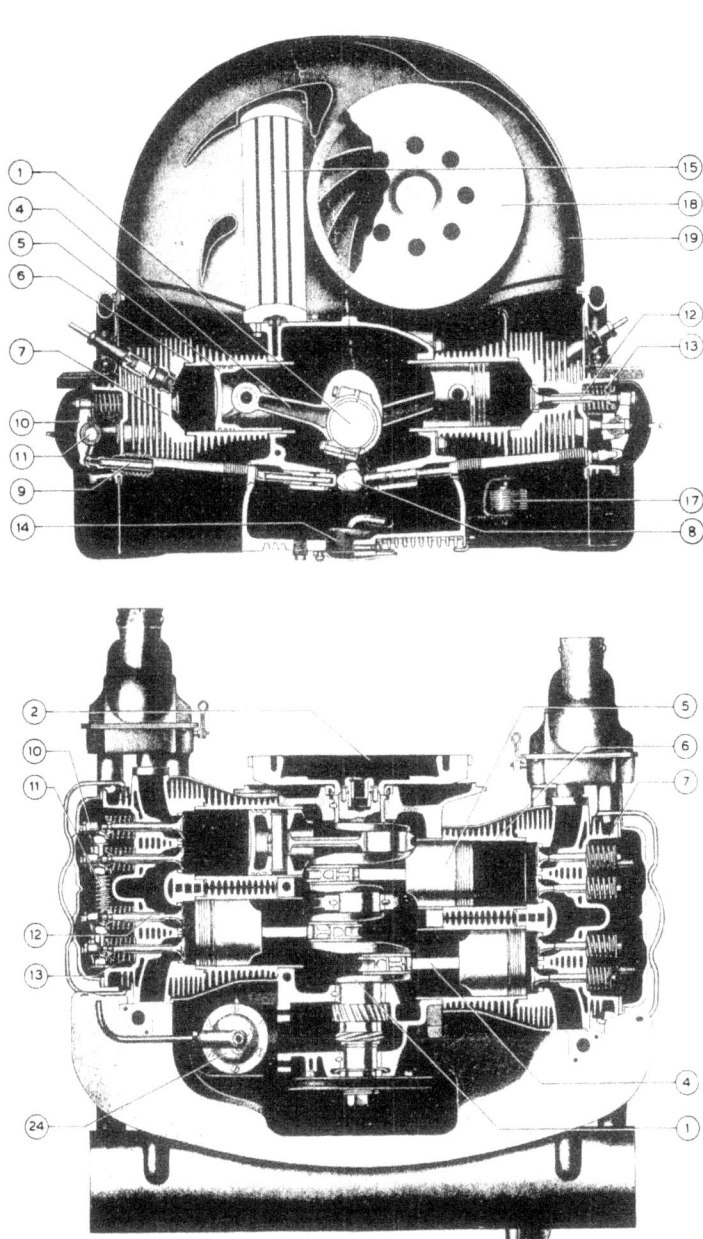

The 1131 cc Volkswagen engine
(up to 1954; later engines are similar
but slightly bigger in capacity)

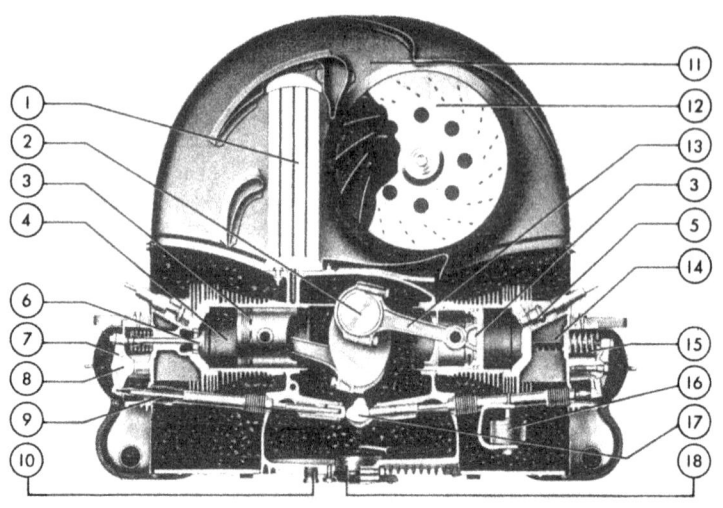

1-Oil cooler
2-Crankshaft
3-Piston
4-Cylinder
5-Spark plug
6-Valve
7-Rocker arm
8-Rocker arm shaft
9-Pushrod
10-Oil drain plug
11-Fan housing
12-Fan
13-Connecting rod
14-Cylinderhead
15-Valve spring
16-Thermostat
17-Camshaft
18-Oil strainer
19-Air filter
20-Carburetor
21-Generator
22-Throttle ring
23-Intake manifold
24-V-belt
25-Distributor drive gear
26-Oil pump

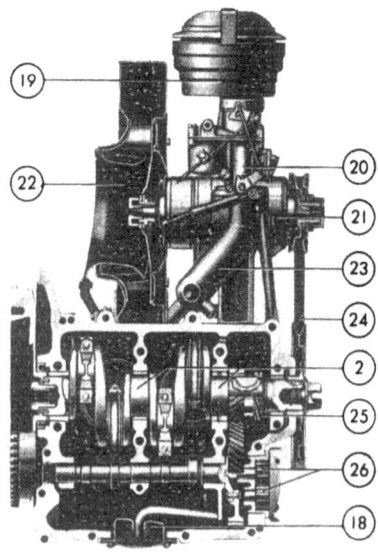

Fig. 1 —The 1192 cc VW engine

The flywheel which is provided with a starter ring gear is accurately located in four dowel pins and fastened by large central nut. An oil seal is fitted on the flywheel end, while there is an oil slinger on the pulley side.

Timing gears and located with Woodruff keys. The fanpulley is keyed to the crankshaft with a Woodruff key and retained by a center bolt.

CONNECTING RODS—The short forged connecting rods are of a very sturdy design. Lead-bronze bearing shells are used. The wrist pin is carried in bronze bushings. It is fully floating and secured endwise by circlips.

LUBRICATION SYSTEM—An important feature of the VW engine is the oil cooler in its lubrication system. A geartype oil pump driven by the camshaft draws the oil from the lowest point of the oil sump from where it is directed to various parts of the engine via the oil cooler. Connecting rod bearings are fed from the mains through passages in the crankshaft. The camshaft also is pressure fed, as are the rocker arms (through the hollow pushrods). Cylinder walls, pistons and pins are splash lubricated. Oil is cleaned by an efficient oil strainer at the lowest point of the sump before being re-circulated.

1- Rear cover
2- Front cover
3- Fan housing
4- Cover plate
5- Lower heating channel
6- Cylinder cover plate
7- Cover

Fig. 3 —Engine with cover plates

13

The oil cooler receives its cooling air from the fan and the temperature drop in the cooler amounts to almost 70° F which is an indication of its effectiveness. In cold weather when the oil is thick, a pressure relief valve protects the oil cooler against excessive pressure. In this case, the oil cooler is by-passed and engine parts are lubricated directly.

An oil pressure warning light is fitted on the instrument panel. This warning light is actuated by an automatic oil pressure switch situated in the oil line between the pump and the cooler. At approximately 5.5 - 8.5 lbs oil pressure the grounding contact opens cutting off the current to the control lamp. The lamp lights up again when the pressure falls below approximately 6.5 lbs (engine stationary with ignition switched on or idling very slowly).

ENGINE COVER PLATES—Fig. 3 shows the engine with the cover plates. Engine rear cover plate should be taken off prior to removing engine. Fanhousing and generator should be removed as a unit. Valve pushrod tubes should be taken out before deflector plates are removed. When replacing deflector plates it is advisable to bend them slightly so that they are slightly preloaded to avoid rattling. When replacing cylinder plates make sure that the rubber spark plug sealing caps are correctly positioned (fig. 4). Worn or damaged caps must be replaced. Cover plates should be correctly positioned to prevent loss of cooling air. Before installing engine front cover plate, check condition of weather strip (fig. 5).

REMOVING AND INSTALLING FANHOUSING

To remove fanhousing proceed as follows (fig. 6): disconnect battery cable, remove rear engine cover, disconnect leads from generator, ignition coil, oil pressure indicator switch. Disconnect accelerator, choke control cables; remove conduit tube. Remove fanbelt, generator strap, fanhousing screws. Disconnect spring for air regulator ring (also called throttle ring) and loosen regulator ring screws.

When installing fanhousing pay particular attention that the guide plates are correctly positioned and in good shape. Any blow-by between fanhousing and cover plate diminishes the efficiency of the cooling unit.

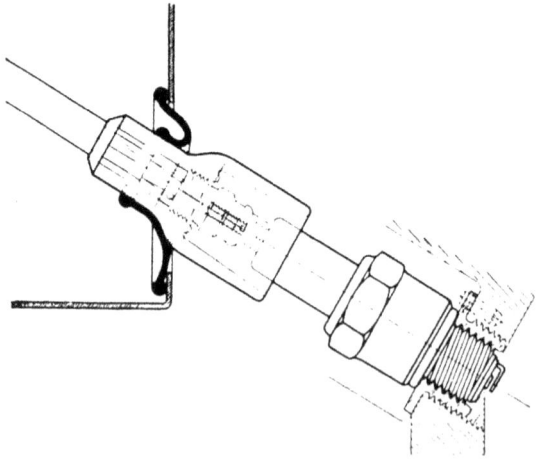

Fig. 4 —Sealing of spark plug

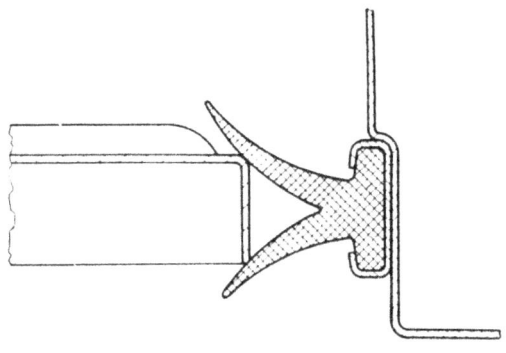

Fig. 5 —Weatherstrip

Fig. 6 —Removing fan housing

AIR REGULATOR RING (THROTTLE RING)—It is normal for the air regulator ring to have a tilted position (fig. 7 and 8) so do not bend holding plate. Ring is centered by moving mounting bolts in their clearance holes. Connect return spring and adjust regulator ring.

COOLING REGULATION—The amount of cooling air necessary to cool cylinderheads and cylinders is automatically regulated by means of a thermostat (to be seen in fig. 1). The blower impeller is fitted onto the end of the extended generator shaft and is driven by a V belt. Regulator adjustment should be inspected regularly especially in countries subject

Fig. 7 —Throttle ring position

Fig. 8 —Adjustment of throttle ring

to extremes in temperatures. Slow or late opening of the ring in hot weather will cause the engine to run excessively hot. If ring opens too soon or remains open permanently, engine will run too cool most of the time causing increased fuel consumption and carburetor flat spots.

ENGINE COLD—With a cold engine, the regulator ring should rest against the air intake flange, slightly loaded. Warm up engine until top of thermostat element reaches end of travel. In this position the distance from the center of induction flange to edge of regulator ring should be .79 in. (20 mm).

ADJUSTMENT (ENGINE IN CAR)—Disconnect regulator ring operating lever. Warm up engine until thermostat reaches upper stop. Adjust ring to .79 in. as previously described. Tighten actuating lever (when engine is being assembled on the bench, adjust by lifting thermostat element to upper stop). Check operating linkage for free operation. Correct thermostat adjustment is very imortant and should if possible be performed by a competent VW mechanic.

ADJUSTING FAN BELT—Correct adjustment of the fan belt is for obvious reasons vital for correct and efficient functioning of the cooling mechanism. When lightly pressed as shown in fig. 9 it should yield approximately 1 in. **(.6 inch in post-1957 cars)** To adjust belt tension proceed as follows: insert screwdriver in slot of inside pulley half (see fig. 10) and rest it behind the upper generator bolt nut (to hold pulley as nut is being loosened). Unscrew nut of pulley shaft and remove outer pulley half. Belt tension is adjusted by fitting the correct amount of spacer washers between the pulley halves. If the belt is too slack, one or more washers have to be removed. If the belt is too tight insert washer(s). Belt should be of the correct length. If belt rides too high or too deep in pulley, the drive ratio is excessively affected and cooling suffers (fig. 11). Never remove or install belt without loosening pulley, using the socket wrench and jack handle that comes with the VW. Replace extra spacers on the shaft after outer pulley half, replace the follower, and then tighten the nut. Inspect tightness of new belt after 50 miles since there is an initial amount of stretch. Since the loss of a belt will put the cooling fan and generator out of operation, be sure to carry a spare belt in the vehicle.

Fig. 9 — Fan belt is adjusted correctly

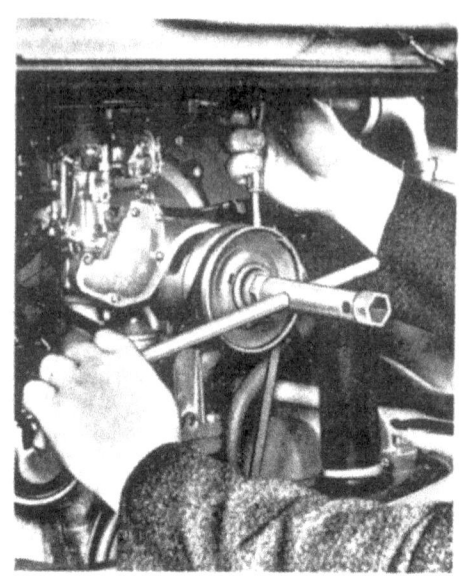

Fig. 10 —Loosening fan pulley nut

Fig. 11 —Fan belt adjustment

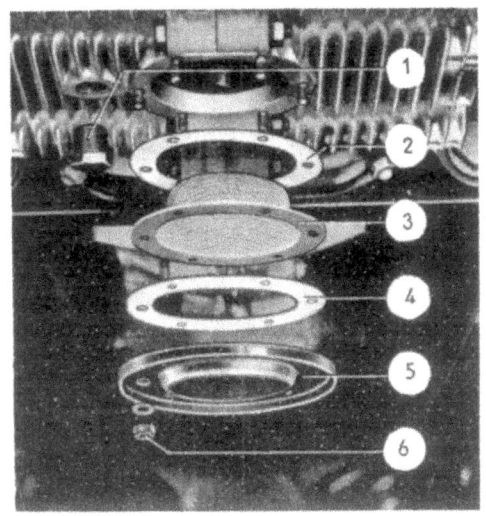

1-Oil drain plug   3-Strainer   5-Bottom plate
2-Gasket   4-Gasket   6-Nut with lockwasher

Fig. 12 —Oil strainer

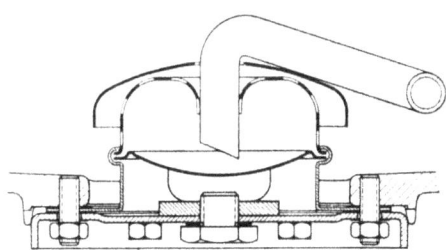

Fig. 13 —Section of oil strainer

OIL STRAINER—Fig. 12 shows a disassembled view of the oil filter. To clean the filter disassemble as shown. When reassembling observe the following: oil pump suction pipe should be a tight fit in the strainer. Renew gaskets. The low side of the strainer should be below the suction pipe. The bottom plate must be perfectly straight. Do not overtighten the nuts.

MAGNETIC OIL FILTER—The magnetic type oil filter as shown in fig. 13 is even more efficient. The illustration shows that the lubricant after passing through the strainer must flow through the magnetic system before it can enter the suction pipe. Through this expedient all ferrous abrasives are caught. To install the magnetic filter drill a 4 mm (.16 in.) hole in center of bottom plate. A washer of sufficient thickness should be placed between bottom plate and magnetic filter. Assembly is riveted together as shown. Test riveting for leaks. Re-install bottom plate using new gaskets.

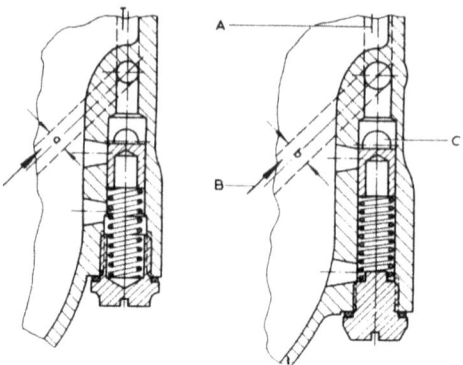

Fig. 15 — **Oil pressure relief valve. Left: early type; right: latest design**

These two types are not interchangeable.

OIL PRESSURE RELIEF VALVE—Fig. 15 shows a disassembled view of the oil pressure relief valve. A correctly adjusted relief valve is of vital importance for efficient operation of the engine. Fig. 16 shows how valve operates. See also fig. 17 showing oil circulating circuit. Oil from the oil pump (a) is fed through the oil cooler (b) to various parts of the engine. Arrow (c) indicates a by-pass directly to the points to be lubricated. Oil can flow back to the oil pan through passage (d) (against the pressure of the valve spring). A sticking valve can be removed by screwing a 10 mm tap into it. Check plunger for correct fit. Free length of the spring (unloaded) should be 2.04-2.08 in. (for the earlier models)

DIMENSIONS FOR LATER MODEL OIL PRESSURE RELIEF VALVE

Condition	Length	Load in kg (lbs.)
unloaded	62—64 mm (2.44"—2.52")	0
loaded	23.6 mm (0.93")	7.75 (17.1)

Oil Pressure (for oils SAE 20)

a - At idling speed with engine warm
　　　　　min. 0.5 kg/sq. cm. (7.1 lbs/sq. in.)

b - Engine at 70° C (158° F) and 2500 r. p. m.
　　　　　min. 2.0 kg/sq. cm. (28.5 lbs/sq. in.)

OIL PRESSURE SWITCH — The warning device which operates a glow lamp on the instrument panel is the oil pressure switch (or sender). When the ignition is turned on the lamp glows. As pressure builds up (5 to 8.5 lb./sq. in.), the pressure deflects a diaphragm and breaks the electrical circuit. When the pressure drops the lamp glows.

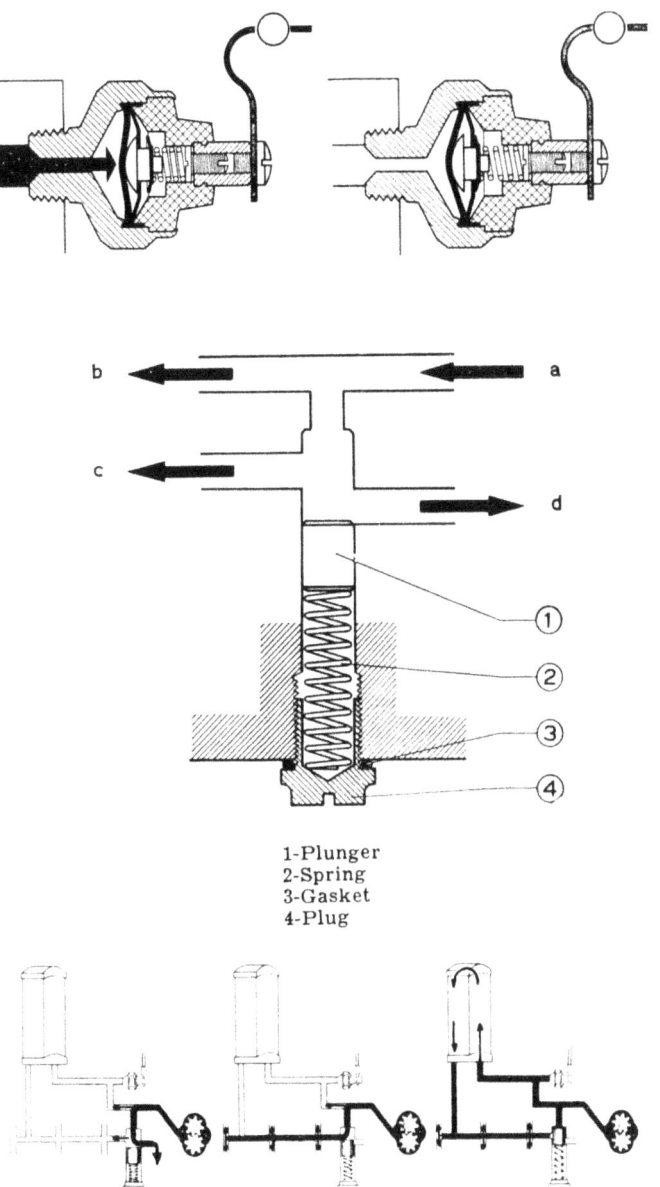

1-Plunger
2-Spring
3-Gasket
4-Plug

Fig. 16 —Operation of relief valve

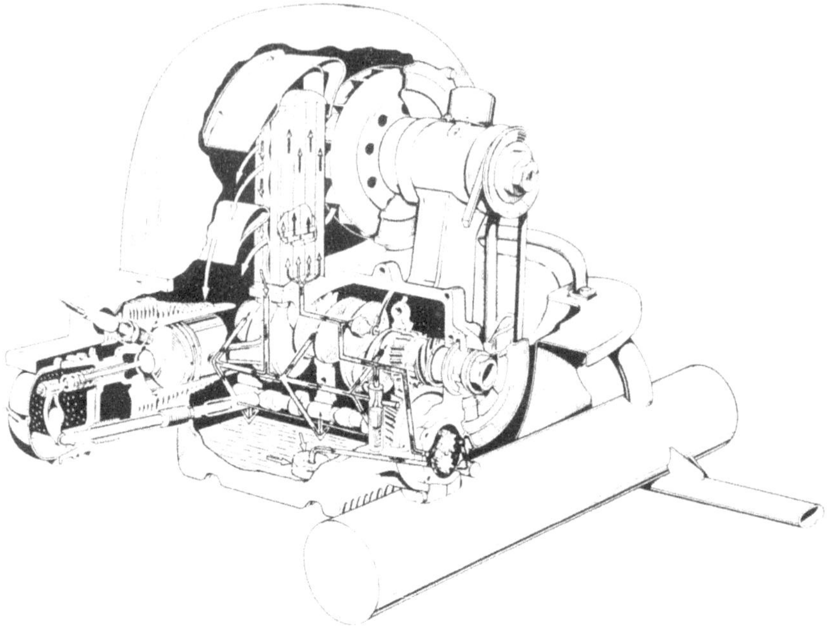

Fig. 17 —Oil circulation diagram

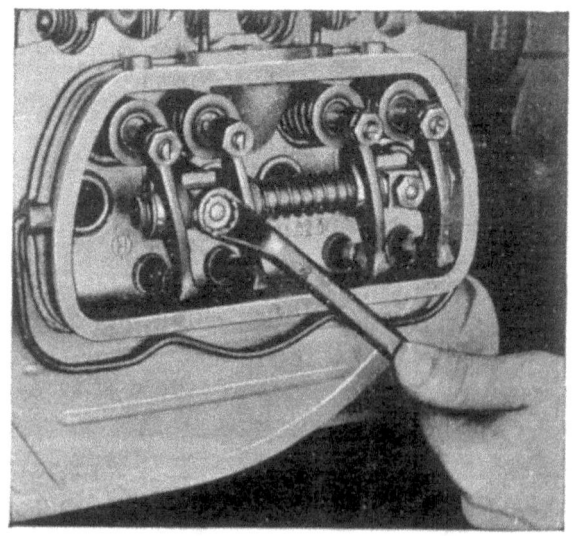

Fig. 18 —Rocker arm mechanism

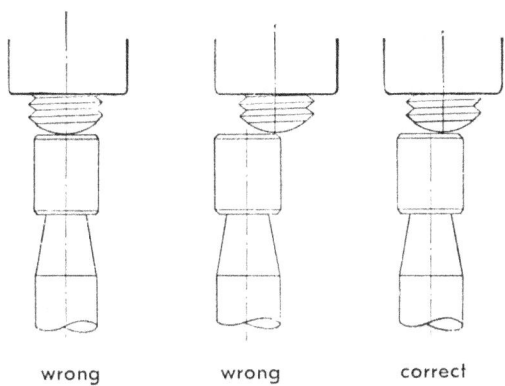

Fig. 19 —Position of rocker arm in relation to valve stem

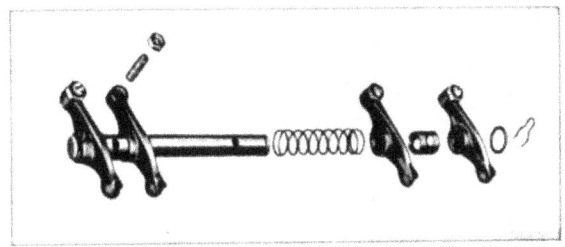

Fig. 20 —Exploded view of rocker arm mechanism

ROCKER ARM MECHANISM—Fig. 18 shows rocker arm mechanism. It is easily removed after undoing nuts as shown. It is important that the ball ends of the push rods are correctly positioned in the rocker arm sockets. To obtain valve rotation during engine operation the rocker arm is placed slightly to the side in relation to the valve stem (fig. 19). Rocker arms can be positioned either by moving the rocker arm shaft (it can be moved slightly after retaining nuts have been loosened) or by fitting washers of different thickness (part 102 135). When refitting cylinderhead covers use new gasket which should be glued to the cover.

Fig. 20 shows rocker arm mechanism disassembled. Check rocker arm shaft and rocker arms for wear, check sockets of rocker arms. Before replacing rocker arm assembly, back off adjusting screws.

CYLINDERHEAD — To remove the cylinderhead (after rocker mechanism has been taken off) use a 15 mm socket wrench to unscrew cylinderhead nuts. Tap head with light mallet blows, then lift straight up (see fig. 21). If cylinders need not be removed, use a clamping device to hold them in place.

Except with reconditioned cylinderheads no gasket is used between head and barrel. There is however a gasket on the outside of the cylinder (see fig. 22) When reinstalling cylinderhead check to see that the oil seals at the push rod ends are correctly seated. Cylinderhead nut gaskets should be dipped in oil before refitting. Cylinderhead nuts should be ccat-

Fig. 21 —Removing cylinderhead

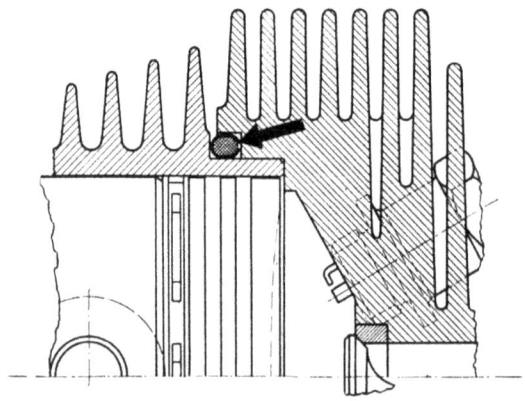

Fig. 22 —Cylinderhead gasket ring

ed with graphite paste, and tightened to 7 lb-ft according to sequence indicated in fig. 23 . Finally tighten nuts to approximately 27 lb-ft in sequence indicated in fig. 24 .

VALVES—Fig. 25 shows cross section of valve assembly. Fig. 26 shows disassembly with VW tool 311. After pressing down on valve spring, remove valve cotters after which the assembly can be taken apart. Check valve stem for wear, especially under the cotter shoulder (see fig. 27). Burrs should be removed with file.

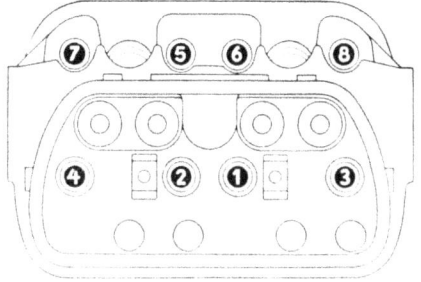

Fig. 23
—Sequence of tightening cylinderhead nuts

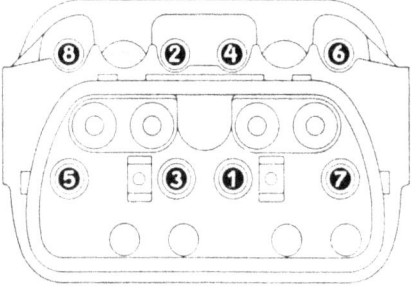

Fig. 24
—Final sequence of tightening of cylinderhead nuts

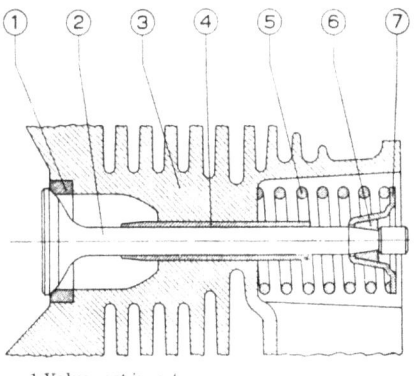

Fig. 25
—Valve assembly

1 Valve seat insert
2-Valve
3-Cylinderhead
4-Valve guide
5-Valve spring
6-Valve cotter
7-Valve spring seat

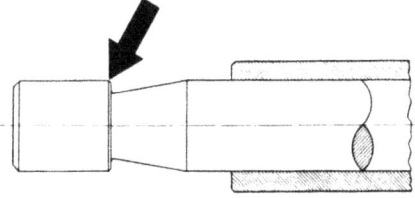

Fig. 27 —Checking valve stem for wear (arrow)

Fig. 26 —Using valve tool

VALVE STEM CLEARANCE IN GUIDE — Stem to guide clearance is .0015—.0025 in. (intake) and .002—.003 in. (exhaust). Valve stem run-out should not exceed .0004 in.

If the clearance should be near the wear limit of 0.16 mm (0.0063") for both the intake and exhaust valve, replace the cylinderhead with a new or reconditioned one. A check is carried out with the Plug Gauge VW311k after the valve guide has been cleaned from deposits that may have accumulated.

Check valve springs for tension in test fixture. Free length is 43 mm (1.69 in.). When compressed to 28 mm (1.10 in.) load should be 73.5 lbs. with a tolerance of 5% either way. Springs can also be tested against a new spring when placed end to end in a vice. The used spring should not compress more than 10% against the new one.

The valve guides are shrunk into the cylinderhead with a heavy interference fit and cannot be removed with methods available in the average workshop. Any attempt to drive out the guides is liable to result in damage to the cylinderhead.

RECONDITIONING VALVE SEATS—Valve seats must be reconditioned with good valve grinding equipment. Valve seats are ground to 45°. Important is that the valve guides are in good shape since they position the pilot of the cutter or grinder. Seat width should be kept to .050 - .063 in. (intake) and .065 - .080 in. (exhaust). Valve seats can be narrowed and positioned with 15° and 75° stones. When chamfering upper edge do not cut into cylinderhead proper (fig. 28).

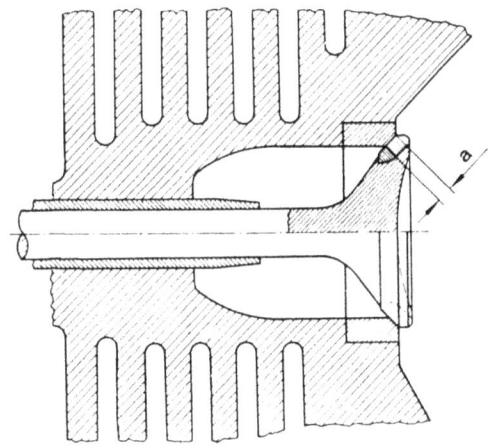

Fig. 28 — Correct position of valve seat
a .050 - .063 in. (intake)
a .065 - .080 in. (exhaust)

VALVES—Valves should be refaced in a valve machine. Fig. 29 gives the tolerance on valve dimensions. Valves with insufficient margin thickness should be renewed (this is especially important for exhaust valves).

To check correct seating of valve, coat valve face with bearing blue. Insert valve and turn it ¼ turn on its seat applying light pressure. If valve is seating correctly blue should be transferred all around the valve seat.

ADJUSTMENT OF VALVE CLEARANCE—Valve clearance should be adjusted when engine is cold (preferably after it has cooled down overnight). Check clearance every 3,000 miles for best results.

Valve lash for both intake and exhaust should be .004 in. Clearance increases after engine warms up. The timing is as shown in valve timing

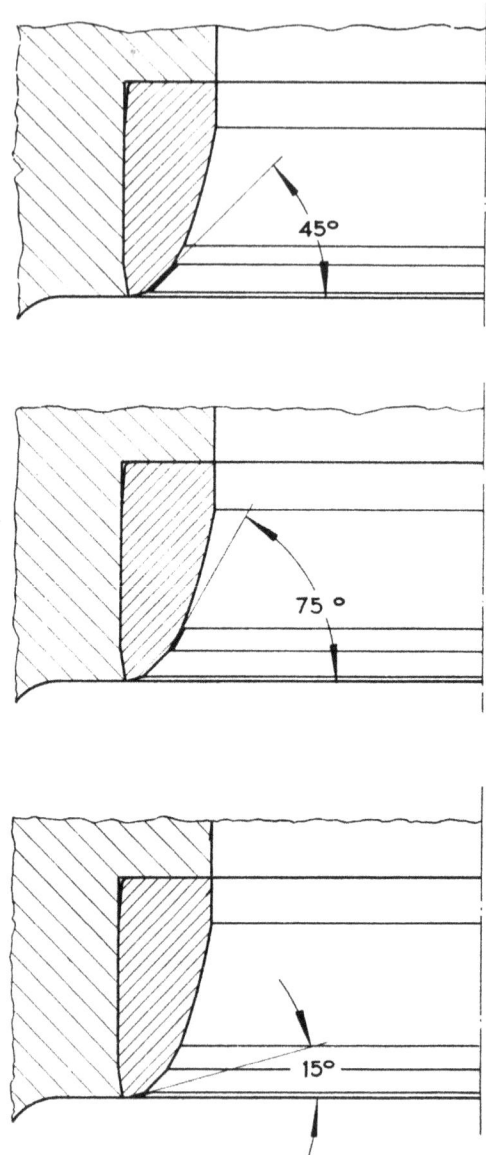

Sequence of Valve Seat Reconditioning Operations

Three cutters are required for reconditioning the valve seat inserts.

1) Cut the 45° seat face. Considerable care must be taken when cutting to obtain a concentric seating surface. Take off only the minimum of metal as otherwise the life of the inserts will be affected. The operation should cease as soon as the whole surface has been cut. 2) Cut the 75° face: Slightly chamfer the lower edge of the valve seat face with the 75° cutter. 3) Cut the 15° face: Chamfer the upper edge of the valve seat fact with the 15° cutter until the correct seat width is reached.

EARLY VALVE

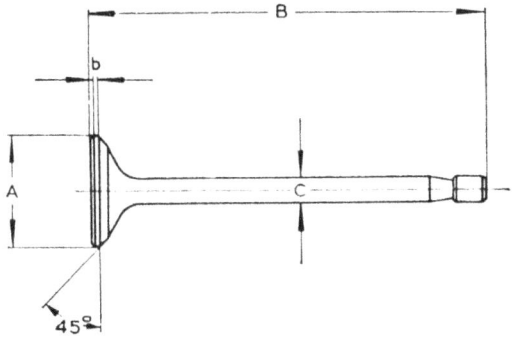

intake valve
A = 29.9 - 30.1 mm (1.177 -1.185 in.)
B = 101.7 -102.3 mm (4.004 -4.023 in.)
C = 6.955- 6.965 mm (.2738- .2742 in.)
b — 1.10 - 1.60 mm (.043 - .063 in.)

exhaust valve
A = 27.9 - 28.1 mm (1.098 -1.106 in.)
B = 101.7 -102.3 mm (4.004 -4.023 in.)
C = 6.945- 6.955 mm (.2734- .2738 in.)
b — 1.10 - 1.60 mm (.043 - .063 in.)

Fig. 29 —Tolerance on valve dimensions

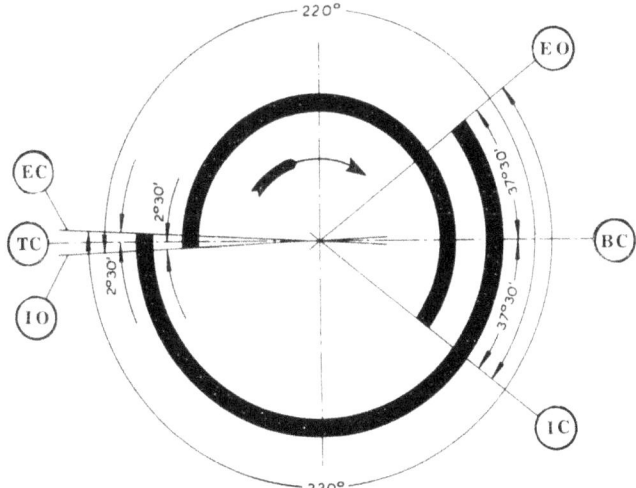

Fig. 30 —Valve timing diagram with .040 in. valve clearance. Running clearance for both valves is .004 in.

29

VALVE CLEARANCE FOR 1131 and 1192 cc ENGINES PRIOR TO ENGINE #5 000 001 (ADJUSTED COLD)
  Intake — 0.1 mm (0.004")
  Exhaust — 0.1 mm (0.004")

LATE VALVE

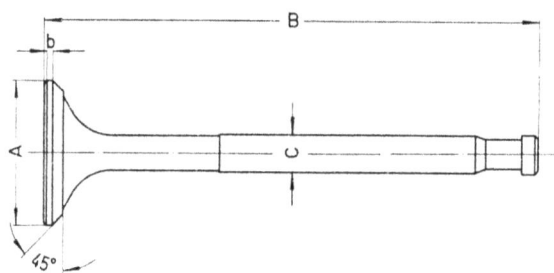

INTAKE
A = 31.4 — 31.6 mm   1.236" — 1.244"
B = 111.4 — 112.2 mm   4.386" — 4.417"
C =   7.94 — 7.95 mm   0.3126" — 0.3130"
b =   0.8 — 1.5 mm   0.031" — 0.059"

EXHAUST
A = 29.9 — 30.1 mm   1.177" — 1.185"
B = 111.6 — 112.4 mm   4.394" — 4.425"
C =   7.91 — 7.92 mm   0.3114" — 0.3118"
b =   1.00 — 1.70 mm   0.039" — 0.067"

Valve Spring Specs.
Free length   — 47.9 mm (1.89")
Loaded length   — 34.3 mm (1.35")
Load   — 46.3 kg (102 lbs.)
Wear limit   — 38.1 kg (84 lbs.)

Valve timing Engines prior to 5 000 001

Intake opens	EÖ	2° 30' before T. D. C.
Intake closes	ES	37° 30' after B. D. C.
Exhaust opens	AÖ	37° 30' before B. D. C.
Exhaust closes	AS	2° 30' after T. D. C.

Valve timing is measured with 1 mm (0.04") clearance. Normal clearance should be restored before operation of the engine.

Fig. 31 —Timing mark lined up

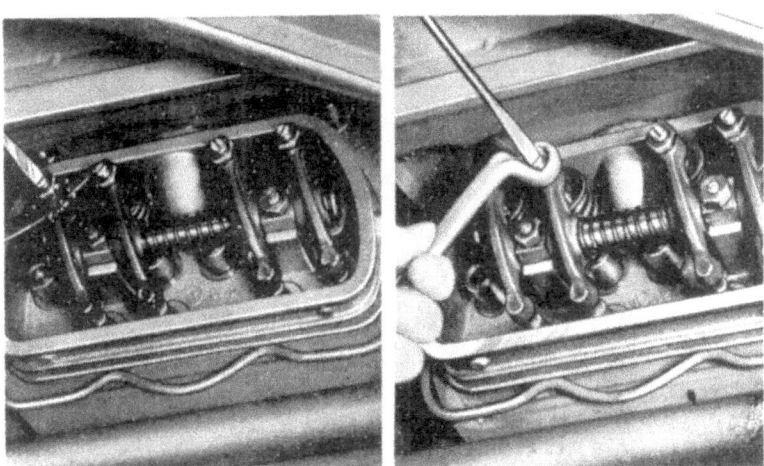

Fig. 32 —Adjusting valve clearance

diagram fig. 30 (this is with a clearance of .040 in. When timing checks out OK it should be reset at .004 in.).

Intake opens 2° 30' before TDC
Intake closes 37° 30' after BDC
Exhaust opens 37° 30' before BDC
Exhaust closes 2° 30' after TDC

Valve clearance should be adjusted with the piston on TDC on firing stroke in the sequence of cylinders 1, 2, 3 and 4. Turn engine slowly count-

Fig. 34 —Marking of pistons

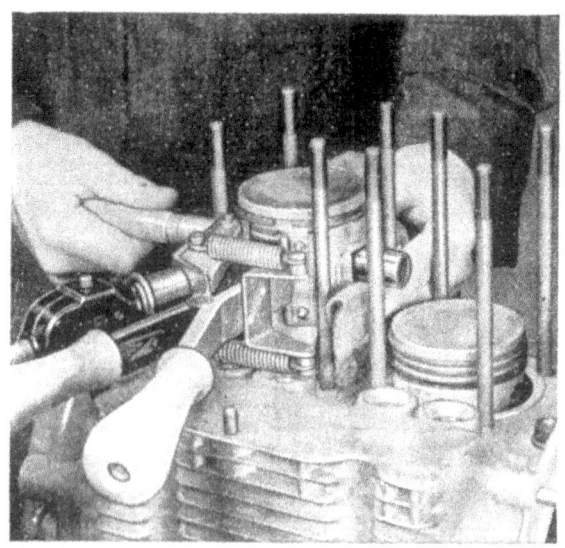

Fig. 35 —Electric piston heating tool

er clockwise until valves to be adjusted are closed with cam follower off the cam ramp (timing mark on pulley should line up with parting line of crankcase halves, see fig. 31). Loosen lock nut of rocker arm adjusting screw. Turn screw to obtain proper clearance. Tighten lock nut while holding adjusting screw with screw driver (fig. 32) and recheck clearance. If this checks out OK, turn engine 180° counter clockwise to adjust the valves of the cylinder that is next in the firing sequence.

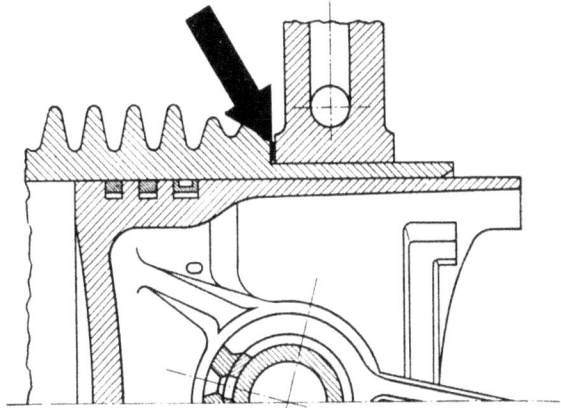

Fig. 33 —Cylinder spigoted in crankcase (Note gasket)

CYLINDERS—Removal: remove cylinderhead, pushrods and tubes, deflector plates, cylinders. Fig. 33 shows how the cylinder is deeply spigoted into the crankcase. If cylinder is excessively worn it should be replaced by a matched cylinder and piston assembly (cylinders should be measured about ½ in. below the upper edge). When reinstalling cylinder(s) make sure that the cylinder-seating surface and its corresponding contact face on the crankcase are perfectly clean. This is very important for correct alignment of cylinders. Always replace gasket (see arrow). Use ring compressor as shown. Ring gaps must be staggered and the oil ring gap should always be at the top. Oil consumption usually is fairly indicative about general condition of engine. When oil consumption exceeds a quart per 650 miles it is safe to say that the engine will be needing an overhaul.

REMOVING PISTONS—Fig. 34 shows the pistons after the cylinder barrels have been removed. If pistons are to be used again they should be marked as shown to insure correct reassembly. Remove wrist pin circlips with pointed nose pliers. Pistons must be heated (to appr. 180° F) for the wristpins to be withdrawn (special electric piston heating device VW 205 is shown in fig. 35). Piston pins may be removed with a suitable extractor (tool VW 207 or 207a). Check piston thrust surfaces for correct wear pattern. Uneven wear indicates misalignment (twisted connecting rod or cocked cylinder). Pistons should be measured for size at the bottom end of the skirt.

The running clearance between the piston thrust surfaces and cylinder wall should be .0014-.0022 in. If this clearance exceeds .008 in. replace cylinder and piston by another pair of the same size and weight grading.

Do not fit a new piston if the cylinder shows signs of wear. If cylinder is unworn a new piston of the correct size and grading may be fitted.

PISTON RINGS—All three piston rings must be fitted with a gap of .012-.017 in. (with a maximum of .037 in.). Gap must be measured after ring has been squared in cylinder (with piston) as shown (fig. 36). Ring gaps must be staggered around the cylinder circumference and the oil scraper ring gap should be at the top.

Piston ring side clearance in grooves should be:

    Compression ring: .0014-.0024 in. (max. .004 in.)
    Oil ring: .001 -.002 in. (max. .004 in.)

The top compression ring is slightly tapered and it should be installed with the marking TOP or OBEN toward top of piston (see fig. 37). Use piston ring compressor for installation.

PISTON PINS (WRIST PINS)—The piston pin should be a push fit in the piston after the piston has been heated. When pin is a push fit in a cold piston, use larger pin (fit selectively).

Paint markings on the piston pin boss and on the pin give the size gradings.

The clearance between piston pin and connecting rod bush is .0002-.001 in. To insert the wrist pin proceed as follows: insert circlip on side that faces flywheel. Heat piston to approximately 180° F. Now quickly push in pin until stopped by circlip. Insert other circlip and check to see that circlips are well seated in their grooves.

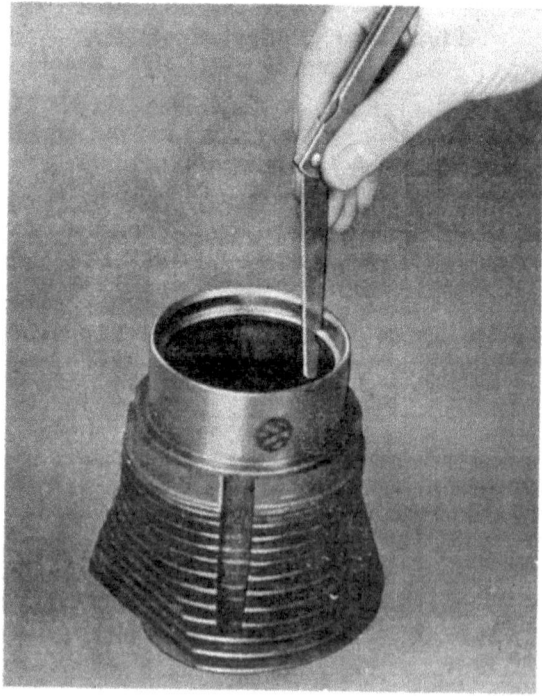

Fig. 36 —Measuring piston ring gap

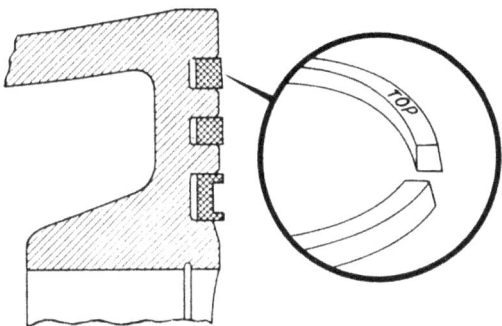

Fig. 37 —Correct position of top compression ring

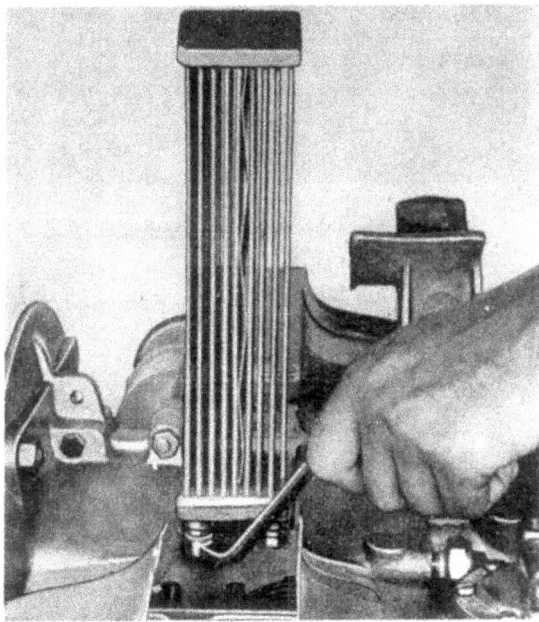

Fig. 38 —Removing oil cooler

OIL COOLER—The oil cooler (fig 38) can be removed after the fan-housing has been removed and the retaining nuts taken off. A leaky oil cooler usually indicates too high an oil pressure and a check of the oil relief valve would be in order. Oil cooler should be checked for leaks at a pressure of 85 lbs./sq. in.

When installing oil cooler use new gaskets (fig. 39) and make sure that the nuts and bracket are tight.

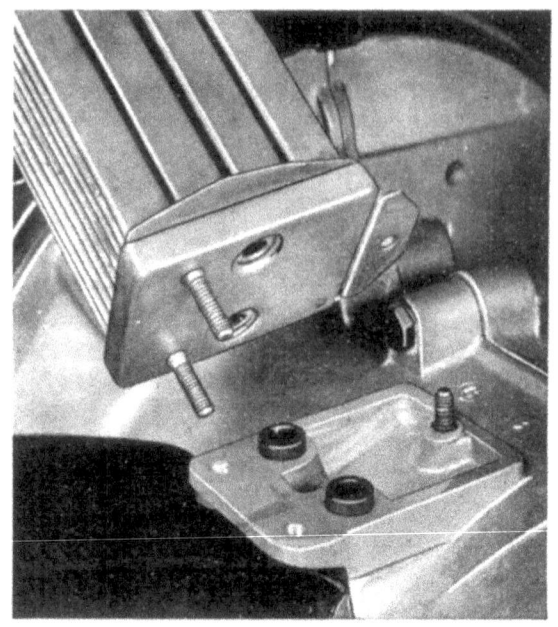

Fig. 39 — Oil cooler gaskets

Fig. 40 —Exploded view of oil pump

Fig. 41 —Removing oil pump housing

Fig. 42 —Measuring clearance

OIL PUMP—Fig. 40 shows an exploded view of the oil pump. It is driven by the camshaft. To remove proceed as follows: remove engine rear cover plate, fan pulley, pulley cover. Now remove nuts on oil pump cover after which the cover, gasket and gears can be withdrawn. Fig. 41 shows how the pump housing is removed with special puller (VW 201).

Check pump housing and gears for wear. Backlash between gears should be .0015 - .003 in. Measure gear side play with cover removed (.0025 - .0075. Max. allowable limit .008 in.). Also check to see that the idler gear pin is securely fastened and if necessary peen into position

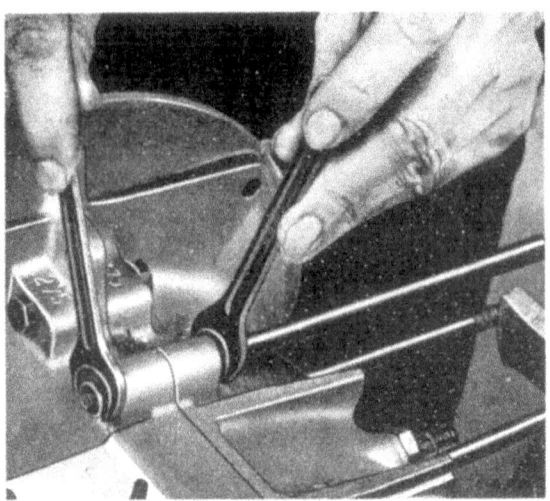

Fig. 43 —Disassembly of crankcase

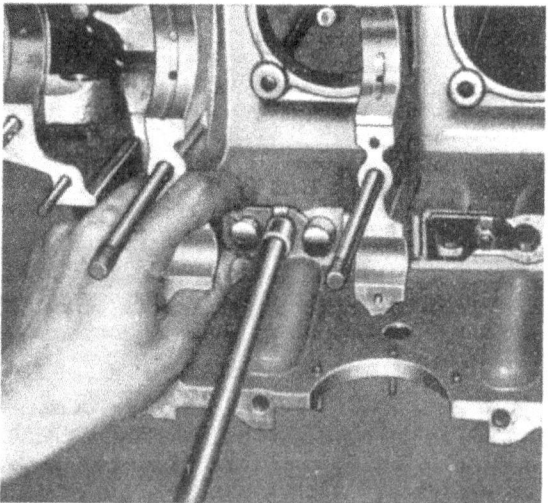

Fig. 44 —Tightening pushrod guide plates

Fig. 42 shows how the clearance is determined between the gears and a steel ruler placed across the housing. This clearance should not be in excess of .004 in. (without gasket). If cover is worn it should be planed. Always use new gasket (.0031 in. thick) without sealing compound. Oil pump mating surface on crankcase should be clean and even.

CRANKCASE—The crankcase which houses the crankshaft and the camshaft is made in two halves. Whenever the crankshaft or camshaft have to be removed, crankcase must be split.

Fig. 45 —Camshaft end plug

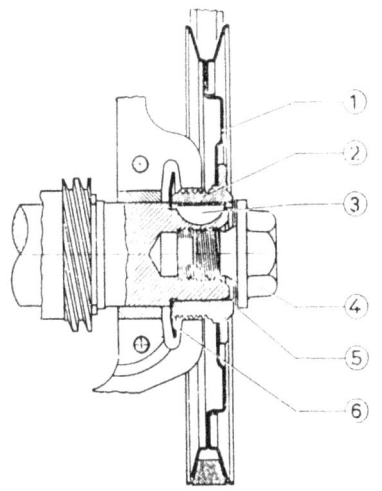

1-Crankshaft pulley
2-Oil return thread
3-Woodruff key
4-Mounting bolt
5-Spring washer
6-Crankshaft oil thrower

Fig. 46 —Section of pulley mounting on crankshaft

Fig. 43 shows crankcase retaining nuts being loosened. The mating faces of the crankcase halves are assembled with sealing compound without a gasket in between and must be perfectly even and straight. A soft hammer should be used to separate the halves, never insert tools in between the faces to pry them apart.

Fig. 44 shows how the curved camfollowers are positioned by the guide plates. The permissible clearance is very small (.0004 - .0008 in.). It is most important that the guide plate is correctly fitted and care should be taken not to alter the position of the plates when they are tightened down. Oversize pushrods may be installed when there is excessive clearance.

Fig. 47 —Removing pulley with puller

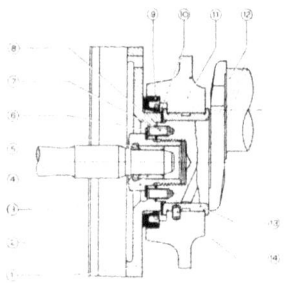

1-Flywheel
2-Retainer nut
3-Pilot bush
4-Main drive shaft
5-Gasket
6-Lockwasher
7-Dowel pin
8-Gasket
9-Oil seal
10-Shims
11-Crankcase
12-Crankshaft
13-Crankshaft bearing
14-Dowel pin

Fig. 48 —Section of flywheel mounting

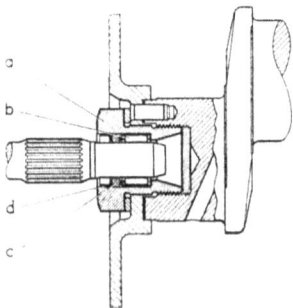

Needle-type clutch shaft spigot bearing replacing bronze bushing formerly used

Fig. 49 —Checking end play with dial indicator

Fig. 50 —Removing flywheel center nut

Fig. 45 shows the camshaft end plug with the camshaft resting in one crankcase half. Use sealing compound. The matching faces of the crankcase halves should be perfectly clean prior to assembly. Care should be taken that sealing compound does not enter oil return passages of crankshaft and camshaft bearings.

Crankcase retaining nuts should be tightened with a torque wrench (10 mm nuts to 22 lb-ft; 8 mm nuts to 15 lb-ft).

Fig. 51 —Determining thickness of shims for correct end play with dial indicator measurements

CRANKSHAFT FAN PULLEY—Fig. 46 shows how the fan pulley is fastened to the end of the crankshaft. The pulley can easily be taken off with a puller as shown in fig. 47, after fan belt, rear cover plate and mounting bolts have been removed. Always clean the oil return thread before reinstalling. Pulleys with oversize return threads are available in the event of oil leakage past the pulley hub.

REMOVING AND INSTALLING FLYWHEEL—Fig. 48 shows how flywheel is fixed to the end of the crankshaft. The flywheel is accurately located by four dowels and retained by a large center nut which also contains the pilot bush for the transmission main drive shaft. A paper gasket is fitted between the flywheel and the crankshaft end face. Crankshaft end thrust is taken by the main bearing at the flywheel end (toward front of car). The amount of end play can be varied by the thickness of shims 10 in fig. 48 . End play should be .003-.005 in. If there is too much end play which can be checked with dial indicator on the fan pulley as shown in fig. 49 thicker shims will have to be installed between flywheel shoulder face and crankshaft end flange of front main bearing shell. This necessitates removal of the engine.

Fig. 50 shows how flywheel center nut is removed with long wrench on special VW fixture. The pilot bush can now be checked for wear (with special plug gauge). The crankshaft oil seal can also be replaced at this stage if it has given signs of leaking. Special VW equipment is available to install new oil seal.

By using a depth micrometer or dial indicator the correct thickness of shims for proper end play can be determined. Fig. 51 shows how the distance of the crankshaft end face to flange of main bearing shell is measured (crankshaft should be pushed forward as far as it will go). Fig. 52 shows how the height of flywheel shoulder is measured (also refer to fig. 49). The thickness of the paper gasket should also be taken into account (it is approximately .008 in. thick and will be compressed to approximately .006 in.). Shims are made in different thicknesses. Do not use more than one paper gasket. The center nut should be drawn up tight (217 lb-ft).

Fig. 52 —Measuring height of flywheel shoulder

HEATER BOX—Fig. 53 shows a cross-section of the heater box. The cooling air drawn in by the fan is heated by engine and exhaust pipe heat.

Whenever exhaust fumes enter the car when the heater control knob is opened, heater box and exhaust pipe should be checked for leaks.

With the heater control knob closed the heat control valve (see fig. 54) must fully close the heater box outlet to prevent entry of hot air into the car. If it does the gasket may be defective or a replacement of the complete valve is in order.

All pivots in the heater box should be lubricated with a mixture of graphite and high melting point grease. Only use so much grease as to hold the graphite.

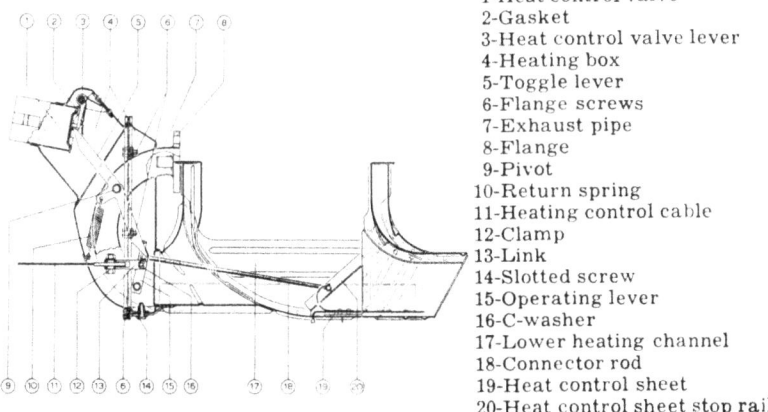

1-Heat control valve
2-Gasket
3-Heat control valve lever
4-Heating box
5-Toggle lever
6-Flange screws
7-Exhaust pipe
8-Flange
9-Pivot
10-Return spring
11-Heating control cable
12-Clamp
13-Link
14-Slotted screw
15-Operating lever
16-C-washer
17-Lower heating channel
18-Connector rod
19-Heat control sheet
20-Heat control sheet stop rail

Fig. 53 —Section of heating box

Fig. 54 — Heating box control valve

REMOVING AND INSTALLING MUFFLER — Raise car at rear and support on trestles. Remove rear cover plate. Take off 4 nuts at flanges of preheating pipe. Loosen clamps on the tail pipes and take pipes out. Loosen clamps at front exhaust pipes. Take off 4 nuts at flanges of muffler. Draw back muffler and take it off from below. Remove gaskets from flanges of cylinder heads, muffler and preheating pipe.

When installing, the following points should be observed: 1) Check muffler and exhaust pipes for cracks and damage. If necessary, the pipes can be straightened. The welded joint of the muffler and the tail pipe is particularly susceptible to damage by impacts. Leaks may result in the exhaust fumes entering the engine compartment and thus into the interior of the car when the heating is turned on. Always replace all bent or out-of-round tail pipes. If the cartridges are no longer serviceable the tail pipes have to be replaced. 2) Use new gaskets. 3) There should be a perfect seal at connection to front exhaust pipes. 4) Push tail pipes into the exhaust pipes and make sure there is a perfect seal at the connection with the exhaust pipes. The tail pipes should protrude approximately 190 mm (7.5") out of the exhaust pipes. The tail pipes must not touch the lower edge of the body. If necessary, remove tail pipes and heat exhaust pipes prior to bending them.

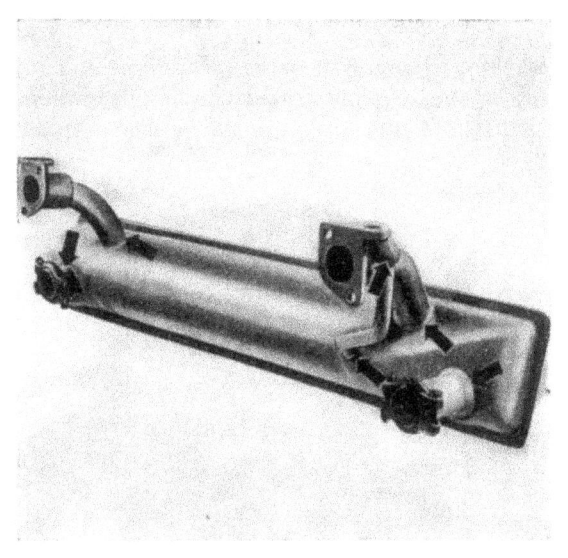

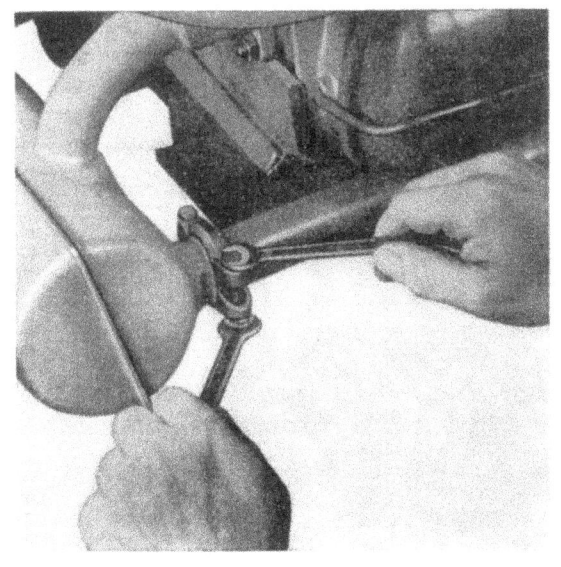

LATER 1200 ENGINE
1192 cc models after August, 1960

The following changes in parts, procedures and measurements pertain only to the engines installed in the Transporter line after August, 1960 (No. 5 000 001). Certain refinements were made be-

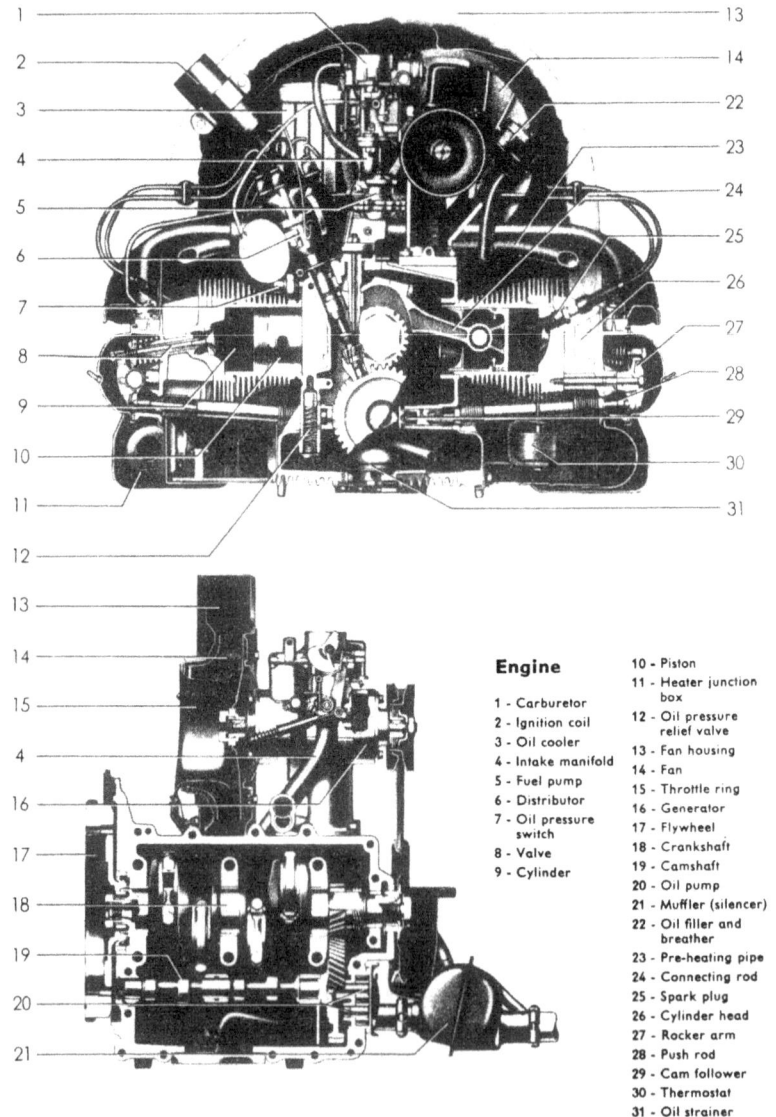

Engine

1 - Carburetor
2 - Ignition coil
3 - Oil cooler
4 - Intake manifold
5 - Fuel pump
6 - Distributor
7 - Oil pressure switch
8 - Valve
9 - Cylinder
10 - Piston
11 - Heater junction box
12 - Oil pressure relief valve
13 - Fan housing
14 - Fan
15 - Throttle ring
16 - Generator
17 - Flywheel
18 - Crankshaft
19 - Camshaft
20 - Oil pump
21 - Muffler (silencer)
22 - Oil filler and breather
23 - Pre-heating pipe
24 - Connecting rod
25 - Spark plug
26 - Cylinder head
27 - Rocker arm
28 - Push rod
29 - Cam follower
30 - Thermostat
31 - Oil strainer

40 HP Engine

ENGINE NUMBER 5,000,001 AND LATER

ginning with engine No. 5 009 663. Where necessary, an engine or chassis number is used to pinpoint a change. External appearance of some parts (for example, the air cleaner) may change from that of the illustrations, but unless noted, the procedure remains the same. When ordering parts, it is best to note the engine or chassis number to avoid mistakes.

Cooling Air Control (Thermostat)

For correct operation of the engine, a metered amount of cooling air is automatically supplied. Regular inspection and attention to the cooling air control is part of maintenance, especially at the beginning and end of hot or cold seasons. If the throttle ring opens prematurely or is jammed open, the engine will not attain operating temperature quickly enough. Symptoms are spitting back through carburetor, flat spot in acceleration and increased fuel consumption. If the ring opens too far it may interfere with the fan and result in noisy operation. Too little opening, on the other hand, creates excessive engine heat.

To provide for "fail-safe" operation, if the thermostat becomes inoperative the throttle ring remains in the open position so that excess heat cannot build up.

When the engine is cold (inoperative) the throttle ring should touch the air intake flange lightly. When warmed up the distance from the throttle ring to the intake flange (at the top) should be 25 to 30 mm (approximately 1 inch to 1 3/16 inches).

To adjust the thermostat when the engine is out of the vehicle;
1. Lift the thermostat to the upper stop of its support.
2. Adjust the throttle ring for open clearance at top as outlined above.
3. Tighten operating lever.

4. Tighten thermostat in position. Be sure the faces milled in the tapped boss of the thermostat fit properly in the guide hole of the support. It may be necessary to rotate the thermostat back ½ turn. When the thermostat has been tightened the throttle ring rests lightly against the intake flange (cold position).
5. Connect return spring.
6. Install right heating channel.

When the engine in the vehicle, this sequence is advised.
1. Detach return spring.
2. Release throttle ring operating lever.
3. Allow engine to warm up until upper end of thermostat touches upper stop of support.
4. Adjust throttle ring for clearance (1 inch to 1 3/16 inches).
5. Tighten operating lever.
6. Connect return spring.

Always make sure that throttle ring operating lever and linkage are moving freely and not binding in any position.

Fan Belt Tension

Correct fan belt tension must be maintained to avoid excessive wear and insure proper cooling and generator operation. This belt is subjected to considerable stress, particularly in downshifts and high speed revving. If the belt is too slack, slippage results, too tight places a strain on generator bearings and is also likely to cause belt breakage.

Correct belt deflection, when pressed with the thumb at a point midway between the crank pulley and the generator pulley should be 15mm, approximately 5/8 of an inch.

To adjust this tension, spacers in the generator pulley are placed either in the sheave or outside the outer flange. (see illustrations). These spacers are flat washers. The greater the number inside the pulley, the smaller the sheave diameter in which the fan belt runs and the slacker the tension. Remove the 21 mm nut on the generator shaft by inserting a large screwdriver into the pulley slot and turning the nut with a box wrench. Take off the outer pulley half and insert or remove washers as needed. Place all surplus washers between the outer pulley half and the retaining nut so that all spacers are kept on the shaft.

New belts will stretch after only a few miles of operation, so it is necessary to check belt tightness after the first 100 miles

---

Butler, New Jersey
March 20, 1961

Floyd Clymer Publications
1268 South Alvarado Street
Los Angeles 6, California

Gentlemen:

The Volkswagen owner's handbook published by you has been most helpful in routine maintenance work.

I would like to offer a suggestion regarding fan belt adjustment. The conventional instructions to check the correct belt tension by pressing the belt sideways and noting the deflection is, I submit, unreliable as no two persons are likely to press with the same force. How much is "lightly"? Furthermore, how can the deflection be measured conveniently?

I offer a simpler method:

Apply a wrench (21 mm.) to the nut on the generator shaft and turn the engine over slowly by the wrench. If the belt slips, it is too loose and should be tightened by shifting <u>one</u> space washer at a time. If the engine can be turned over, the tension is sufficient.

Owners should be cautioned against tightening the belt too much. Not only does a tight belt have a short life, but it is likely to ruin the generator bearings.

When checking the valve setting or the ignition timing, I never turn the engine over by pulling the belt by hand. I use the wrench and get my fan belt test at the same time.

Very truly yours,
Howard E. Russell

Mr. Russell's suggestion seems logical and worth passing on to the readers of this book. --Ed.

Cooling System

Heating air is no longer drawn over the engine where it can pick up oil fumes, but instead the fan blows part of the air down two large diameter flex hoses to heat exchangers surrounding the exhaust pipes. Strip the engine of cover plates as follows: Loosen clips holding large flex hoses to remove, then remove front engine cover plates. Remove carburetor heater flex hose, air cleaner assembly, then remove sealing plate screws from manifold heater pipes. Remove rear engine cover plate, then fan housing with generator. Remove intake manifold, then lift off the cylinder cover plates. After removing the cylinder head, pull out the deflector plates.

When removing the fan housing, first remove the fuel hose and vacuum lines from the carburetor, then pull the accelerator cable along with its conduit tube through the front of the engine. Remove spark plug cables from clips on fan housing, and cables from coil. Fan housing and generator are removed as a unit.

When reinstalling the plates, first the deflector plates are installed before replacing the pushrods, pushrod tubes and cylinder heads. Tension the plates against the cylinder head studs by bending the plates slightly to secure in position. Check that the weatherstrip around the edge of the engine compartment is over and under the engine cover plate.

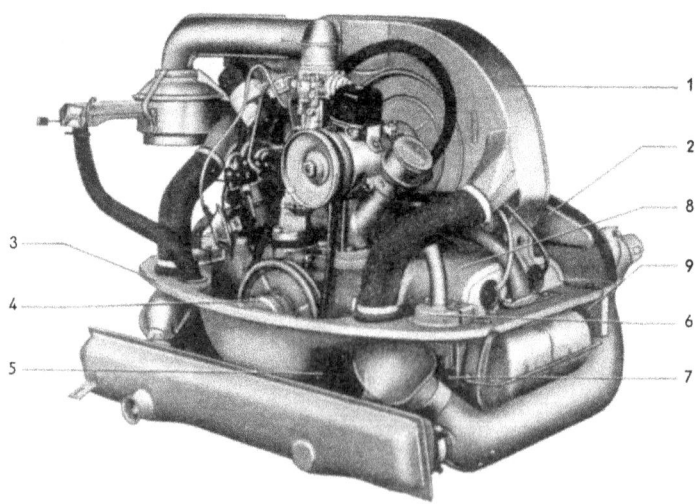

1 - Fan housing
2 - Front engine cover plate
3 - Rear engine cover plate
4 - Fan pulley cover
5 - Fan pulley lower plate
6 - Pre-heater pipe sealing plate
7 - Air deflector plate
8 - Cylinder cover plate
9 - Screening plate

Oil Strainer

Cleaning of the oil strainer in the bottom of the sump every 6,000 miles is good practice. Removal of the nuts around its outside edges permits it to be separated from the sump for cleaning in solvent. When replacing the unit, be sure that the mating surfaces are all clean and all traces of gasket material removed, use a new gasket and install the strainer so that the lower side comes to rest below the bend of the oil pickup tube and the tube is a snug fit in the strainer opening. When making up the retaining plate, tighten the nuts evenly and avoid warpage to insure against leakage.

The later model has a drain plug for easier servicing. A magnetic ring may be installed in the strainer with a retaining spring. This will ensure that all ferrous abrasives are trapped.

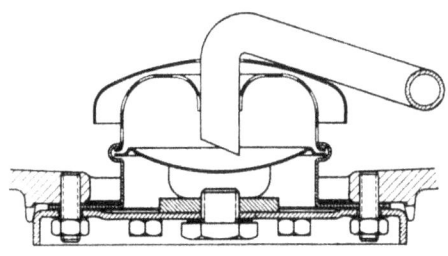

1 - Oil drain plug
2 - Gasket
3 - Bottom plate
4 - Gasket
5 - Oil strainer
6 - Lock washer
7 - Nut

Oil Pressure Switch

The warning device which operates a glow lamp on the instrument panel is the oil pressure switch (or sender). When the ignition is turned on the lamp glows. As pressure builds up (2.1 to 6.3 lb./sq. in.) the pressure deflects a diaphragm and breaks the electrical circuit. When the pressure drops the lamp glows. It is normal for the light to glow dimly at slow idle. If it comes on at speed, stop as soon as practical and check the engine for oil leaks. If oil temperature stays down, the dipstick level does not drop, and there is no visible evidence of a gusher, assume the sender to be faulty.

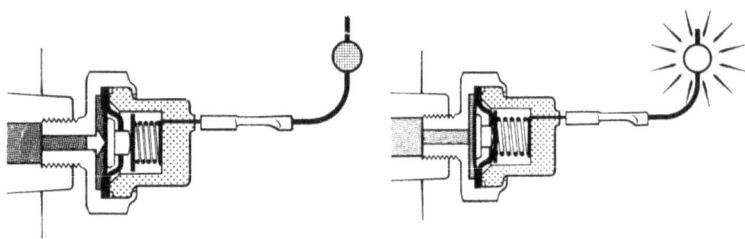

Pressure Relief Valve

The pressure relief valve should not be overlooked when disassembling engine and cleaning the case. If it sticks or cocks in the bore a 10 mm tap can be screwed into it to assist in removal.

1 - Plunger
2 - Spring
3 - Gasket
4 - Plug

Rocker Arm Assembly

The rocker arm assembly differs in that no coil spring is used and the bearing supports are stronger. After removing retaining nuts, remove shaft and pull off spring clips. After replacing shaft, position rocker arms as previously described. Tighten retaining nuts to 14 ft. lb. A drilling from the rocker arm bearing through to the adjusting screw lubricates the valve end.

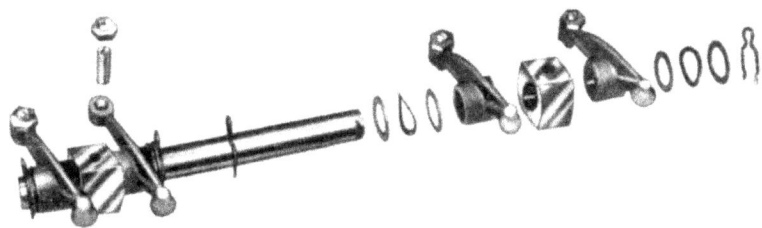

Cylinder Head and Pushrod Seals

After removing a cylinder head, remove the cylinders by pulling straight off. Be sure that most of the dirt has been removed from the area where the cylinder seals with the crankcase prior to removing the cylinders if no further disassembly is contemplated. Whenever the cylinder head is removed, the cylinder tends to unseal itself from the crankcase, so it is best to remove the cylinder and install a new seal between the cylinder and the crankcase. Be sure to clean off this area prior to installing the cylinder. This procedure also prevents the possibility of a cylinder falling off.

There is no gasket between the upper edge of the cylinder and the cylinder head, but a gas sealing ring is placed between the cylinder head and the cylinder shoulder. Renew this gasket, making sure the seam side of the gasket faces the head. Slightly stretch the corrugated sections of reused pushrod tubes over a bar, being careful not to crack the tube. This will insure a tight fit between tube, crankcase and cylinder head. As the head is lowered into place, make sure the oil seal at the ends of the push rod tubes are properly seated. The seam in the tubes should be upwards in the operating position of the engine. See "Removing and Installing Cylinders".

a = 190—191 mm (7.48—7.52")

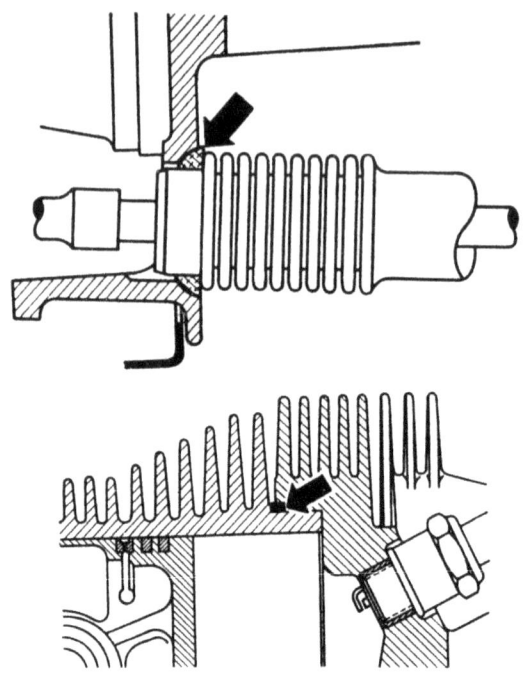

Valves

A different type of keeper is used on the valve stem, necessitating a change in the shape of the valve stem. Arrows point to areas where a burr may be encountered after the keeper is removed. The burr should be filed off prior to removing valve from the guide. If keepers are burred, file off burr. It should be just possible to turn the valve when the keepers are pressed together. If not, replace the keepers. A cap (see arrow) can be placed on the stem end of the valve to compensate for wear prior to installation of the rocker arms. The valve stem clearance in the guide is .002 to .003" for the intake valve, and .0031 to .0041" for the exhaust valve, with a wear limit of .006". Use previous procedure for remaining instructions.

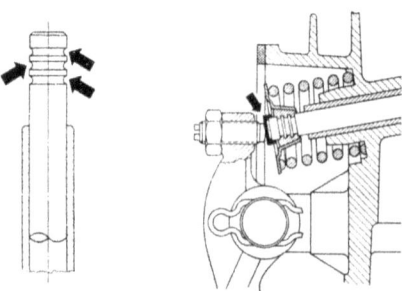

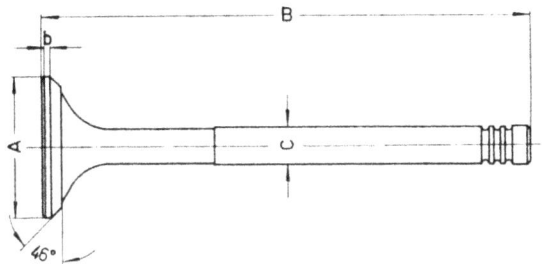

Valve Dimensions

	Intake	Exhaust
A.	31.4 mm — 31.6 mm dia. (1.236" — 1.244" dia.)	29.9 mm — 30.1 mm dia. (1.177" — 1.185" dia.)
B.	111.4 mm — 112.2 mm (4.386" — 4.417")	111.6 mm — 112.4 mm (4.394" — 4.425")
C.	7.94 mm — 7.95 mm dia. (0.3126" — 0.3130" dia.)	7.91 mm — 7.92 mm dia. (0.3114" — 0.3118" dia.)
b	0.8 mm — 1.5 mm (0.031" — 0.059")	1.00 mm — 1.70 mm (0.039" — 0.067")

valve springs

Loaded length 33.4 mm (1.32")
Load 43.8 ± 3 kg (96.7 ± 6.6 lbs.)

Valve Adjustment and Timing

Note that the valves are adjusted after the right-hand notch (10° before T.D.C.) is lined up with the split in the crankcase. Engine rotation is clockwise. Use the previous procedure.

On both the 40 hp 1200 and the 1500 engines there are two valve clearance settings possible. Rocker arm shafts are held in blocks of metal mounted on the cylinder head. The base (known as a boss) on which each block mounts may be either round or square. **Note:** Make sure that the boss that is being observed is actually part of the head casting and NOT part of the rocker arm mechanism. Use a flashlight or droplight to illuminate the area under the rocker arm mechanism.

If the boss is round, the intake valves are set at .008" and the exhaust valves are set at .012". If the boss is square in shape, then both valves are set at .004" clearance. On many of the 40 hp 1200 engines, a modification kit has been used with which the valve clearance is set at .004", no matter how the boss is shaped. Normally, the rocker arm mechanism is held on the cylinder head with studs coming through the metal blocks and nuts holding down the blocks. With the modification kit, however, there are boltheads showing where there were formerly studs and nuts.

An adjustment of the valves must only be carried out with the engine cold and at moderate outside temperature (approx. $20° C = 68° F$).

The clearance changes as the engine warms up. It should be carefully checked at the prescribed intervals.

Valve adjustment gives the desired result only if: the valves seal tightly, there is no undue clearance in the valve guides, and the stem face is not pitted.

Valve clearance insufficient:
Burning of valves and valve seats.
Distortion of valves.
Poor performance by reduced compression.
Uneven engine running.
Unsteady valve timing.

Valve clearance excessive:
Noisy timing mechanism.
Uneven engine running.
Unsteady valve timing.
Poor performance resulting from insufficient cylinder charge.

Valve Timing Diagram

Valve Timing Engines #5 000 001 to 5 009 663

Intake opens	EÖ	2° after T. D. C.
Intake closes	ES	24° after B. D. C.
Exhaust opens	AÖ	32° before B. D. C.
Exhaust closes	AS	10° before T. D. C.

Engine #5 009 663 and later

Intake opens EO	4° before T. D. C.
Intake closes ES	32° after B. D. C.
Exhaust opens AÖ	41° before B. D. C.
Exhaust closes AS	1° before T. D. C.

This diagram applies to a valve clearance of 1 mm (0.04") with the engine cold. After having checked the valve timing, the normal valve clearance should be restored.

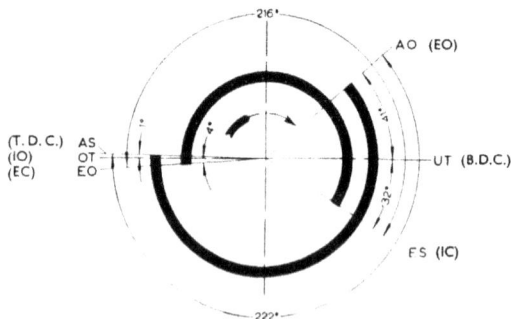

Valve Timing

1 - Mark the position of T.D.C. of cylinder No. 1 on the crankshaft pulley: 16 mm (0.47") to the right of the timing mark.

2 - Make a mark 3 mm (0.12") to the left of the T. D. C. mark.

3 - Adjust valve clearance of cylinder No. 1 to 1 mm (0.04").

4 - Crank the engine clockwise. The inlet valve should open when the mark on the crankshaft pulley lines up with the vertical crankcase jointing faces.

Displacing the camshaft gear by one tooth alters the valve timing by approx. 22 mm (0.87").

Removing and Installing Cylinders

With the engine in the process of disassembly, the removal of cylinders is a prelude to separation of the case, replacement of piston rings, etc. With the heads removed, take out the pushrods and the pushrod tubes, then remove the deflector plates before lifting the cylinders off the case.

In replacing the cylinders the mating surfaces between the cylinders the thin gasket and the case must be perfectly clean since foreign matter would cause distortion. It is well to use new gaskets in all instances. Then:

1. Apply engine oil to piston, pin, and cylinder walls.
2. Compress the piston rings (tool VW 123a). Rings must be staggered so that gaps are not in line vertically.
3. Shove cylinder down over piston. Do not allow the long studs to contact the fins.
4. Install deflector plates, bending slightly to prevent rattling.
5. Install pushrods and tubes, then lower head into place. Tighten cylinder head nuts slightly in sequence previously shown. Tighten nuts to 7 ft. lb. (using first diagram), finally tightening nuts to 22–23 ft. lb. (using second diagram).

Pistons and Rings

Volkswagen uses the selective assembly method of matching components by tolerance in finished dimensions. Pistons and cylinders are so mated and if it becomes necessary to replace a piston, the proper size and weight should be chosen.

57

A - Weight grading.

> Brown = — weight
>
> Grey = + weight

B - Size grading paint mark.

C - Arrow and the word "vorn" (indented or stamped) must point towards the flywheel when installing the piston.

D - Weight grading paint mark.

E - Size.

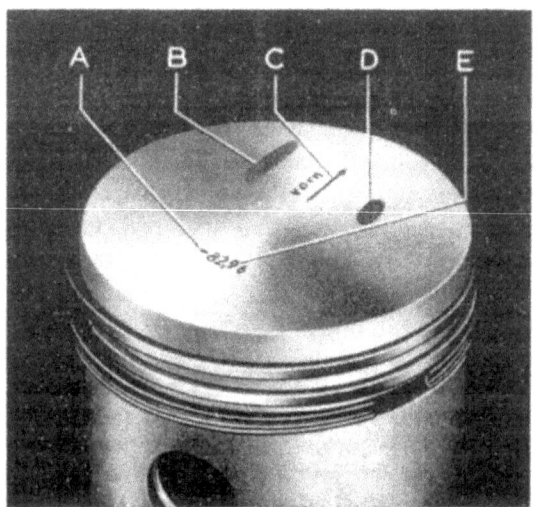

Piston rings should not be removed unless necessary; use piston ring pliers to prevent breakage. Check rings for gap and clearance as previously described, using the following dimensions:

Check piston ring side clearance in grooves with a feeler gauge.

Compression ring, top 0.065—0.092 mm; max. 0.12 mm (.0026—.0036"; max. .0047").

Compression ring, lower 0.045—0.072 mm; max. 0.1 mm (.0018—.0028"; max. .004").

Oil ring 0.025—0.052 mm; max. 0.1 mm (.001—.002"; max. .004").

Compression ring gap: 0.30—0.45 mm (.012—.018"); max. 0.95 mm (.037").

Oil scraper ring gap: 0.25—0.40 mm (.010—.016"); max. 0.95 mm (.037").

Piston Pins

Piston pin holes are offset in the piston to effect less wear and noise during engine operation. For this reason, it is very important that the pistons are installed with the arrow or the word "vorn" pointing toward the flywheel. Piston pin fit can range from a tight fit (in which the piston needs to be heated for pin removal) to a loose fit (in which the pin will slide out under its own weight). In none of these cases is it necessary to replace the pin, piston or both. Both the pin and piston hole are color marked, as shown in the chart. For a piston pin hole over .7874", use a green marked pin.

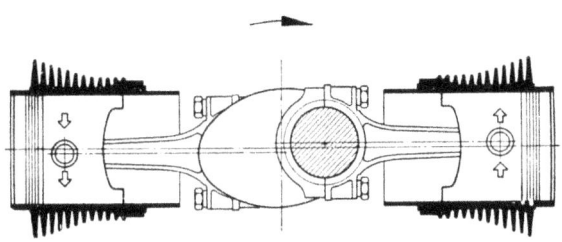

Color	Piston pin dia. (mm)	Pin bearing dia. (mm)
Black	19.994—19.997	19.996—19.999
White	19.997—20.000	19.999—20.001
Green	20.001—20.004	Pin only

The clearance between the piston pin and the connecting rod bush is .0001 to .0006". If clearance is near the wear limit of .0016", it is best to renew the piston pin and the connecting rod bush. If piston is a tight fit on the pin, use the heating method previously described to remove or replace, starting by inserting the circlip on the side facing the flywheel, inserting the oiled pin with one movement until it is stopped by the circlip, then inserting the other circlip. All circlips should be double checked for correct seating.

Matching Cylinders and Pistons

Measure the diameter of the cylinder .4—.6" below the upper edge of the cylinder with an inside micrometer, then measure the diameter of the piston at the bottom end of the skirt at right angles to the piston axis. Compare the readings with the nominal values stamped on the crown of the piston and on the cylinder base. If the measurement proves that the clearance is about .008", the wear limit, replace the piston and cylinder with another set of the same size grading. Make

	Colour	Cylinder mm ⌀	Corresponding Piston mm ⌀
Standard Size Nominal Dimension 77 mm ⌀	Blue Pink Green	76.990—76.999 77.000—77.009 77.010—77.020	76.95 76.96 76.97
1st Oversize Nominal Dimension 77.5 mm ⌀	Blue Pink Green	77.490—77.499 77.500—77.509 77.510—77.520	77.45 77.46 77.47
2nd Oversize Nominal Dimension 78 mm ⌀	Blue Pink Green	77.990—77.999 78.000—78.009 78.010—78.020	77.95 77.96 77.97

sure the difference in weight between the pistons in one engine does not exceed 10 g. Since the compression ratio should remain the same when installing reconditioned cylinders, the distance from the crown to the boss of the oversize pistons is appropriately reduced. Cylinders (new or reconditioned) may be reused when the cylinder of a corresponding damaged piston does not show signs of wear. Simply renew the piston with one of the same size and weight grading.

Distributor Drive Pinion

With distributor, fuel pump with intermediate flange, gaskets and push rod removed, withdraw distance spring by placing a thin rod through it and using a wire hook to pull it up. Working through the fuel pump opening, lever the distributor drive pinion upward slightly, then make sure the washer is resting on its base before removing the pinion completely. Remove the washer the same way as the distance spring, using a rod and hook (a bar magnet may also be used, or if the engine is out of the car, turn the engine upside down and let the washer drop out). In any case, if the washer is dropped

into the interior of the crankcase, it will be necessary to remove it to prevent damage to the timing gears. Check the eccentric and spiral gear of drive pinion for wear, and if gear is badly worn, check the distributor drive gear on the crankshaft. Also check the washer for wear, replace any parts as necessary. Replace washer carefully as it was removed, using a rod to guide washer into place so it does not fall into crankcase interior.

Note: If distributor drive pinion is removed when the engine is in the vehicle, set cylinder No. 1 to TDC as follows: With the engine completely assembled and the valve covers off, use a wrench on the crankshaft pulley nut to rotate the engine clockwise (which is normal direction of engine rotation) until No. 1 cylinder intake valve goes down and returns (opens and closes). Continue turning the crankshaft in the same direction until the "TDC" mark on the crankshaft pulley is lined up with the mark on the crankcase. This locates the TDC of the No. 1 cylinder.

Replace the distributor drive pinion after the oil pump, cover plate below the crankshaft pulley and the pulley itself have been installed. As drive pinion shaft is inserted, it will rotate clockwise about 20°. With the No. 1 cylinder at TDC (see note), the offset slot in the top must be at right angles to the driving direction and the smaller segment must be towards the crankshaft pulley.

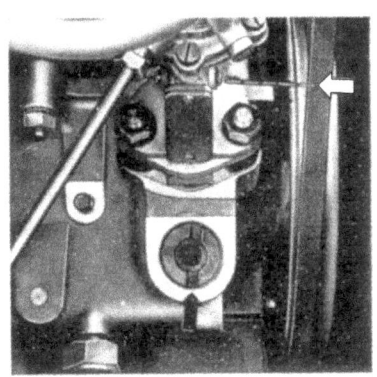 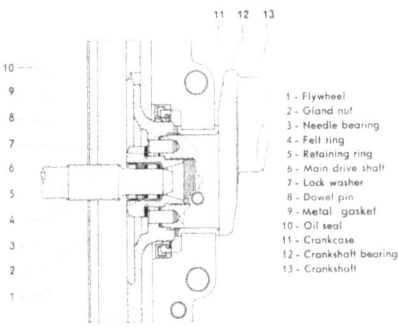

1 - Flywheel
2 - Gland nut
3 - Needle bearing
4 - Felt ring
5 - Retaining ring
6 - Main drive shaft
7 - Lock washer
8 - Dowel pin
9 - Metal gasket
10 - Oil seal
11 - Crankcase
12 - Crankshaft bearing
13 - Crankshaft

Removing and Installing Flywheel

The flywheel is attached by the gland nut to the crankshaft and is held by four dowel pins. A metal gasket replaces the paper gasket between the flywheel and the crankshaft, and a needle bearing in the gland nut supports the main drive shaft. To install, check the flywheel teeth, remove any burr if necessary, then check the dowel pin holes in the flywheel and crankshaft for wear. Any repair must

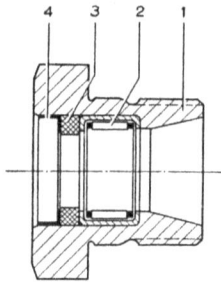

1 - Gland nut
2 - Needle bearing
3 - Oil seal
4 - End ring

Parts	Mark
Crankshaft	Paint dot **inside** hole for gland nut.
Flywheel	Paint dot and 5 mm (.2") dia. hole on the face which is towards the clutch.
Clutch	Paint line on the outer edge of the clutch pressure plate.

be carried out with the correct special equipment. Renew dowel pins if necessary. Check the needle bearing for wear, then lubricate with about one-third ounce of universal grease and wipe away any excess. Ensure that the needle cage is adequately greased.

Check the flywheel for runout, then adjust the end play by taking the measurements previously described, taking into account the .0078" thick metal gasket, which is compressed by .0019" on assembly, leaving .0059" to be considered when deciding the thickness of the shim. The crankshaft end play is between .0028 and .0047" (best set between .004 and .0045" because of extreme heat conditions causing engine seizure), with a wear limit of .006". Shims of different thicknesses (a total of three and only one metal gasket) must be used in each case. Following the computation of this thickness, put the shims in place, replace the metal gasket, then check the unbalance marks as described in the chart. Taking the mark on the crankshaft into consideration, install the flywheel and clutch so that the marks are about 120° offset. Install with an offset of 180° if only two parts are marked, then tighten the gland nut down to 217 ft. lb.

Crankshaft Oil Seal

Procedure for the oil seal remains the same, however, it should be noted that in certain cases the outer diameter of the seal expands to a lesser degree than the respective crankcase bore when the engine is at operating temperature. With oil seals in the lower tolerance range, leaks may occur in time. This may lead to the faulty conclusion that oil losses at the flywheel side have occurred from leaks at the crankcase joint, leading to expensive and unnecessary repairs. Therefore, it is best to check the crankshaft oil seal first whenever oil losses are noticed at the flywheel side, and replace oil seal if necessary.

Crankcase, Camshaft, Crankshaft and Connecting Rods

The camshaft followers have been provided with a mushroom head and are no longer held in place with guide plates. Since they are loose, use a clip to hold them in place before lifting off the right-hand crankcase half. Clean crankcase and check for wear, cracks, uneven jointing faces, and inspect oil suction pipe for tightness and leaks; if necessary, peen into place with a hammer and drift. Check studs for tightness and peen if necessary. Use Heli-Coil inserts if tapped holes are worn. Remove sharp edges from oil passages, crankshaft bore, and camshaft bearing bores. Insert cam followers and crankshaft bearing dowel pins before installing the camshaft and crankshaft. Make sure the dowel pins are tight (use a small punch to upset soft metal near pin to tighten), then make sure the timing marks are together on the gears. Use Liquid Aviation Permatex gasket compound to coat the entire camshaft end plug and lay a film on all jointing surfaces prior to putting together the case halves. Install the thrust washers and the crankshaft oil seal, bedding the seal squarely in the crankcase recess, then use clips to hold the cam followers in the right half of the crankcase. Make sure none of the sealing compound enters the oil passages of the crankshaft and camshaft bearings, then join the case halves and screw on the nuts. First, tighten the M8 nut which is beside the M12 stud of the No. 1 crankshaft bearing. Only then must the M12 nuts be tightened fully. Torque the M12 nuts to 24—26 ft. lb., and the M8 nuts to a 14 ft. lb. setting. Finally, turn the crankshaft to test for ease of movement.

Slight damage to the cam faces may be smoothed down with an oilstone (silicone carbide) — a 100 to 120 grain stone should be used before polishing with a 280 to 320 grain stone. See the List Of Tolerances and Wear Limits for camshaft end play and backlash adjustment.

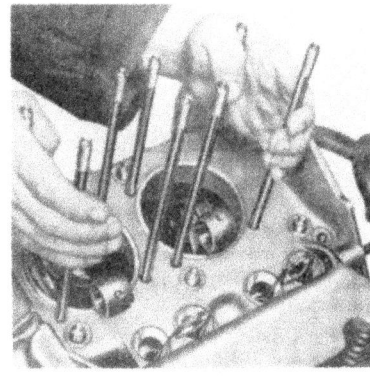

 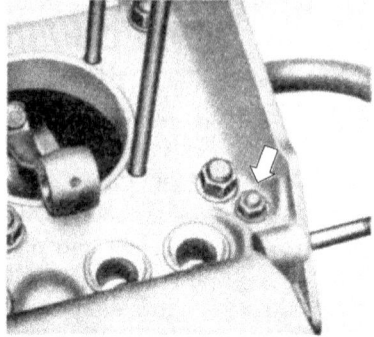

If backlash is excessive, timing gears will be noisy. Check by rocking the gears back and forth with both hands while gradually revolving the camshaft timing gear until it has made a complete turn, and if gearlash is excessive at any point, the camshaft with its gear should be replaced. New camshafts can be purchased with timing gears in various sizes under different part numbers.

The crankshaft has removable bearing shells, and clearance is measured by the Plastigage method. This plastic wire, available at auto parts stores, is placed across the bearing shell, the crankshaft is installed, and the crankshaft halves tightened to the prescribed torque. Remove crankshaft, making sure not to turn it during the complete procedure. The flattened wire will probably be found stuck to the bearing shell, and its width is compared to the scale on the reverse of the paper container. From this the clearance can be ascertained, and a decision made as to whether it is practical to save the old bearings or replace them. If the car uses one quart of oil in 650 miles, and the engine is being overhauled, it is usually most practical to replace all bearings at the same time. The above method is also

 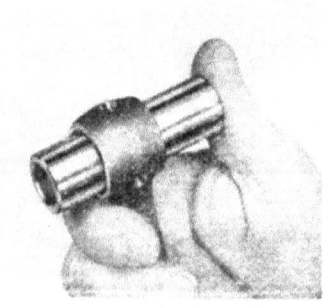

best for checking the connecting rod bearings. However, this had best be done one connecting rod at a time, being sure not to turn the rod on the crankshaft while torqueing the bolt to 36 ft. lb. After bearings are replaced, it is best to use this method to check that the new crankshaft bearings are adequate, and it is not a case of a badly worn crankshaft that should be reconditioned.

The crankshaft needs to be disassembled to remove both the No. 4 and No. 3 bearings. With bearing No. 1 removed, remove the Woodruff key and oil thrower, then pull off bearing No. 4. Use circlip pliers to remove the distributor drive gear retaining ring. Remove the connecting rods and keep them in order for replacement with mating parts. To remove the No. 3 bearing, a machine shop press is needed to remove the distributor drive gear, spacer, and crankshaft timing gear. It would be best to clean and inspect the crankshaft at this time and blow out the oil passages with compressed air, then hold the crankshaft at one end and strike a non-bearing surface with a hammer. If there is a clear, ringing tone, there is little chance of cracks being present.

If there is equipment available, check the crankshaft for runout, then coat the parts removed with clean engine oil and press into place. Replace any gears that show signs of seizure and wear. The gears must first be heated to about 180° F. in an oil bath prior to being pressed into place. Check gears for tight seating after they have cooled, then replace remaining parts. The annular groove in the running surface of No. 4 bearing must be towards the oil thrower, and the oil thrower must be installed so that the concave surface faces the pulley. Blow out all oilholes before installing crankshaft. As long as the crankcase is open, it is wise to replace all bearings.

Connecting rods should be checked for wear or damage, and if any rods are replaced, re-weigh all of them since replacement rods are supplied in the upper weight range only. Metal may be removed from the shaded areas to reduce the weight of a connecting rod, being sure to remove metal from both sides to balance the rod. Final weights should not exceed 5.6 drams difference between the weights of all rods in one engine. Check the piston pin bush, pushing a piston pin through. It should be merely a thumb push, and if it falls through, the bushing will have to be replaced. It is inadvisable to fit oversize piston rings in such cases, since they will be too tight in the piston. Oil all parts and re-insert the connecting rod bearings, then assemble the connecting rods, making sure the identification numbers on both parts are on one side. Tighten the connecting rod bolts to 36 ft. lb., then check that the rod will fall smoothly through an 180° arc under its own weight. Release any pre-tension between the bearing halves, which is likely to occur when tightening the connecting rod bolts, by

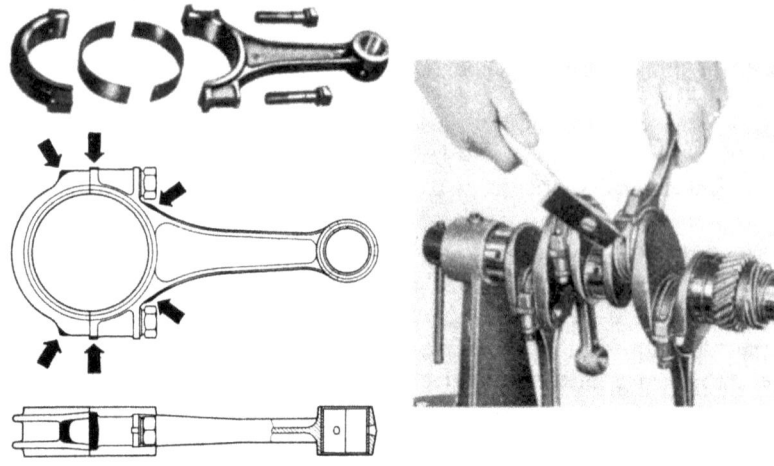

tapping both sides of the connecting rod with a hammer. Never file, scrape or ream the bearings. Finally, check the end play of the connecting rod bearing with a feeler gauge, using the List Of Tolerances and Wear Limits, then secure the bolts in several places with a peen.

Oil Filler

The oil filler is removed by unscrewing the threaded ring inside and pulling off the hose. Tool VW 170 is recommended. When installing, be sure to replace the gasket between the generator support and the oil filler. Be sure to install the pipe as illustrated, with the adapter pipe directly to the front, or the oil will not flow back and there will be gurgling noises.

Servicing Fan

To remove the fan from the housing and generator shaft, first remove the screws on the fan cover with a T-wrench, then remove the generator and the fan. With one mechanic holding the fan, remove the nut on the fan, then remove the fan, spacer washers and hub. Do not loose the Woodruff key.

To install the fan, place the hub on the generator shaft, making sure the Woodruff key is properly seated. Insert the same number of spacer washers, then place the fan in position. Place the remaining spacer washers on the shaft. Use a socket and torque wrench to tighten the special nut to 40—47 ft. lb. Check the distance between the fan and the fan cover as shown in the diagram. If distance is not correct, remove special nut and add or subtract washers between the hub and thrust washer as necessary. Place unused spacer washers between the thrust washer and fan, then retighten the special nut to 40—47 ft. lb. Insert the fan into the housing and tighten the screws on the cover.

1 - Thrust washer
2 - Fan hub
3 - Woodruff key
4 - Spezial nut
5 - Generator shaft
6 - Lock washer
7 - Spacer washers
8 - Fan
9 - Fan cover

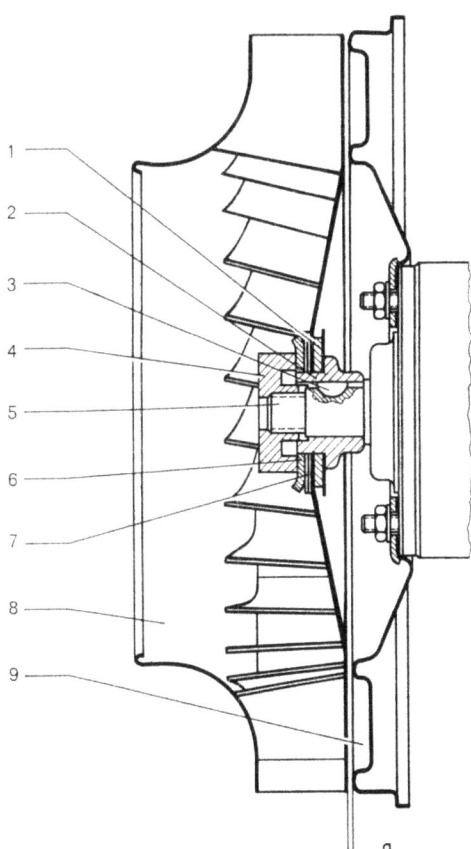

a = .08" (2.0 mm)

Performance Graph

34 bhp Engine

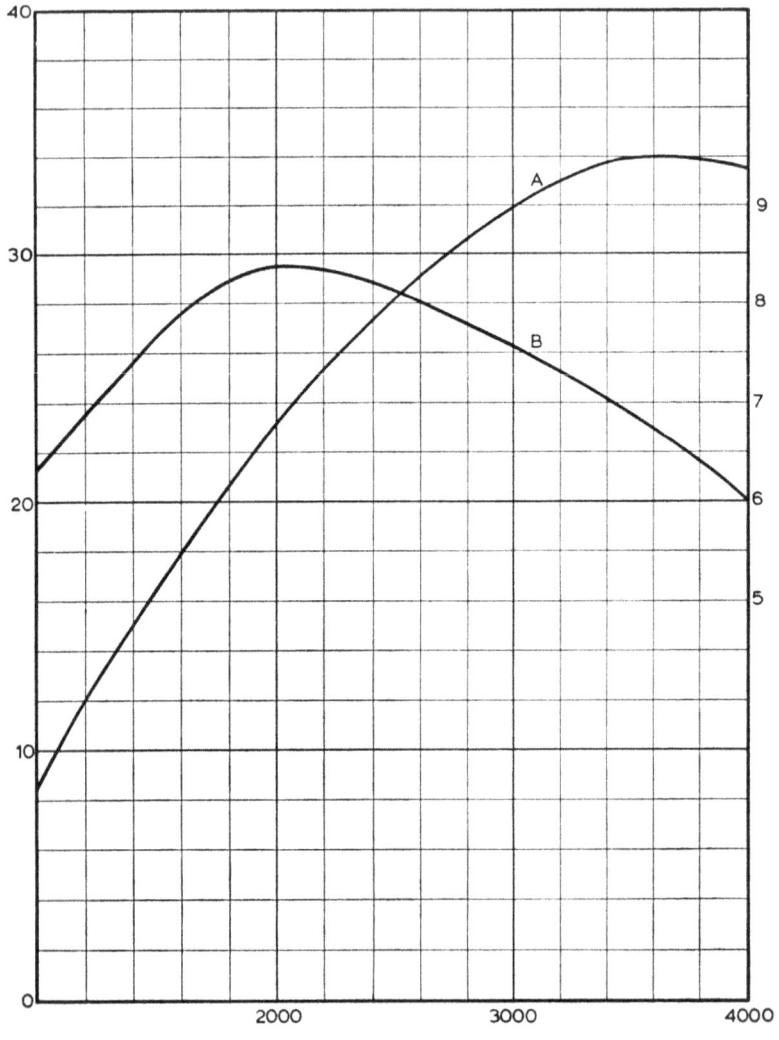

A—Ne = Output (bhp.)

B—Md = Torque (ft. lbs.)

(1 mkg = 7.233 ft. lbs.)

1500 Repair Supplement
1943 cc models after August, 1963

Beginning with cars manufactured in August, 1963 and thereafter, a larger engine has been used, putting out 50 (S.A.E.) bhp. Those changes in maintenance and repair procedures which apply are set forth in the following pages. If a part or method is not described here, the technique and components which apply to the 1200 models remain the same.

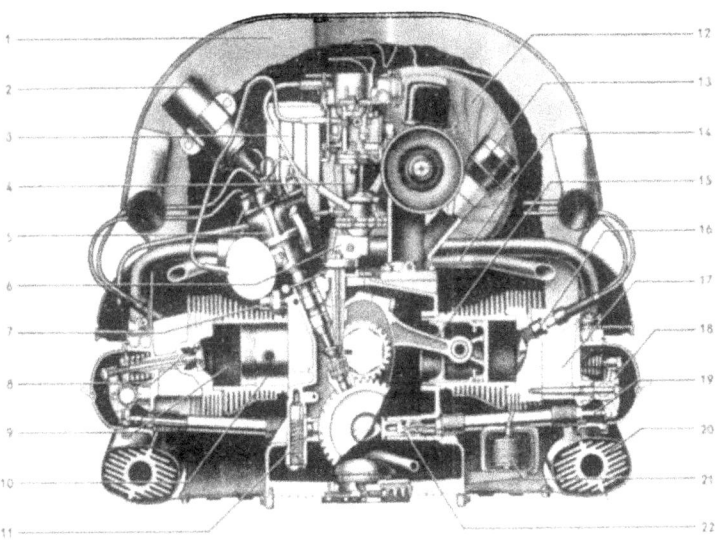

The Volkswagen Engine

1 - Fan housing
2 - Ignition coil
3 - Oil cooler
4 - Intake manifold
5 - Distributor
6 - Fuel pump
7 - Oil pressure switch
8 - Valve
9 - Cylinder
10 - Piston
11 - Oil pressure relief valve
12 - Fan
13 - Oil filler neck
14 - Pre-heater pipe
15 - Connecting rod
16 - Spark plug
17 - Cylinder head
18 - Rocker arm
19 - Push rod
20 - Heat exchanger
21 - Thermostat
22 - Cam follower
23 - Throttle ring
24 - Carburetor
25 - Generator
26 - Flywheel
27 - Crankshaft
28 - Camshaft
29 - Oil pump
30 - Oil strainer

Rocker Arms

There is a difference in dimensions between the rocker arms on the 1200 and the 1500 series engines, so one must not be substituted for the other. **A** is the 1200 rocker arm and **B** is the 1500 rocker arm.

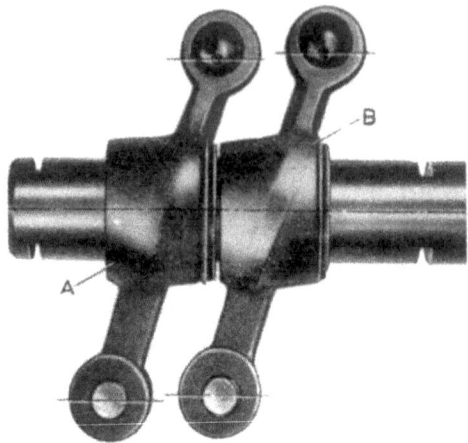

Cylinder Head

See previous instructions for installing the cylinder head, dispensing with the sealing ring instructions. No sealing ring is used with the improved design.

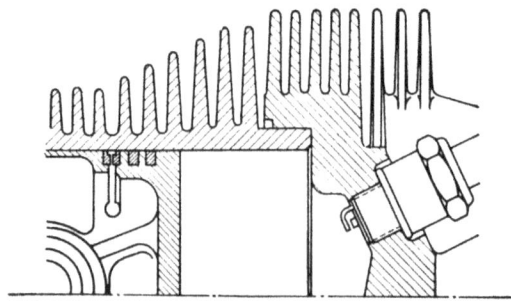

Valves and Valve Seats

Valve seats in serviceable and uncracked heads can be reconditioned with proper tools. Use the illustrations and measurements as a guide. Cut the 45° face first, being very careful to ensure a perfectly concentric seating surface and the minimum amount of metal removal. Lift up on cutting tool as soon as the complete surface has been cleaned up or else the life of the insert will be affected. Next, slightly chamfer the lower edge of the exhaust valve seat insert with the 75° cutter. Slightly chamfer the lower edge of the intake valve seat insert with the 60° cutter. Finally, cut the upper edge of the valve seat insert with the 15° cutter until the correct seat width is reached.

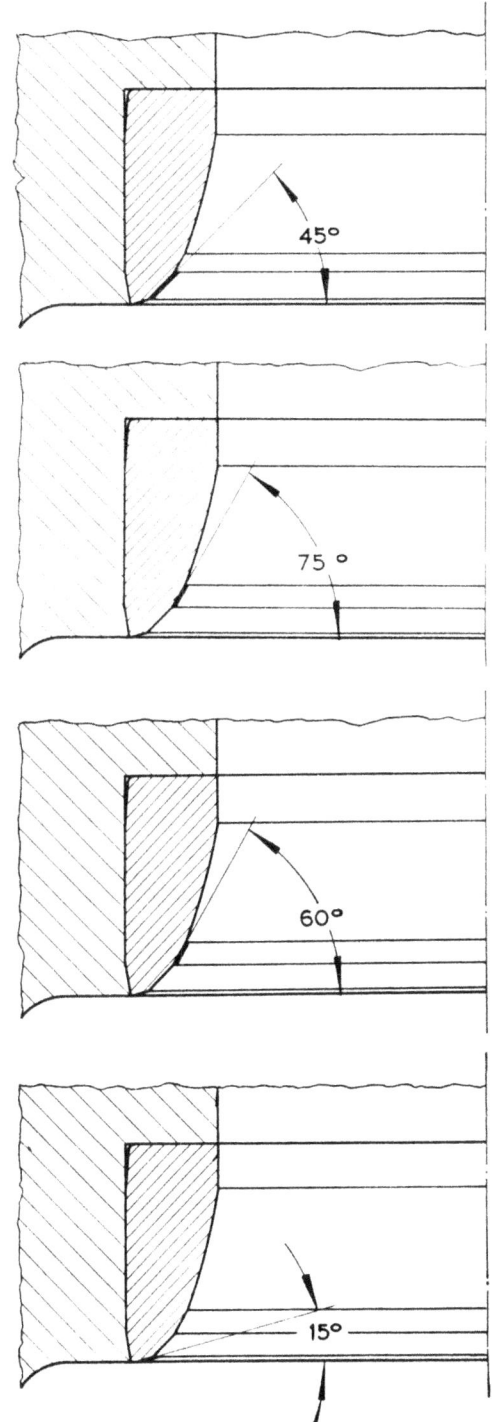

Cut the 45° face.

Intake: Cutter 45°/37 mm dia.

Exhaust: Cutter 45°/34 mm dia.

Cut the 75° face.

Exhaust: Cutter 75°/30 mm dia.

Cut the 60° face.

Intake: Cutter 60°/37 mm dia.

Cut the 15° face.

Intake: Cutter 15°/37 mm dia.
Exhaust: Cutter 15°/34 mm dia.

Valve Clearance and Valve Timing

The valve clearance must only be checked or adjusted with the engine cold or at a maximum oil temperature of 50°C (122°F).

Valve clearance: **Intake** 0.30 mm (.012")

Exhaust 0.30 mm (.012")

The clearance decreases as the engine warms up. It should be carefully checked at the prescribed intervals.

Valve adjustment gives the desired result only if: the valves seal tightly, there is no undue clearance in the valve guides, and the stem face is not pitted.

Valve clearance insufficient:

- Burning of valves and valve seats.
- Distortion of valves.
- Poor performance due to low compression.
- Uneven engine running.
- Altered valve timing.

Valve clearance excessive:

- Noisy timing mechanism.
- Uneven engine running.
- Altered valve timing.
- Poor performance resulting from insufficient cylinder charge.

	Intake Valve	Exhaust Valve
A	31.4 — 31.6 mm dia.	29.9 — 30.1 mm dia.
B	111.4 —112.2 mm	111.6 —112.4 mm
C	7.94— 7.95 mm dia.	7.91— 7.92 mm dia.
b	1.4 — 1.9 mm	1.6 — 2.1 mm

Intake Valve

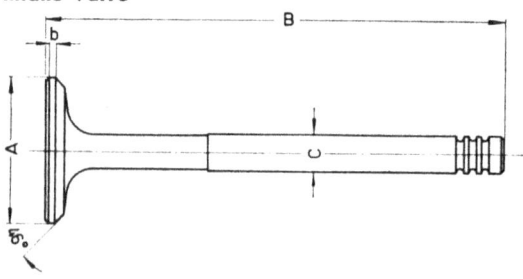

Exhaust Valve

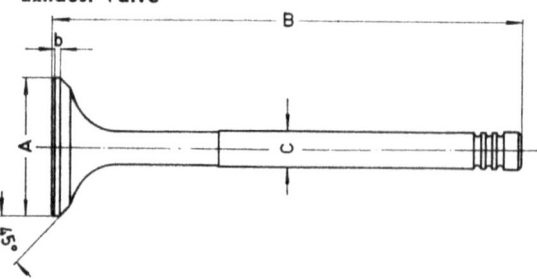

Pistons and Cylinders

When installing the rings with the piston ring tool (to avoid damaging the piston), be sure to locate the expander spring as indicated in the illustration, and install the compression rings with the word "Top" or "Oben" toward the top of the piston. Use the previous instructions for the remainder of the procedure.

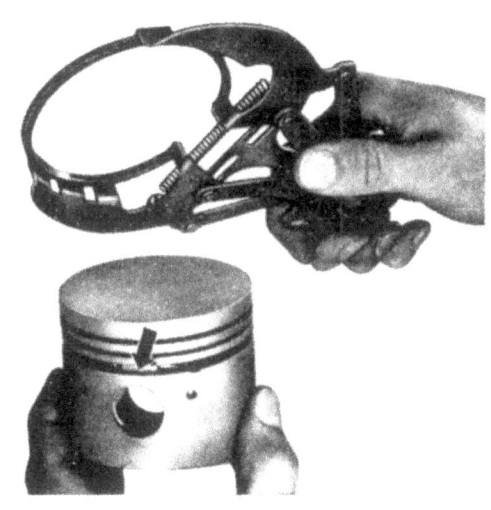

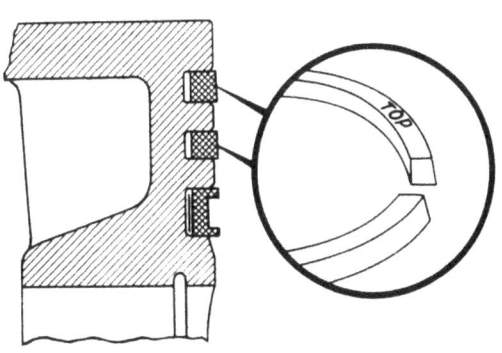

Piston pins have been enlarged over the previous model; however, they retain the same marking system, with a green-marked oversize pin for a piston pin hole diameter in excess of .8662".

Color	Piston pin dia. (mm)	Pin bearing dia. (mm)
Black	21.994—21.997	21.995—21.998
White	21.997—22.000	21.998—22.001
Green	22.001—22.004	Pin only

Pistons and cylinders come in three size gradings as shown in the table. Use an inside micrometer to check the internal dimensions of the cylinder about ½" below the top. Piston/cylinder clearance should be .0014 to .0024". Use the previous instructions for the remainder of the procedure.

	Colour	Cylinder mm dia.	Corresponding Piston mm dia.
Standard Size Nominal Dimension 83 mm dia.	Blue Pink Green	82.990—83.001 83.002—83.013 83.014—83.025	82.95 82.96 82.97
1st Oversize Nominal Dimension 83.5 mm dia.	Blue Pink Green	83.490—83.501 83.502—83.513 83.514—83.525	83.45 83.46 83.47
2nd Oversize Nominal Dimension 84 mm dia.	Blue Pink Green	83.990—84.001 84.002—84.013 84.014—84.025	83.95 83.96 83.97

Engine Power Curve

42 bhp Engine

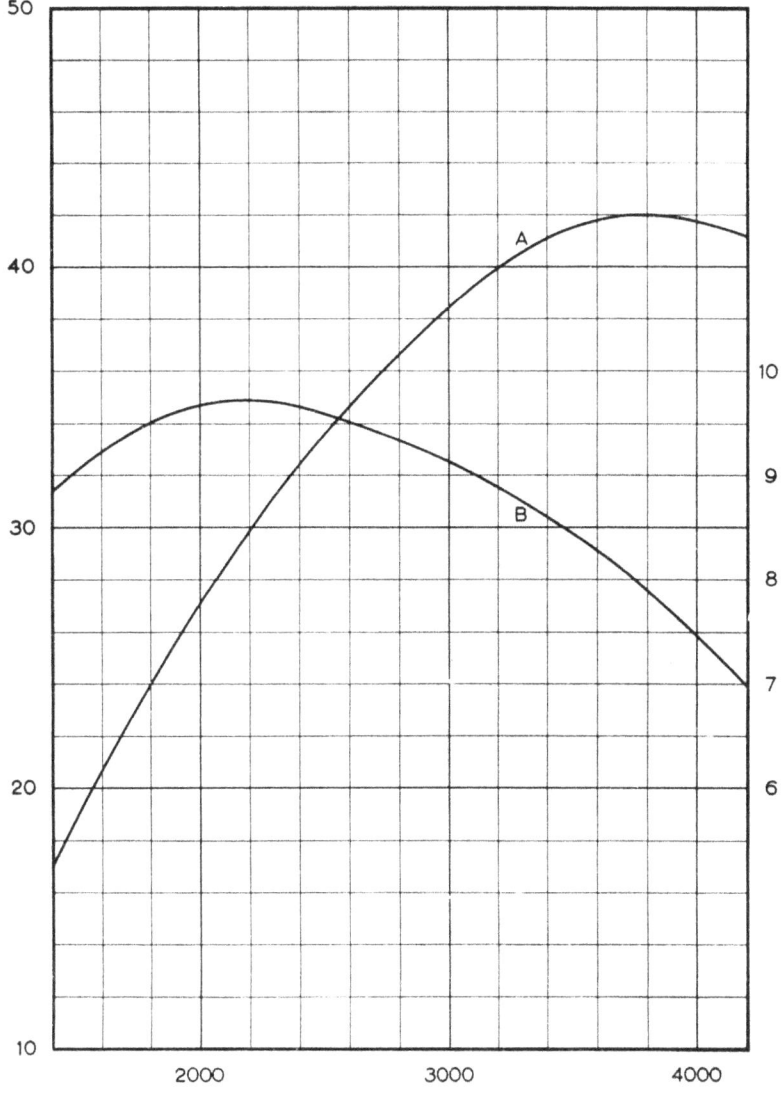

A—Ne = Output (bhp.)

B—Md = Torque (ft. lbs.)

Later 1500 Changes

The following changes were made during production of the 1500 cc engine. Refer to the engine number when ordering repair parts. The bhp was increased to 53 (S.A.E.) after August, 1965, although the total displacement remained 1493 cc (91.1 cu. in.).

Rocker Arm Assembly

Bearing supports for the rocker arm mechanism are split. Be sure the supports are fitted with the chamfered edges outwards and the splits upwards, and torque the nut on the studs to 18 ft. lb. Cylinder head covers should be wiped clean of road dirt prior to removal, and all exposed parts of the valve mechanism should be wiped completely clean before replacing the covers. Check that the cylinder head covers are not leaking after test running the engine.

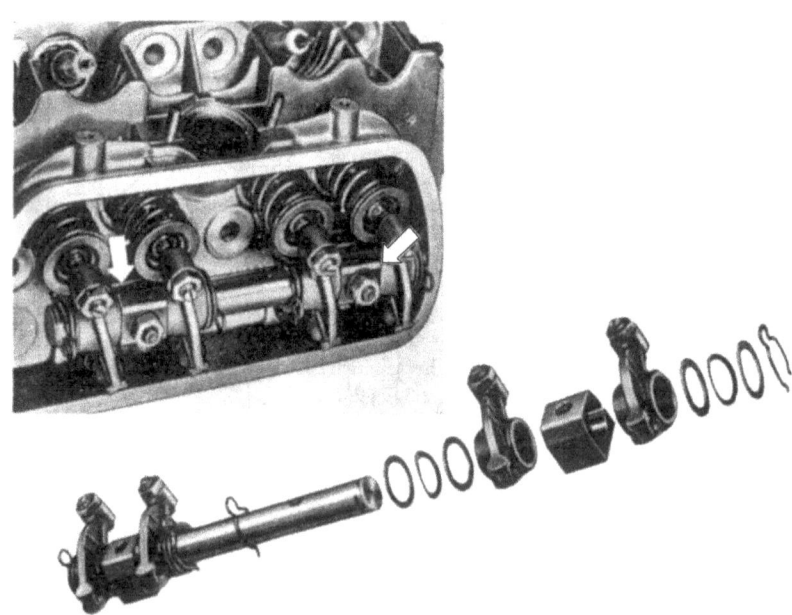

FIG. A-1

Intake Manifold

The diameter of the intake pipe is 28 mm (1.10″). It is fitted to the cylinder heads with a slight inward angle.

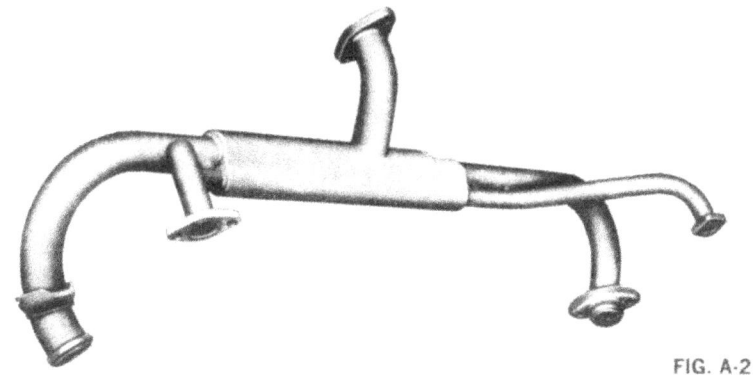

FIG. A-2

Cylinder Head and Valves

There is no sealing ring between cylinder shoulder and cylinder head. The rocker arms have two forged-on identification marks and push rods have internally-fitted ball ends (Figure A-3). An oil deflector ring has been added to the valve stems.

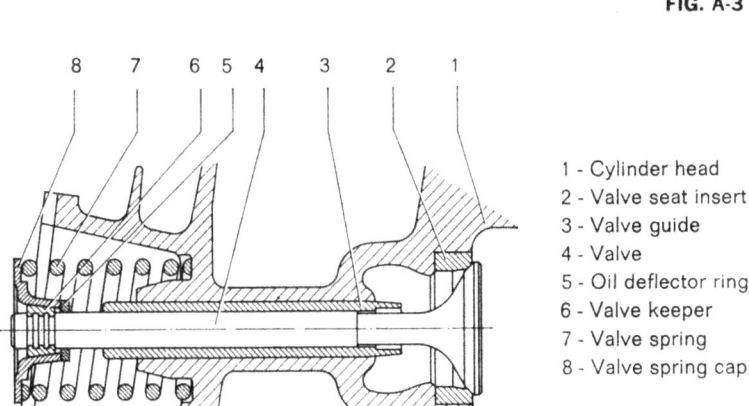

FIG. A-3

1 - Cylinder head
2 - Valve seat insert
3 - Valve guide
4 - Valve
5 - Oil deflector ring
6 - Valve keeper
7 - Valve spring
8 - Valve spring cap

Valve spring data: Loaded length: 31 mm (1.220"). Pressure: 57 ± 4 kg (125 9 ± lbs.) All other measurements, including those of the exhaust valves, are unchanged. Valve clearance (up to a maximum oil temperature of 50°C.) is inlet and exhaust 0.1 mm (.004"). The valve clearance is given on a sticker on the fan housing.

Color	Piston pin dia.	Piston pin bore dia.
Black	21.994 – 21.997	21.995 – 21.998
White	21.997 – 22.000	21.998 – 22.001
Green	22.001 – 22.004	pin only

FIG. A-4

Cylinders and Pistons

The cylinders have 19 cooling fins. Diameter of piston pin bore is 22 mm (.866″).

Oil Circulation

Oil flow has been increased by using a larger oil pump.

The openings in oil suction pipes and oil strainer have also been enlarged.

The oil strainer is marked with an annular groove (see illustration). a = 14 mm dia. A = Annular groove

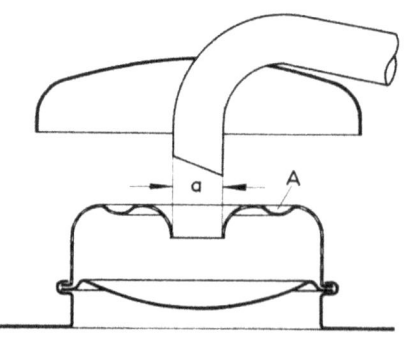

FIG. A-5

FIG. A-6

FIG. A-7

Camshaft

The camshaft runs in three lead-coated split steel bearings. Axial thrust is taken by No. 3 camshaft bearing. The bearing shells on the left are provided with shoulders on each side to prevent play. The mark "O" on the outer face of each camshaft timing gear is to help locate the camshaft in relation to the crankshaft timing gear, and this tooth should be situated between the two teeth of the crankshaft marked with a punch.

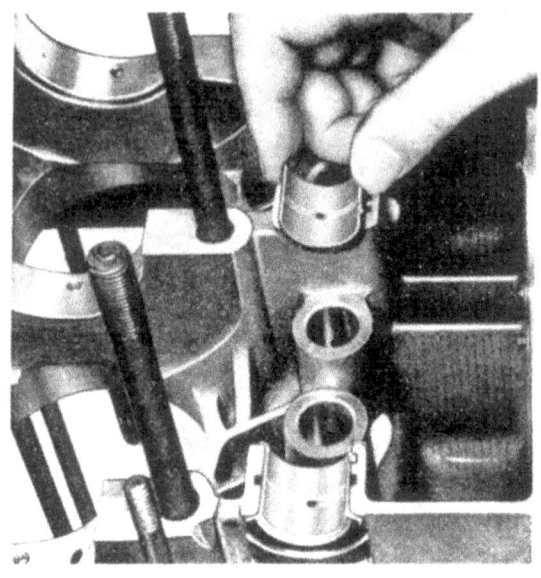

FIG. A-8

Removal
1 — Disassemble crankcase.
2 — Take camshaft out.
3 — Take bearing shells out.

Installation
Note the following points when installing:

1 — Break the edges of the camshaft bearing bores at the crankcase joining faces to prevent seizure due to pressure on the bearing shells.
2 — Check bearing shells for wear and damage. Fit new bearing shells if necessary.
3 — Install the bearing shells so that the tongues engage in the recesses in the crankcase.
4 — Coat all bearings with oil.
5 — Insert camshaft.

FIG. A-9

Clutch Operating Shaft
The clutch operating shaft A-9 has a plastic bush on the left-hand side and is sealed on both sides with rubber bushes. Removal and installation procedure has not changed.

Generator

Generators of 105 mm diameter with separately installed regulators have been installed together with the fan cover. The cooling air slots must face downward.

A - Cooling air slots   B - Connections

Valves

When replacing new or used valve keepers, be sure it is just possible to turn the valve when the keepers are pressed together. This is necessary to avoid valve noise. If valve is too tight, replace keepers.

Crankshaft

All 1500 and later engines are being equipped with a crankshaft incorporating a second oilhole leading from main bearings 1 through 3 to the connecting rod bearings. This crossover or "X" oiling system allows more oil per crankshaft revolution to flow to the connecting rod bearings. Along with this new crankshaft, a stepped piston ring is used in place of the bottom ring as is a new oil control ring with spiral expander spring.

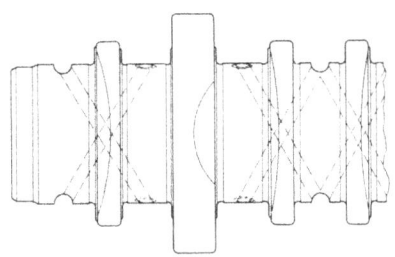

Piston Rings

Since there is a larger quantity of oil pumped under pressure out of the connecting rod bearings, special piston rings are required to prevent an increase in oil consumption. This is accomplished with a stepped piston ring instead of the bottom ring and a scraper ring with spiral expander spring instead of the scraper ring with or without the previous type expander spring. The compression ring gap is .012 - .018", with a wear limit of .035". The oil scraper ring gap is .010 - .016", with a wear limit of .037". Use a feeler gauge to measure the piston ring gap and side clearance. The upper compression ring side clearance is .003 - .004" with a wear limit of .004". The oil ring is .001 - .002", with a wear limit of .004".

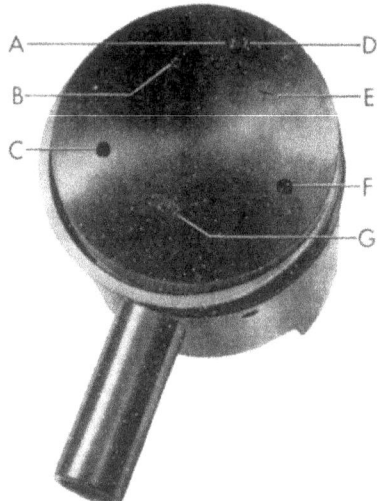

Piston Markings

A - Arrow (indented or stamped) which must point towards the flywheel when piston is installed.

B - Details of piston pin bore size indented or stamped (s = black, w = white).

C - Paint spot indicating matching size (blue, pink, green).

D - The letter near the arrow corresponds to the index of the part number of the piston concerned. It serves as an identification mark.

E - Details of weight grading (+ or −) indented or stamped.

F - Paint spot indicating weight grading (brown = − weight, grey = + weight).

G - Details of piston size in mm.

Pistons

Piston pin holes are offset to prevent slapping noise as the piston moves inside the cylinder. Therefore, it is most important that the piston be installed with the arrow or word "vorn" pointing toward the flywheel when installed. Fitting clearance between cylinder and piston is .0016 - .0019", with a wear limit of .008".

Flywheel

The metal gasket between the crankshaft and the flywheel has been replaced by a rubber seal, necessitating a change in the axial end play adjustment of the crankshaft. Assemble engine, then add flywheel without shims or rubber seal. Measure end play with dial gauge as previously described (no paper gasket used), then remove flywheel and install rubber seal and 3 shims to make final dimension .0028 to .0004" (.07 to .010 mm). Recheck end play.

Connecting Rods

Larger connecting rods with fitted bolts and nuts are being installed and only the hexagon nuts may be replaced. The connecting rod bolts must never be replaced. Should the bolts be damaged somehow, replace the complete connecting rod. Also note that the small end is offset .040" in relation to the big end so that it is exactly in the center of the piston pin. The forged mark on the connecting rod shank must be upwards on installation, with each connecting rod viewed so it points toward the cylinder to which it belongs. Be sure to remove the protective coating with solvent prior to installation. Tightening torque for the connecting rod bolts is 22 - 25 ft. lb.

Cylinder 1   Cylinder 2

Cylinder 3   Cylinder 4

1600 Repair Supplement

The 1600 (actually 1584 cc) engine went into production in August, 1967 (Engine No. H O 183 373), resulting in more torque and better pickup. Changes in repair and maintenance will be found herein, while the balance of procedures will be found first in the LATE 1500 CHANGES, then the 1500 REPAIR SUPPLEMENT and finally the sections dealing with the 1200 engine. This 96.6 cu. in engine, putting out 57 bhp (S.A.E. rating at 4400 rpm) or 47 bhp (German D.I.N. rating), compared to the 53 bhp (S.A.E. rating at 4200 rpm) or 44 bhp (German D.I.N. rating) of the previous 91.1 cu. in. 1500 model, is still of the same configuration overall. Engine capacity is upped by using an 85.5 diameter cylinder and piston size.

Valves

Dimensions for valves are 1.396" diameter for intake valves, and 1.259" diameter for exhaust valves. All other valve dimensions remain the same.

Piston Rings

Compression ring side clearance for the top ring is .0031 - .0043", with a wear limit of .005". The fitting clearance between the cylinder and piston is .0016 - .0023", with a possible wear limit of .008".

Oil Strainer

A valve incorporated into the oil strainer will ensure that the engine is still provided with oil even if the oil strainer is blocked (ex. with ice). When needed, this spring-loaded valve will automatically pull the wire mesh away from the shoulder of the funnel-shaped insert, causing the oil to bypass the strainer and flow directly into the intake pipe.

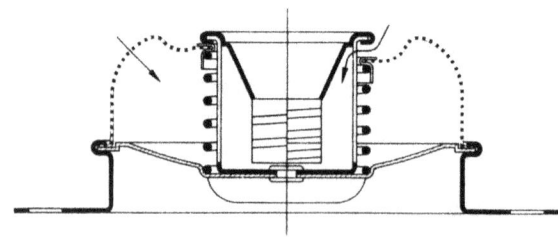

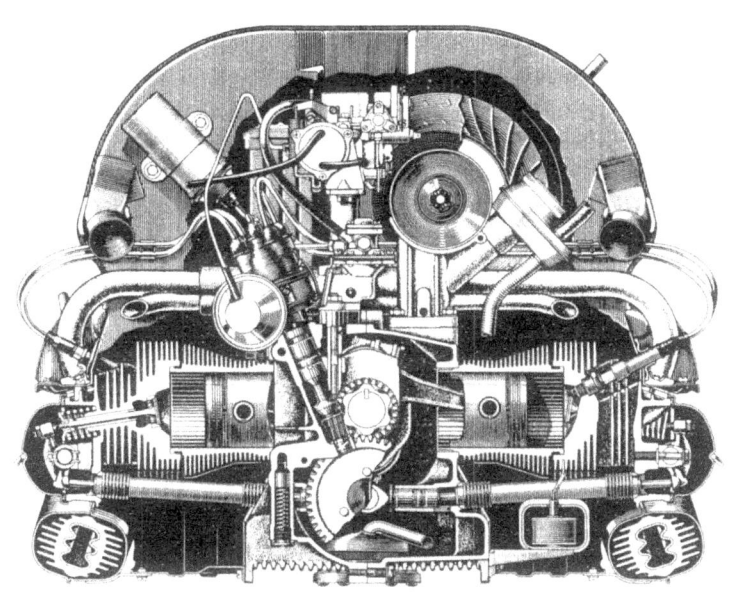

Oil Pressure Relief Valve

The piston for the oil pressure relief valve is modified with an annular groove to lower the engine oil temperature. On the 1970 models, a second oil pressure relief valve was installed in the main oil-passage to ensure that a constant supply of oil would be delivered to all bearing surfaces. Should the oil temperature or engine speed affect the lubrication system, the pressure relief valves would hold the pressure below 28 psi. In addition, the main oil passages in the crankcase were enlarged to ensure an increased flow of lubricant to all bearings.

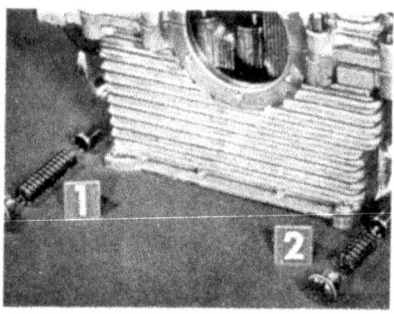

Oil Pump

On 1970 models, the oil pump was enlarged to provide a more constant supply of lubricant to the engine no matter what the operating conditions. The contact surface of the oil pump flange and the main oil-passages in the oil pump housing were enlarged.

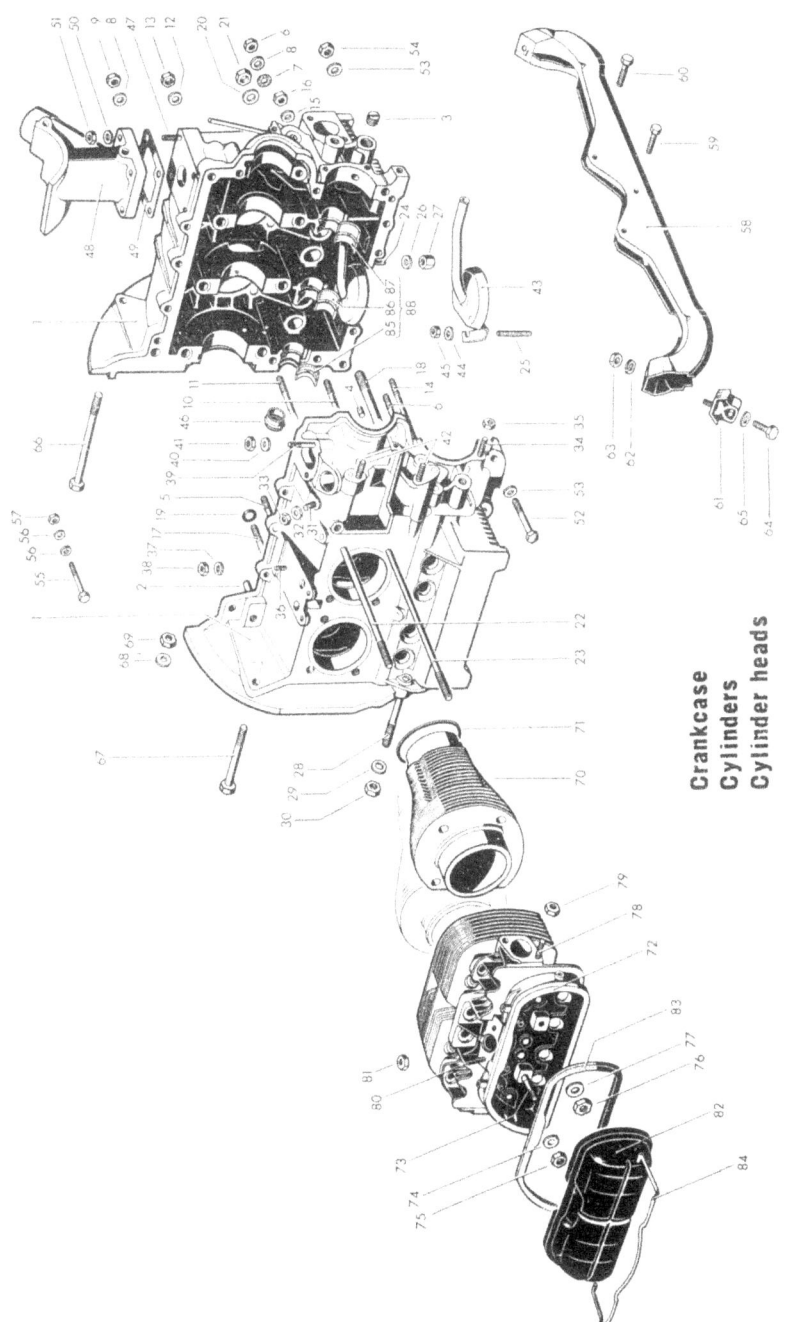

Crankcase
Cylinders
Cylinder heads

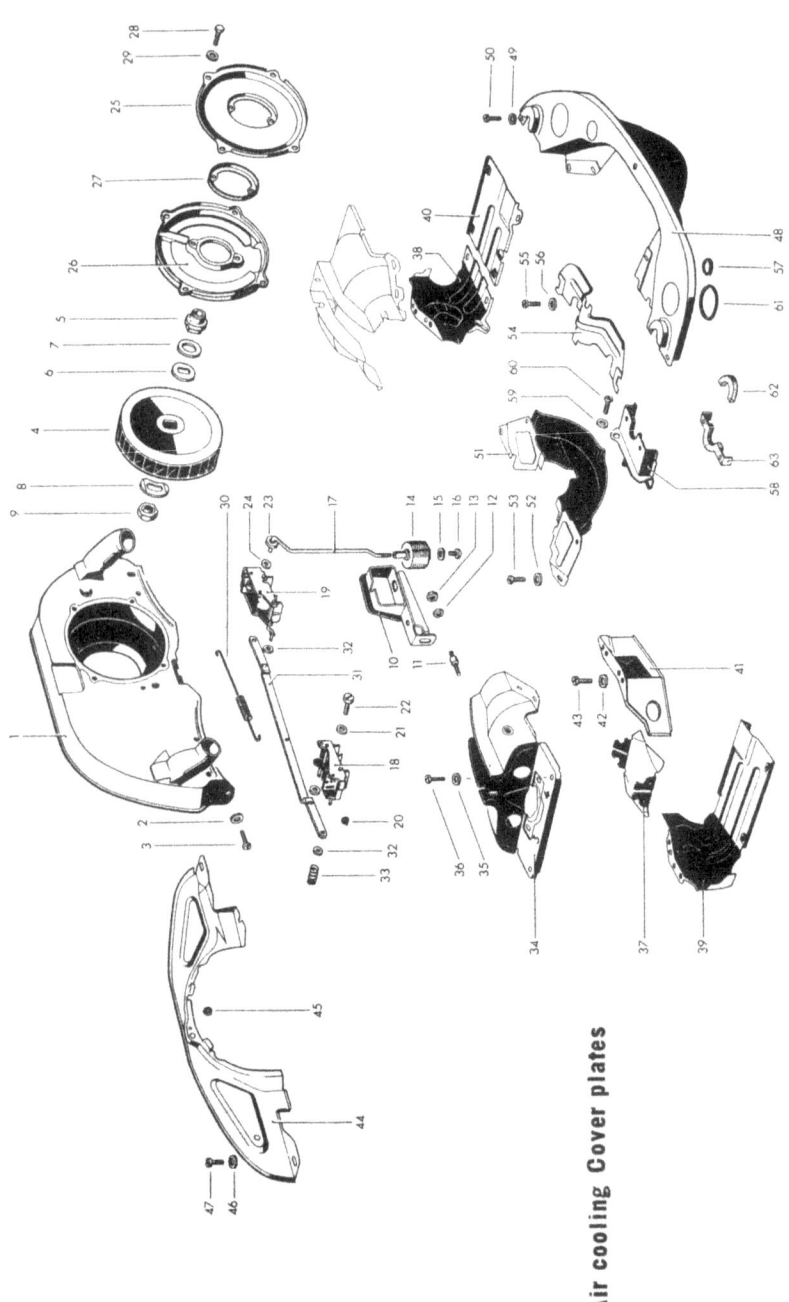

Air cooling Cover plates

Flywheel

The flywheel now has 130 teeth instead of 109 and its outside diameter has been increased by 4 mm to 276 mm. A new starter is being used. This change has also necessitated an increase in the size of the transmission housing, and space for the clutch has been made with additional machining. The diameter of the hole for the starter pinion shaft has been reduced from .491" to .432".

Generator Support

Since the new crankshaft throws off more oil, an oil deflector plate is being fitted between the crankcase and the generator support to prevent the oil from being thrown out via the crankcase breather. Make sure the three depressions in the plate are hanging down with the slightly longer part of the center depression pointing to the rear. Be sure to place a gasket on the crankcase, the plate with the word "Top" showing, then another gasket.

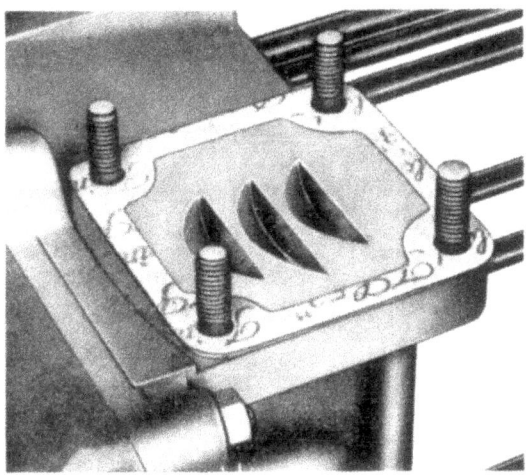

Crankcase

The six crankcase studs M 12 X 1.5 are now sealed with rubber seals. The seals are located between the crankcase halves, and the stud holes in both crankcase halves have been countersunk. To install, slide the seals over the studs until seated, prior to assembly.

Prior to the introduction of the above seals, the center M 12 X 1.5 crankcase studs adjacent to No. 2 bearing were sealed in production with sealing nuts. Washers are **not** to be installed at these locations. The plastic rings pressed into the sealing nut faces the crankcase. Torque the sealing nuts to 18 ft. lb. instead of the former 25 ft. lb. setting.

ENGINE TROUBLE SHOOTING

I. ENGINE WILL NOT START, MAY TURN OVER SLOWLY.

Diagnosis

Poor internal contact in ignition switch.

Loose connection

A. At battery or starter

B. At ignition switch

C. At light switch

D. At fuse box

Dead or partially discharged battery.

Cure

Move key around in switch as temporary cure.

A. Check connections at both ends of battery cables and at solenoid on starter.

B. Check switch connections behind dash board.

C. Check switch connections behind dash board.

D. Check fuse box connections behind dash board.

Check electrolite level, refill and recharge. Push to start as temporary cure.

II. ENGINE TURNS OVER BUT WON'T START.

Diagnosis

No gas in tank

Loose connections in ignition's primary system.

Loose connection in ignition's secondary system.

If no spark at terminal 15, juice from battery does not reach coil.

If spark at terminal 15, trouble likely in secondary system.

Cure

Most common cause of emergency road calls.

Turn ignition on, remove wire from terminal 15 at coil (labeled) and scratch on a ground to check.

Check coil, distributor and spark plug connections and spark plug wires. Check that coil is bolted tightly to fan housing.

Check connections at choke, ignition switch and fuse box.

Check for spark at plugs by inserting conductor into spark plug connector and hold $1/4''$ from a ground while cranking

If no spark at plugs and there is a spark at terminal 15, problem is in secondary system.	engine, if possible by starter. Wipe distributor, coil, plugs, wires and inside of distributor cap, removing dirt and moisture. Check points for gap and timing.
If spark at plugs is good, trouble is in fuel system.	Remove gas line from carburetor to check that gas travels this far. Usually gas pump is working if gas runs from line. Gas should squirt out when engine is cranked.
If gas does not squirt from fuel line, problem may be cloggage.	Remove gas line coming from tank from fuel pump and blow through line. With front hood open and gas tank cap removed, listen for bubbling sound. If line is free, check fuel pump and push rod.
If carburetor is wet outside or odor of gasoline is obvious, carburetor may be flooded, possibly due to stuck float needle valve or choke.	Lightly tap outside of carburetor with wooden handle of a tool. After a short wait turn ignition. If automatic choke, wait again for choke valve to open, then try to start while holding accelerator to floor.
If air cleaner is clogged or throttle linkage stopped.	Remove air cleaner to check flow of air and examine linkage.

III. ENGINE RUNS ROUGHLY OR STALLS.

Diagnosis	Cure
Poor fuel supply.	See above.
Incorrect idling mixture.	Correction procedure described in owners manual.

IV. DASH BOARD WARNING LIGHT GLOWS

Diagnosis	Cure
If red warning light flashes, generator is not producing enough juice to charge battery.	Check for slipping or broken fan belt. If O.K., push lightly on ends of generator brushes with pencil to check brush-armature contact.
If green warning light flashes, oil pressure is low.	Stop the car and check oil level. On curving roads, light will usually blink before staying on permanently.

FUEL SYSTEM

The fuel system of the VW transporter consists of a 10.6 gallon fuel tank, fuel tap and filter, lines, mechanical fuel pump and carburetor. Solex 28 PCI carburetors were standard on models prior to 1960, later units employ the 28 PICT which is distinguished by the automatic choke. Each will be discussed in turn.

The tank is situated in front of the engine above the rear axle of all models except the Pickup where the tank is in a separate compartment in front of the engine compartment. The tanks are deep drawn so that the fuel tap connection is at the lowest point.

Fuel Tap

The remote control tap underneath the tank regulates flow of fuel in three positions: "ZU" (shut off), "AUF" (open) and "RES" (reserve). The reserve can only be used when the tap is turned to the reserve position (operating knob fully pulled out). It contains 1.3 gallons.

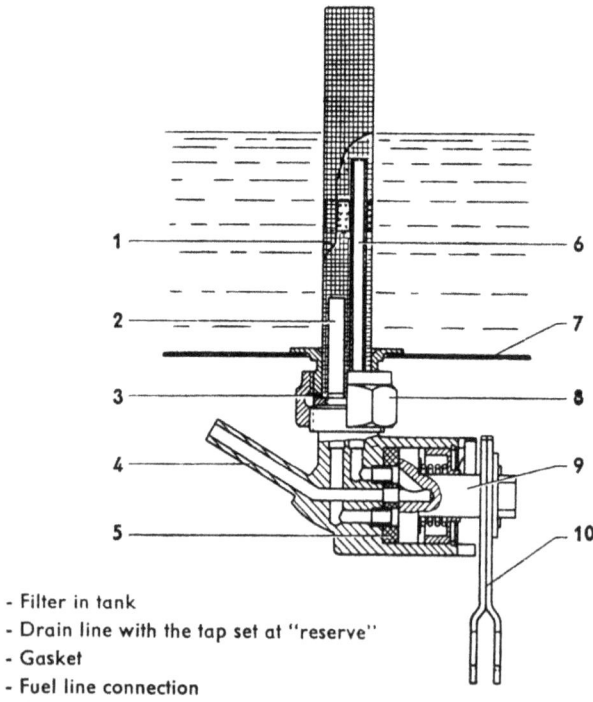

1 - Filter in tank
2 - Drain line with the tap set at "reserve"
3 - Gasket
4 - Fuel line connection
5 - Gasket
6 - Drain line with the tap set at "open"
7 - Fuel tank
8 - Union nut
9 - Three-way tap
10 - Operating lever

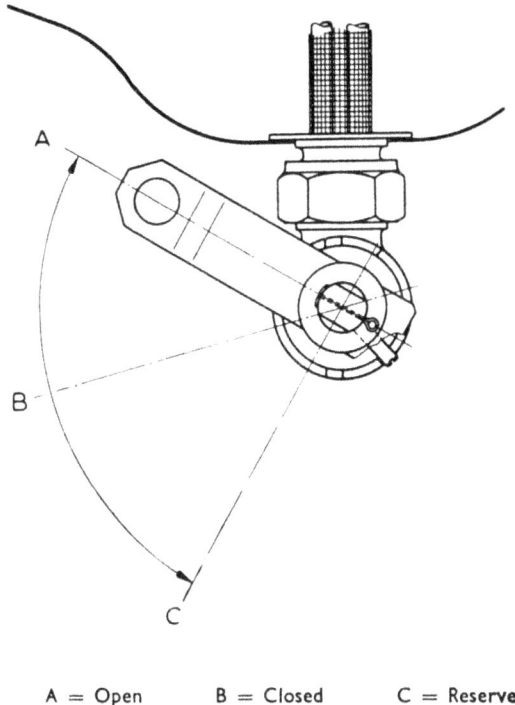

A = Open   B = Closed   C = Reserve

On occasion the fuel tap operating cable becomes kinked or is difficult to move, and the control knob returns to original position, refusing to stay on Reserve. It is important that the cable be in a straight line and not sag and should be lubricated with Universal grease. In installing a replacement, straighten the guide bracket, if necessary, attach the cable sleeve to the bracket. If the sleeve protrudes over the clamp so as to interfere with operation, shorten it as needed. If advisable to prevent hanging, add more sleeve clamps with a space of about 10" between them.

Renew cable by loosening clamp screw at fuel tap, then loosen cable sleeve clamp and slide off rubber boot. Bend up cable sleeve retaining loops at the heating cable guide tube, then lift the cab seat and remove the union nut from inside the seat bench, screw off the operating knob and pull out the cable sleeve from below the vehicle. Lubricate the used or new cable with universal grease, insert into sleeve, then insert sleeve from the front to the clamp. Attach front end to the seat bench, making sure rubber grommet is properly seated in the tool compartment floor. Replace knob and tighten sleeve clamp, push knob in, then attach cable to operating lever with lever to full open position.

Accelerator Cable

The accelerator cable is connected to a swivel pin on the throttle valve lever at one end, passes through the fan housing, a plastic tube and a guide tube under the body, and is hooked to the accelerator pedal crank lever just below the floor pedal. The spring over the conduit (3 in diagram) returns the accelerator cable. A sleeve (4) prevents the spring from buckling.

1 - Accelerator cable conduit tube
2 - Accelerator cable
3 - Accelerator cable spring
4 - Spring guide sleeve
5 - Spring seat
6 - Accelerator cable swivel pin

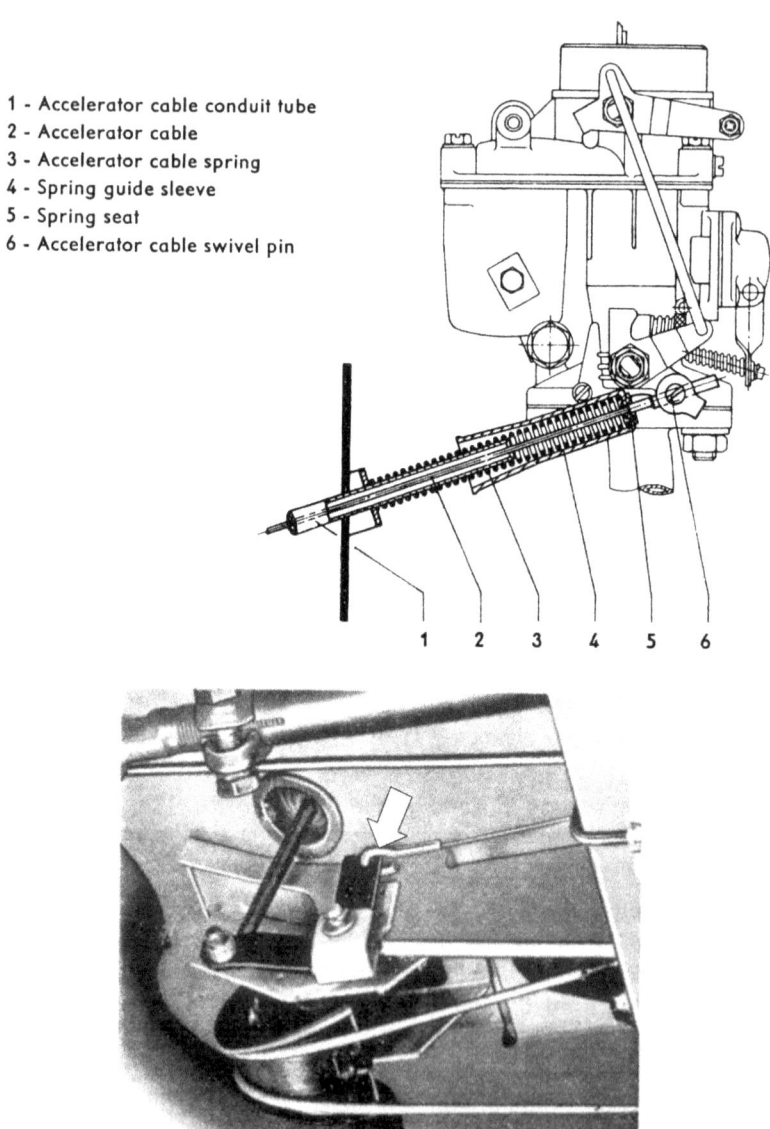

To remove the cable, hoist the vehicle to permit creeper travel below the chassis, disconnect the swivel end from the throttle lever, compress the spring and remove the spring seat, then remove guide sleeve and spring. Pull the cable out of guide tube in the fan housing towards the front. Remove the cover plate under the pedal linkage, then hook cable out of lever. Pull complete cable towards the front.

When installing a new cable, first apply Universal grease to the entire length of the cable. Attach pedal end, then feed it from the front toward the back making sure it is in the conduit over the transmission case. At the carburetor end, re-install spring and sleeve then fully depress accelerator pedal and connect cable to throttle lever so that there is still approximately 0.04" clearance between the throttle lever and the stop on the carburetor body at wide open throttle to avoid possible damage to carburetor.

Choke Control Cable

The choke cable passes through a plastic-coated flexible conduit from the knob on the front of the seat-bench through the tool compartment and under the chassis through the rear cross member and through the fan housing. It is clipped to the accelerator cable conduit under the body.

The cable is attached to the choke level at the carburetor by a clamp screw and the control knob unscrews.

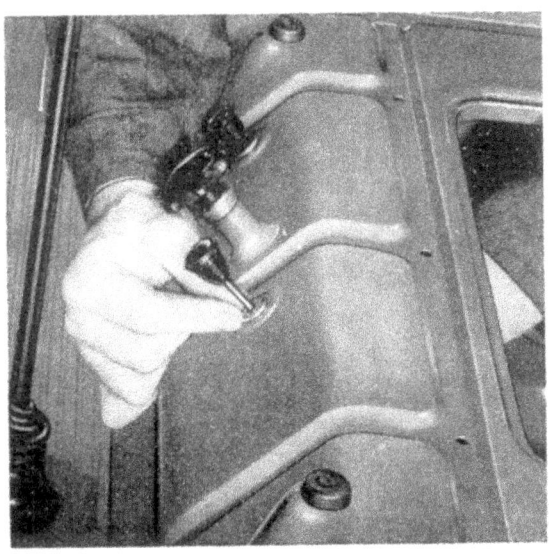

To remove and replace it is best to jack up the vehicle for floor clearance to permit a creeper to be used. First disconnect the carburetor end of the cable from the choke lever, then remove the seat cushion and unscrew the union nut inside the bench, remove the knob and remove the cable from the tool compartment. Under the van, unclip the choke cable from the accelerator cable and pull the cable forward through the fan housing and rear cross member.

Before installing a new cable grease it with Universal grease. Shove the new cable into the rear cross member and fan housing first, but do not attach it to the choke lever. Clip it to the other cable and feed it through the compartment and re-affix the control knob. Shove the knob fully home against the panel, then attach the cable to the choke lever in the **open** position. Be sure that the cable is not entwined with the clutch or accelerator cables above the transmission case.

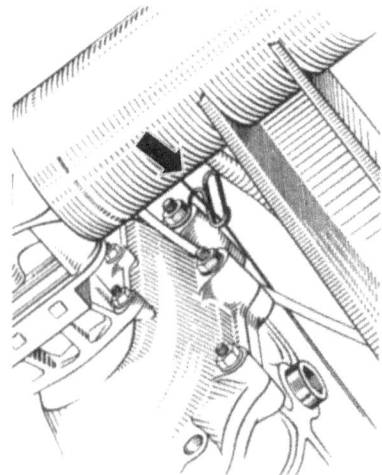

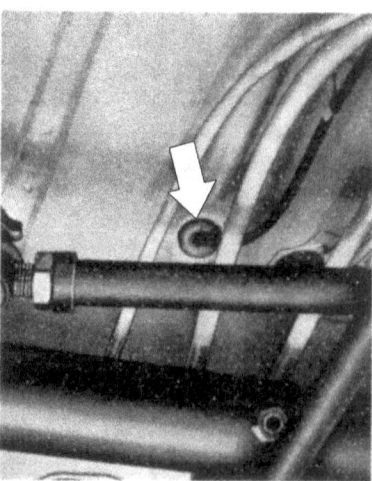

Fuel Pump

Fuel is fed to the carburetor by a diaphragm pump attached to the crankcase. It is operated by a pushrod and an eccentric on the distributor drive shaft. The top half of the pump contains the suction and delivery valves (one way). The bottom half houses the rocker mechanism. The diaphragm and spring are situated between the two halves.

Reference to the cutaway drawing will make the operation and part nomenclature clear.

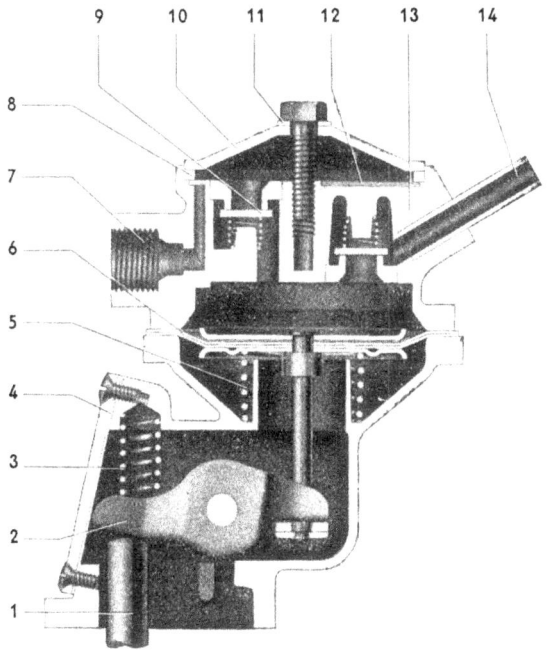

1 - Push rod
2 - Rocker arm
3 - Rocker arm spring
4 - Inspection cover
5 - Diaphragm spring
6 - Diaphragm
7 - Fuel intake
8 - Filter
9 - Suction valve
10 - Fuel pump cover
11 - Gasket
12 - Filter
13 - Delivery valve
14 - Fuel outlet

As the distributor shaft revolves, the eccentric causes the pushrod (1) to move against the rocker arm (2) which pulls the diaphragm (6) downward against the diaphragm spring (5). This movement causes a vacuum above the diaphragm which pulls the inlet valve (9) down and admits fuel from the intake (7). When the pushrod moves down the spring returns the diaphragm, pushed the delivery valve (12) open and forces fuel into the line to the carburetor. The flow is regulated by the carburetor float needle valve reacting against the spring.

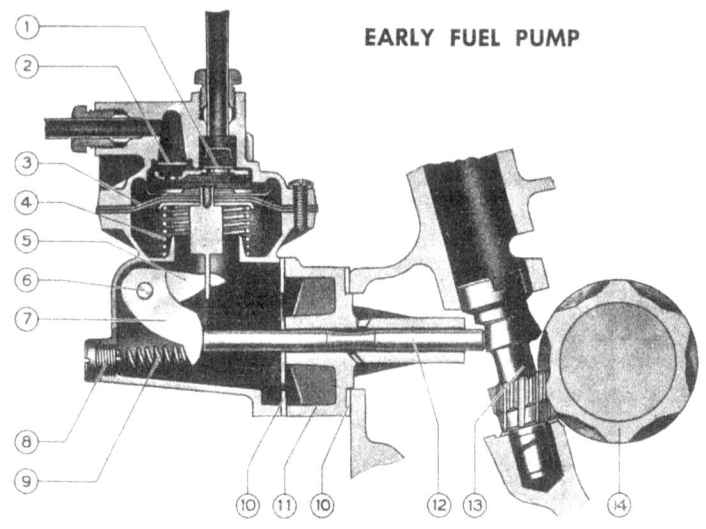

EARLY FUEL PUMP

1-Pressure valve
2-Suction valve
3-Diaphragm
4-Diaphragm spring
5-Link
6-Rocker arm pivot
7-Rocker arm
8-Spring end plug
9-Rocker arm spring
10-Seal
11-Intermediate flange (plastic)
12-Pushrod
13-Distributor drive-shaft
14-Distributor drive gear

Operating pressure depends on the length of the return spring and the adjustment of the pushrod stroke. A manometer with a range of 0 to 6 lbs./sq. in. is used to check output pressure or fuel

delivery can be checked against the minimum requirement of 167 cc per minute with the engine running 1,000 to 3,000 rpm.

Correct pressure is 1.3 to 1.85 lbs/sq. in. @ 1,000 to 3,000 rpm with the float needle valve closed. Adding or removing fuel pump flange gaskets is the accepted method for shortening or lengthening pump stroke. If adjustment does not correct the situation replace the spring or compress or extend it.

If pump pressure is too low, insufficient fuel will be delivered resulting in faulty performance. Too much pressure causes flooding and dilution of engine oil.

VW gage 328c is used to check pushrod stroke with the gage installed in place of the pump with two new gaskets. The proper amount of travel is .2" (5 mm) which is marked on the gage. In the absence of a gage, this distance can be measured with a millimeter rule of the pocket type or any rule with 1/64" graduations. .2" equals approximately 13/64".

If the pump is removed, the lower chamber should be filled with Universal grease and when re-installed, be certain that the inspection cover is faced toward the left. Tighten nuts at engine working temperature.

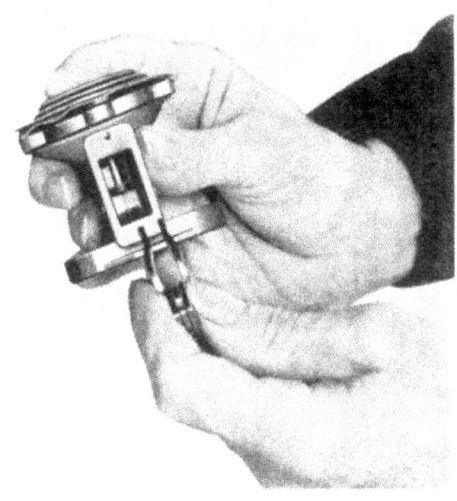

FUEL PUMP
Prior To 1966

Maximum fuel pressure is 2.8 lb. per square inch, with the needle valve closed and the engine running at 3000 RPM. At this speed, the minimum fuel delivery should be 16.3 cu. ins. (267 cc). Pressure is determined by effective length of push rod stroke and diaphragm spring tension. The stroke is adjusted by adding or removing flange gaskets (4). If push rod stroke is approximately .2" and fuel pump pressure is still incorrect, adjust by stretching or compressing diaphragm spring. Too high a pressure results in flooding and dilution of crankcase oil. Poor engine performance will result from too low a pressure. Fuel pressure is checked by T-connecting a pressure gauge in the line between pump and carburetor. Before measuring pressure, check for freedom of movement of push rod in hole through intermediate flange. With fuel pump removed, push rod stroke can be measured with a dial indicator while slowly cranking engine over by hand.

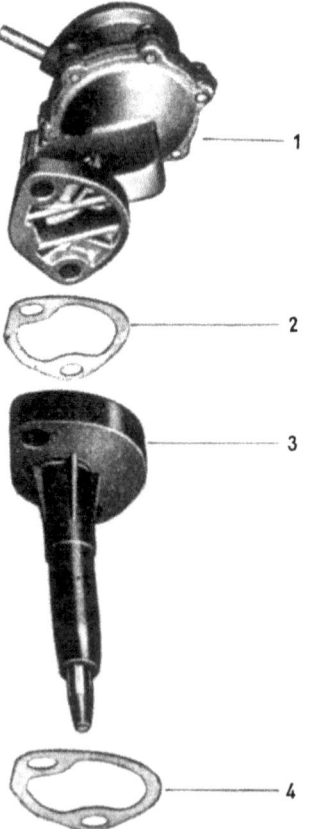

1 - Fuel pump
2 - Gasket
3 - Intermediate flange
4 - Gasket

Checking

Pump pressure with closed needle valve:

	1200	1500
Engine speed (rpm)	3600	3800
Pressure (psi)	2.8	2.8
Capacity (pints per hour)	31.7	42.3
Capacity (cu. ins. per min)	18.3	24.4

FUEL PUMP
1966 Models And Later

To remove the fuel pump, pull off the hoses, unscrew the flange nuts, then remove pump, push rod, intermediate flange and gaskets. Note the number of gaskets removed. To install (after adjusting pump stroke or replacing the same number of gaskets), fill the lower pump chamber with universal grease, then be sure to place the intermediate flange with its gasket into position before inserting the push rod. If not, the push rod could

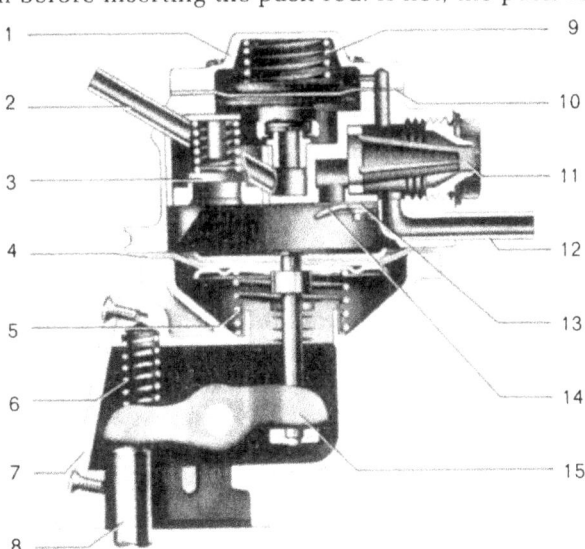

Fuel pump cross section

1 - Fuel pump cover
2 - Delivery pipe
3 - Delivery valve
4 - Diaphragm
5 - Diaphragm spring
6 - Spring
7 - Inspection cover
8 - Push rod

9 - Cut-off diaphragm spring
10 - Cut-off diaphragm
11 - Fuel filter
12 - Intake pipe
13 - Suction valve
14 - Suction valve retainer
15 - Pump operating lever

slip into the crankcase interior, necessitating engine disassembly. Install the pump so the inspection cover is facing toward the left. Tighten nuts, replace fuel hoses along with their clips, then run the engine until operating temperature has been reached. Retighten the nuts (but do not overtighten), then check that the fuel line grommet is properly seated in the engine front cover plate. Clean filter as part of the regular maintenance procedure.

Fuel Pump Adjustment

The correct fuel pump delivery quantity is 1.3 to 1.6 cc per stroke. To adjust, fit the intermediate flange onto the crankcase with 2 new gaskets and insert the pushrod, with the rounded end toward the camshaft. Measure the total stroke from the pump contact surface on the intermediate flange (including gaskets) using a depth gauge. The stroke should be .16 in. (4 mm).

Use a wrench on the crankshaft pulley to turn the engine until the push rod end has reached the highest point. The measurement from the push rod tip to the surface of the intermediate flange should be .5 in. (13 mm). Turn the crankshaft once more until the push rod has reached its lowest point. Here the measurement should be .3 in. (8 mm). If the measurement is incorrect, adjust the stroke with a suitable number of flange gaskets.

Fuel Pump Filter

Check and clean the fuel pump filter every 6,000 mi. Clamp off the fuel hose between the tank and the engine compartment, then remove the screw in the cover of the pump. Remove the cover and the filter, clean the filter in solvent, then replace filter and cover with a new gasket (if necessary).

Fuel pump trouble shooting

Symptom	Cause	Remedy
1 - Pump leaky at joining faces: Loss of fuel	a - Slotted screws loose b - Diaphragm cracked	a - Tighten screws b - *Renew diaphragm*
2 - Diaphragm leaks at rivets: Loss of fuel	Diaphragm damaged by careless assembly	*Renew diaphragm*
3 - Diaphragm material leaky: Loss of fuel	Diaphragm material damaged by solvent substance in fuel	*Renew diaphragm*
4 - Excessive pump stroke: Overstraining the diaphragm	Pump incorrectly installed, gasket too thin	a - *Install pump correctly, check diaphragm, if necessary* b - *Check push rod stroke, check diaphragm if necessary*
5 - Pump pressure low	a - Pump incorrectly installed, gasket too thick b - Spring pressure low	a - *Install pump correctly* b - *Renew spring or, if necessary stretch it apart*
6 - Pump pressure excessive: Float needle valve forced down	a - Pump incorrectly installed, gasket too thin b - Spring pressure excessive	a - *Install pump correctly, check push rod stroke* b - *Renew spring or, if necessary, bring intermediate turns closer together*
7 - Fuel pump inoperative or insufficient fuel delivery	Valves leaky or sticking	*Renew top half of pump*

Operations shown in italics should be carried out by an authorized VW workshop

Carburetor

On the pre-1960 models, a 28 P.C.I. carburetor was used. It is shown later in this chapter. It was used in conjunction with the 36 hp. engine that powered the Transporter prior to the introduction of the 40 hp. engine in 1960. In that year, the 28 P.I.C.T. carburetor with automatic choke replaced the 28 P.C.I. model with manual choke. In 1964 the number 1 was added after the 28 P.I.C.T. to designate the substitution of a diaphragm for the automatic choke vacuum piston. There are many similarities between the old and new models, although the new one is a more sophisticated mechanism. We will consider the post-1960 type first.

Carburetors

The 28 P.I.C.T. carburetor, (Fig. 60), mounts on top of the intake manifold by two studs and takes an oil bath type air cleaner. Fuel is fed from the pump to the needle valve controlled float bowl. The carburetor has idling, normal running, and power and acceleration systems. It consists of the bowl or base piece (Fig. 61), including float, venturi, accelerator pump (Fig. 61A), and the jet system; and the top part (Fig. 61B), the bowl cover which includes automatic choke, float needle valve, and pump jets. It is a simple single barrel downdraft design.

The various systems in the carburetor are designed to allow it to efficiently meter the correct amount of fuel in to the air stream on the many different conditions of engine load and speed, and air temperature.

Pre-Heater

Air enters the air cleaner through a small extension or horn. Coming into the bottom of the horn is a small hose that robs warm air from the car's heating system. A pivoting, weight-loaded flap, (Fig. 62), closes off the open end of the horn. When idling in the winter, there is insufficient vacuum inside the horn to open the flap and most of the air comes into the horn via the air tube. This prevents the jets from icing and the car from stalling. As engine speed increases, vacuum increases, the flap opens and cool air is drawn in. When open all the way, the flap blocks the warm air entrance and only cold air is inhaled. Since warm air is only needed during the winter, the flap should be fixed in its open position when air temperature is regularly above 68°.

Choke

Starting, (Fig. 63), requires a richer mixture than normal run-

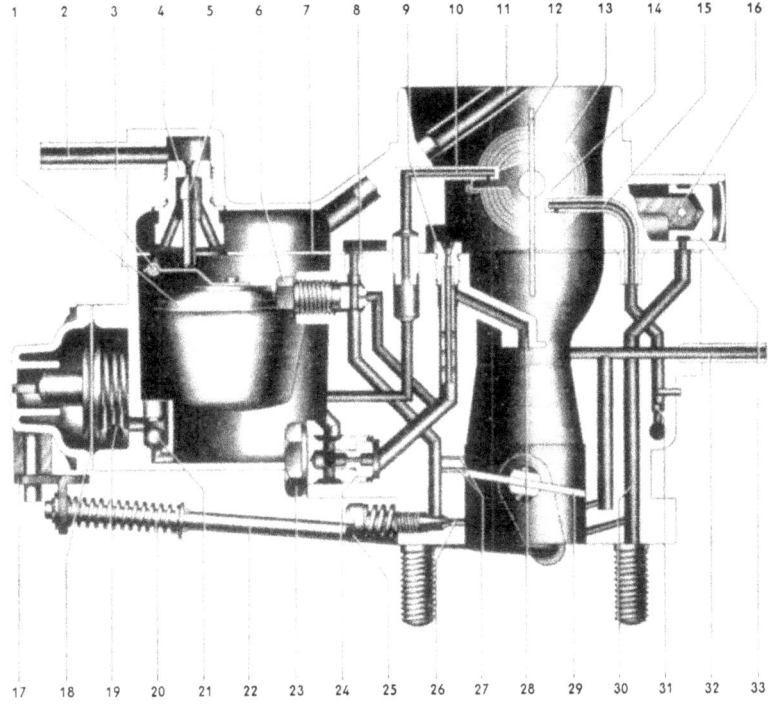

Solex 28 PICT

1 - Float
2 - Fuel line
3 - Float toggle
4 - Float needle valve
5 - Float needle
6 - Pilot jet
7 - Gasket
8 - Pilot air drilling
9 - Air correction jet with emulsion tube
10 - Power fuel tube
11 - Float bowl vent tube
12 - Choke valve
13 - Bi-metalspring
14 - Operating lever
15 - Accelerator pump discharge tube
16 - Piston rod
17 - Pump lever
18 - Pump diaphragm
19 - Diaphragm spring
20 - Spring
21 - Ball check valve for accelerator pump
22 - Pump connector rod
23 - Main jet carrier
24 - Main jet
25 - Volume control screw
26 - Idle port
27 - By-pass port
28 - Discharge arm
29 - Throttle valve
30 - Vacuum drilling
31 - Ball check valve in accelerator pump drilling
32 - Vacuum connection
33 - Vacuum piston

FIG. 60

105

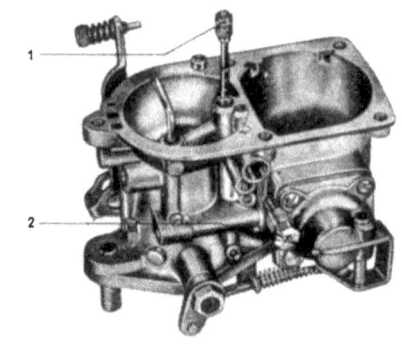

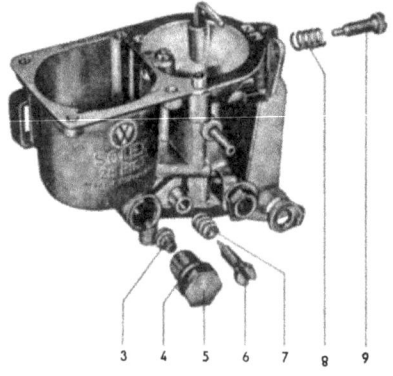

1 - Air correction jet with emulsion tube
2 - Pilot jet
3 - Main jet
4 - Gasket
5 - Main jet carrier
6 - Volume control screw
7 - Spring
8 - Spring
9 - Idle adjusting screw

FIG. 61

ning and this is arranged automatically by the choke. The basic principle of choking, whether manual or automatic, is to restrict the entrance of air between the float bowl vent and the venturi in order to increase the vacuum which then "draws out" more gasoline and enrichens the mixture. While the manual choke model had a centrally pivoted butterfly valve with a spring loaded poppet valve to allow the entrance of extra air in order to prevent the mixture from becoming too rich at high speed with the choke closed. With the automatic choke, three devices accomplish this task; the butterfly is pivoted off center so that inrushing air tends to open the valve all by itself. The valve then flutters according to air pressure. The freely pivoting, fast idling cam is a weight that also tends to open the choke. Finally there is a vacuum piston connected by a passage to the underside of the throttle valve that unloads the choke during high vacuum conditions such as over-run when coasting.

All three devices act counter to a spiral-shaped, bi-metallic

1 - Screw
2 - Accelerator pump cover
3 - Pump diaphragm
4 - Diaphragm spring
5 - Washer
6 - Connecting rod
7 - Connecting rod spring
8 - Washer
9 - Cotter pin

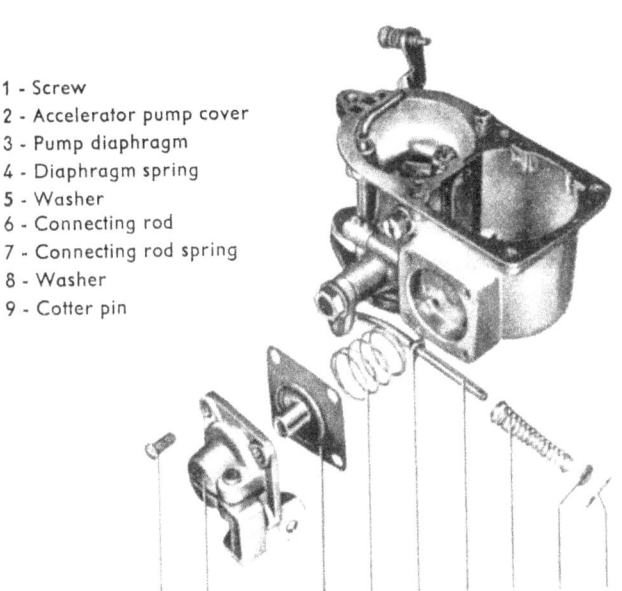

FIG. 61A

1 - Heater element
2 - Bi-metal spring
3 - Ceramic plate

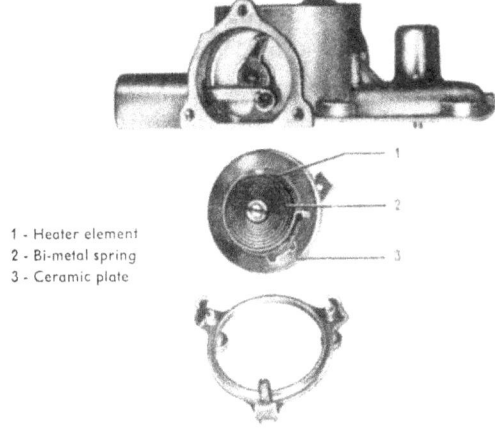

FIG. 61B

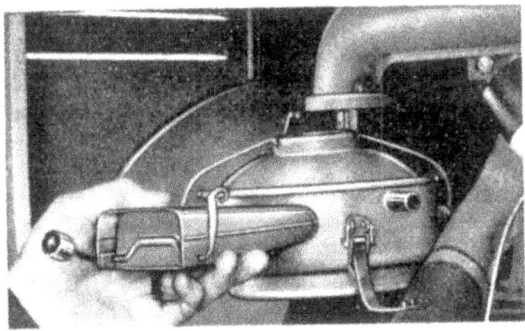

FIG. 62

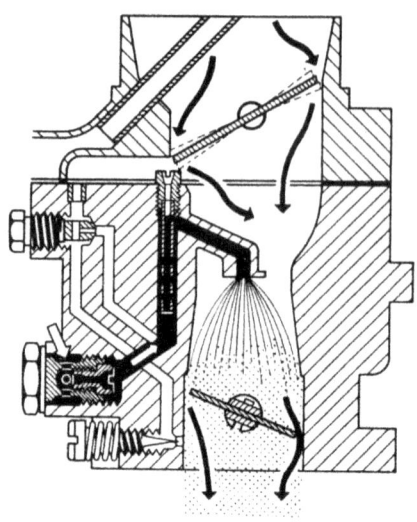

FIG. 63

spring that tries to rotate the choke closed. Next to the spring in a ceramic housing, is an electric heater coil that turns on and off with the ignition switch. When cold, the spring coils the choke shut to enrichen the mixture and the three unloading devices balance its action under certain conditions. As the coil heats the bi-metallic spring, the spring unwinds and opens the choke in varying degrees until it is finally held open all the way, according to air temperature and length of time after starting. A lever from the throttle shaft comes up to the stepped cam balance weight on the choke. An adjusting screw (throttle stop) in the end of the lever rests on one of the steps. This has the action of assuring a minimum throttle valve opening when the choke is closed, so that the engine will continue to run at idle when cold. In cold weather, pressing the accelerator pedal to floor before starting frees the cam from the throttle adjusting screw so the choke, which was last positioned fully opened, can then seek its own degree of closing.

When starting, the gas flows from the float chamber through the main jet up through the emulsion tube and out through the main spraying arm into the small of the venturi where it mixes with the slowly moving air drawn past the fluttering choke valve. The venturi is a restriction in the carburetor barrel which increases the speed of the air flow and thus creates a pressure drop or vacuum that "pulls" gas from the jets. If engine is flooded, turning on the ignition and waiting before starting (with accelerator held to floor) will allow the coil to open choke for easier starting.

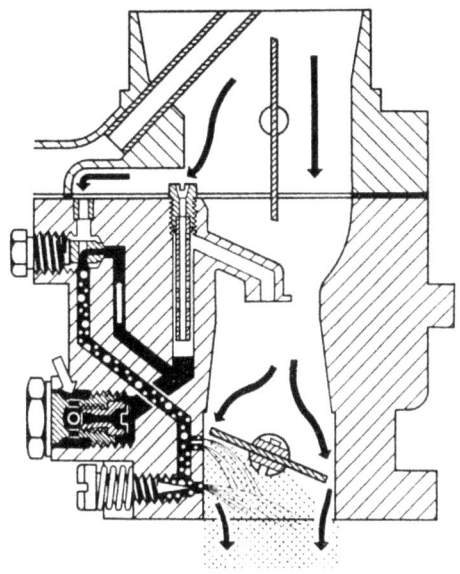

FIG. 64

Idling System

When the engine warms up the choke fully opens, (Fig. 64). When idling, the idling system comes into play. Because the throttle valve is only slightly open, there is little air speed and thus insufficient vacuum to draw gas out through the main spraying arm. Gas then comes through the main jet and up to a pilot jet which restricts gas flow and pre-mixes the gas with correct amount of air coming in through a pilot jet air bleed. From here the "bubbled" gas flows down and out through three small ports below, level with, and just above the throttle valve. Fuel is metered according to the amount of throttle opening. These three ports smooth the tranfer to the main jet system during normal running.

The idling mixture is adjusted by turning the volume control screw which moves a tapered needle in or out of the lowest port.

Normal Running

During normal running speeds, the same spraying arm that squirted the mixture for starting is used again, but now these is sufficient air speed and vacuum in the venturi. The emulsion tube which didn't function during starting is now activated by the increased vacuum. It's function is to pre-mix the gas coming in from the main jet with air entering through an air correction jet before the gas is sprayed. This action helps atomize the fuel for more efficient mixing in the venturi.

The emulsion tube is a small tube with holes along its length. It is situated in the vertical passage between main jet and spraying arm. At its top is the air correction jet. As the throttle opens, the rising vacuum in the venturi increases gas flow from the spraying arm and the gas level around the emulsion tube sinks. This exposes more of the holes in the tube to allow more air to mix with fuel to constantly adjust the pre-mixture according to needs.

Power Fuel System

The power fuel system adds more fuel to enrichen the mixture at full load and high engine speeds (Fig. 65). It has its own spraying arm, the power fuel tube, which, because it is situated above choke level, is only subject to vacuum at high air speed. The power fuel tube connects directly to the float chamber and a ball check valve assures that it only functions under high vacuum. Once started, its delivery is progressive right up to top engine speed. Since it only passes fuel at high engine speed it aids gas economy during part load conditions.

Accelerator Pump

Lastly there is an accelerator pump which is a miniature diaphragm-type pump linked to the throttle valve so that the mixture gets an extra shot of gas during acceleration, (Fig. 66). The system works only while the accelerator is being depressed and stops when speed is attained and the pedal stops moving. A spring on the link between throttle shaft and accelerator pump insures that the accelerator pump functions only during initial accelerator pedal travel. On highways when varying speed between medium and high, the accelerator pump doesn't continually waste gas since vacuum is sufficiently high for the power fuel system to do its job.

The carburetor is thus a form of computer varying mixture and quantity according to road conditions.

Idling Adjustment

If the idling mixture is too rich, the engine may stall when vehicle is braked or idling speed too slow. Adjust it with screw on lowest step of cam. Turn idling speed screw, (Fig. 67), for an engine speed of 550 rpm. Turn volume control screw, (Fig. 68), to the right until speed begins to drop and then back to the left $1/4$ to $1/3$ turn. Again regulate the idling speed. Turn volume control screw slowly to avoid damaging tapered needle in fully closed position. (When correctly adjusted, the volume control screw will usually be $1^{1}/_{4}$ to $1^{1}/_{2}$ turns opened from the fully closed position.) Finally, test the adjustment by flipping accel-

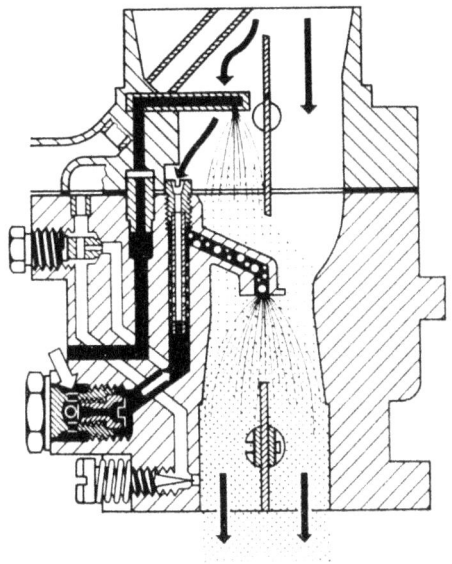

FIG. 65

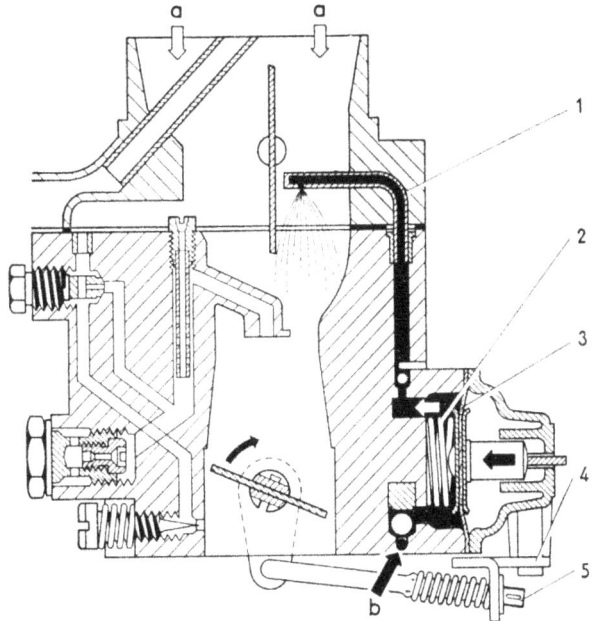

a - Air
b - Fuel from float bowl
1 - Pump discharge tube
2 - Diaphragm spring
3 - Diaphragm
4 - Pump lever
5 - Pump connecting rod

FIG. 66

FIG. 67

erator and by depressing clutch at idle. If engine stalls, the mixture is too weak and the volume control screw should be turned left $1/8$ of a turn. The carburetor should only be adjusted with engine warm.

Cable Adjustment

The accelerator cable is adjusted at carburetor, (Fig. 69), by loosening the cable swivel-pin and depressing the accelerator all the way to floor, while opening the throttle valve lever so that the clearance between throttle lever and stop at carburetor is .04". Tighen cable swivel pin in this position. This guarantees that the accelerator pedal bottoms before the throttle lever, so that foot pressure cannot break the accelerator cable.

Specifications

	1200	1500
Venturi (cast-in) .... mm dia.	22.5	22.5
Main jet	122.5	115
Air correction jet	145 y	145 y
Pilot jet	g 55	g 45
Pilot air bleed................. mm dia.	2.0	1.55
Pump jet	0.5	0.5
Power fuel jet	1.0	0.7
Float needle valve .... mm	1.5	1.5
Float weight	5.7 g	5.7 g
Pump delivery quantity .. cm³/per stroke	0.8—1.0	1.2—1.3

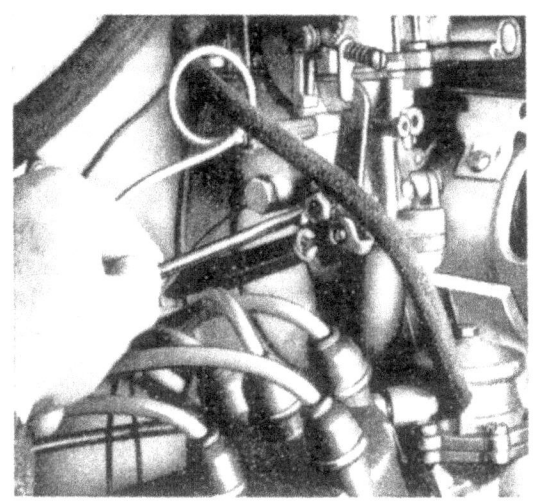

FIG. 68

FIG. 69

Optional Air Filter

A Cyclone air filter (Optional Extra M 155) is fitted on some 1200 Transporters at the factory along with a carburetor (Part No. 141 129 023 E) which uses a 122 or 125 main jet, and a 170 Z air correction jet.

Along with this air cleaner and carburetor combination, the distributor and timing point have been altered. The Bosch VJU 4 BR 8 distributor is used, and the ignition timing point is 12.5° before TDC.

Early Carburetor

Fig. 72 shows the Solex 28 P.C.I. used on pre-1960 VW's. It is a downdraft carburetor with accelerating pump, a fixed main jet, additional air correction, and manual choke.

There is a separate idle system (for idling and low speed range) and a power system (for high speed range). The carburetor float bowl is supplied with fuel by the engine-driven fuel pump. The float and needle assembly keeps a constant level in the float bowl. With normal operation (part load), fuel from the float bowl flows through the main jet into the mixing- (also called spraying-) well, and it is discharged through the radial outlet holes by the depression (partial vacuum) in the choke tube (venturi). This fuel then is mixed with the air drawn in through the carburetor throat. The depression in the venturi is a function of engine speed and throttle opening.

As the throttle is opened wider the fuel level in the mixing well decreases (fuel flow is limited by the size of the main jet) and air is drawn in through the air correction jet (13). This air passes through the holes of the emulsion tube (14) where a "pre-mixing" process takes place with the fuel drawn from the main jet. This rich fuel-air mixture then passes through the discharge holes in the narrowest part of the venturi where it is mixed with the air drawn in through the carburetor throat (primary air) to form a combustible mixture of the correct consistency. Jet and venturi sizes are combined in such a way that the correct fuel-air ratio is maintained throughout the speed range.

Idling Circuit

At very small throttle openings the depression in the venturi is insufficient to draw fuel out of the mixing well. The carburetor therefore is provided with a separate idle and low speed system. The pilot jet, adjustment of control screw 12 and pilot

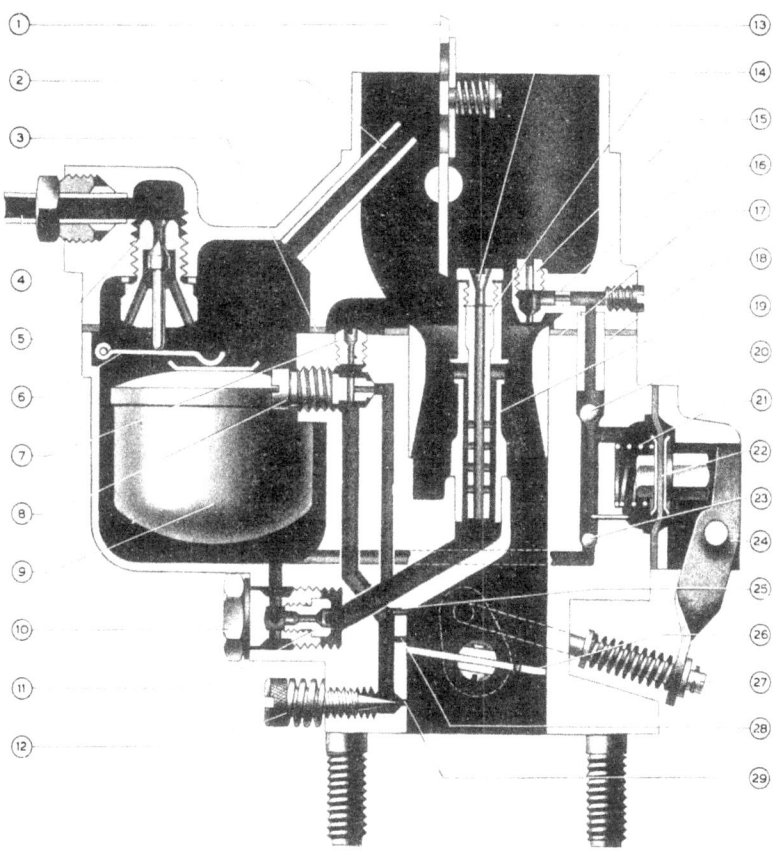

1-Choke valve
2-Vent tube
3-Gasket
4-Fuel line
5-Float needle valve
6-Needle valve lever
7-Pilot jet air bleed
8-Pilot jet
9-Float
10-Main jet carrier
11-Main jet
12-Mixture adjusting screw
13-Air correction jet
14-Emulsion tube
15-Air correction jet (pump)
16-Pump jet
17-Venturi
18-Fitting tube
19-Spraying well
20-Upper ball check valve
21-Diaphragm spring (pump)
22-Diaphragm (pump)
23-Lower ball check valve
24-Pump lever
25-Idle air bleed passage
26-Throttle valve
27-Throttle valve link
28-Accelerator port
29-Idle port

FIG. 72

a-Fuel from main jet
b-Primary air
c-Fuel from float bowl

1-Pump discharge nozzle and air correction jet
2-Pump jet
3-Diaphragm spring
4-Diaphragm
5-Pump lever
6-Throttle valve link

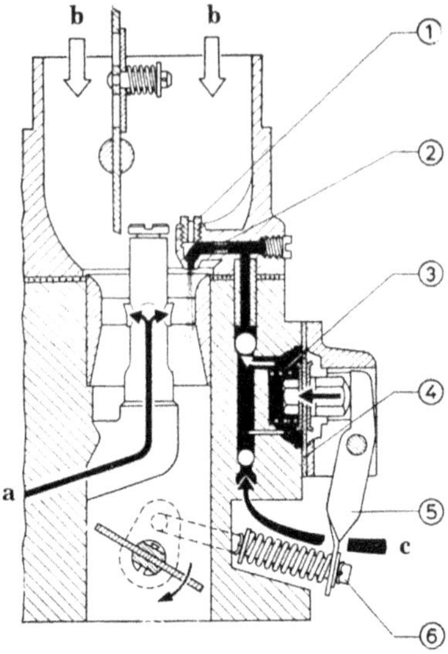

FIG. 73

jet air bleed combine to supply the correct mixture for this speed range. The depression **under** the throttle valve in the low speed range is considerable and it is here that the idling port discharges its fuel. This rich mixture is mixed with the air flowing past the partially opened throttle valve to give a mixture of the correct consistency. The flow of fuel is regulated by control screw 12. Screwing in weakens the mixture.

To insure smooth take over from idling range to part-load range, two accelerating ports (28) are provided in the carburetor throat. As the throttle is opened wider, the depression above the throttle increases and additional fuel is drawn from these orifices. A little above these ports is an idle air bleed passage (25) the purpose of which is to lean out the mixture when the throttle is snapped shut, thus preventing stalling of the engine.

Accelerating System

(Fig. 73) — The carburetor is provided with a diaphragm type accelerating pump to be seen in the illustrations. The spring-loaded diaphragm (4) is linked to the throttle. When the throttle valve closes, the diaphragm is pushed back by the spring and fuel is drawn in the suction chamber from the float bowl through the lower ball check valve (23). When the throttle is opened, the pump diaphragm is pushed back and fuel is discharged through the upper ball check valve (20) through the pump jet (2) on out through the discharge nozzle into the ven-

FIG. 74

FIG. 75

turi. This additional fuel prevents "flat spots" and insures instantaneous pick-up when throttle valve is suddenly opened. The pump chamber fills up only when throttle is near closing point.

Power System

In the higher speed range at wider throttle openings, the accelerator pump system also serves as power system. Under these conditions, additional fuel is supplied through the pump

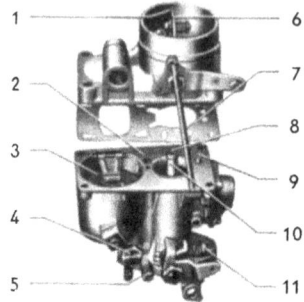
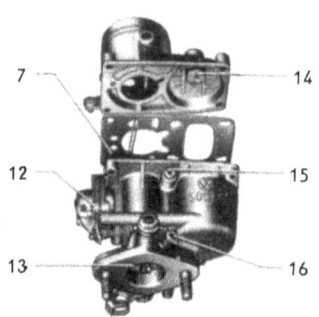

1-Choke valve
2-Pilot jet air bleed
3-Float
4-Main jet
5-Idle mixture adjustment
6-Poppet valve
7-Gasket
8-Air correction jet
9-Fitting tube
10-Emulsion tube
11-Idle adjusting screw
12-Accelerator pump
13-Throttle valve
14-Float needle valve
15-Pilot jet
16-Connection for vacuum line

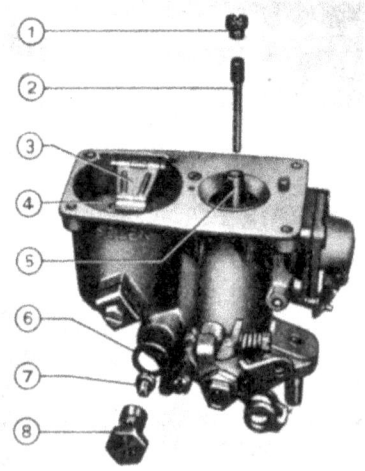
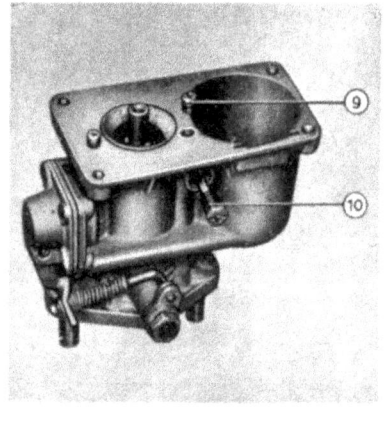

1-Air correction jet
2-Emulsion tube
3-Float toggle lever
4-Float
5-Spraying well
6-Gasket
7-Main jet
8-Main jet carrier
9-Pilot jet air bleed
10-Pilot jet

FIG. 76

discharge nozzle.

Adjustments

A correctly adjusted idling mixture is very important. Mixture should only be adjusted after engine has attained operating temperature, as described previously.

VW Engine 1946-1960	Engine	1131 c.c. — 25 b.h.p.		1192 c.c. — 30 b.h.p.		
	Carburetor Type	26 VFI	26 VFIS	28 PCI		
	Up to Eng. No.	194 695	481 712 695 281	849 904	3 919 979 991 589	3 919 979 3 538 143
Venturi ....mm dia.		21.5	21.5	20.0	21.5	21.5	21.5
Main jet		120	120	105	122.5	117.5	117.5
Air correction jet		170	180	190	200	195	180
Pilot jet		45 g	45 g	50 g	50 g	50 g	50 g
Pilot jet air bleed........mm. dia.		1.5	1.0	0.8	0.8	0.8	0.8
Emulsion tube		0	0	10	29	29	29
Spraying well...............mm dia.		5.3	5.3	5.5	5.0	5.0	5.0
Float needle valve..............mm		1.2	1.2/1.5	1.5	1.5	1.5	1.5

Removing and Installing Carburetor

Remove aircleaner, disconnect fuel line, accelerator cable, choke cable. Unscrew carburetor flange nuts. When installing always use new manifold flange gasket. Adjustment of accelerator cable is described on page

Cleaning Carburetor

To dismantle carburetor for cleaning, remove as described above, remove carburetor bowl cover, then cover and gasket. Choke control cable is disconnected as described prior in this chapter.

Remove float assembly, main jet plug. Clean main jet and float bowl Clean pilot jet air bleed, pilot jet, air correction jet, emulsion tube.

Jets and passages should be cleaned with compressed air. Fig. 76 shows the various parts of the disassembled carburetor. The venturi can be removed after the retaining screw has been taken out. Fig. 77 shows the various parts of the accelerating pump. (Flat spots when pressing on accelerator usually indicate a faulty accelerating pump.)

Inspection

Check needle valve for correct seating. Check accelerating pump diaphragm. Check float for leaks (dip in hot water and check for air bubbles and if necessary replace). When reinstalling venturi make sure that it is installed correctly (Fig. 78). Do not overtighten retaining screw. Check clearance of throttle shaft. Air leaks at this point will upset the mixture. Inspect

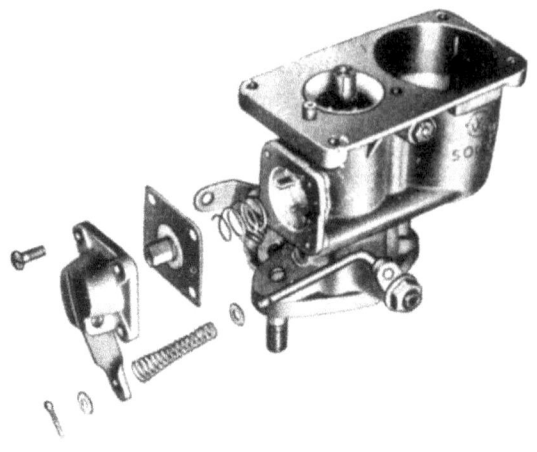

FIG. 77

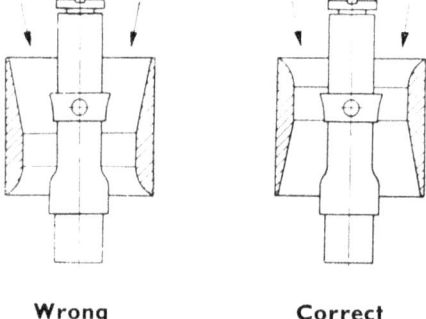

Wrong   Correct   **FIG. 78**

idling mixture control screw for correct seating.

NOTE: This same procedure can be used on the later model carburetor. Do not forget to connect the choke heater element wire.

30 PICT — 1 Carburetor (1961 Models And Later)

The model following the 28 PICT—1 was the 30 PICT—1 carburetor, which remains basically the same in principle of operation but incorporates several important changes. First, in place of the vacuum piston to unload the choke during engine overrun, there is now a vacuum diaphragm. On one side of the diaphragm there is a passage leading to the underside of the throttle valve. When the throttle valve is barely open there is a high vacuum at this point, actuating the diaphragm. The diaphragm is attached to a pull rod, and the other end of this rod is hooked to a lever on the choke valve shaft, opening the choke. This

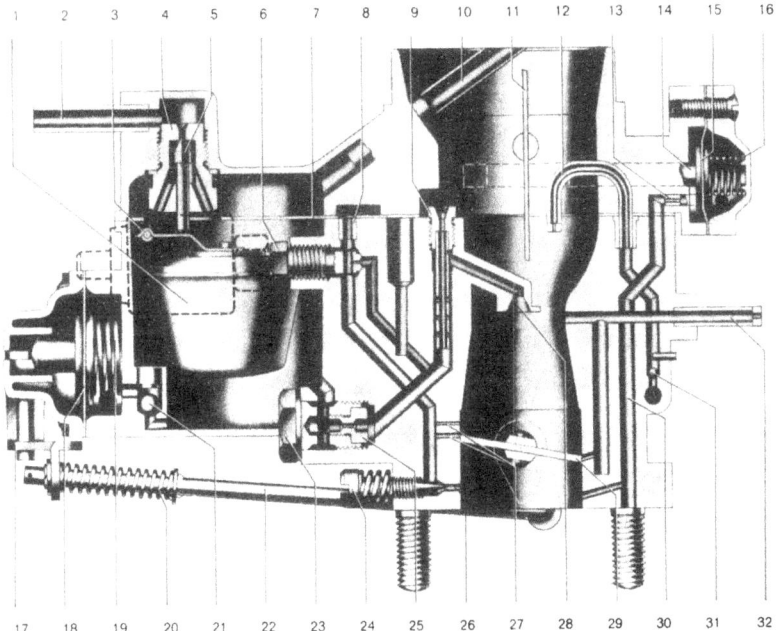

SOLEX 30 PICT-1

1 - Float
2 - Fuel line
3 - Float lever
4 - Float needle valve
5 - Float needle
6 - Electro-magnetic pilot jet
7 - Gasket
8 - Pilot air drilling
9 - Air correction jet with emulsion tube
10 - Float bowl vent tube
11 - Choke valve
12 - Accelerator pump discharge tube
13 - Jet in vacuum drilling
14 - Diaphragm rod
15 - Vacuum diaphragm
16 - Spring for vacuum diaphragm
17 - Pump lever
18 - Pump diaphragm
19 - Pump spring
20 - Spring
21 - Ball check valve for accelerator pump
22 - Pull rod for accelerator pump
23 - Main jet carrier
24 - Volume control screw
25 - Main jet
26 - Idle port
27 - By-pass port
28 - Discharge arm
29 - Throttle valve
30 - Vacuum drilling
31 - Ball check valve in accelerator pump drilling
32 - Vacuum connection

ensures that the rich mixture is weakened enough to suit the operating conditions, such as pulling away from the curb after starting the car on a cold morning. The automatic choke has also been redesigned, including a plastic insert in the choke housing for lateral support and heat insulation for the bi-metal spring.

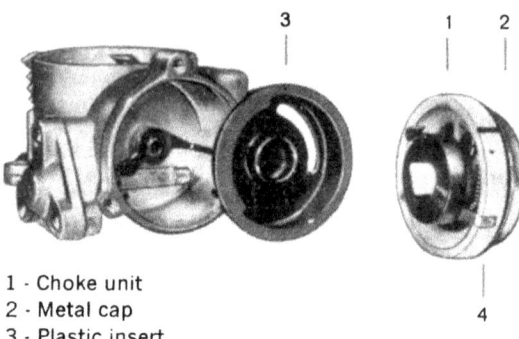

1 - Choke unit
2 - Metal cap
3 - Plastic insert
4 - Ceramic rod

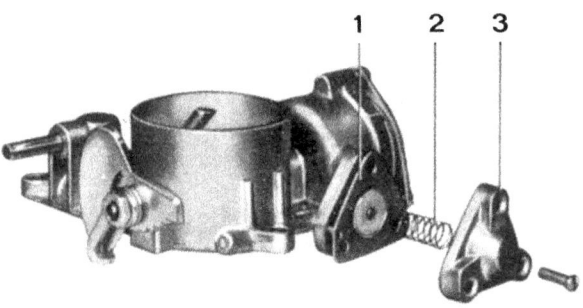

1 - Vacuum diaphragm
2 - Diaphragm spring
3 - Cover for vacuum diaphragm

The second major change is the addition of an electro-magnetic pilot jet. Basically, this is a solenoid-operated cutoff valve incorporated into the pilot jet of the idling circuit. When the ignition is turned on, this unit is activated, pulling the needle back and allowing fuel to flow into the pilot jet. When the ignition is turned off, the spring-loaded needle again shuts off the supply of fuel, preventing engine dieseling (after-running). The same electrical cable that operates the automatic choke actuates the electro-magnetic pilot jet. For those who often drive at high altitudes, an altitude corrector may be used to replace the main jet. This will automatically change the fuel mixture as the altitude varies. This unit may not be available in all parts of the country.

1 - Air correction jet with emulsion tube
2 - Electro-magnetic pilot jet

30 PICT—1 Carburetor Repair

The previous repair procedure still provides the basic information needed, with the following differences: Note the marks on the automatic choke prior to removal so it can be replaced properly, then remove the three screws and disassemble. Assuming the repair kit has been purchased, disassemble the vacuum diaphragm by removing the three screws. Use carburetor cleaner solution to clean all metal parts.

Note: Carburetor cleaner, although necessary for a thorough job, is highly caustic and can cause burns on skin if not washed

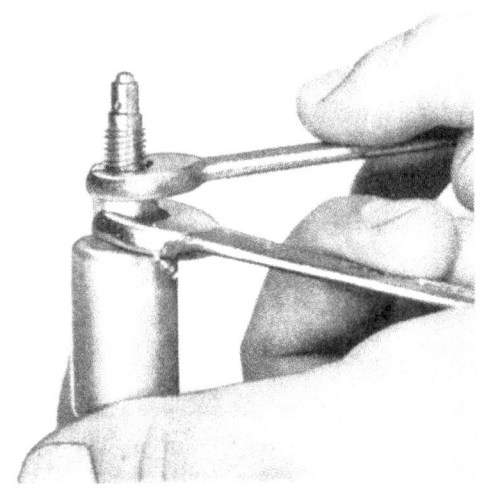

off quickly. **Do not immerse the automatic choke cover or plastic insert in the solution, nor the accelerator pump and vacuum diaphragm if they are to be reused.**

Screw pilot jet off the electro-magnetic actuator using two wrenches. Do not try to clamp the actuator in a vise as the needle may stick later. Before assembling carburetor, blow out all jets, valves and drillings with a high-pressure airhose. Never poke pins or wire into these as the calibrated drillings may be enlarged.

Check the bimetal spring and heater element on the automatic choke and replace as necessary. Place the new vacuum diaphragm in place, making sure the pull rod is in the correct position and the shaft slides easily. Hold the shaft steady with one finger while compressing the spring with the cover, then finger tighten one screw to hold the cover in place. Made sure the choke valve shaft and the fast idle cam are free moving, then be sure to fit the plastic insert so the lug engages in the notch in the automatic choke housing. The ceramic cover must be installed so the ceramic rod between the heater element and bimetallic spring is located properly, and the operating lever engages the hooked end of the bi-metallic spring as the cover is installed. After replacing the outer cap, distance pieces, and tightening the screws finger tight, be sure to turn the cap until the mark on the ceramic cover is in line with the center lug on the automatic choke housing. Do not overtighten the screws. When replacing the pump rod, place circlip on the rod so there is .012 to .020" axial play, then insert the cotter pin into the inner hole.

Testing Electro-Magnetic Jet

With the pilot jet removed from the actuator (see Carburetor Repair) and the cable disconnected, first check to see that the grubscrew is intact. If the grubscrew is missing, replace the whole valve. The screw is factory preset, so do not attempt to alter the setting except under emergency conditions. Turn on the

FUEL SYSTEM TROUBLE CHECKING

Symptoms	Cause	Remedy
1 - Engine will not start (with fuel in tank and ignition in order)	a - Automatic choke not working properly	a - Check the vacuum piston for freedom of movement and, if necessary squirt easing oil through the spring housing
	b - Choke valve sticking	b - Free the choke valve shaft with easing oil (or tapping lightly with a hammer)
	c - Bi-metal spring unhooked or broken	c - Re-connect spring, or if broken, replace complete ceramic plate
	d - Ceramic plate broken	d - Replace ceramic plate. Note marks when installing
	e - Float needle valve sticking and carburetor flooding	e - Clean or replace float needle valve Attention: If a large quantity of fuel has passed from the flooded carburetor into the engine, switch on the ignition and wait 1 minute before starting and then open throttle fully.
2 - Engine runs continually at a fast idle	a - Automatic choke not switching off	a - Check heater element and both connections
	b - Heater element defective	b - Replace complete ceramic plate
3 - Engine idles unevenly or stalls	a - Idling adjustment incorrect	a - Adjust idling correctly (550-600 engine revolutions or 1000 generator revolutions, with clutch pedal depressed)
	b - Pilot jet blocked	b - Clean jet
4 - Engine "runs-on" when ignition is switched off	a - Idling mixture too rich	a - Weaken idling mixture
	b - Idling speed too fast	b - Regulate idling speed
5 - Backfiring in the exhaust when vehicle is over-running the engine	Idling mixture slightly weak	Enrich mixture by turning the volume control screw approximately $\frac{1}{8}$ of a turn

6 - Poor transfer from idling to normal running	a - Accelerator pump dirty (pump passages blocked, ball sticking)	a - Clean accelerator pump and check action
	b - Torn diaphragm	b - Replace diaphragm
	c - Idling adjustment incorrect	c - Adjust idling correctly
7 - Engine stalls when accelerator pedal is released suddenly	Idling mixture too rich	Adjust idling correctly
8 - Engine runs unevenly (surges) with black exhaust smoke at low idling speed and smokes badly as idling speed increases. Spark plugs soot up quickly and mis-fire	a - Excessive pressure on the float needle valve	a - Check fuel pump pressure and reduce if necessary
	b - Leaky float	b - Replace float
	c - Float needle valve not closing	c - Check needle valve and replace if necessary
9 - Engine runs unevenly at full throttle, misfires and cuts out or loses power	Fuel starvation	a - Clean main jet and power fuel system b - Clean float needle valve c - Check fuel pump pressure and increase if necessary d - Clean fuel tank and tap
10 - Excessive fuel consumption	a - Jet sizes not properly matched	a - Install correct set of jets. Check spark plug condition
	b - Excessive pressure at float needle valve	b - Check fuel pump pressure and reduce if necessary
	c - Leaky float d - Float needle valve not closing	c - Replace float d - Check needle valve and replace if necessary
	e - Automatic choke not working properly	e - Check as at Point 2

Special care should be taken when filling the tank from cans to avoid dirt and foreign matter entering the tank. It is recommended that the fuel is filtered through a clean piece of chamois when filling the tank.

The air cleaner should be serviced in accordance with the instructions given under "Maintenance." Under severe dust conditions, the air cleaner must be serviced more frequently than indicated in the Maintenance Chart, in extreme cases even daily.

The fuel pump requires no service attention apart from regular filter cleaning.

ignition and touch the terminal with the cable end while grounding the unit. The needle should pull in and the actuator should emit a ticking noise as the cable makes and breaks contact. If not, or if the engine still tends to run-on (diesel), replace the actuator.

Note: Should the engine fail to start, idle, or accelerates roughly, check that the electro-magnetic pilot jet is connected and tight. Should the above test show that the unit has failed, the engine can still be operated until repairs are accomplished by turning the grubscrew to the left until the engine operates. This procedure will switch off the unit so the needle is withdrawn and the pilot jet is open continuously. This is only a temporary repair as the engine may diesel when hot and break a crankshaft. To stop the engine when dieseling, put in first or reverse gear, hold down brake pedal and let up on the clutch. Renew the electro-magnetic pilot jet as soon as possible.

EXHAUST EMISSION CONTROL SYSTEM

To meet U.S. Federal requirements to control carbon monoxide gas and hydrocarbon emission from auto exhaust systems, Volkswagen developed a new carburetor, since the air/fuel ratio is the chief factor to keep pollutants to a minimum. Engine temperature, condition, and ignition timing are also factors.

As the vehicle is operated, the mixture varies according to conditions, which also changes the composition of the exhaust gases. When the vehicle is over-running the engine, such as on a downhill run, a throttle positioner opens the throttle valve slightly in accordance with the intake manifold vacuum to prevent the increase of hydrocarbons being emitted into the air.

When performing the following service procedures, be sure to stay with the specifications in order to maintain a low emission level. To repair the 30 PICT—2 carburetor, use the previous instructions. Special emission control settings for the ignition will be found in the ignition system section.

Adjusting Carburetor Idle

With timing nearly set correctly, warm the engine to operating temperature by driving the car at least ten city blocks, then immediately adjust the ignition system as previously described in the ignition system chaper. Use a tachometer (set on high scale) to set the idling speed to 850 rpm with the idle adjusting screw, shown in illustration. Next, turn the volume control screw (2) to the right until the speed starts to drop, and from this position turn the volume control screw to the left until the engine runs fastest. **Note:** This procedure should be done immediately after the engine is warmed up to DRIVING operating temperature by driving the car at least ten city blocks.

It will be noticed that only minimal changes will occur when adjusting the volume control screw. The engine can still run when the volume control screw is turned right in, so make corrections very slowly so as not to damage the cone tip of the screw. When this adjustment is completed, return the engine speed to 850 rpm with the idle adjusting screw. Immediately adjust throttle positioner, using the following instructions.

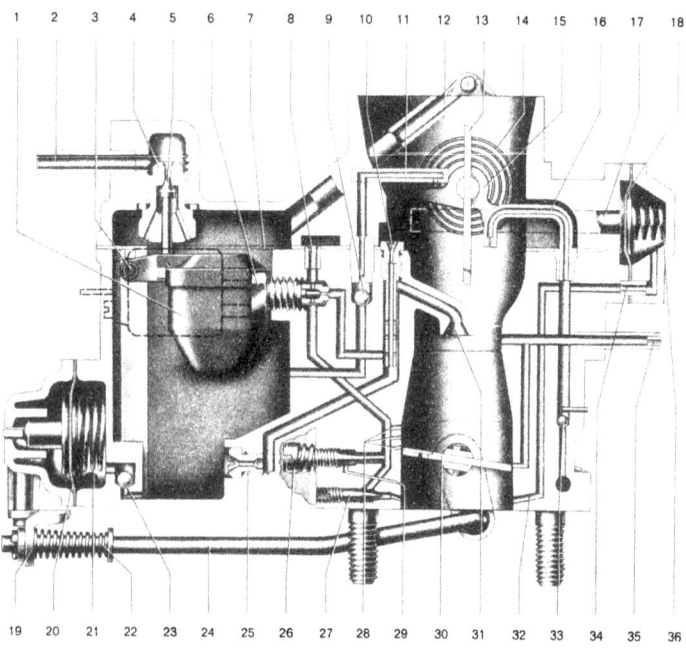

SOLEX 30 PICT-2

1 - Float
2 - Fuel line
3 - Float lever
4 - Float needle valve
5 - Float needle
6 - Pilot jet
7 - Gasket
8 - Pilot air drilling
9 - Ball check valve in power fuel system
10 - Air correction jet with emulsion tube
11 - Power fuel tube
12 - Float bowl vent tube
13 - Choke valve
14 - Bi-metal spring
15 - Operating lever
16 - Accelerator pump discharge tube
17 - Diaphragm rod
18 - Vacuum diaphragm
19 - Pump lever
20 - Pump diaphragm

21 - Spring
22 - Push rod spring
23 - Ball check valve for accelerator pump
24 - Pump connector rod
25 - Main jet
26 - Volume control screw
27 - Fuel metering screw*)
28 - By-pass port
29 - Idle port
30 - Throttle valve
31 - Discharge arm
32 - Vacuum drilling
33 - Ball check valve in accelerator pump drilling
34 - Jet in vacuum drilling
35 - Vacuum connection
36 - Diaphragm spring

Caution:
*) Do not change the adjustment of this screw

SOLEX 30 PICT-2 carburetor

No.	Designation	Qty.	Important
1	Screw for carburetor upper part	5	Tighten screws evenly and not too firmly.
2	Spring washer	5	—
3	Carburetor upper part	1	—
4	Float needle valve 1.5 mm diameter	1	Check.
5	Washer for float needle valve	1	Ensure correct thickness
6	Screw for retaining ring	3	Do not tighten screws too firmly.
7	Retaining ring for cap	1	—
8	Spacer for retaining ring	3	—
9	Choke unit with spring and heater element	1	Ensure correct voltage and installation position.
10	Plastic cap	1	Cap projection must engage in housing notch.
11	Fillister head screw	3	—
12	Cover for vacuum diaphragm	1	Ensure correct installation position.
13	Diaphragm spring	1	—
14	Vacuum diaphragm	1	—
15	Gasket	1	Replace.
16	Return spring for accelerator cable	1	—
17	Carburetor lower part	1	If damaged, replace complete carburetor.
18	Float and pin	1	Ensure correct weight, check.
19	Bracket for float pin	1	—
20	Air correction jet	1	—
21	Plug for main jet	1	—
22	Plug seal	1	Replace.
23	Main jet	1	—
24	Volume control screw	1	Cone must not be scored. On replacing, use only screws with designation "A".
25	Spring	1	—
26	Pilot jet cut-off valve "A"	1	Ensure correct voltage and designation "A", functional check.
27	Circlip	2	Connecting rod must have .012–.02 in. (0.3–0.5 mm) axial play at throttle valve lever.
28	Fillister head screw	4	Set pump arm to pressure stroke, then tighten screws.
29	Cover for pump	1	—
30	Pump diaphragm	1	—
31	Spring for diaphragm	1	—
32	Cotter pin 1.5 x 15 mm	1	Installation position inner drilling.
33	Washer 4.2 mm	2	Thickness 1 mm.
34	Spring for connect rod	1	—
35	Connecting rod	1	—
36	Injector tube for accelerator pump	1	Injection direction into the opening throttle valve gap.

Jets:
For all vehicles with exhaust control system

Venturi diameter	24 mm
Main jet	X 116
Air correction jet	125 z
Pilot jet*)	55
Pilot air jet (pre-adjusted)	130
Accelerator pump jet	50
Power fuel jet	60
Float needle valve diameter	1.5 mm

Washer under float needle valve	1 mm**
Float weight	8.5 grams
Accelerator pump capacity cc per stroke	1.30–1.60
Fuel level in float chamber	17–19 mm

*) with electro-magnetic cut-off valve and designation "A"

**) 1.5 mm on carburetors without throttle positioner. Fuel level in float chamber 18.5–20.5 mm.

Exhaust emission control trouble shooting

Symptoms	Cause	Remedy
1 - Poor idling, idle cannot be adjusted	Dirt in idle system	Clean carburetor, adjust idle as prescribed.
2 - Engine idle too fast	a - Throttle valve sticking	Free throttle valve lever and pull rod, or replace. A bent pull rod must be replaced
	b - Throttle valve positioner maladjusted	Adjust throttle valve positioner as prescribed
	c - Throttle valve positioner cannot be adjust	Replace throttle valve positioner
3 - Back-firing when coasting	Throttle valve positioner maladjusted	Adjust throttle valve positioner as prescribed, or replace it. In extreme cases, set cut-in speed to max. 1900 rpm

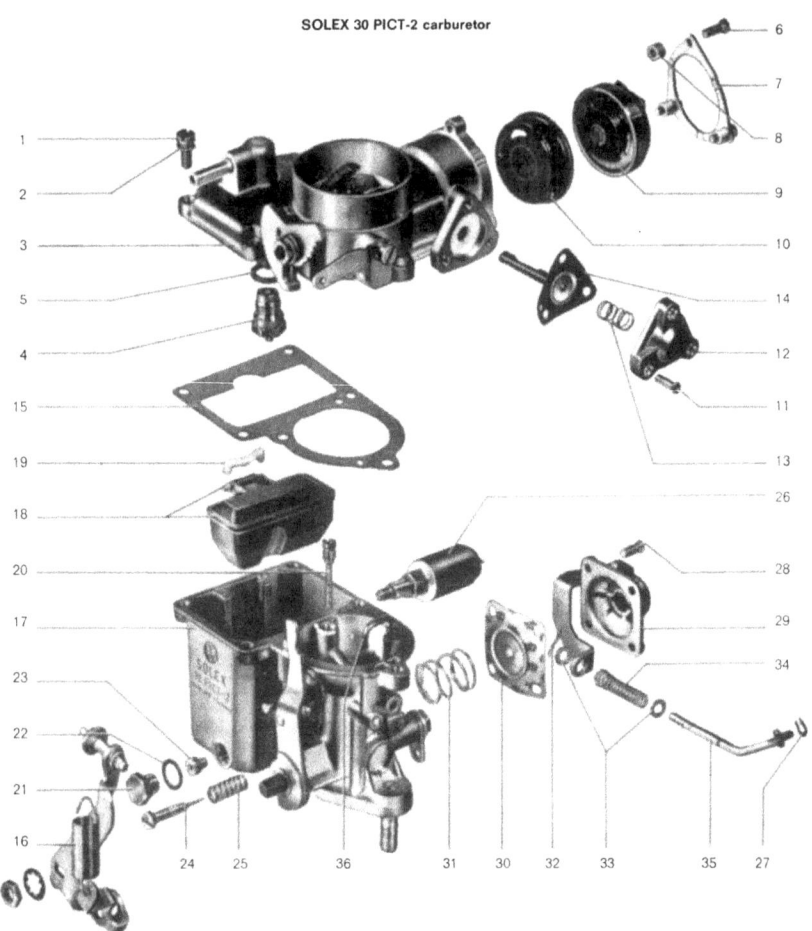

SOLEX 30 PICT-2 carburetor

30 PICT—3 Carburetor

For 1970 models and later, the idling circuit has been completely changed and the carburetor designation has been changed to 30 PICT—3. The major difference between it and the previous carburetors is the air bypass drilling (1) which allows all the air necessary for idling to bypass the throttle valve (2). The throttle valve now remains completely closed whenever the engine is idling; air and fuel are mixed in the air bypass chamber, and the mixture is regulated by the air bypass screw (3). All routine idling adjustments are performed with the air bypass screw, and the throttle valve need not be opened with the idle adjusting screw. Also, this screw must not touch the fast idle cam at idle speed. The volume control screw (4) is factory pre-set and must not be changed or tampered with. The amount of idling air/fuel mixture remains the same in the system even when the air volume changes. Fuel is drawn in from the idling system via a drilling (5), and the amount of fuel depends on the vacuum existing in the air bypass drilling (1), so that an adjustment of the air by-pass screw (3) does not influence the idling mixture, just the amount of that mixture used. Once again, the only adjustment necessary with the 30 PICT—3 carburetor is the idle speed, using the air by-pass screw.

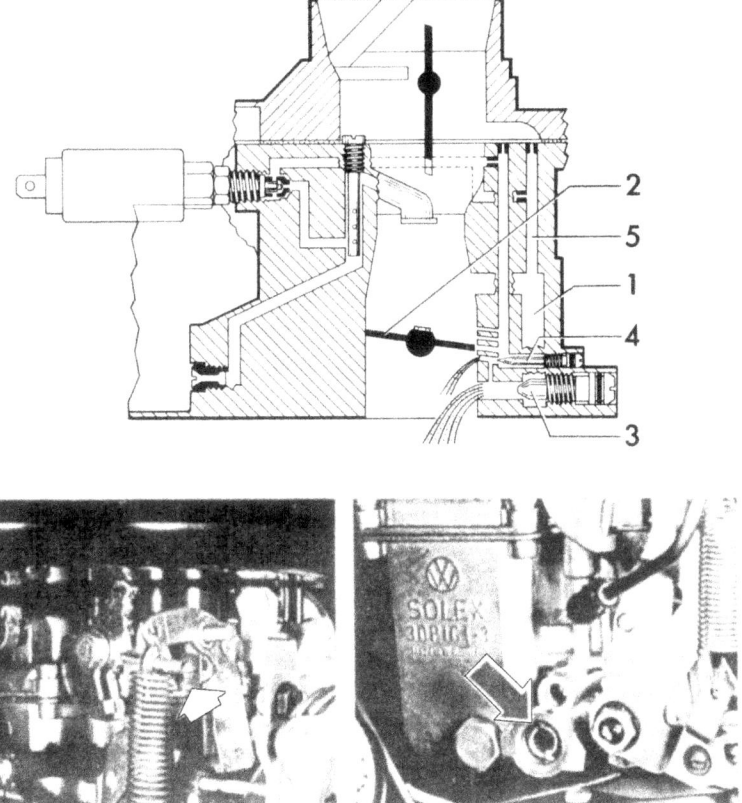

Throttle Positioner

The throttle positioner has the function of opening the throttle a bit when the car is over-running the engine, such as on a downhill run. This prevents fuel from passing into the atmosphere in

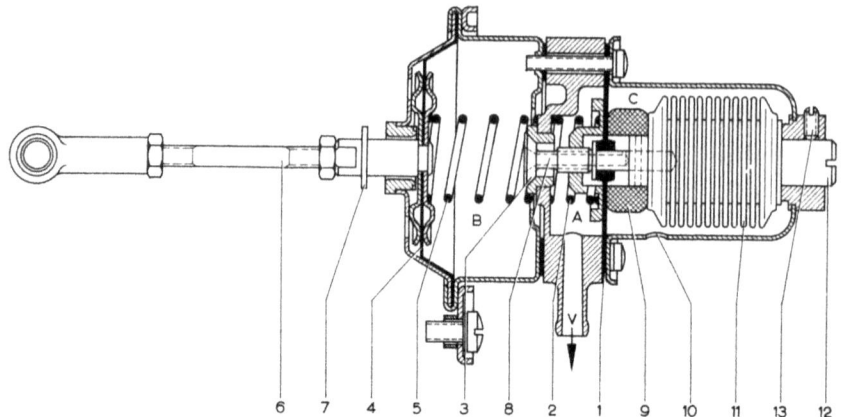

an unburned state, and also prevents backfiring in the muffler. The first purpose is naturally to prevent the emission of large amounts of carbon monoxide and hydrocarbons (prime ingredients of smog) from the vehicle's exhaust. As the throttle valve is opened by the positioner, the intake manifold vacuum is prevented from rising as high as it would with a closed throttle. Thus, even on deceleration, the engine is sure to receive an adequate charge of combustible air-fuel mixture rather than an over-rich mixture which will not burn, and will pass into the atmosphere in this form, or else cause backfiring in the muffler.

As the vacuum rises below the throttle valve upon deceleration, it becomes effective in chamber (A) through connection (V). The vacuum pulls diaphragm (1) to the left against the pressure of the spring (2), and valve (3), fixed to the diaphragm (1) opens and the vacuum existing in chamber (A) becomes effective in chamber (B) and pulls the diaphragm (4) to the right against the pressure of spring (5). This movement is transmitted to the pull rod (6), connected to the throttle shaft via the damper lever, thus opening the throttle valve.

Stop washer (7) limits the travel of the pull rod stroke. As the intake manifold vacuum decreases, the spring (2) presses the diaphragm (1) to the right, which closes valve (3). Spring (5) now moves diaphragm (4) to the left because the vacuum in chamber (B) is eliminated via a connection to the atmosphere. The outside air passes through hole (10) into the housing (C) of the altitude corrector, through the plastic foam filter (9) and into chamber (B) via the drilling (8) in valve (3). The altitude corrector (11) is set with a slight preload and presses on valve (3). The preload varies according to the existing atmospheric pressure so that the operation of the throttle positioner is never affected by the actual atmospheric pressure. The throttle positioner can be adjusted with adjusting screw (12) which is locked with grubscrew (13).

Throttle Positioner Adjustment

With the engine warmed up to operating temperature, all ignition and carburetor adjustments made, and choke valve of the automatic choke held completely open, proceed as follows:

1. Connect a tachometer to the operating engine and turn the adjusting screw on the altitude corrector (1) (see illustration) clockwise until the stop washer on the pull rod contacts the throttle positioner housing. At this point the engine speed should be between 1,700 and 1,800 rpm.
2. To correct any variation, lengthen or shorten the pull rod by turning it one way or the other, then tighten the locknuts. If speed is higher, lengthen the pull rod; lower, shorten the pull rod.
3. Use the adjusting screw on the altitude corrector to bring the idle speed down to 850 rpm by turning it counterclockwise.
4. Increase the engine speed to 3,000 rpm, then release the throttle lever. The time taken to drop from 3,000 rpm to 1,000 rpm must not exceed two to three seconds. If the time taken is shorter, turn the adjusting screw (1) on the altitude corrector clockwise, if longer, turn the screw counterclockwise. Lock the adjusting screw into place with the grubscrew and check the throttle closing time again.

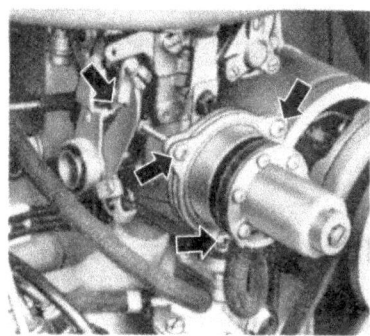

Servicing Throttle Positioner

To remove and replace the throttle positioner, first pull off the hose, then unscrew the three screws and remove the retaining ring and throttle positioner. Disconnect the pull rod at the carburetor. Install in reverse order, then check the adjustment. Replace as a unit if throttle positioner is faulty.

Throttle Positioner Changes

On 1970 models and later, the throttle positioner is separated into two parts connected by a vacuum line. The actuator section is attached to the carburetor with a bracket, while the control part is attached on the left in the engine compartment. The basic function of the throttle positioner remains the same, except that it also functions as a damper by preventing the throttle valve from closing immediately upon deceleration. An additional vacuum connection between the actuator section and the vacuum drilling in the carburetor performs this function. Use the procedure under "Throttle Positioner Adjustment", making the adjustment using the adjustable stop-screw. Hold the lever against the stop-screw with the engine running and the tachometer attached; adjust rpm with the adjustable stop-screw if necessary. All other corrections remain the same.

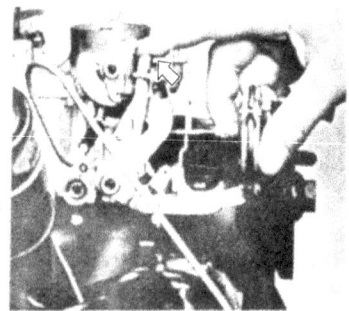

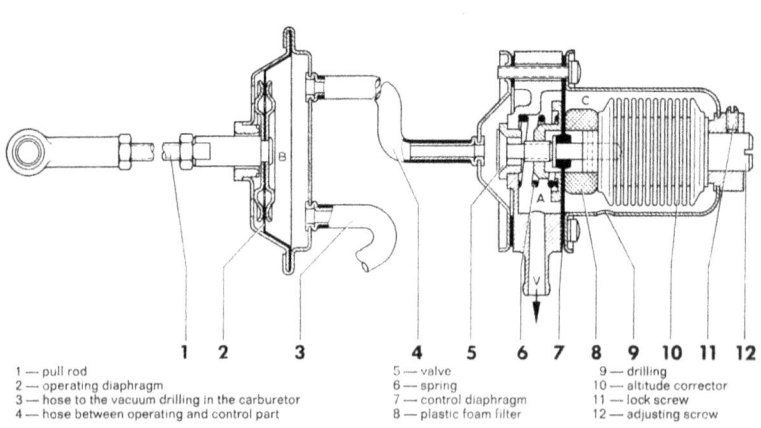

1 — pull rod
2 — operating diaphragm
3 — hose to the vacuum drilling in the carburetor
4 — hose between operating and control part
5 — valve
6 — spring
7 — control diaphragm
8 — plastic foam filter
9 — drilling
10 — altitude corrector
11 — lock screw
12 — adjusting screw

Fuel Evaporative Emission Control

All 1970 and later vehicles sold in California are equipped with an activated charcoal filter system to provide fuel evaporative emission control. All VW vehicles use a similar system, except that there is no need for an expansion tank with the Type 2 vehicles since the upper part of the fuel tank provides an additional space for fuel displaced due to heat expansion.

Prior to the introduction of this control system, hydrocarbon vapors originating in the fuel tank were expelled through the tank vent into the atmosphere. With the control system, hydrocarbon vapors originating in the fuel tank reach the activated charcoal filter via the expansion tank (1) and the fuel vapor line (2). When the engine is not operating, fuel vapors are absorbed by the activated charcoal. When the engine is operating, the engine cooling air blower is utilized to force air into the filter container through a pressure hose (3). This air flow through the filter regenerates the activated charcoal, at the same time the air with the hydrocarbon vapors is drawn off for combustion via the suction hose (4), connected to the air cleaner.

Fuel Evaporative Emission Control Servicing

No regular maintenance is necessary with this activated charcoal filter system other than checking hoses for condition and tightness. Remove the activated charcoal filter container by pulling off hoses and removing screw on clamp strap.

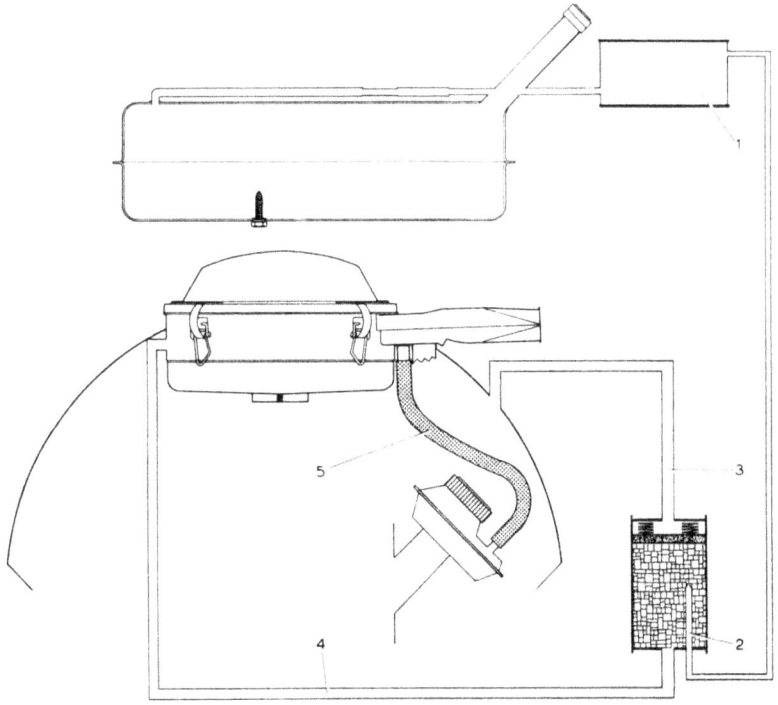

Air Cleaner

The air cleaner should be removed and cleaned every 6,000 miles or twice a year at least. Should the normal atmosphere in which the vehicle is operated be at all dusty, the air cleaner should be checked more often, even daily if necessary. The filter element retains the dust in the air as the air is pulled into the cleaner. As the vehicle moves, the dust settles into the oil in the bottom of the cleaner and is retained. To check whether

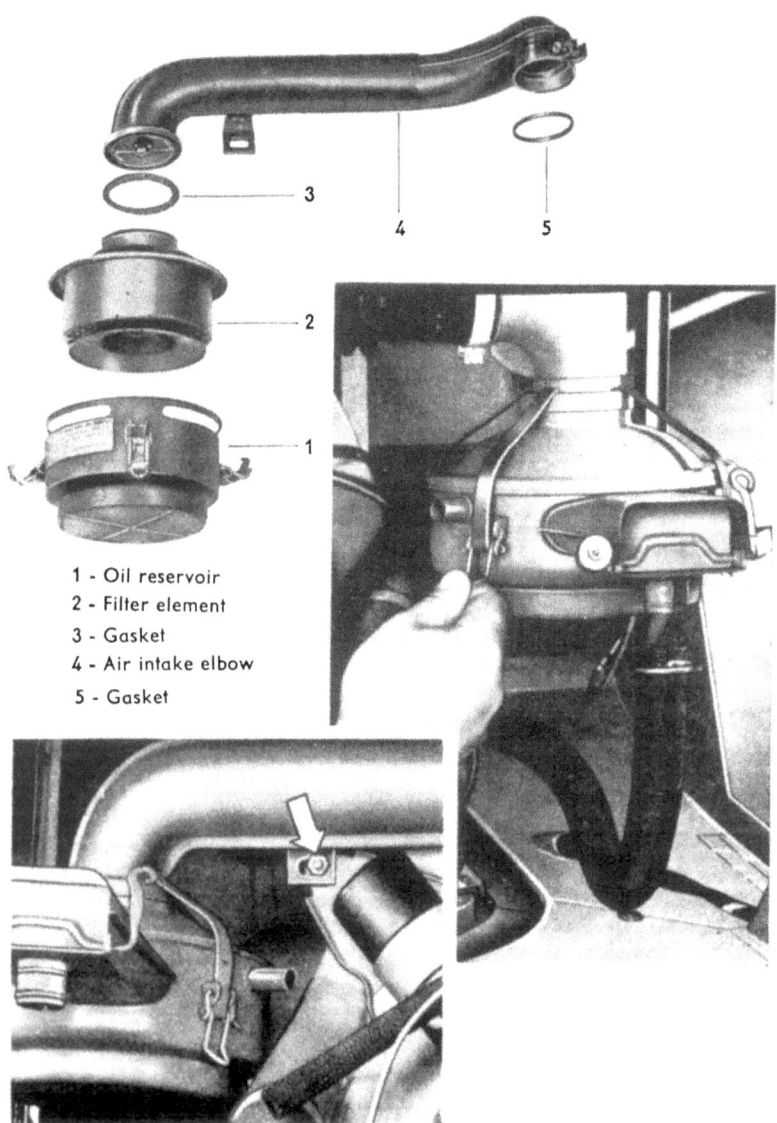

1 - Oil reservoir
2 - Filter element
3 - Gasket
4 - Air intake elbow
5 - Gasket

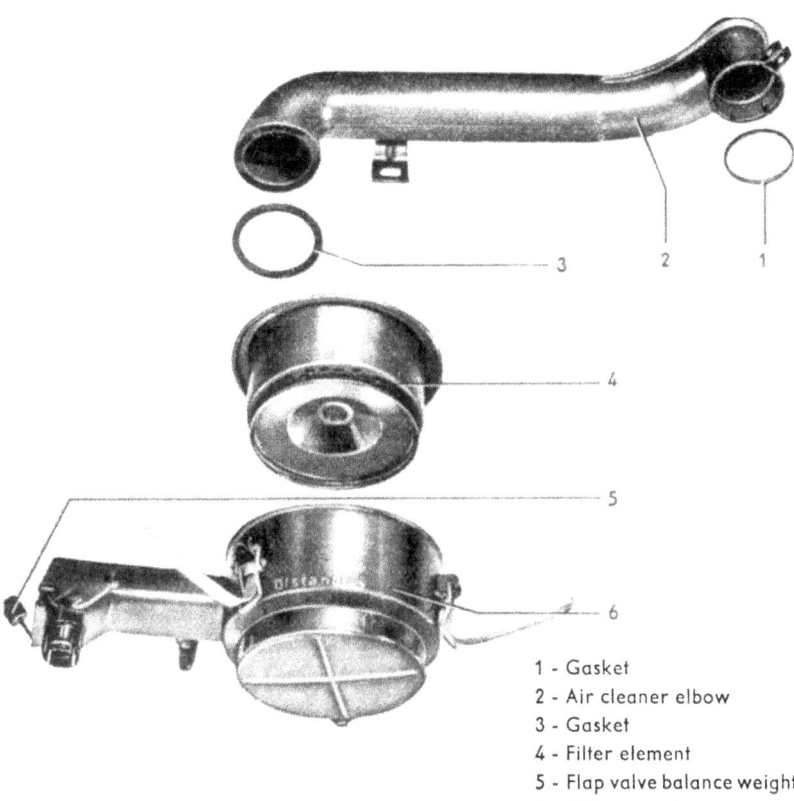

1 - Gasket
2 - Air cleaner elbow
3 - Gasket
4 - Filter element
5 - Flap valve balance weight
6 - Oil reservoir

or not the cleaner needs to be cleaned, check the amount of oil above the layer of sludge in the bottom of the lower part. When there is only 3/16 in. of oil above this layer, the lower part must be cleaned and filled with clean oil. If the cleaner is not properly serviced regularly, not only will be engine output drop, but the engine will also be worn prematurely.

On models produced prior to 1958, turn the complete oil reservoir to unscrew it from the filter element. On models following that, disassemble the air cleaner by pulling up on the clips, folding out the hooks, and lowering the oil reservoir without tipping it to any radical angle. This model has a wing nut under the filter element. After removing the oil reservoir, the wing nut can be removed to lower the filter element. Do not turn the element upside down. The element does not need to be cleaned out unless the air inlet holes are partly blocked; use a piece of wood to remove this crust. Use solvent to clean the oil reservoir, wipe dry, then put in fresh SAE 20 engine oil up to the mark ($^1/_2$ pint).

If it is necessary to remove the air intake elbow, as prior to taking off the carburetor (and always before removing the engine), first remove the air cleaner. Then loosen the clamping screw at the carburetor, leaving the bolt at the elbow for last. When replacing cleaner and elbow, check that connections and gaskets are tight and free of gaps, but do not overtighten the clamping screw at the carburetor.

Air enters the air cleaner through a small extension or horn. Coming into the bottom of the horn is a small hose that robs warm air from the car's heating system. A pivoting, weight-loaded flap, (No. 5), closes off the open end of the horn. When idling in the winter, there is insufficient vacuum inside the horn to open the flap and most of the air comes into the horn via the air tube. This prevents the jets from icing and the car from stalling. As engine speed increases, vacuum increases, the flap opens and cool air is drawn in. When open all the way, the flap blocks the warm air entrance and only cold air is inhaled. Since warm air is only needed during the winter, the flap should be fixed in its open position when air temperature is regularly above 68°.

On models produced prior to 1968, remove the air cleaner by pulling the crankcase breather and pre-heater hoses off, then loosen the clips and remove the cleaner from the elbow. Remove the top part, being careful not to turn it over, but set it down in the same position it was when removed. Use solvent to clean the bottom part, wipe dry, then put in .6 pint of fresh 30 W engine oil (10 W in arctic climates). Check the filter element in the upper part from underneath. Only if the filter element has become so dirty due to delayed cleaning of the bottom part or oil shortage that the air inlet holes on the underside are partly blocked, should the encrusted dirt be scraped off with a piece of wood.

Reverse the removal procedure to install the air cleaner, ensuring that it fits properly on the intake elbow, then check that the warm air flap (if so fitted) is free-moving. At temperatures above 50° F. this flap should be fixed in the open position with the wire loop tucked under the flange. Should the temperatures dip below 50° F. at times, the flap should be free to move and regulate the flow of warm air according to the speed of the engine.

On models produced after 1968, use the above instructions to clean the unit with the following differences: The preheater hose clip (C) must be loosened before the hose can be removed, the screw (D) should be held with a pair of pliers while the hexagon nut is loosened so the warm air control flap cable is not bent, then loosen the screw (E) on the outer cable retainer and pull out the cable. First release the lower clips (F) securing the lower part to the bracket, remove cleaner, then release the three upper clips (G) and remove the upper part, being careful not to turn it over and checking it for encrustation from the underside. Use solvent to clean the bottom part, wipe dry, then put in about a pint of fresh 30 W engine oil (10 W in arctic climates).

Assemble the cleaner, clip it back onto the bracket, then check that the warm air control flap moves freely before reconnecting the cable. Push the outer cable into the retainer, and the cable into the clamp screw as far as they will go, then secure both properly. Be sure to tighten all clips and hoses securely.

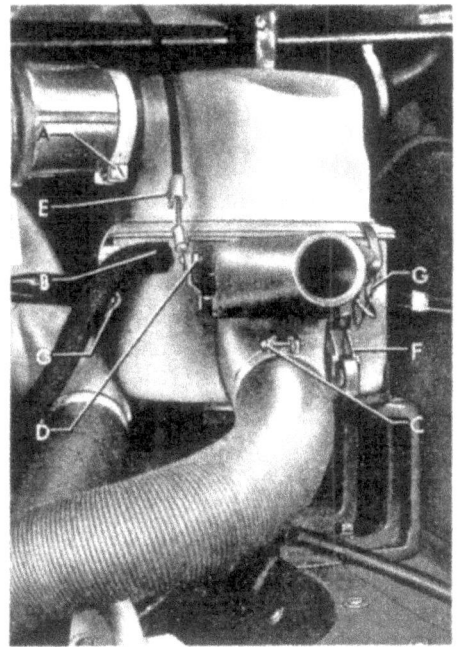

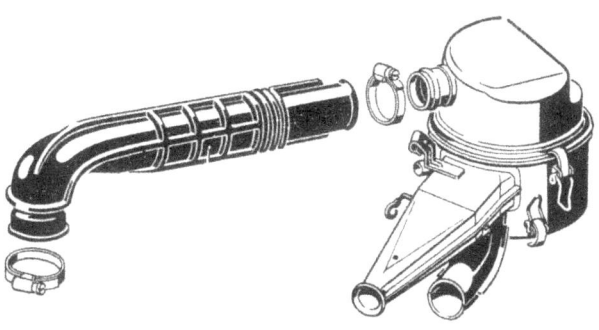

IGNITION SYSTEM
Early Models

The coil-battery ignition employs a Bosch TE 6 B1 coil, a Bosch VJR 4 BR 8 distributor with centrifugal advance and 14mm spark plugs, Bosch W 175T1 or W 175 T1-A.

COIL

The coil mounts on the fan housing adjacent to the distributor and connections are as follows: Terminal 1 to contact breaker of distributor, Terminal 15 to ignition switch, Terminal 4 to distributor cap (high tension lead). To test the coil, disconnect the high tension lead at the distributor cap and hold about 3/8 of an inch away from a ground, such as the engine crankcase and turn the engine on the starter. A strong spark should result, otherwise the coil is faulty.

Always keep the insulating cap dry and free from oil to prevent leaking of high tension current.

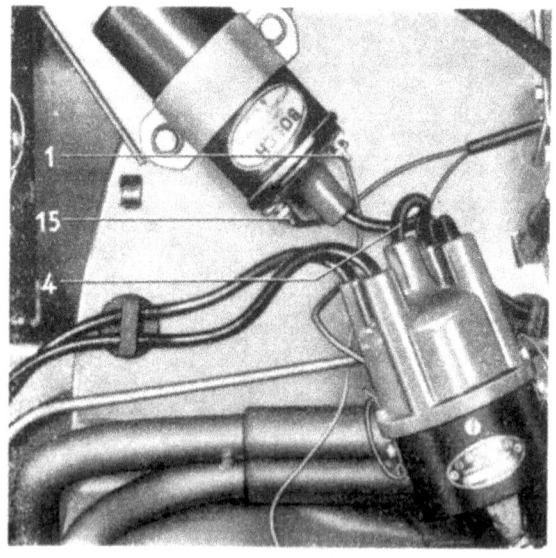

Connections:
Terminal 1 to distributor (contact breaker)
Terminal 15 to ignition/starting switch
Terminal 4 to distributor cap (high-tension lead)

DISTRIBUTOR

At the beginning of the cold season apply 4 or 5 drops of oil to the felt wick in the center of the rotor. Keep both the outside and the inside of the cap clean and dry. Otherwise, outside cleaning, adjusting and renewing breaker points, there is no maintenance required on the distributor. The centrifugal advance is correctly set at the factory. It can be checked against the reprinted chart.

To adjust breaker points, crank the engine over by turning the generator pulley with a wrench until the contact arm is at the highest point on the cam lobe, loosen the set screw of the other breaker point, turn the eccentric screw until the gap between the sprung contact and the fixed contact is 0.4mm (0.016"). A slight drag fit on a feeler gage is correct. Re-tighten locking screw.

To dress the points, use a point file, not emery cloth or sandpaper, and make sure that surfaces are clean, unpitted and parallel. Be sure that there is no oil or grease on the surface of the points.

NOTE: After dressing and adjusting the points it will be necessary to re-time the ignition.

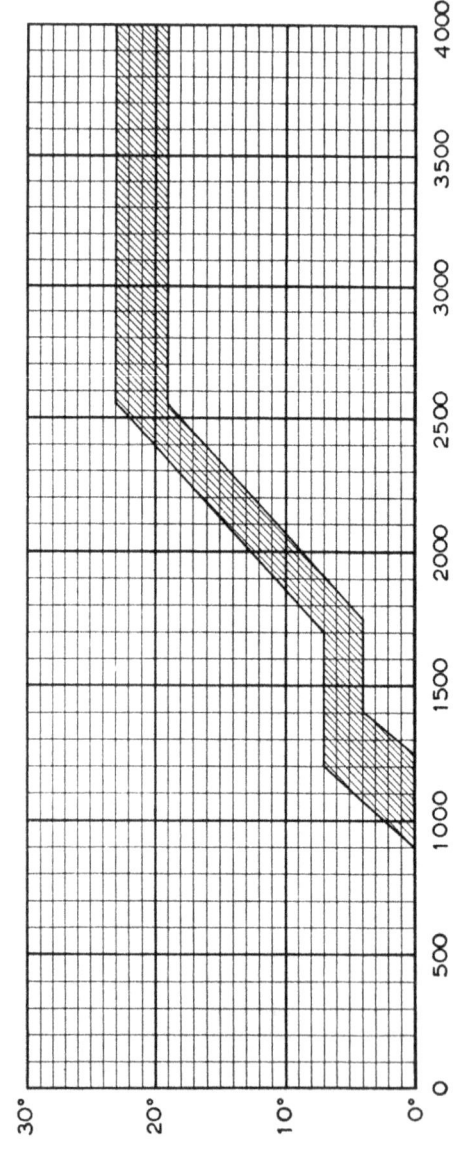

IGNITION TIMING

Crank the engine until the mark on the pulley lines up with the vertical split in the crankcase and the distributor rotor is adjacent to #1 spark plug terminal. (Filed mark in distributor body). Loosen clamp screw of distributor. Insert a small piece of paper torn from a cigareett between the contact points and pull gently on it. Turn the distributor until the paper is just released by the points. Re-tighten clamp.

A timing light (static) can be used to the same effect. Connect one lead to terminal 1 at distributor, the other to ground switch on ignition. The lamp will light up just as the points begin to open.

Note: Do not use a stroboscope light inasmuch as the mark on the pulley is for static setting and will be incorrect with engine running.

1 - Breaker point
2 - Breaker point lock screw
3 - Breaker point adjusting screw
4 - Cam
5 - Cam hole
6 - Primary lead connection
7 - Insulating washer
8 - Insulating piece
9 - Angle plate
10 - Terminal screw
11 - Insulation
12 - Breaker arm

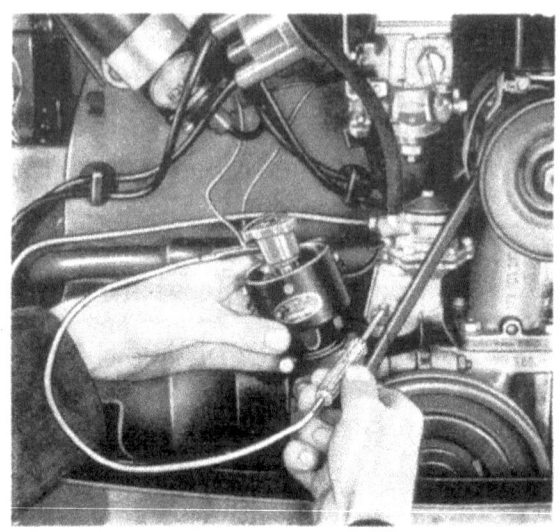

If the distributor is removed, be sure to replace it with the rotor in #1 position (toward filed mark) and with the engine cranked to #1 piston on firing position (split in crankcase lined up with pulley mark) then the slot of the distributor drive pinion will be offset towards the rear and nearly parallel to the fan pulley and it will slide into position. An exploded view identifies the various components.

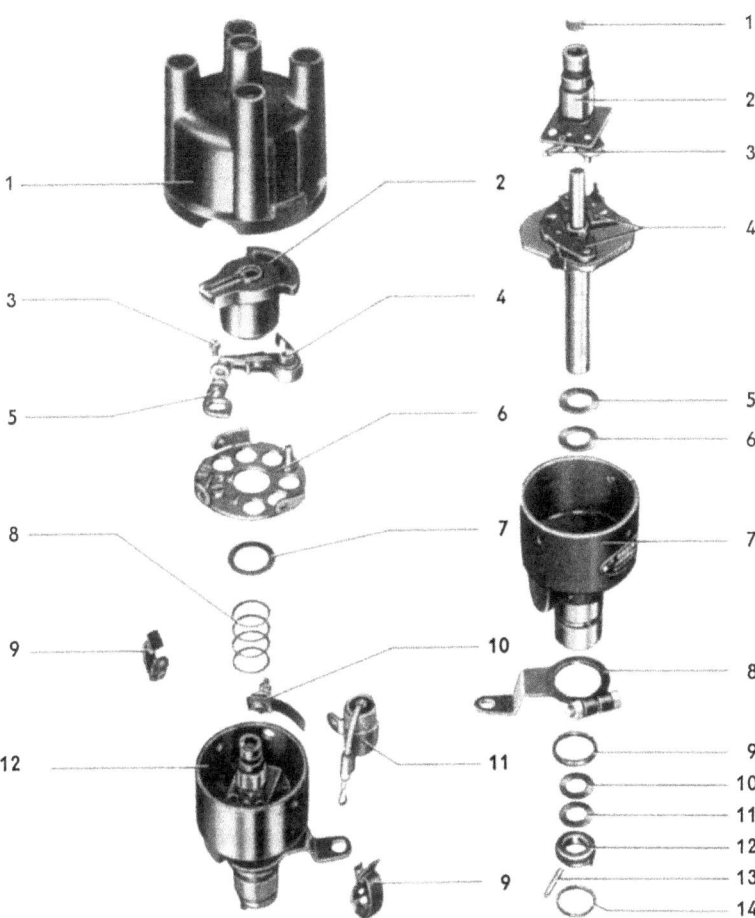

1 - Distributor cap
2 - Rotor
3 - Breaker point lock screw
4 - Fixed breaker point
5 - Breaker arm
6 - Breaker plate
7 - Fiber washer
8 - Shim
9 - Cap retaining spring
10 - Primary terminal
11 - Condenser
12 - Distributor housing

1 - Cam Lubrication felt
2 - Cam
3 - Return spring
4 - Centrifugal weights
5 - Fiber washer
6 - Steel washer
7 - Distributor housing
8 - Distributor lock plate
9 - Rubber ring
10 - Fiber washer
11 - Steel washer
12 - Coupling
13 - Coupling pin
14 - Coupling pin retaining spring

SPARK PLUGS

Plugs should be cleaned and serviced (gap renewed) every 2,500 miles, more frequently if much stop-and-go driving is encountered. The condition of the plugs reveals much about the engine's condition and fuel mixture. The following rough guide can be followed as to appearance of electrodes and center insulator:

Medium gray: Ideal mixture and correct spark plug.
Black: Too rich mixture, plug too cold.
White: Too lean a mixture, plug too hot.
Oiled or carboned: Plug failure or bad piston rings.

SPECIFIED PLUGS
Bosch W 175 T1
Autolite AE 6 or AER 6
Champion L 10 S or L 85

Ignition — Prior To 1968

VW Type Prior To 1968

Two different ignition coils and distributors were used consecutively, either made by Volkswagenwerke or by Bosch. In common with other automobiles, the ignition system consists of battery, ignition switch, coil, distributor and spark plugs. The six-volt current of the battery is converted to approximately 15,000 volts by the coil when the distributor points make and break the low tension circuit. The condensor prevents the points from being burned and assures a sharp drop in current when points break. The rotor in the distributor distributes the high tension voltage from the coil to each cylinder at the proper time. The distributor is driven from the rear end of the crankshaft and either a diaphragm-type vacuum unit, a centrifugal weight unit or a combination of both advances the timing (beyond the initial $7^1/_2$ or 10 degree static setting) according to engine demand. This is required because mixture burning time varies with engine load and speed. Because maximum efficiency requires that maximum pressure on the piston head reach a peak at a comparatively constant number of degrees after top dead center, the mixture must be ignited at varying degrees before top dead center.

Coil

Both Bosch and Volkswagen coils have been used alternately. Coils should be checked for tight mounting to fan housing. Terminal #15, (Fig. 91), takes in the current from the battery and terminal #1 takes the low tension current to the distributor

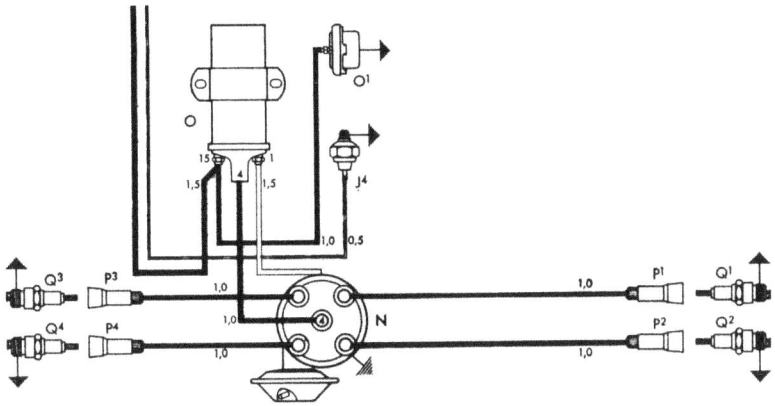

FIG. 91

points. The condenser is wired in parallel with the points. The automatic choke also feeds off terminal #15. Terminal #4 is the high tension lead to the center of the distributor cap. When removing or installing any of the high tension wires, grasp the wire by the terminal connector and not by the wire itself. This prevents breaking up the graphite core high tension wires that are used to prevent radio interference.

Distributor

Fig. 92, shows an exploded view of the currently-used VW distributor. Both Bosch (condenser inside) and Volkswagen distributor (condenser outside) have been fitted. Earlier models used a different type, but the procedure in tuning or repair is the same.

To remove distributor, take off vacuum pipe and disconnect primary cable at terminal #1 of coil. Take off distributor cap and remove distributor bracket screw. Lift distributor out. Installation is the reversal of this procedure, watching the following points. With #1 cylinder at firing point, the slot in the drive pinion (Fig. 93), will then be pointed across the engine and offset toward the back of the engine. To insert distributor, turn rotor to point to the notch for #1 cylinder on the distributor housing, (Fig. 94).

When checking on distributor testing machine, the dwell angle for the Bosch distributor is 51-55° and for the Volkswagen distributor 48-52°.

Setting Point Gap

Fig. 95 shows the top of a VW distributor. Points are easily replaced by removing retaining screw and screw at terminal bracket. Points are adjusted by turning engine over by hand until cam follower or fiber block on the breaker arm rests on the top of one oft he four lobes of the cam so that the points are the farthest apart. Check gap with feeler gauge for a measurement of .016". If not correct, loosen the lock screw, move breaker points until gap is correct and lock screw again.

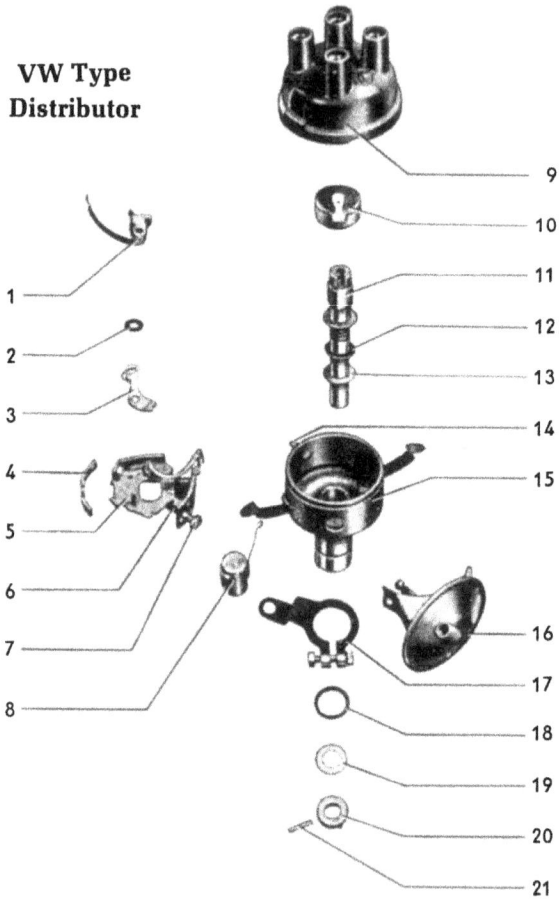

1 - Breaker arm
2 - Insulating washer
3 - Fixed breaker point
4 - Stop bracket
5 - Breaker plate
6 - Spring
7 - Threaded rod with nut and lock washer
8 - Condenser
9 - Distributor cap
10 - Rotor
11 - Distributor shaft
12 - Steel washer
13 - Plastic washer
14 - Low-tension cable
15 - Distributor housing
16 - Vacuum advance unit
17 - Clamp bracket
18 - Sealing ring
19 - Plastic washer
20 - Driving dog
21 - Pin

FIG. 92

FIG. 93

FIG. 94

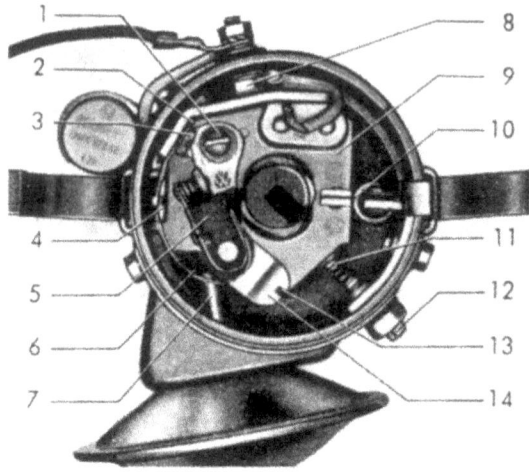

1 - Securing screw
2 - Leaf spring
3 - Hexagon head screw
4 - Stop bracket
5 - Breaker arm
6 - Breaker arm spring
7 - Pull rod
8 - Primary connection
    with cable
9 - Breaker plate
10 - Leaf spring for breaker
    plate
11 - Spring
12 - Threaded rod
13 - Adjusting slot
14 - Fixed point

FIG. 95

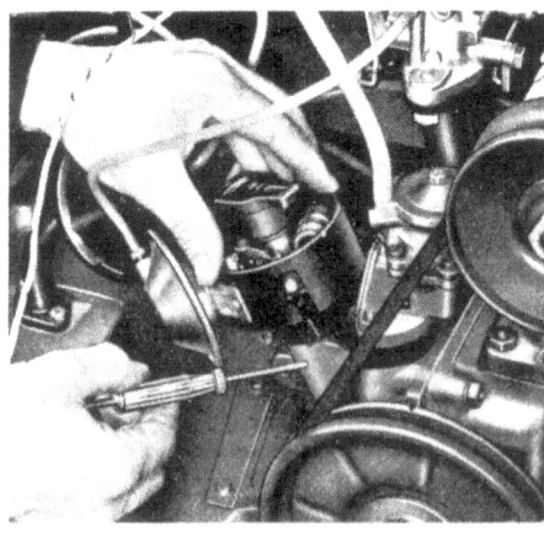

FIG. 96

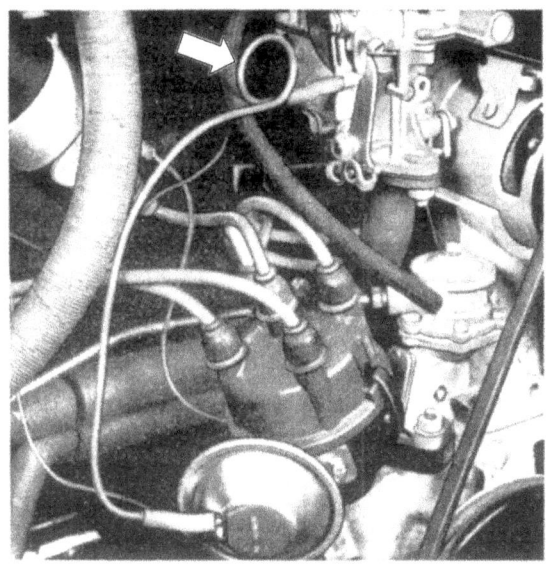

FIG. 97

After adjusting points, it is important to check the ignition timing. There are either one or two timing notches on crankshaft pulley. If only one, it indicates that #1 piston is $7^1/_2°$ before top dead center when it is lined up with the crankcase jointing faces and the piston is at the end of the compression stroke. If there are two notches, the left indicates $7^1/_2°$ and the right 10°. (Crankshaft pulley rotates clockwise.) Use right-hand notch.

Wire a six-volt light bulb between the primary lead to distributor (terminal #1 of the coil) and a ground. Rotate engine by hand until distributor rotor points to #1 mark (notch) on distributor housing and crankshaft pulley notch is at the top of pulley opposite the crankcase jointing face. Turn on ignition and slowly rotate crankshaft pulley clockwise, (Fig. 96). Light should go on just as notch passes jointing face. If incorrect, loosen pinch bolt at base of distributor and rotate distributor counter-clockwise to advance ignition, clockwise to retard. Tighten pinch bolt when timing is correct.

Ignition is adjusted with engine cold. Do not use strobe light in secondary circuit of ignition system but rather the six-volt bulb in the primary circuit as described, because a strobe light can give a false reading.

The 10° advance came with the forty-hp engine. If a low grade of fuel causes pinging, retard ignition back towards $7^1/_2°$.

If a test lamp is not available the following procedure can be resorted to in an emergency: With point gap correctly set and

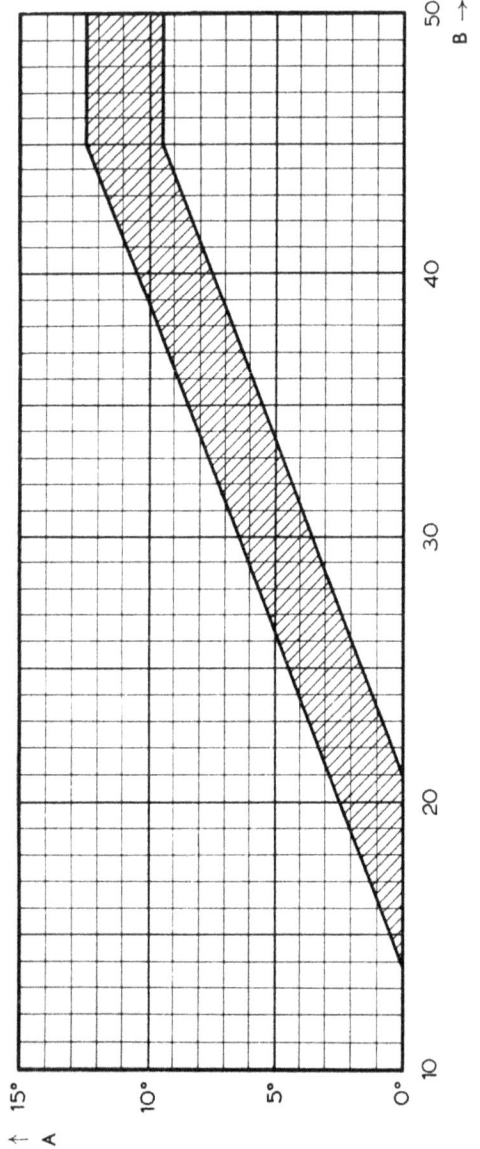

A - Advance in crankshaft degrees B - Vacuum in mm Hg

VW Distributor Vacuum Advance Curve

marks on crank pulley and crankcase aligned as described above; loosen clamping screw on distributor, insert a piece of very thin paper (cigarette paper will do) between the points; rotate distributor clockwise until points are fully closed; grasp the piece of paper between thumb and first finger with one hand, tug at it firmly and rotate the distributor slowly counterclockwise with the other hand until the paper is just released. Then re-tighten clamping screw, install rotor and cap.

The diaphragm type vacuum unit can be checked for leaks by pulling the hose from the unit, moving the breaker plates as far as they will go, holding a finger over the vacuum unit pipe and releasing the breaker plate. Plate should move only small amount and stay in that position for at least a minute. On recent engines there is a loop in the vacuum line between the vacuum advance unit and carburetor to prevent gas from running down to the vacuum unit. This is easily installed using a rubber hose, (Fig. 97).

Spark Plugs

14 mm spark plugs are used in the VW engine. The factory recommends any of the following makes:

36 H.P.	40 H.P.
Bosch W 225 T 1	Bosch W 175 T 1:
Beru 225/14 u 2	Beru 175/14
AC F 10	Lodge H 14 or HN
Auto-Lite AE 6 or AER 6	Champion L87Y or W175 T 1
Champion L 10S	AC 43 L or 43 F
Lodge H 14 or HN	Auto-Lite AE 6 or AER 6
KLG F 70	KLG F 70

Gap should be adjusted to .026 in.

.026 in.

FIG. 98

The electric spark jumps the gap between the two electrodes to ignite the fuel-air mixture in the combustion chamber. Starting, idling, acceleration and maximum performance greatly depend on the right choice of spark plug to suit engine operating conditions. For operating under severe heat or load conditions, use either Champion or Bosch W 225 T1 spark plugs. Check spark plugs every 6,000 mi. and do not use over 12,000 mi. Check for appearance to determine the engine's operating condition. If possible, clean plugs with a sand blaster, dress center electrodes with a file, gap, then check pressure plugs will stand before failing to fire. Otherwise, clean the carbon from the plug with a chip of wood, dress center electrode, then gap. Remove filings with solvent and a blast from an air hose, drying plug exterior to avoid shorting and tracking. Always install with a new washer, being careful not to crossthread the plugs and tightening until the washer is just heard to crush.

Electrodes and Insulator

medium brown — good carburetor setting and correct performance of spark plug;
black — mixture too rich;
light grey — mixture too lean;
oiled up — failure of spark plug or leaking cylinder.

In the case of fuel containing tetra-ethyl-lead (anti-knock fuel), the insulator will show a grey color, provided the engine is correctly adjusted.

During operation, the plug gap increases due to natural burning. If the gap has increased too much, the plug may fail to operate. The gap is checked by means of a gauge and adjusted by bending the ground (outer) electrode to the correct value.

NORMAL CONDITIONS CARBON FOULING

BURNED OR OVERHEATING OIL FOULING

FIG. 98A

Vehicles which are used mainly in towns and on short runs will start more readily during the winter if plug gap is reduced to .016 to .020". **Note:** Engine idle will be rougher at this setting, and engine may tend to die. To overcome this problem, reset the carburetor volume and idle speed adjustments so the engine idles faster.

Bosch Type Prior To 1968

Details of the Bosch ignition coil have been previously outlined. Only the items unique to the Bosch distributor will be detailed, so it will be necessary to refer to the previous sections for the remainder of the information. Distributor maintenance involves general lubrication and adjustment or renewal of the breaker points. With every point adjustment, renewal or check, carefully blow out the interior of the distributor after unsnapping the clips holding the distributor cap in place. Adjust the contacts as described further in this section, reset timing, then use distributor cam grease or (if necessary) lithium multi-purpose grease to lubricate the fiber block on the breaker arm. Press a pea-size quantity of grease into the corner between the fiber block and the breaker arm. At the same time, apply 4 or 5 drops of light oil (engine oil will do) to the felt ring in the contact breaker baseplate. **Caution:** Make sure no oil is left on the breaker points, and that the felt ring is not over-oiled, since in either case the oil could cause the points to burn prematurely or misfire. If the points have been dressed, be sure to clean out any filings or grease.

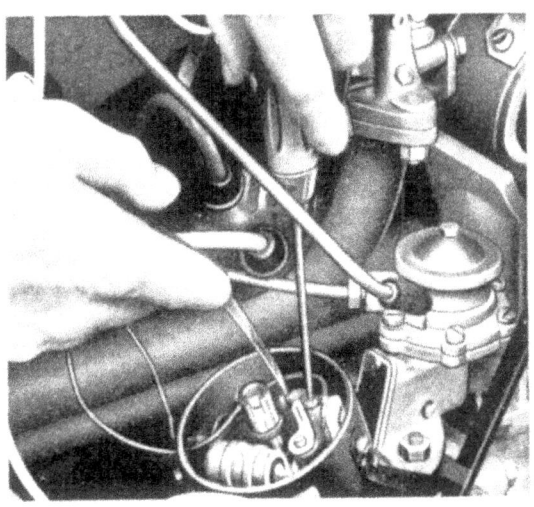

Adjust the breaker points as described previously, noting that the breaker gap can be measured by inserting the feeler blade at the edge of the points when the points are pitted only slightly. After adjusting points, reset the ignition timing since an alteration of .004" (.1 mm) in the point gap alters the ignition timing about 3°. Check the radial (side) play in the distributor shaft bearings. If it is excessive, replace the complete distributor since the points will not open and close at the proper time.

Should the breaker points need to be renewed (shop practice is to renew the points each 6,000 miles) replace the parts in the reverse order, making sure that the washers for the breaker arm are in the correct order. Adjust as noted previously, then time the engine.

1 - Retaining screw
2 - Pins and adjusting slot
3 - Breaker point
4 - Oil drilling
5 - Ground connection
6 - Return spring
7 - Low tension cable
8 - Pull rod
9 - Hexagon screw
10 - Insulator
11 - Breaker arm spring
12 - Breaker arm
13 - Condenser cable
14 - Condenser

Servicing Distributor

Both distributors are disassembled, examined, and assembled nearly the same way. Differences between the two are noted. See the appropriate exploded view for parts placement. With

Bosch Type Distributor

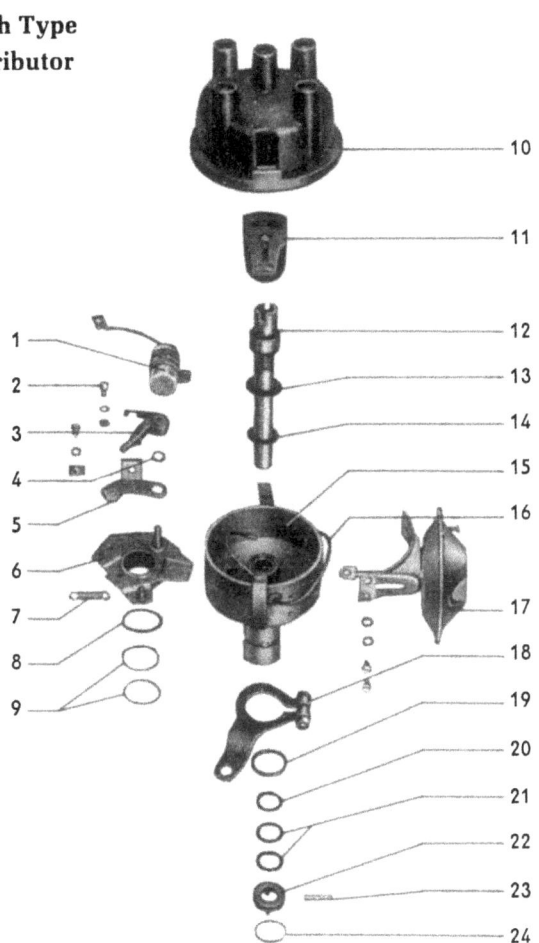

1 - Condenser
2 - Securing screw with flat and spring washers
3 - Contact breaker arm
4 - Insulating washer
5 - Contact breaker point
6 - Breaker plate
7 - Return spring
8 - Plastic washer
9 - Shim
10 - Distributor cap
11 - Rotor
12 - Distributor shaft
13 - Steel washer
14 - Fiber washer
15 - Distributor housing
16 - Low tension cable
17 - Vacuum advance unit
18 - Clip
19 - Sealing ring
20 - Fiber washer
21 - Shim
22 - Driving dog
23 - Pin
24 - Locking spring

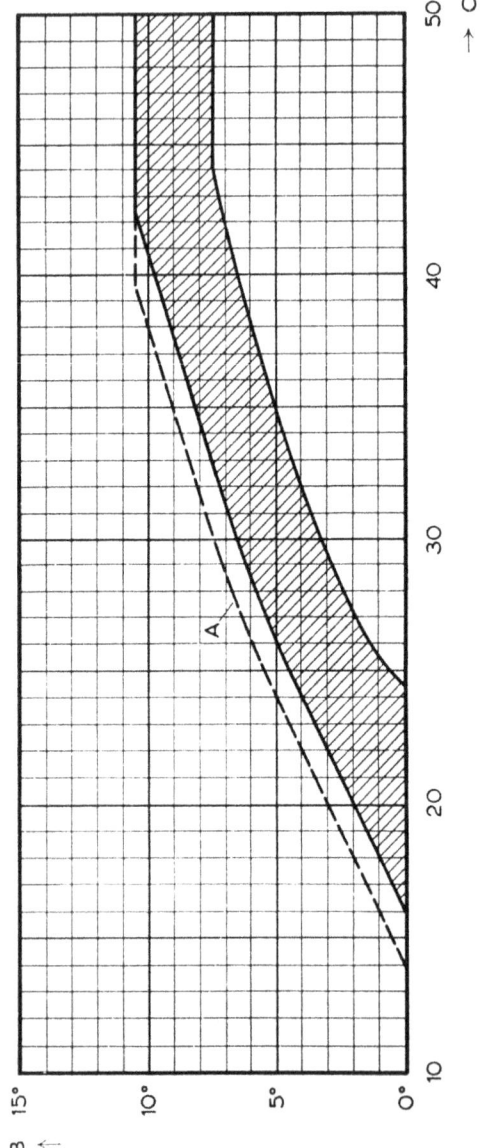

Vacuum Advance Curve for the BOSCH ZV PAU 4 R 5 Distributor

A - Wear limit when measuring with falling vacuum
B - Advance in distributor shaft degrees
C - Vacuum in mm Hg

the distributor removed from the vehicle and the distributor cap and rotor removed, follow this procedure: On the VW distributor, unscrew the nut from terminal 1 and take off the low tension cable and washers. Pull out the connecting cable to the breaker plate, on the Bosch distributor also remove the rubber sleeve on the low tension cable. Remove the condensor and the breaker points. On the Bosch unit, detach the breaker plate ground cable on the housing and take off the retaining spring, then remove the vacuum unit return spring. Take out the three screws holding the vacuum unit and remove the unit.

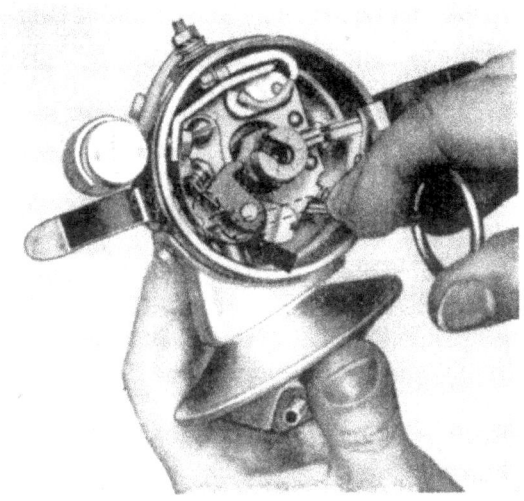

VW Type

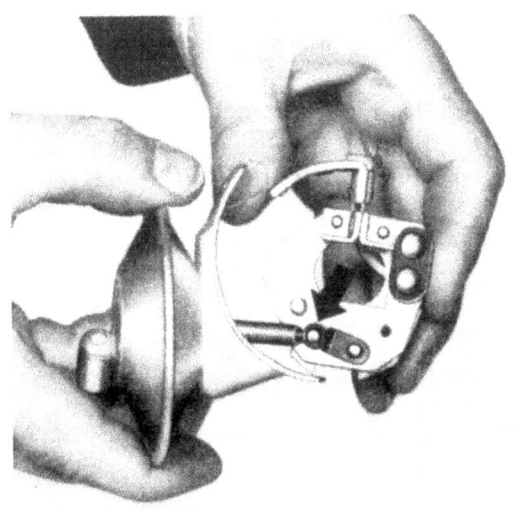

On the VW distributor, push the vacuum unit pull rod out of the ball joint by inserting a suitably bent wire hook in the hole provided in the pull rod. Take off the nut with the threaded pin and the vacuum unit securing screw, then remove the vacuum unit. Remove the screw holding the breaker plate retaining bracket, then remove the breaker plate and stop bracket from the distributor housing. Pull out the low tension cable. On both distributors knock out the driving dog pin and remove the driving dog and fiber washer. Remove the distributor shaft with the steel and fiber washers, and on the VW unit remove the rubber ring and clamp arm from the distributor base. On the Bosch unit, remove the contact breaker plate and plastic washer.

Inspect distributor components after washing in solvent. Do not wash the self-lubricating bush in the distributor housing. Examine the contact breaker points for wear and renew if necessary, then examine the distributor shaft bearing areas for wear. If radial (side) play is excessive, replace the complete distributor. Axial play is eliminated with shims. Check the steel leaf spring, the insulation of the low tension connection and the engagement of the spark advance pull rod in the ball joint on the VW unit. Replace the complete breaker plate if necessary. On the Bosch unit, replace the breaker plate if the plastic bushes are worn. On both units, renew the sealing ring for the distributor shaft.

Assemble the distributor after oiling the distributor shaft. On the Bosch distributor also lubricate the felt ring for the breaker plate with 1 or 2 drops of engine oil. On the VW unit, fill the space in the housing between the bushes with Bosch Special Grease FT 1 v 8 or equivalent. On either unit, check the correct order and quantity of steel and fiber washers and insert the shaft into the distributor housing. Compensate for axial play with shims. Turn the securing slot for the rotor towards the No. 1 cylinder notch on the cylinder housing edge. Place the steel and fiber washers on the shaft end (fiber only on the VW unit), and install the driving dog so that the lugs are offset towards the notch on the housing edge. Insert the pin and install the lockring in the groove on the driving dog for the Bosch unit. On the VW unit, peen both ends of the hole to keep the pin in place.

The remaining important items to watch on the Bosch distributor are the retaining spring with the guide piece for the distributor cap, which should be on the same side as the breaker plate ground connection. Lubricate the fiber block with universal grease. See the illustration of the VW distributor body and condenser to insure that the washers are in the correct order to insure the proper insulation from that unit. Lubricate the ball

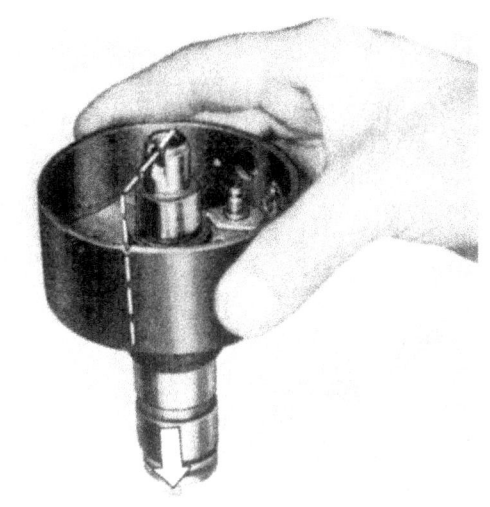

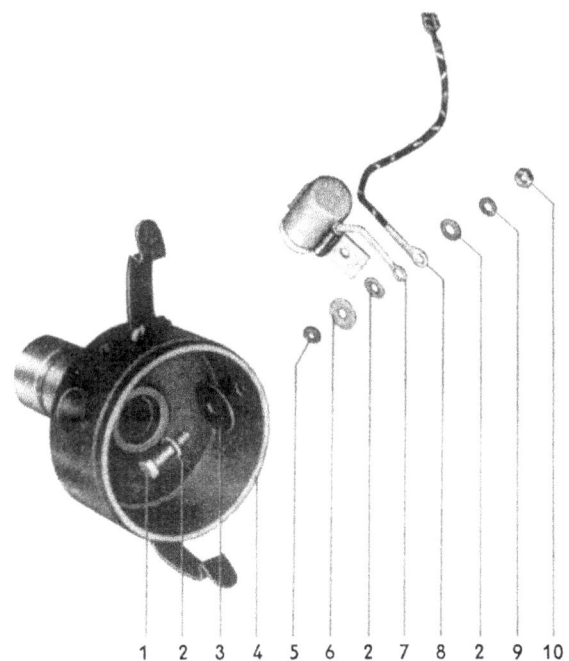

1 2 3 4 5 6 2 7 8 2 9 10

1 - Hexagon head screw
2 - Washer
3 - Insulating washer
4 - Distributor housing
5 - Insulating bush
6 - Insulating washer
7 - Condenser cable
8 - Low-tension cable
9 - Lock washer
10 - Nut

socket underneath the breaker plate with multi-purpose grease, then place the stop bracket and breaker plate in the distributor housing and secure with a screw. Attach vacuum advance unit to the housing, then press the unit pull rod into the ball socket in the breaker plate from underneath with a suitably shaped wire hook. Install the condenser and breaker points, then adjust the breaker point gap. **Caution:** When securing the vacuum advance unit on the VW distributor, the threaded rod must only be screwed in to set the correct total advance. The adjustment of the spring influences the spark advance curve of the distributor. After rebuilding the distributor, the advance curve must be readjusted on a distributor test stand by altering the spring tension.

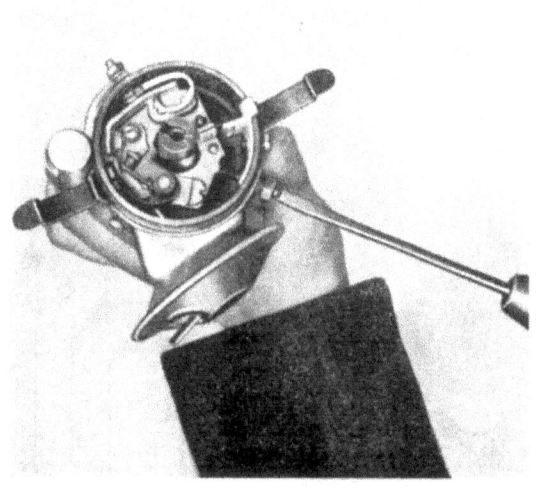

Ignition — 1968 And Later

Models With Exhaust Emission Control

On engines with exhaust emission controls, be sure to have the engine, the ignition timing, and the carburetor adjusted in accordance with the manufacturer's specifications. This is essential in order to maintain a low emission level.

Dwell Angle (Bosch Distributors Only)

The dwell angle for all models equipped with a Bosch distributor is $47°$ to $53°$. Adjusting the distributor points with a dwell angle meter rather than with a feeler gauge as previously described will give a more accurate setting to the points.

Automatic Spark Advance With Curve

The carburetor vacuum line connected to the vacuum unit on the distributor will automatically advance the spark. Use the following data to test:

Vacuum mm Hg	Advance Crankshaft degrees
4 – 8	advance starts
10	4 – 6
30	17 – 19
50	26 – 28
70	31 – 35
80	32 – 35 end

Advance curve:

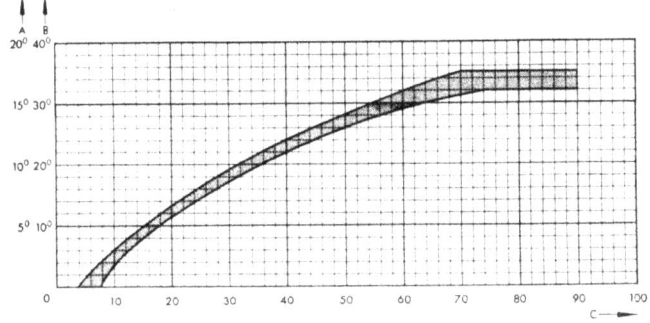

Measure with increasing vacuum.

A = Advance in distributor shaft degrees
B = Advance in crankshaft degrees
C = Vacuum in mm Hg

Ignition Timing

There are three notches on the crankshaft pulley (viewed facing the crankshaft pulley) as follows:

Left	**0° (TDC)**
Center	**7.5° before TDC**
Right	**10.0° before TDC**

The following procedure using a stroboscopic timing light is necessary to time models with exhaust emission control, but first set timing approximately with a stationary light as previously outlined. Make sure that engine, fuel system, spark plugs and breaker points are in good condition.

1—Warm engine by driving the car at least 10 city blocks (oil temperature 158° F.), then set idling speed to 850 rpm with a portable tachometer, turning the idle adjusting screw (1) if necessary.

2—Loosen the clamp screw on the distributor bracket until the distributor can just be turned by hand.
3—Connect a stroboscopic timing light to the engine, making sure to connect to the No. 1 (front right) cylinder ignition cable.
4—Remove vacuum hose from the vacuum unit on the distributor, then start the engine and run it at idling speed.
5—As the stroboscope flashes, direct the beam at the pulley. Turn the distributor until the TDC mark (the separate left hand line) on the pulley is in line with the crankcase joint.

6—Turn off the engine and tighten the distributor clamp screw, then recheck the ignition timing with the engine running at 850 rpm and connect the vacuum hose to the distributor at the same time. If the distributor is in order, the timing as set before must not change by more than .160" (distance from pulley mark to crankcase joint).

1 - Primary connection with cable
2 - Securing screw
3 - Leaf spring
4 - Hexagon head screw
5 - Stop bracket
6 - Breaker arm
7 - Breaker arm spring
8 - Pull rod
9 - Fixed point
10 - Adjusting slot
11 - Threaded rod
12 - Spring
13 - Leaf spring for breaker plate
14 - Breaker plate

7—Briefly speed engine up to 3,000 rpm and direct stroboscope beam onto pulley once more. The mark should move about 2 to 2.2" to the left (32 to 35° crankshaft). If not, either the vacuum unit or the distributor is at fault. Test the vacuum unit by pulling the vacuum hose off at the

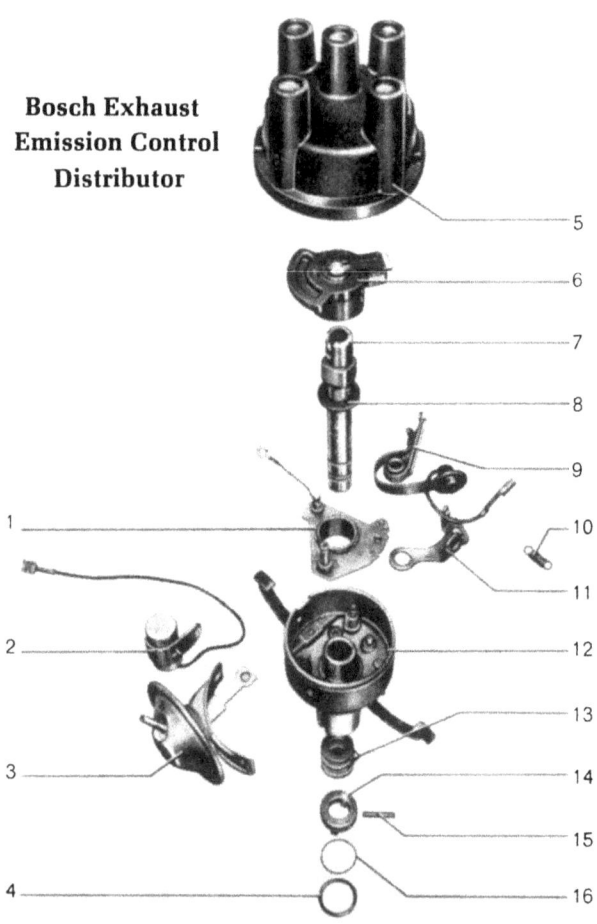

Bosch Exhaust Emission Control Distributor

1 - Breaker plate with ground
2 - Condenser
3 - Vacuum advance unit
4 - Sealing ring
5 - Distributor cap
6 - Rotor
7 - Distributor shaft
8 - Fiber washer
9 - Contact breaker arm with spring
10 - Return spring
11 - Contact breaker point
12 - Distributor housing
13 - Steel washers
14 - Driving dog
15 - Pin
16 - Locking ring

distributor and removing the distributor cap. Turn the contact breaker point to the left as far as it will go and close the small pipe in the vacuum unit with a finger. The breaker plate will be pulled back about 3/16 in. by the return spring and then should remain in this position for about a minute. If it moves further to the right with the small pipe sealed, the vacuum unit is leaking and must be replaced.

Installing Distributor

Turn the distributor shaft one tooth to the left (—30°) when installing. Correctly positioned, the slot of the drive shaft will face the front of the stud attaching the fuel pump, while the small segment faces the pulley. With the firing point correctly set, the vacuum unit will be at right angles to the longitudinal axis of the vehicle. Make sure the engine has not been turned over while the distributor is out of the vehicle. When the distributor has been replaced after the distributor drive shaft has been positioned at #1 cylinder (see previous instructions), it will be similar to the following illustration.

ELECTRICAL SYSTEM

GENERATORS FOR EARLY MODELS

The VW Transporter's 6-volt electrical system incorporates a Bosch LJ/REG 180/6/2500 L3 generator fitted intermittently in production with a similar 160 watt model. Geared to a nominal maximum output speed of 2500 rpm at 25 mph in 4th gear for the vehicle. Cut-in speed is 1560 rpm, corresponding to 785 rpm at the crankshaft. The generator is contiguous with the cooling fan and is driven by an adjustable-tension V-belt from the crankshaft. (See fan-belt tension).

A Bosch RS/TA 180/6 A 3 regulator controls output. It is mounted atop the generator.

Connections:

Terminal 61 to generator warning lamp

Terminal B+(51) to terminal 30 on starter
(and thus to battery)

Caution: Disconnect or connect the regulator cables when the engine is stationary and not operating. Prior to removing any other cables, disconnect the B+ (51) cable to prevent a short circuit which will ruin the regulator. Accidentally switching the cables on the terminals ⊥ (D+) and F (DF) will also ruin the regulator. All regulators can only be renewed, since repair or adjustment is impossible.

Quick Regulator Check (1200 and 1500 Models)
The regulator can be checked independently of the battery with a voltmeter, an ammeter and a sliding 50 A resistance (R). Disconnect cable from regulator terminal B+ (51), then connect the resistance in series with the ammeter between the terminal B+ (51) and ground on the regulator. Connect the voltmeter positive terminal to terminal B+ (51) and the negative terminal to ground. Be sure to use only short cables with a minimum cross section of ¼ in.² Make sure all connections and groundings are good to avoid high resistances and false readings. Start the engine and accelerate slowly to 3500 — 4000 generator rpm (1950 — 2200 engine rpm). With a resistance loading of 45 A (1200 model), or 50 A (1500 model), the voltage should be at least 6.6 to 7.2 Volts (1200 Model), or 6.6 to 7.2 Volts (1500 Model). If the readings are not within these limits, renew the regulator, check the connections prior to applying power, then recheck the circuit. No repair of the regulator is possible, and do not use this procedure for early 160 Watt models.

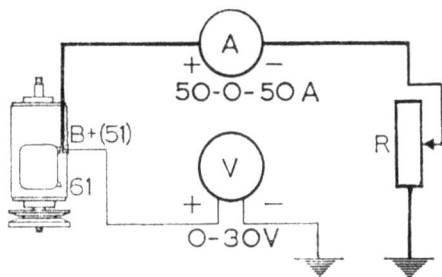

Generating System Check (1200 and 1500 Models)
Should there be any doubt about the generating system adequately charging the battery, in spite of the fact that the generator warning light goes out when the engine speed increases, use a voltmeter to test the system. Disconnect the battery ground cable when working on the regulator to prevent short circuits. Disconnect the cable from the regulator post B+ (51) terminal. Connect the voltmeter positive terminal to the regulator post B+ (51) and the negative terminal to ground.
Start the engine and accelerate slowly to 3500 — 4000 generator rpm (1950 — 2200 engine rpm). At just above idling speed, the needle should jump from 0 to 6 — 7 Volts and remain at 7.4 to 8.1 Volts. If this is not so, the regulator should be replaced and the generator checked (if voltage is low). When the engine is switched off, the voltmeter needle should spring from about 6 to 0 Volts just before the engine stops completely as an indication that the regulator points are not sticking.

GENERATOR FOR 1200 MODEL

Quick Generator Check

Disconnect the two feed cables from the regulator, then connect the cable F (DF) on the generator to ground (D—). Connect the voltmeter positive terminal to the plus cable (D+) on the generator and negative terminal to ground (D—). **Important: Run the generator for only a few seconds since the field wings will heat up and burn out.** Operate the generator at the speeds indicated and quickly check the voltage produced. If the generator produces only a low voltage or none at all, it must be removed and checked.

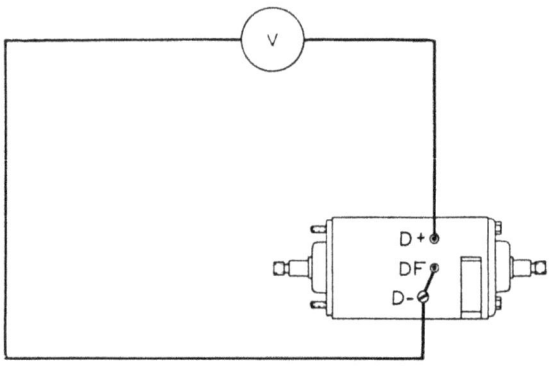

Rpm	Voltage
1500	approx. 6 V
3000	approx. 18 V

Servicing Regulator

Remove regulator by disconnecting cables B+ (51) and 61 from regulator, then remove screws securing regulator and remove regulator. Disconnect both cables from generator to regulator at terminals + (D+) and F (DF) underneath the regulator. When reinstalling the regulator, connect the thick cable from the positive brush to the + (D+) terminal underneath the regulator. Connect the thinner cable from the field coils to the F (DF) terminal underneath the regulator. If the correct readings cannot be obtained after replacing the regulator, the generator is defective. The regulator is non-adjustable and can only be renewed.

Important: If a new regulator is being installed, connect wires as noted above, then remove the fanbelt and place a jumper wire between B+ (51) and 61 for about 5 seconds. This will cause the generator to spin as a motor, establishing the direction of current flow.

Checking Brushes and Commutator

The brushes and commutator can be examined with the generator installed. If brushes no longer protrude from the holders, they are worn out and must be replaced with new brushes of the same type. Clean an oily or dirty commutator with a clean cloth moistened with alcohol, then check it for grooves or burns. If so, the generator must be overhauled. To replace the brushes, loosen the screw and remove the wire to the brush, then pull back the spring and pull out the brush. Make sure new brush is seated properly. In an emergency, the commutator can be cleaned of graphite with fine polishing cloth held over the end of a flat stick.

Generator

Remove the generator by disconnecting the battery ground cable, spark plug cables for cylinders 1 and 2, then detaching heater pipes between the fan housing and the heat exchangers. Remove the air filter and intake elbow, then remove the carburetor and the fan belt (be sure to loosen the fan belt pulley on the end of the generator). Remove the generator clamping strap, then remove the two fan housing securing screws and lift the fan housing. Remove the four screws in the fan housing cover and remove the generator and fan. When installing, be sure to locate the fan housing so that it contacts the cylinder cover plates all around.

BOSCH GENERATOR AND REGULATOR

No-load voltage	Charging current	Cut-in rpm *)	Cut-in voltage	Rated output
7.4—8.1 V	max. 45 A at 6.0—7.2 V	1800—1850	5.5—6.8	180 W at 6 V and 2500 rpm *)

*) generator rpm   All values apply at a generator housing temperature of 20° C, 68° F

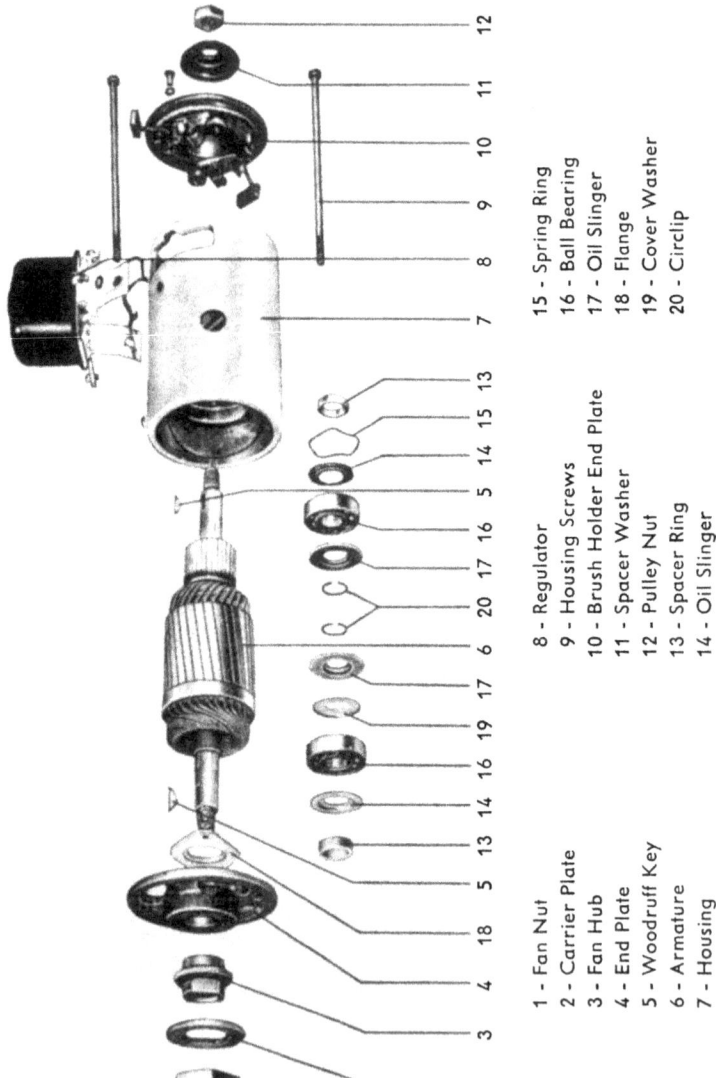

BOSCH GENERATOR AND REGULATOR

1 - Fan Nut
2 - Carrier Plate
3 - Fan Hub
4 - End Plate
5 - Woodruff Key
6 - Armature
7 - Housing
8 - Regulator
9 - Housing Screws
10 - Brush Holder End Plate
11 - Spacer Washer
12 - Pulley Nut
13 - Spacer Ring
14 - Oil Slinger
15 - Spring Ring
16 - Ball Bearing
17 - Oil Slinger
18 - Flange
19 - Cover Washer
20 - Circlip

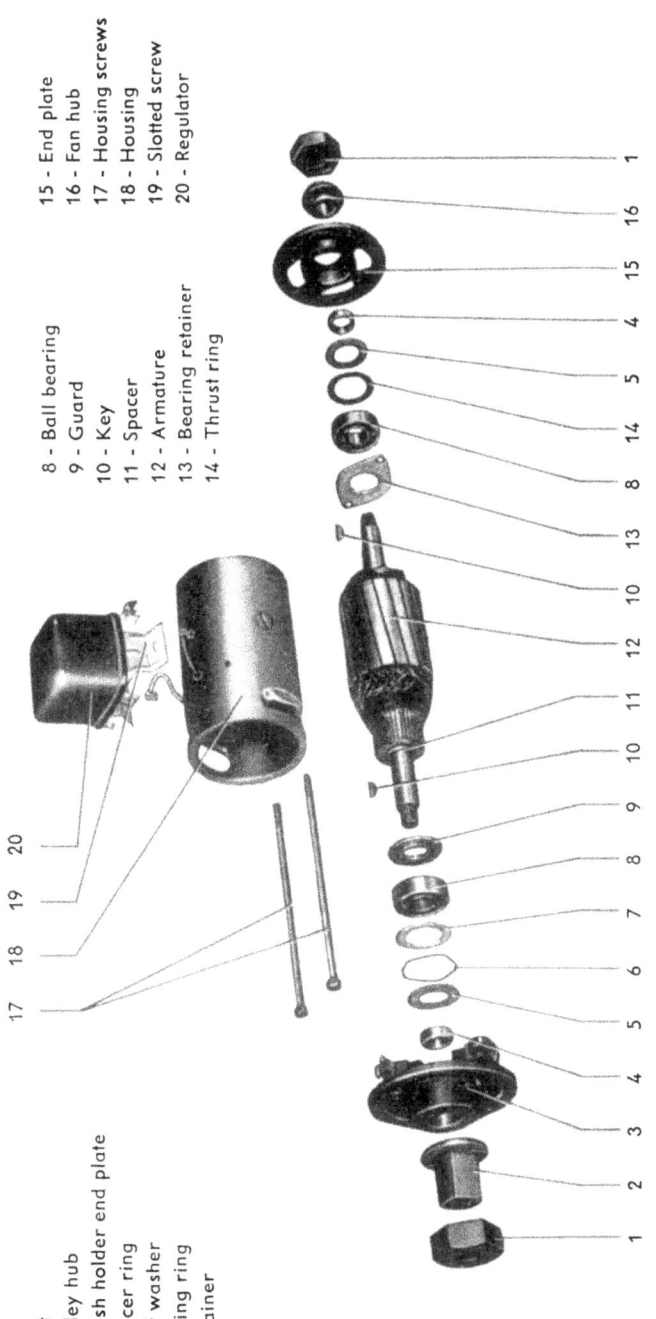

1 - Nut
2 - Pulley hub
3 - Brush holder end plate
4 - Spacer ring
5 - Felt washer
6 - Spring ring
7 - Retainer

8 - Ball bearing
9 - Guard
10 - Key
11 - Spacer
12 - Armature
13 - Bearing retainer
14 - Thrust ring

15 - End plate
16 - Fan hub
17 - Housing screws
18 - Housing
19 - Slotted screw
20 - Regulator

VW GENERATOR AND REGULATOR

VW GENERATOR AND REGULATOR

No-load voltage	Charging current	Cut-in rpm *)	Cut-in Voltage	Rated output
7.4—8.1 V	max. 45 A at 6.0—7.2 V	1350—1660	5.9—6.6	180 W at 6 V and 2500 rpm*

*) generator rpm   All values apply at a generator housing temperature of 20° C, (68° F).

GENERATOR FOR 1500 MODELS

Fitted to the VW Transporter with the 1500 engine is a 200 Watt generator (nominal output), with a separately mounted regulator, Bosch variode type. The regulator is mounted on the right-hand wheel housing in the engine compartment. The nominal voltage is 6, with maximum output of 300 Watts at a nominal speed of 2600 rpm and a cut-in speed of 1820 rpm. The nominal output can be continually exceeded by up to 50% without damage to the generator.

Use the previous procedure to quick-check the generator and to check the generating system, using the following set of figures as a guide. Be sure to terminate the test in a few seconds to prevent damage to the field windings. The previous procedure to remove and install the generator should also be followed. The separate regulator can be removed by disconnecting the battery ground strap, the four cables from the regulator, then remove the screws and remove the regulator. The regulator is installed in the reverse order, then check against the wiring diagram to ensure that all connections are correct. Check the readings with the replacement regulator (a faulty regulator can only be renewed, not repaired). If the correct readings cannot be obtained, the generator is defective and must be repaired.

Generator connections
Terminal D+ to terminal D+ on the regulator
Terminal DF to terminal DF on the regulator

Regulator connections
Terminal D+ to D+ on generator
Terminal DF to DF on generator
Terminal 61 to generator warning lamp
Terminal B+ (51) to battery positive terminal via terminal 30 on the starter

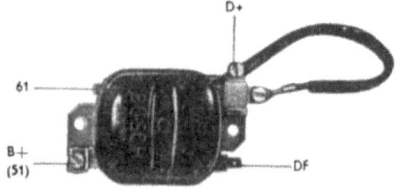

BOSCH GENERATOR AND REGULATOR
FOR 1500 MODELS

Rpm	Voltage
1750	approx. 6
3000	approx. 15
4500	approx. 24

No-load voltage	Regulating Current under Load	Cut-in rpm *)	Cut-in voltage	Rated output
6.9—7.5 V	6.2—7.0 V at 200 Watt	approximately 1820	5.9—6.5 V	200 W at 6 V and 2600 rpm *)

*) generator rpm. All values apply at a generator housing temperature of 20 C. (68 F)

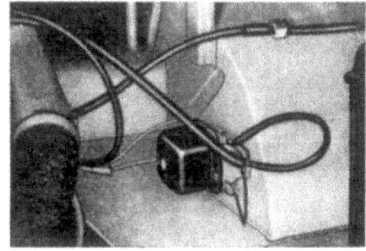 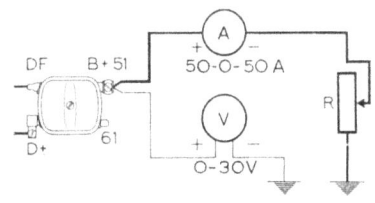

GENERATOR FOR 1600 MODEL
12 VOLT SYSTEM

The 12-Volt electrical system used on late model VW Transporters uses a Bosch generator of 360 Watts nominal output at 2000 rpm. Cut-in speed is 1450 generator rpm, creating a current of 12.4 — 13.1 volts. The regulator is mounted on the engine compartment wall.

When conducting the generating system check previously described, the no-load voltage should be 13.5 to 14.5 volts for the system. The quick generator check is also run in the same manner as previously described, being sure to conclude the test in a few seconds so as not to burn out the field windings, and using the same chart. The quick regulator check is conducted in the same manner, with the sliding resistance set at 45. The voltage reading should be 12.8 — 14.2.

Generator

Use the procedure previously outlined to remove and install

Generator Trouble Shooting

The red generator lamp lights up when the ignition is switched on and should go out when the engine has been started and the speed increases.

Symptom	Cause	Remedy
Generator lamp does not light up when ignition is switched on	a - Battery discharged b - Battery defective c - Bulb burned out d - Corroded or loose battery terminals e - Loose connections or broken cables f - Steering-ignition lock defective g - Generator brushes do not make contact with commutator	a - Charge battery b - Renew battery c - Renew bulb d - Clean or tighten terminals respectively e - Tighten or repair cables f - Renew steering-ignition lock g - Free the brushes or renew them. If necessary renew the brush springs
Generator lamp does not go out or flickers when engine is accelerated	a - Fan belt loose or faulty b - Regulator faulty c - Charging cables loose or disrupted d - Generator faulty e - Graphited commutator	a - Adjust belt tension or renew belt b - Renew regulator c - Check cables and connections d - Check generator e - Clean commutator with fine polishing cloth
Generator lamp goes out only at very high speed	a - Generator faulty b - Regulator faulty	a - Check generator b - Renew regulator
Generator lamp remains on when the ignition is switched off	a - Regulator contact points sticking (burned)	a - Renew regulator
Warning lamp glows at all engine speed	a - Poor connections in cable from B+(51) on regulator to electrical equipment	a - The following connections should be checked Terminal B+(51) Regulator Terminal 30 starter Terminal 30 on light switch Terminal 30 fuse box Terminal 30 ignition/starter switch Terminal 15/54 ignition/starter switch The connections should be cleaned carefully to ensure good metal-to-metal contact

the regulator and generator, adding the following information: Generators used (105 mm in diameter) are presure ventilated and use a modified fan cover. When assembling the generator / fan cover, install both parts together as illustrated. When installing the generator in the fan housing, have the cooling air slots face downwards, or the generator will receive insufficient cooling and will be damaged.

A - Cooling air slots.
B - Connections.

STARTER

Caution: A very common problem is for the cable connector AT THE STARTER SOLENOID (observed from under the vehicle) to come loose, in which case the battery will not receive the output of the generator, even though the red ignition warning light will only glow dimly when the engine is running. This connector joins one cable from the voltage regulator and a separate cable from the battery to the starter solenoid.

Through the years various Bosch and VW starting motors have been used on the Transporters, but all share the same basic principles of operation. Maintenance is limited to checking the armature brushes. The motor is bolted to the back right side of the transmission case at the front of the engine.

When the starter switch is turned on, the solenoid engages the starter motor pinion with the teeth on the flywheel ring gear. The final movement of the solenoid closes the starting

Connections:
1 - Battery lead (positive terminal).
2 - Terminal 51 at generator and terminal 30 at lighting switch.
3 - Terminal 50 ignition/starting switch.

motor electrical circuit. When the engine catches, the starting motor solenoid still passes current until key is released. When the ignition key is released and spring tension disengages the clutch, the over-running clutch helps to prevent the engine from driving the starter if the key is held on too long. On later model cars, a non-repeat lock in the ignition switch prevents the starter from being accident engaged when the engine is running by requiring that the key be turned fully off before the starter can be turned on again.

Checking

Use the following tables to determine the condition of the starter motor, using appropriate testing instruments. Check the starter motor battery voltage, being sure to check first that the battery used is in good condition and is fully charged. Check the no-load current and speed; the current intake, torque and voltage drop of the battery when loaded (speed of starting motor about 1000 rpm); the current, torque and voltage drop in the event of short circuit (load starting motor until it stalls); then check the engagement of the pinion under load. If the starter is a reconditioned unit with new brushes, it will not give accurate readings as the commutator and the brushes take some time to settle and bed-in properly.

Removing and Installing

With the battery negative ground strap disconnected, remove

Type: BOSCH EEF 0.5/6 L 1

No-load test			Load test				Stall torque test		
Current Amp.	Voltage	Speed* rpm.	Current Amp.	Voltage	Speed* rpm.	Torque ft. lbs.	Current Amp.	Voltage	Torque ft. lbs.
55—65	5.5	5500—6700	250—290	4.5	1000—1200	4.3	440—500	3.5	8

Type: VW 113 911 021 A

No-load test			Load test				Stall torque test		
Current A	Voltage	Speed rpm	Current A	Voltage	Torque ft. lbs.	Speed rpm	Current A	Voltage	Torque ft. lbs.
40—50	5.5	3500—5500	260	4.5	4	1000—1200	450—520	3.5	8.6

Type: BOSCH EGF 0,6/6 L 5

No-load test			Load test				Stall torque test		
Current Amp.	Voltage	Speed* rpm	Current Amp.	Voltage	Speed* rpm	Torque ft. lbs.	Current Amp.	Voltage	Torque ft. lbs.
55—65	5.5	6000—7000	240—280	4.6	800—1000	4.3	450—520	3.5	9.4—10.8

The values apply to a 77 Ah battery and a temperature of 20 C (68 F).

Deviations from the above values should not exceed ± 10%.

* = Speed of starting motor

the three cables from the starter terminal 30, then disconnect the cable from the starter/ignition switch from starter terminal 50. Remove the starter securing nuts and screws, then remove the starter.

With the starter removed, the bushing in the transmission housing may be checked. Wiggle the starter shaft in the hole. **Important:** If necessary because of wear, remove the bush with a withdrawal tool (VW 228a), then soak a new bushing in hot engine oil, cool off, then insert it with the VW 222 pilot. Install starter motor after lubricating the bush with multi-purpose grease. Seal the starter flange mounting surface on the transmission with Genuine VW Sealing Compound D 1a or equiva-

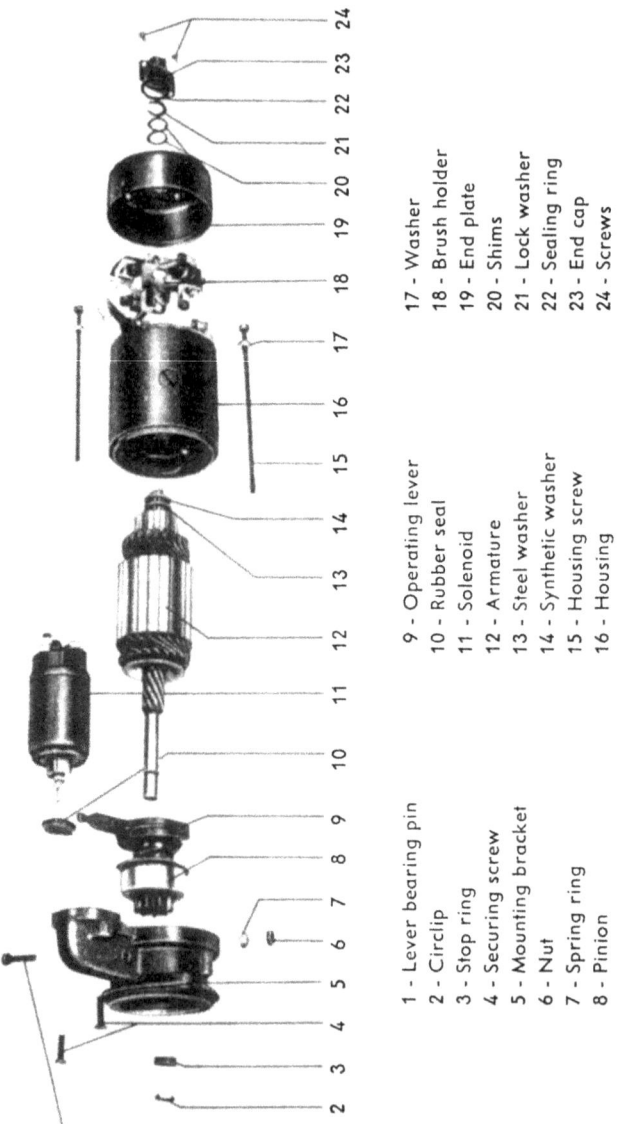

EXPLODED VIEW OF BOSCH STARTER

1 - Lever bearing pin
2 - Circlip
3 - Stop ring
4 - Securing screw
5 - Mounting bracket
6 - Nut
7 - Spring ring
8 - Pinion
9 - Operating lever
10 - Rubber seal
11 - Solenoid
12 - Armature
13 - Steel washer
14 - Synthetic washer
15 - Housing screw
16 - Housing
17 - Washer
18 - Brush holder
19 - End plate
20 - Shims
21 - Lock washer
22 - Sealing ring
23 - End cap
24 - Screws

lent. Place the screw in the hole in the flange and locate the starter on the transmission housing. Check that the cable connections are clean and tight.

Checking Brushes and Commutator

On the Bosch starter motor, remove the end cap with the sealing ring, then remove the lockwasher and steel shims from the starter shaft. Remove the housing screws and remove the commutator end plate, then lift the brushes out of the holders. Pull the brush holder off the armature shaft. Assemble the unit in the reverse order, being careful to correctly seat the rubber gasket for the solenoid cable and the sealing ring for the end cap. On the VW starter motor, pry off the two brush inspection covers, lift up the brush springs, and pull out the brushes. Reverse the procedure to replace the brushes and covers.

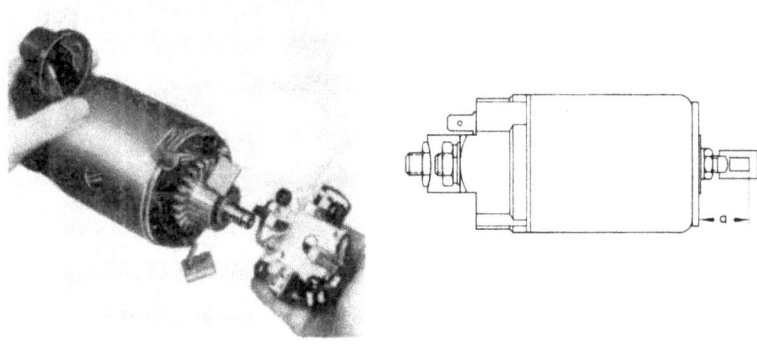

Check the brushes and commutators for wear and damage. Brushes should be replaced when the carbon is worn sufficiently to make the flexible connector touch the holder edge. On the Bosch unit, unsolder the two brushes at the field coil connections and the two brushes on the brush holder, then solder on new brushes. On the VW unit, unscrew the connector to remove the brushes. Replace brushes with the flexible connector free to avoid sticking of the brushes during operation. General shop practice is to slip off the springs and replace these also, but at least check them for weakness. Inspect the commutator for wear, pitting, roughness and burned spots. Repair starter if any of these conditions are present. If the commutator is only oily or dirty with carbon dust, clean it with a clean cloth moistened with solvent and wrapped around a piece of wood.

Removal and Installation of Solenoid Switch

On the Bosch unit, remove the hexagon nut and detach the connector strip, then remove the two solenoid screws on the mounting bracket. Pull out the solenoid by lifting up the pull

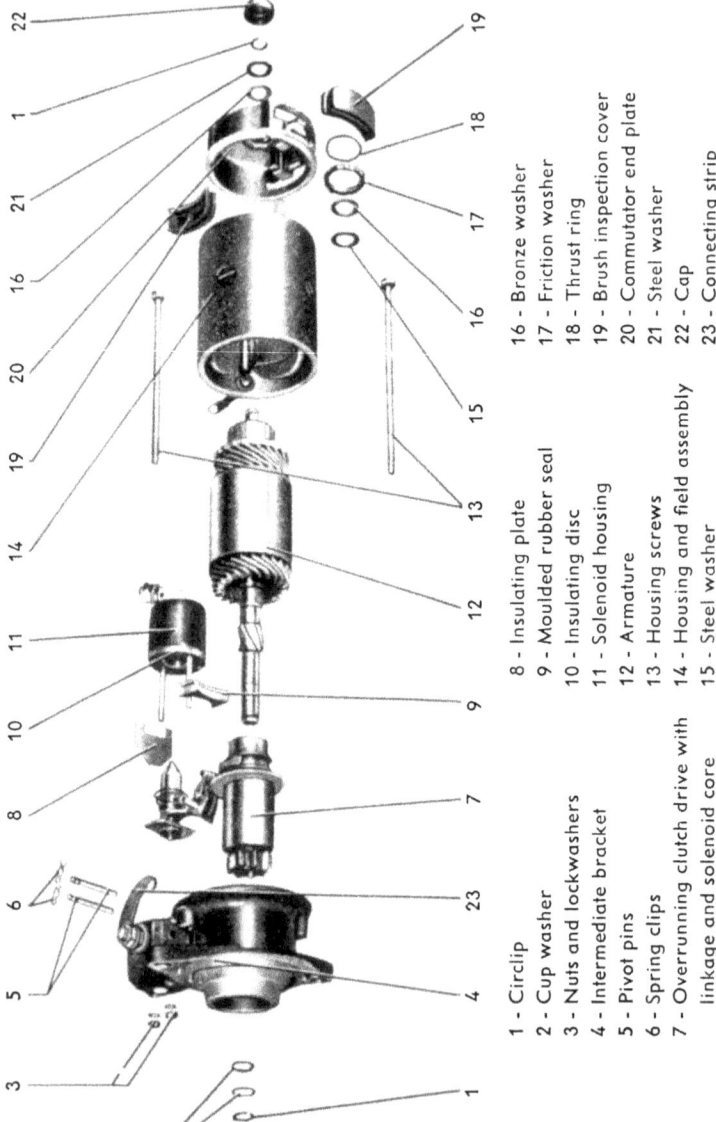

1 - Circlip
2 - Cup washer
3 - Nuts and lockwashers
4 - Intermediate bracket
5 - Pivot pins
6 - Spring clips
7 - Overrunning clutch drive with linkage and solenoid core
8 - Insulating plate
9 - Moulded rubber seal
10 - Insulating disc
11 - Solenoid housing
12 - Armature
13 - Housing screws
14 - Housing and field assembly
15 - Steel washer
16 - Bronze washer
17 - Friction washer
18 - Thrust ring
19 - Brush inspection cover
20 - Commutator end plate
21 - Steel washer
22 - Cap
23 - Connecting strip

EXPLODED VIEW OF VW STARTER

rod off the operating lever. Replace defective solenoid switches since it is impossible to correct a switch by altering the settings. The distance **"a"** from the switch flange to the pull rod eye with the magnet drawn in should be .748 ± .004 in. If not, the nut should be loosened and the rod turned to adjust the length. When installing, check that the rubber gasket on the starter mounting bracket is properly seated, and the outer edge of the solenoid end has a small strip of Genuine VW Plastic Sealing Compound D 14 on it. Pull the operating lever fork or the pinion out as far as possible to ease the insertion of the solenoid.

The VW starter solenoid is removed by disconnecting the connector strip, removing the nuts, then withdrawing the housing and insulating disc. Remove the nut at the field coil lead, then remove the molded rubber seal. Test the solenoid current draw of the pull-in winding and the hold-in winding with a suitable car battery. This is done by inserting the ammeter in lead from the positive battery terminal to terminal 50. Check the pull-in winding by connecting the negative battery terminal with pull-in winding terminal. The current draw should be 35 to 40 amps. Check the hold-in winding by connecting the negative battery terminal to the cover plate. The current draw should be 10 to 12 amps. If any part is defective, replace the whole solenoid housing. When installing, make sure that the terminal makes good contact and that the molded rubber seal is properly seated.

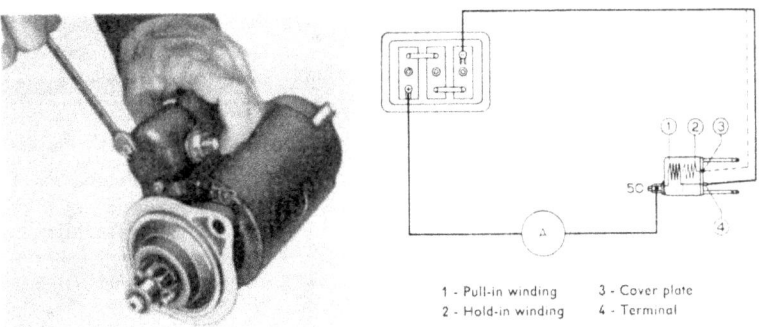

1 - Pull-in winding
2 - Hold-in winding
3 - Cover plate
4 - Terminal

Starting Motor Trouble Shooting

Symptom	Cause	Remedy
Starter does not turn when the ignition switch or steering lock is operated	Switch on the lamps when testing: a - Lights do not burn. Loose cables or poor ground connection. Battery discharged b - Lights go out when ignition or steering lock key is moved to starting position. Insufficient current due to loose connections or corroded terminals c - Lights go dim when ignition or steering lock key is moved to starting position. Battery run down d - Lights burn brightly. Starter turns when terminals 30 and 50 are bridged. Cable 50 to ignition or steering lock faulty, ignition or steering lock defective e - Lights stay bright and solenoid switch operates. Disconnect battery cable from terminal 30 at starting motor and connect it directly to the connector strip terminal. If the starting motor operates, the contacts of the solenoid switch are worn or dirty	a - Check battery cables and connections. Test voltage of battery, charge if necessary b - Clean battery terminals and cable clamps, clean and tighten connections between battery, starting motor and ground c - Charge battery d - Eliminate open circuits, replace defective parts e - Replace solenoid switch
Starting motor does not operate when battery cable is connected directly to the connector strip terminal	a - Brushes sticking b - Brushes worn c - Weak spring tension. Brushes do not make contact d - Commutator dirty e - Commutator rough, pitted, or burned f - Armature or field coils defective	a - Clean brushes and brush guides b - Replace brushes c - Replacing springs d - Clean commutator e - Overhaul starting motor f - Overhaul starting motor
Starter turns slowly or does not turn engine	a - Battery run down b - Insufficient current flow due to loose or corroded connections c - Brushes sticking d - Brushes worn e - Commutator dirty f - Commutator, rough pitted, or burned g - Armature or field coils defective	a - Charge battery b - Clean battery terminals and cable clamps, tighten connections c - Clean brushes and brush guides d - Replace brushes e - Clean commutator f - Overhaul starting motor g - Overhaul starting motor
Starter engages and attempts to turn, but engine turns erratically or not at all	a - Drive pinion defective b - Flywheel gear ring defective	a - Replace drive pinion b - Replace flywheel or remachine gear ring
Drive pinion does not disengage	a - Drive pinion or armature shaft dirty or damaged b - Solenoid switch defective	a - Overhaul starting motor b - Replace solenoid switch

BATTERY

The battery supplied as original equipment on the early models is 6 volt, 77 amp-hours rating (20 hours). Later models use a 12 volt, 44 amp-hours (20 hours) battery. The system is **negative** ground. The battery negative post is definitely smaller than the positive terminal. Use a battery puller to remove connectors rather than prying on the connector, since the battery may be damaged otherwise.

To provide fast starts on cold mornings, the battery should be checked regularly, kept filled to the mark with electrolyte, and cleaned of harmful deposit buildup on terminals. Just because the battery is in a difficult place to reach, and must be removed to check, doesn't preclude proper care and attention.

To remove the battery from the right-hand side of the engine compartment, first remove the oil bath air cleaner as outlined in the lubrication section of this book. Then remove the battery holddown clamps and terminal clamps. Be careful not to short-circuit the terminals, as this causes rapid and possibly harmful heat buildup in the battery. Check that the electrolyte is above the plates and up to the mark if there is one. Some common VW batteries have a bar across the top of the plates, while

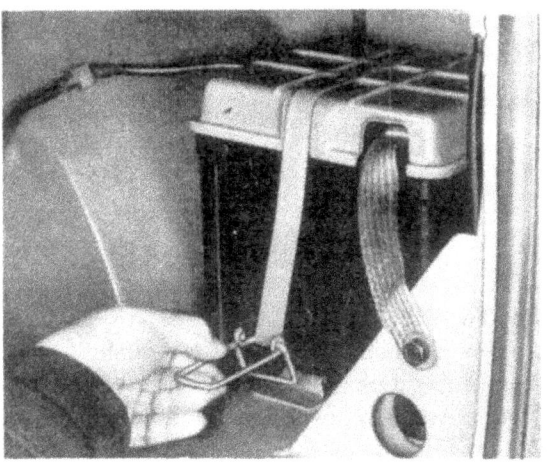

others have a small plastic cup in the filler hole to designate the full mark. However, it is best to remove the cup to check the level since a bubble could be formed in the bottom of the cup. **Caution:** Electrolyte should barely cover the plates ($1/8$ in. max.). If battery is overfilled, the electrolyte will overflow when the battery is being charged and cause damage to the surrounding metal, battery cables and paint.

An alternate method adopted by VW service technicians is to use a mirror and flashlight to judge the electrolyte level. However, this does take some practice to judge the reflection. Also, filling the battery cells from this cumbersome position requires a method of closely metering the distilled water so the level may be checked frequently, preventing possible overfilling.

The frequency of battery checks and topping up depends upon how the vehicle is used and the weather conditions. The general rule is that the battery should be checked more frequently in the summer, and for vehicles that are driven hard in hot weather, a weekly check should be considered mandatory. A vehicle that is often driven long distances in the daytime with hardly any current being used will also require that the battery be topped up with distilled water more often than a vehicle that is usually used for short trips day and night. This is because the electrolyte level drops when the battery is charged due to the disassociation of the water used to dilute the acid, and to a lesser extent, to evaporation.

Other items of care that will ensure fast starts and long battery life are cleaning and greasing the battery terminals to prevent corrosion buildup and making sure the ground connection to the body is tight and free of corrosion or rust behind the cable. If the VW is to be taken out of operation for an extended period of time, or the battery is to be stored for such a period, charge the battery at four week intervals with a trickle of about 4 amps to prevent deterioration of the plates. In this case, discharge the battery prior to each third charging at a rate of 2 to 4 amps until the low limit of 1.75 volt per cell has been reached, then fully recharge the battery. To discharge the battery, load the battery and discharge it.

Fuses

Fuses (Prior To 1968)

The fuse box is located under the parcel shelf near the center of the cab, and has a plastic cover over it that snaps into place. When a fuse blows, it is best to determine the cause of the overload or short circuit. Be sure to carry spare fuses in the car for quick repairs, 16 amp fuses for the brake lights, interior lights,

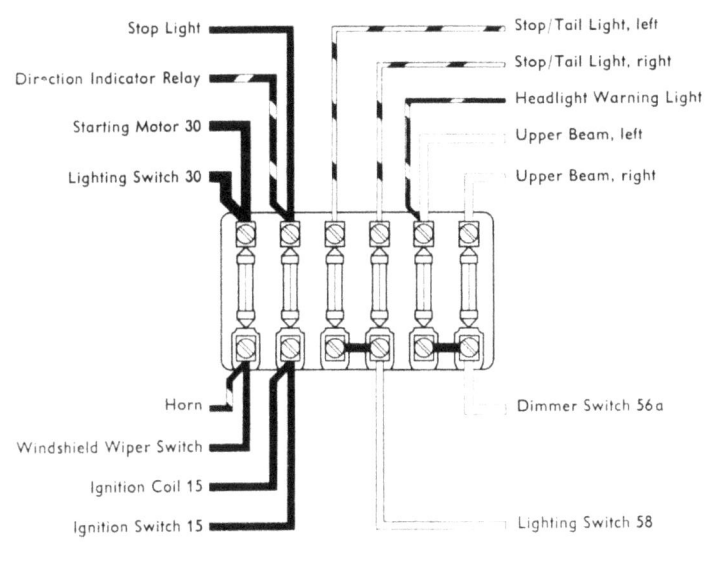

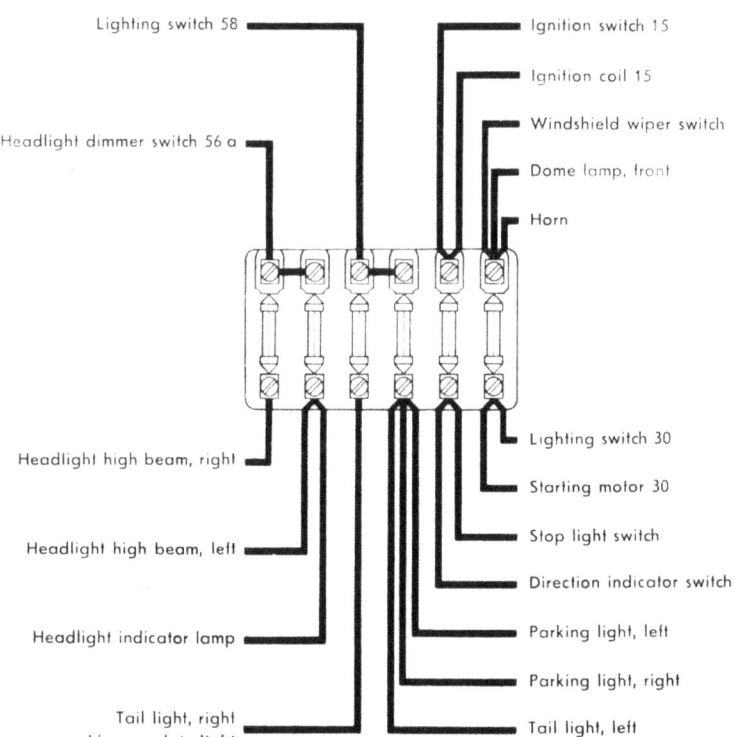

turn signals, wipers and horn, and 8 amp fuses for all other electrical items. **Caution:** Never patch up a fuse with tin foil or wire as this can cause serious damage elsewhere in the electrical system or a flash fire under the dashboard and through the cab. Burning wires emit black clouds of noxious smoke.

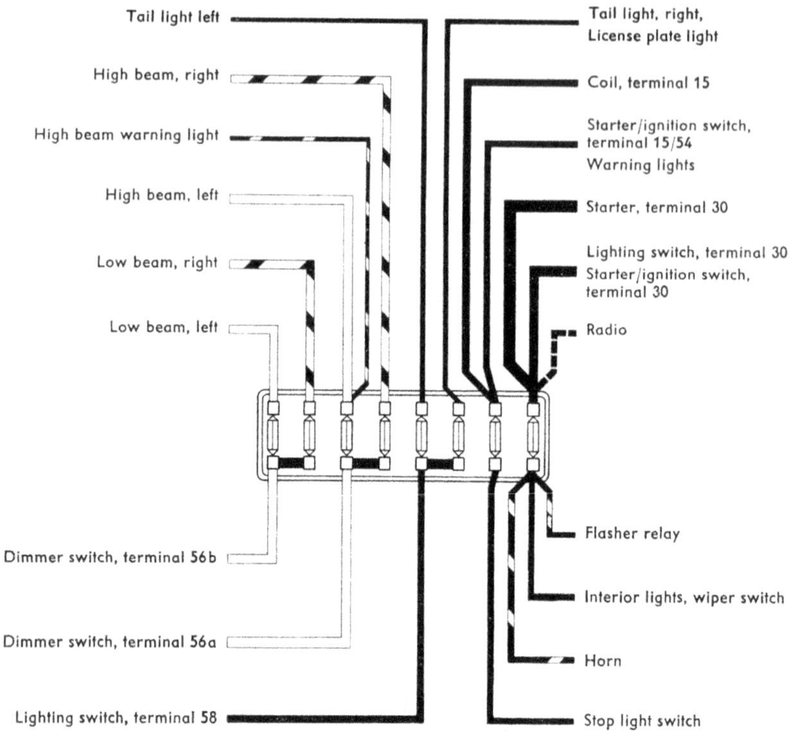

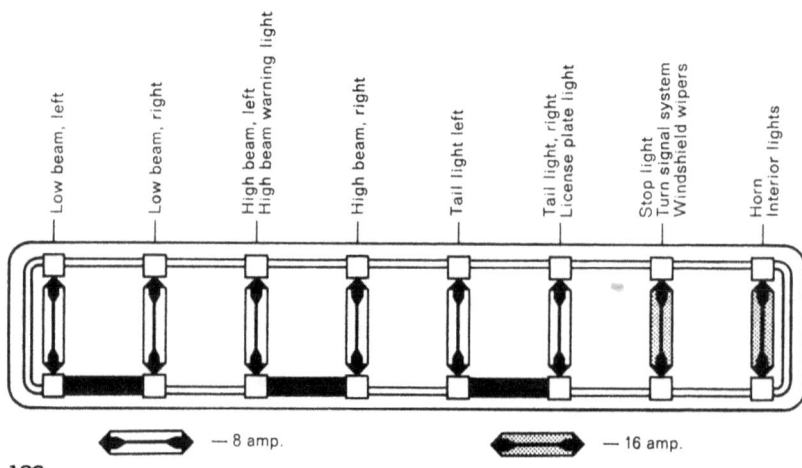

Fuses (After 1968)

The fuse box is located under the dashboard to the left of the steering wheel, and is covered with a snap-on plastic lid. When a fuse blows, it is best to determine the cause of the overload or short circuit. Be sure to carry several spare 8 amp fuses in the vehicle for quick repairs. **Caution:** Never patch up a fuse with tin foil or wire as this can cause serious damage elsewhere in the electrical system or a flash fire under the dashboard and through the cab. Burning wires emit black clouds of noxious smoke.

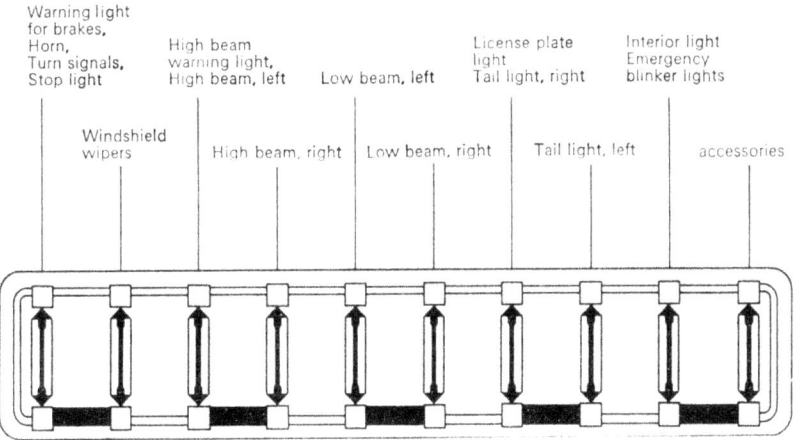

INSTRUMENT PANEL

Note: See the Emergency Procedures section of this book for explanation of the warning lights. The dark green light and the blue light indicate parking lights and high beams respectively. Normally, the red and light green warning lights glow when the engine is stationary and the ignition switch is on. They should both go out slowly, the red light as the generator reaches cut-in speed and begins to charge, and the light green bulb as the oil pressure builds up. It is also normal for either or both of these lights to glow after the engine has been run fast and then allowed to idle slowly, with the vehicle stationary and the engine running.

Fascia (1968 And Later Models)

The fascia contains the fuel gauge, warning lights, speedometer, clock (optional), heating and ventilating controls, and dual brake system warning light. To service all instruments, it is often easier (but not mandatory) that the fascia be pulled out of the dashboard. The alternative is working in close quarters from underneath the dashboard. If only a warning light bulb is to be replaced, for example, leaving the fascia in place should prove the easiest method.

First, disconnect the battery to prevent short circuits. From under the dashboard, remove the white plastic plugs from all four levers controlling the heater and the fresh air ventilator system. Use pliers to squeeze the plugs if necessary, then use the pliers to pull out the spring clips. Remove the four knobs from the levers from the driver's side of the dashboard. Remove the screws from the front of the fascia, then slide the fascia toward you and unscrew the speedometer cable connector, allowing the fascia to be pulled still further toward you. When replacing fascia, make sure that all instruments are upright, do not over-tighten any screws, and note that the control levers are in the proper location.

Fuel Gauge

On early models, the fuel gauge is separate, and is held into the dashboard with a rear bracket. Remove knurled nuts and bracket, then remove gauge toward the interior of the cab. On later models, the gauge is attached to the warning light unit with two screws. A bimetal vibrator keeps the gauge under a continuous, even voltage. Another piece of bimetal keeps the needle

balanced between itself and a spring. A resistance coil wound around the bimetal, and in series with the variable resistance of the sender unit in the fuel tank, is heated by current flowing through the circuit. As the coil is heated, the bimetal bends and moves the gauge needle coupled to it. The stronger the current, the more movement to the gauge needle.

To test the vibrator, install a voltmeter as shown, attaching it between the connector and terminal 15. When the ignition is switched on, the voltmeter needle should show a pulsating reading. If not, replace the fuel gauge unit. To test the gauge itself (assuming the vibrator is good), detach the cable from the sender unit at the gauge (after removing the gauge as described below), and hold the terminal from the gauge briefly to ground. If there is no gauge reading, replace the gauge unit. If the gauge needle moves, there is either a defect in the cable or the sender.

To renew the gauge and vibrator unit, the easiest method is to first remove the fascia from the dashboard as previously described. In either case, first disconnect the battery. Remove screws holding the backplate in place, being sure not to damage any connectors as the backplate is pulled off. Pull off the fuel gauge harness connectors, labeling wires if necessary, then remove the two screws holding the fuel gauge unit in place and remove gauge. When replacing unit, make sure that the instruments are correctly located and the figures on the faces are upright. Do not overtighten any screws.

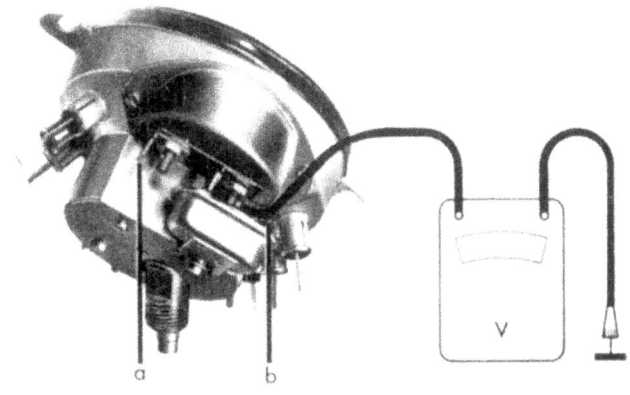

a - to sender unit   b - terminal 15

Servicing Fuel Tank Sender Unit

The sender unit can only be serviced by removing the engine and fuel tank. Disconnect the plus cable at the sender unit and ground the cable on the partition. Remove the five screws from the sender unit flange, then remove unit and pull off cork gasket. When re-installing, reverse the order of removal and align the sender unit and gasket holes with the threaded holes in the tank (which are not uniformly spaced). **Important:** If a new sender unit is being installed, be sure to pull out the float retaining pin.

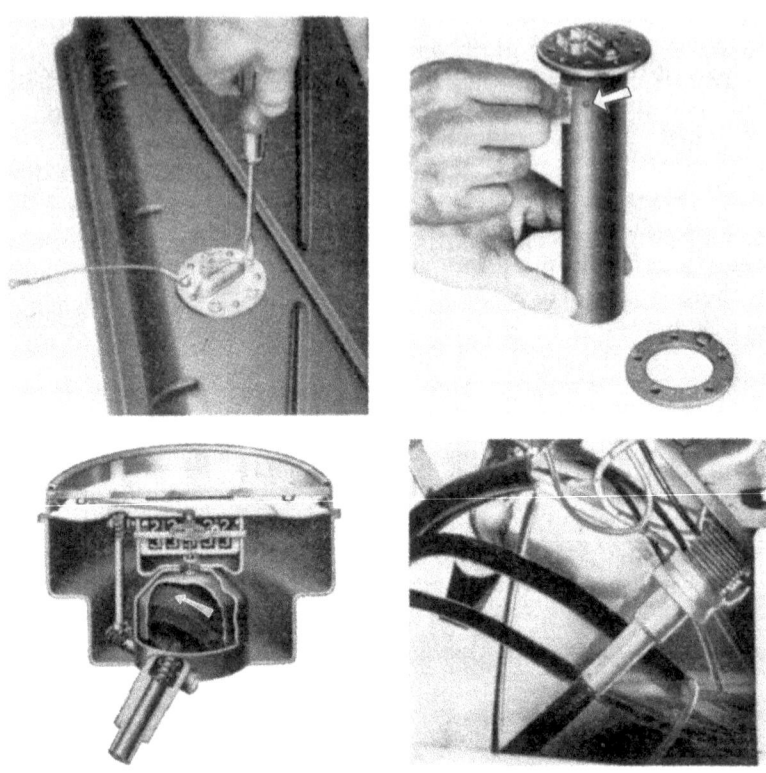

Speedometer

The speedometer and mileage recorder are driven by a cable from the left-hand road wheel. The speedometer operates on the eddy-current generator principle, the drive shaft rotating a ring-shaped magnet. This armature is located within an aluminum cup, which is free to rotate without touching the armature. The magnetic eddy current set up by the rotating armature forces the cup to rotate, while a counterbalancing spring controls the amount of cup movement. The speedometer needle is attached to the cup. A mileage recorder is driven through a triple worm mechanism. This powers five numeral rolls. The speedometer cable is composed of several strands of wire housed in a flexible metal hose protected by a plastic covering.

To remove the speedometer on early models, pull out the cable at the bottom of the speedometer by unscrewing the union nut. Remove the instrument light bulb and warning light bulbs from their sockets, labeling wires for later identification. Loosen the screws holding the speedometer to the dashboard, then turn the speedometer counterclockwise to remove it. When the screws clear the slots in the retaining prongs, remove the speedometer and the gasket from the instrument panel, then remove the black cable from the upper and lower terminals. When installing the speedometer, make sure that the speedometer is properly seated (so that the figures on the face are upright), prior to tightening the slotted screws.

To remove the speedometer on later models, the easiest method is to first remove the fascia from the dashboard as previously described. In either case, first disconnect the battery. Remove screws holding the backplate in place, being sure not to damage any connectors as the backplate is pulled off. Disconnect the speedometer drive cable, then pull connector off the bulb. Squeeze the spring clips on the sides of the speedometer body and remove the unit from the fascia. When replacing unit, make sure that the speedometer is properly snapped in and the figures on the face are upright. Do not overtighten any screws.

Servicing Speedometer Cable

The speedometer cable is removed by first taking off the left front trim panel, then unscrewing the nut at the speedometer. Remove the left front wheel hub cap and remove the cotter pin in the square end of the speedometer cable at the hub cap. Pull up the cable clips at the front axle and body, then remove the guide sleeves from the steering knuckle with a pair of pliers. Pull cable from the steering knuckle. Attach a wire to the square end of the speedometer cable to pull the cable from the cab. The wire facilitates the installation of the cable. If the old cable is to be reused, check it for wear and replace if necessary. In any case, lubricate the cable with cold-resistant and water-repellent grease; never use oil.

Attach the wire to the square end of the cable and pull the cable through with the wire. Make sure cable does not bend

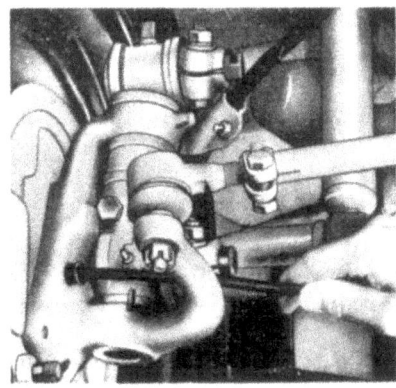
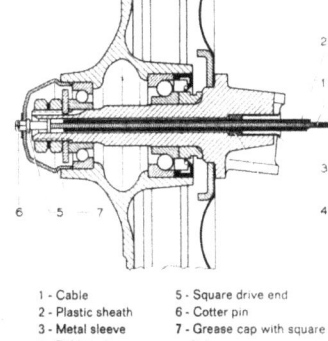

1 - Cable
2 - Plastic sheath
3 - Metal sleeve
4 - Rubber sleeve
5 - Square drive end
6 - Cotter pin
7 - Grease cap with square hole

sharply. Note the correct position of the rubber grommet in the floor panel, and make sure the cable is tightly clipped in position. Check that the upper square end fits correctly in the square hole in the connecting piece, then install a new rubber sleeve in the steering knuckle. If this sleeve is not properly seated, splash water may enter, leading to possible bearing trouble and freezing of the speedometer cable in winter. Check that the bends in the cable are not sharper than a 66" radius. With the front wheels in the straight-ahead position, the speedometer cable must run in a smooth curve. The cable must not be pulled tight or kinked when turning the wheels from one steering lock to the other. The cable will also run noisily under adverse conditions. Finally, install a new cotter pin for securing the square end of the cable to the hub cap.

Clock Servicing (Early Models)

The clock can be set with the knob on the right-hand side. The knob is accessible from the parcel shelf and has to be pulled out to alter the time. The clock light is switched on automatically, and its brightness controlled, when the light switch is actuated. Remove the clock by unscrewing the two knurled nuts on the back of the unit and remove the retainer. Pull clock out of the instrument panel, then disconnect the cable and remove the bulb from its socket. Installation is a reversal of the above procedure.

Instrument Panel Lights (Early Model)

All lights in the speedometer unit, fuel gauge, and clock are serviced by pulling out the socket from under the dashboard, pressing the bulb into its socket, and turning the bulb so the pin

disengages. To replace, reverse the procedure, pressing the bulb in and turning, pulling on it slightly to make sure the pin is engaged, then replacing bulb and socket in unit. Either disconnect the battery ground strap prior to performing the repair or be careful not to ground other connectors while performing the repair since this could cause a short circuit. Since there are many bulbs under the speedometer unit, be careful that the correct bulb is being replaced. Test lights after completing repair.

Clock And Instrument Lights (Later Models)

To reset the clock, push in the centered knob and turn to the correct time. The clock light comes on at the same time as the rest of the instrument panel lights, and is also affected by the rheostat control. There is no speed regulator that can be adjusted, so have this performed by a watchmaker if necessary. To replace the clock as a unit, the easiest method is to first remove the fascia from the dashboard as previously described. In either case, first disconnect the battery to prevent short-circuits, then remove the bulb by pulling it out. Disconnect the clock supply cable, then remove the attaching screws and remove the clock from the back. Replace the clock by reversing the removal procedure, making sure the clock is positioned upright.

Instrument illumination bulbs are removed by pulling out the holder, then pressing bulbs in and twisting so they unlock. The warning lights are of a smaller design than the other instrument lights. They are held in the warning light unit with plastic retainers. The cable connecting shoes are also smaller, but are attached to the cable in a similar manner. To remove these lights, either work from under the instrument panel or remove the fascia as previously described, remove the backing screws, then remove the backing and the unit, complete with the fuel gauge. Turn the plastic retainer on the bulbs 90° to the left (using needle-nosed pliers if necessary), then pull out the retainer. Pull out the warning light. To install, reverse the sequence, making sure the instruments are upright.

On the switch for the emergency blinker system, the bulb may be replaced by first unscrewing the plastic insert marked "EMERGENCY". Use tweezers to remove and replace the bulb. The whole surround and button for the dual brake system may be screwed out for replacement as a unit.

Oil Pressure Warning Light

Although the oil pressure warning light is a part of the lubricating system of the engine, it is also in the electrical circuit and must be considered here. A flickering of the warning

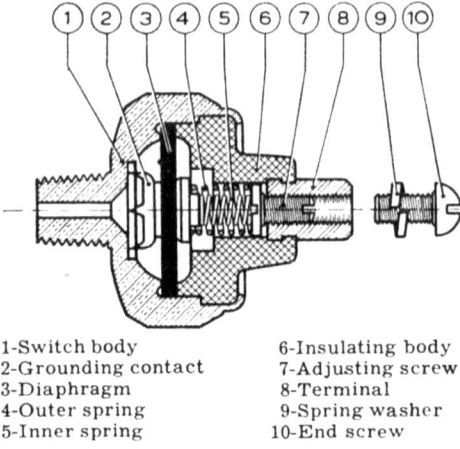

1-Switch body
2-Grounding contact
3-Diaphragm
4-Outer spring
5-Inner spring
6-Insulating body
7-Adjusting screw
8-Terminal
9-Spring washer
10-End screw

light at any time when the car is moving should be cause for investigation. Check first for a loose connection at the instrument panel and at the sender end screw (Fig. 10) then tap the unit with a screwdriver handle or small wrench. Check oil level on dipstick. If there is a good supply of oil and the warning light continues to flicker or goes out, replace it with a new one.

Instrument Panel Switches

Among instrument panel switches are the following: The push/pull switch (3 or 10) to control the passenger compartment light, so that light may be turned on or off from the switch built into it (1968 models and later). The regular light switch (3 or 4) has two stops. The first stop illuminates the parking, license plate, tail and instrument lights. On 1968 and later models, the dark green warning light is also illuminated since it is illegal to drive with only parking lights on in some states. When the headlights are illuminated by pulling the knob out to the next stop, the warning light goes out. Turning the knob at either setting adjusts the brightness of the instrument lights.

The windshield wipers and washer are controlled by a single knob (4 or 5). After 1968, the wipers are set for either fast or slow speed by turning the knob to the desired setting. After 1968, a button in the center of the knob operates the windshield washer. On the prior models, the washer is operated by pressing the rubber bellows on the water container (5). The emergency warning system switch (7 or 9) causes all four turn signal lights to blink at once. A warning light in the switch knob blinks when the system is operating. Another warning light is in the switch for the dual brake system (10). After turning on the ignition, this switch should be pressed before driving off to ensure that the

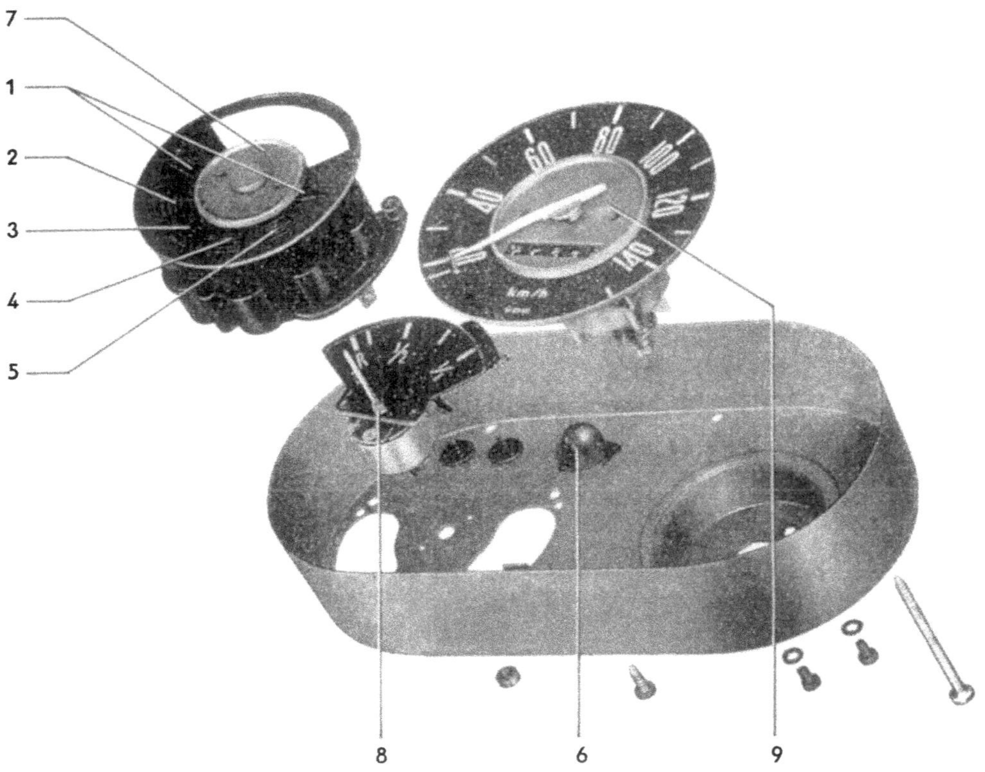

1 - Turn signal warning lamp
2 - Generator warning lamp
3 - High beam warning lamp
4 - Parking light warning lamp
5 - Oil pressure warning lamp
6 - Instrument light
7 - Warning lamp holder
8 - Fuel gauge
9 - Speedometer

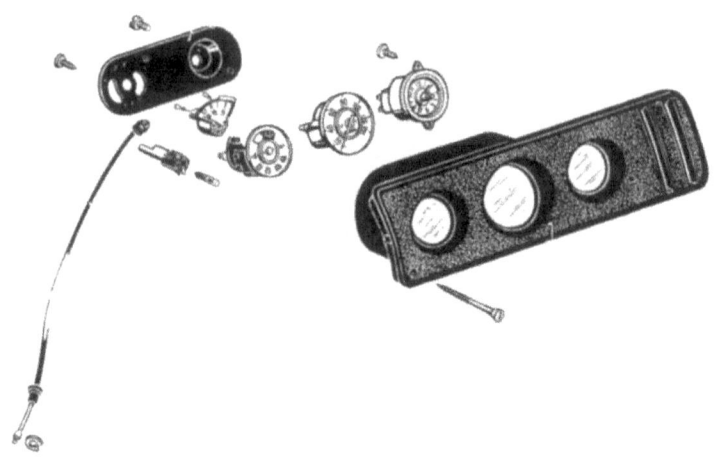

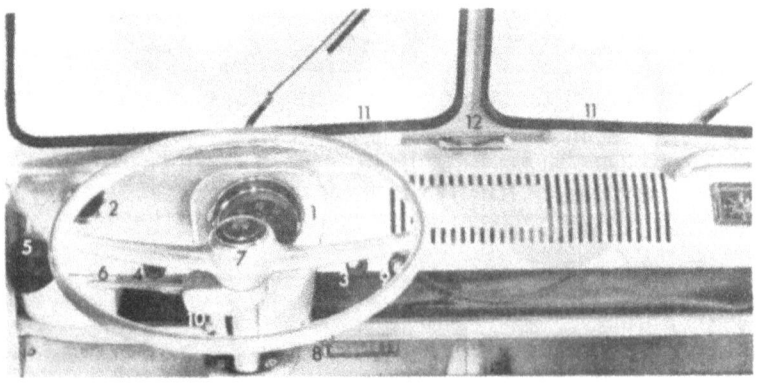

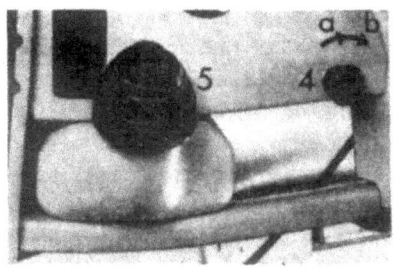

warning light in the system is operating. The warning light will come on when the brakes are applied ONLY IF one of the dual brake circuits is faulty. The brakes will still operate, but the safeguard is gone and the existing brakes will not stop the car as quickly. Have the brake system repaired as soon as possible.

Servicing Switches (Early Models)

Most of the instrument panel switches are removed as follows. Be sure to disconnect the battery ground strap prior to performing repair to prevent the possibility of short circuits: Unscrew the switch knob, then remove the securing screw from under the dashboard. Pull switch out of shaft hole from behind and lower under the dashboard. Disconnect cables and label for correct replacement. After installing, check the operation of the switch. Unscrew the cap to remove the overhead light switch.

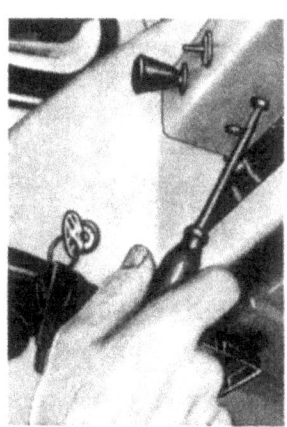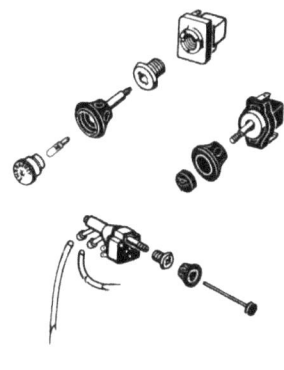

Servicing Switches (Later Models)

To remove some instrument panel switches requires a VW Special Tool to remove the bezel. Be sure to disconnect the battery prior to any work to prevent short circuits. Hold the shaft of the switch with a stiff wire through the hole in the shaft or with needle-nosed pliers, then unscrew the knob. Hold the switch from behind the instrument panel with one hand while unscrewing the bezel with the wrench, or else the switch could turn and twist the cables or hoses. Other switches are held into the dashboard with a screw underneath the dashboard, and only need to have the knob removed. In either case, pull the switch below the instrument panel, then remove the connectors, noting their position for replacement. On the windshield wiper/washer switch, be sure to release pressure in the washer tank prior to disconnecting hoses from the switch. Pull the washer knob straight out until it releases, then remove the wiper knob as previously described. Should the hose split at the connector, cut off about 1" of hose, replace remainder, and wrap tightly with soft wire since the inside of the hose is probably cracked and it could burst once more when pressure is applied to the washer tank.

Interior Lighting

The overhead lights used are either controlled by a switch on the instrument panel or have individual switches built into the housing. To replace bulbs, pull the plastic lens downward from the housing, then change the bulb. Make sure the bulb and switch are tight and have proper contact. A front door switch has been added to 1970 models to operate both the cab light and the ignition switch key buzzer. Use a screwdriver to remove the switch or to pry out the overhead light housing.

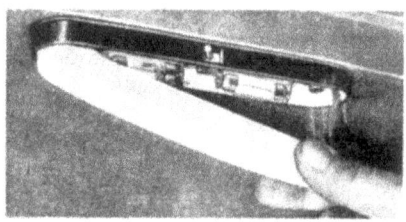 

ROAD LIGHTS AND WARNING SYSTEMS

Sealed-Beam Headlight (Later Model)

To remove, loosen the screw in the trim ring and remove the trim ring. Then remove the three screws in the sealed beam unit retaining ring and remove the ring. Remove the sealed beam unit from the support ring and pull off the cable connector. Replace with a double filament, type two, seven inch sealed beam unit. Make sure that the three glass lugs engage properly in the support ring, then reverse the removal procedure to install. Headlight settings should be checked after replacement of a sealed-beam unit.

Sealed-Beam Headlight And Parking Light (Early Model)

To remove, unscrew the large slotted screw in the headlight rim and remove the complete headlight unit. If necessary, remove screw holding parking light bulb holder, then remove holder. To change bulb, push into socket, turn so pin disengages, then pull out bulb. After replacing bulb, turn and pull up to ensure that it is locked in place. Pull the cable connector from the sealed beam unit. To remove the five retaining springs, hold the unit with one hand, and with the thumb of the other hand remove the springs (**Caution:** Do not use any tools since the spring could jump out and cause injury). Renew the sealed-beam unit after removing the springs, then clean the interior of the unit if necessary. Replace the spring by reversing the removal procedure. The lugs and slots of the retaining ring ensure that the sealed-beam unit is properly located. Be sure that the sealing ring between the lamp and the fender are properly located upon installation. Headlight settings should be checked after replacement of a sealed-beam unit.

 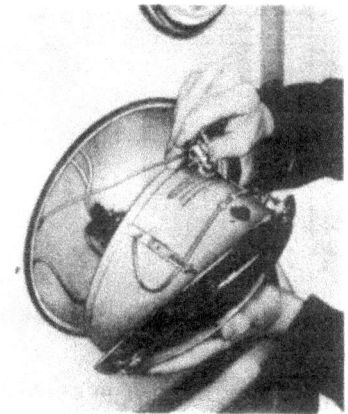

Aiming Headlights

A regulation screen or aiming device is best for aiming the headlights, but it may be accomplished using these directions. First check tires for correct pressure and fill as necessary. Park the vehicle on a level surface squarely facing a wall or screen 25 feet in front of the headlights. Have a person of about 154 lbs. or an equal weight on the front seat. Measure height (a) of center of headlights from ground and draw a horizontal line (H) on the screen at this height the full width of the vehicle.

Opposite the center of each headlight, draw (V) vertical lines intersecting the horizontal. These lines should be (b) distance apart (as noted by year). Drawing a vertical line for the center

Models Produced Before 1968   Models Produced After 1968

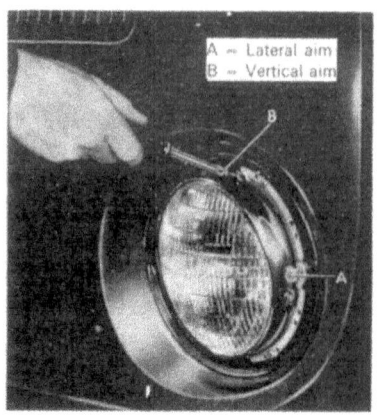

a = Height of headlight centers from ground
b = Distance between headlights = 39½ in.
c = 2 in.

a = Height of headlight centers from ground
b = Distance between headlights = 42½ in.
c = 2 in.

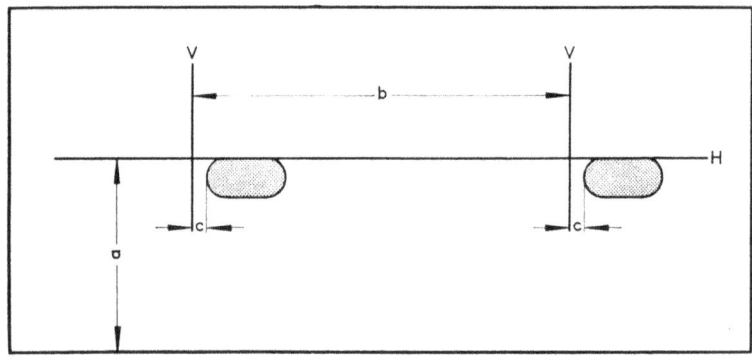

Models Produced Before 1968

Adjustment	Right headlamp	
Vertical	upper screw:	
	clockwise	- lowers
	counter-clockwise	- raises
Horizontal	lower screw:	
	clockwise	- to right
	counter-clockwise	- to left

Adjustment	Left headlamp	
Vertical	lower screw:	
	clockwise	- raises
	counter-clockwise	- lowers
Horizontal	upper screw:	
	clockwise	- to left
	counter-clockwise	- to right

US replacement bulbs

Headlight	- 6012
Parking Light	- 67
Front Turn Signal	- 1073
Tail / Stop / Rear Turn Signal	- 1034
License Plate Light	- 89
Back-up Light	- 1073

Models Produced After 1968

Bulb for	US replacement bulb	VW Part No.
Headlight	6012	111 941 261 A
Front turn signal/parking light	1034	N 177382
Rear turn signal and stop light/tail light	1034	N 177382
License plate light	89	N 177192
Warning and instrument lights	—	N 177512
Warning light for emergency blinker system	—	N 177512
Warning light for dual brake system	—	N 177512
Interior lights	—	N 177232
Back up lights	1073	N 177332

The 8 Ampere fuse for the back-up lights is located in a separate fuse holder above the generator in the engine compartment.

of the vehicle might help aligning vehicle with screen. On the early body style, aim the headlights individually by turning the two aiming screws with low beams switched on. Place a cover over the second headlight. Correct aiming is achieved when the top edge of the high intensity zone is on the horizontal line (H) and the left edge is 2" to the right of the vertical line (V).

On the 1968 and later body style, first loosen the screw in the trim ring and remove the ring. Aim the headlights individually by turning the two aiming screws with low beams switched on. Place a cover over the second headlight. Correct aiming is achieved when the top edge of the high intensity zone is on the horizontal line (H) and the left edge is 2" to the right of the vertical line (V).

In either of the above cases, check with your state department of motor vehicles for variations from these dimensions.

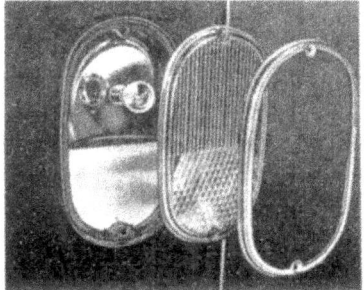

Exterior Lights Except Headlights

Remove the Phillips screws, remove lens, then press bulb in lightly, turn and remove. Insert a new bulb (refer to bulb chart for correct replacement bulb), then press in and turn. On the double-filament tail light, make sure that the retaining pin nearest to the bulbglass engages in the lower recess in the bulb socket. Pull up lightly on all bulbs to make sure they have locked into place. Make sure that gasket is properly located, or that rubber seal is properly located in rim, then tighten lens securing screws evenly but do not overtighten.

License Plate Lights

On the early model, open the engine compartment lid, pull off the rubber cap, then press the bulb holder spring to the right and remove the holder. Press the bulb lightly into the holder, turn and remove. When replacing, insert the holder on the right first, then press in on the left until the retaining spring engages. On the later model, remove the two Phillips screws from the outside, remove lens and bulb holder, then press bulb in lightly, turn, and remove. Reverse the procedure to replace, making sure the gasket is properly located and tighten the screws but do not overtighten.

Turn Signal and High-Low Beam Switch Servicing

The turn signal switch is mounted on the steering column below the steering wheel, and has an automatic neutral return arrangement to turn off the signal when the turn is completed. Prior to working on the switch, disconnect the battery ground strap to avoid short circuits. Remove left-hand front trim panel, then disconnect the two cables from the connector and the one cable from the flasher unit. Remove the two turn signal switch clamp screws and remove the clip. Pry up the cable clip at the

body and remove the switch with the cables. Screw off the switch lever knob, then remove the switch cover attaching screws and remove the cover. If switch is to be renewed, do not unsolder switch from cables since new switch includes the cables. To install, reverse the removal procedure, noting the following points: Make sure the cables are not strained at the switch and at the body. Leave a gap (at "**a**" on the illustration) of .04 to .08" so the signal switch does not interfere with the steering wheel. If the lever does not return to the neutral position when the turn is completed, correct the position of the switch by turning it either clockwise or counterclockwise on the steering column. The flasher may be serviced after the battery is disconnected and the left-hand front trim panel is removed. Disconnect and label the three cables from the flasher unit, then turn the flasher unit to the left to unscrew. Reverse the procedure to replace the flasher unit. Pull the turn signal switch toward the steering wheel to raise or lower the headlight beams. An audible click will be heard and a blue warning light will show on the warning light unit when the headlight high beam is turned on. Use the previous procedure to service the switch.

Backup Light Switch

A speedometer cable switch operates the backup light when the vehicle begins to move in reverse and the speedometer cable begins to turn backward. The switch is located between the speedometer and the cable. When moving backwards, a slip clutch and switch in the cable completes the circuit for the reversing light.

To replace the switch, disconnect the cables from underneath the instrument panel, then remove the speedometer cable union nut from the cable switch and take the cable off. Turn the switch

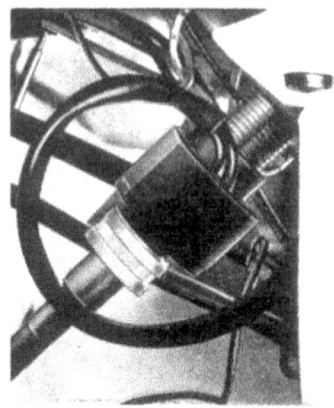
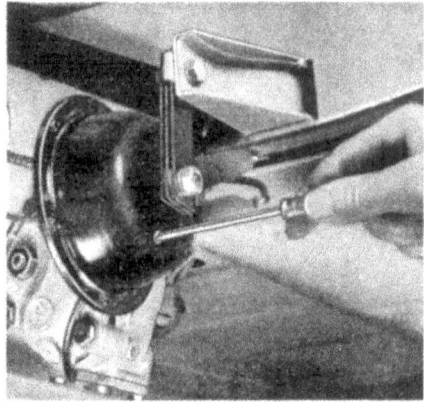

to the left and remove it from the speedometer. To install a new unit, reverse the removal procedure, then note whether the drive pin is properly located. Make sure the speedometer drive cable is not bent sharply or kinked.

Horn

Ensure that the horn bracket is not damaged (such as after an accident), causing the horn to touch the body, since the vibration will otherwise be damped. Other causes for the loss of horn sound could be from worn or dirty breaker points, entry of water into the unit, and a defective condenser. When removing the horn, remove complete with the bracket by removing the bolt under the left-hand front wheel arch, then disconnect the cables and remove the horn. To install the horn, reverse the procedure, making sure that the unit does not contact the body and that the rubber grommets seal the cable connections properly. The horn may be adjusted on the vehicle by removing the sealant over the

Emergency Warning Light System

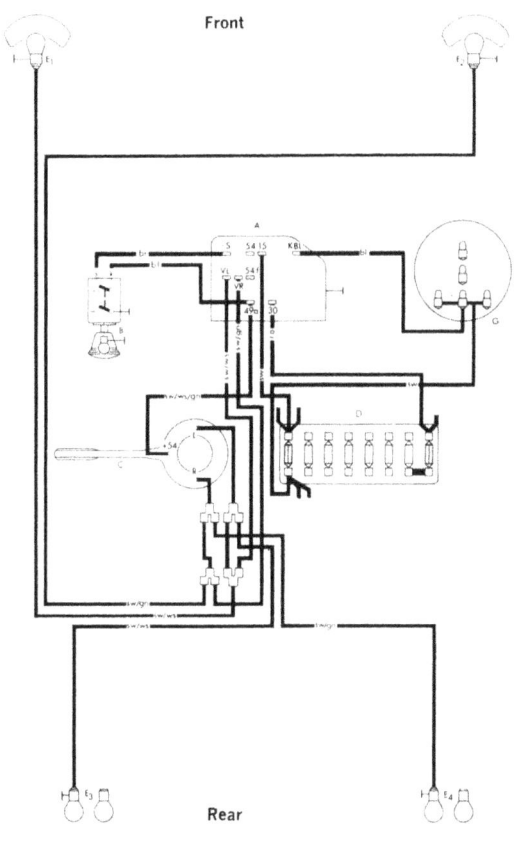

Color Codes

bl - blue   sw - black
li - lilac   gn - green
br - brown   ws - white
ro - red   gr - gray
ge - yellow

For instance:
sw/ws/gn = black-white-green

Explanation

A - Flasher and emergency warning light relay
B - Warning light switch
C - Turn signal switch
D - Fuse box
E_1 - Turn signal lights
E_2 - Turn signal lights
E_3 - Turn signal lights
E_4 - Turn signal lights
F - Stoplight switch
G - Turn signal indicator light

adjusting screw on the back of the housing, then holding the horn button in while slowly turning the adjusting screw clockwise or counterclockwise until the volume is greatest and the pitch of the tone is normal. If this performance cannot be reached, replace the unit. In any case, make sure there is sealant or paint covering the adjusting screw to prevent the entry of water. If shorted, check cable and connectors between fuse box and horn or between ground, horn button, and horn.

The horn button is removed by inserting a screwdriver in the slot between the button and the housing, then disconnecting the cable at the horn button and removing the button. The horn button can be cleaned by removing the parts. Bend back the lugs on the retaining ring. The ring with button and the contact plate can then be pulled apart. Clean and remove any corrosion from the contact surfaces to ensure a good contact.

Emergency Flasher

Remove the switch as previously described for all instrument panel switches. To service the relay, disconnect the battery ground cable, then remove the right-hand front panel lining. Disconnect the four cables on the relay, then remove the relay. Be sure to label the cables for correct replacement.

Stop Light Switch

This is a diaphragm-operated, normally off switch screwed into the front of the brake master cylinder. It is replaced by removing the cover below the pedal cluster, cleaning the area thoroughly to prevent entry of dirt, then detaching the two cables and unscrewing the switch. Renew the switch, tighten, then press pedal to check for leakage. After installing the switch, the brake system must be bled.

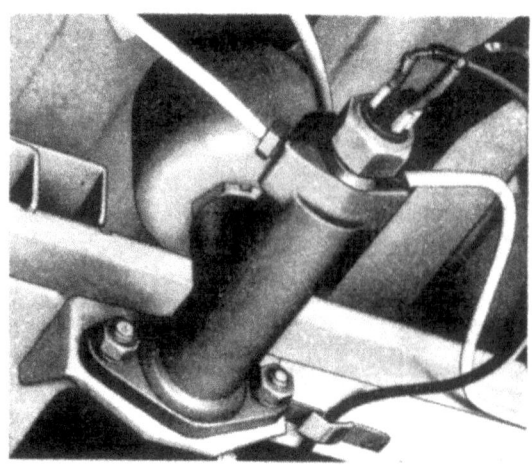

SAFETY EQUIPMENT
Windshield Wipers

The windshield wipers operate off two spindles powered by one motor. The switch is located on the dashboard, and is a push-pull single speed control on early models. On later models, a twist of the knob to the right starts the wipers operating at low-speed, and another twist to the right is the high-speed setting. The window washer button is combined with this later control.

The wiper motor and the spindles are mounted on a common frame connected with linkages, and are accessible from beneath the dashboard. When the windshield wiper motor is switched off, the wiper arms swing automatically to the right and come to a standstill at the correct point. **Caution:** Make sure the movement of the wiper blades, especially in the right side parking area, is not hindered by ice or dirt since the current supply to the wiper motor will continue even though the wiper system has been turned off. Should this occur, the motor armature windings will burn out in a few minutes and ruin the motor.

A double contact in the wiper motor, operated by an eccenter cam on the wiper shaft, continues to supply current to the motor after the wiper switch has been turned off until the contact is opened by the eccenter cam. Simultaneous with the break in current flow is a short circuit by the second contact to rapidly stop the motor and keep the blades in the end position. Only by turning on the wiper switch once more can the blades be moved from the end position.

To prevent damage to the wiper motor for the above reason, free blades from the windshield when frozen in place prior to turning on the switch. Also, should falling snow build up on the windshield right end position, clear the ice or snow away before turning off the switch, since the current supply to the motor will continue despite the switch having been turned off. Another cause of damage to the motor could come from the windshield being dry and the voltage being low from a nearly dead battery, creating enough resistance to stop the blades in the center of their arc. Should this happen, immediately move the blades to the end position and turn off the wiper switch.

Wiper Blades (Early Models)

The wiper blades can be adjusted by folding the arms forward, loosening the screw on the bracket, and turning the bracket on the wiper shaft until the blade covers the correct area. Adjust the blade height by loosening the grubscrews in the bracket. When replacing, do not overtighten the screw in the wiper arm

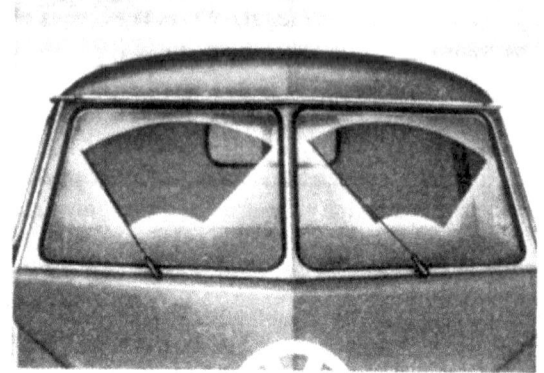

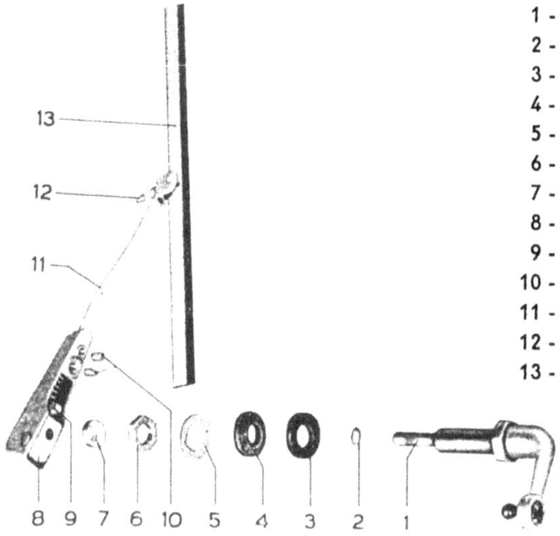

1 - Wiper shaft
2 - Circlip
3 - Inside rubber grommet
4 - Outside rubber grommet
5 - Cap washer
6 - Nut
7 - Pivot bearing cap
8 - Wiper arm bracket
9 - Clamp screws
10 - Grub screws
11 - Wiper arm
12 - Grub screw
13 - Wiper blade

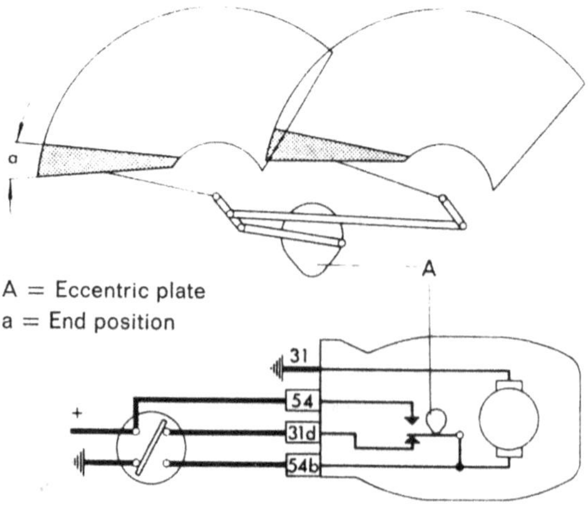

A = Eccentric plate
a = End position

bracket and replace any wiper arms which cannot be properly tightened. Loosen grubscrew to renew wiper blade.

Wiper Blades (Later Models)

To replace the wiper rubber filler blades (which should be done about once yearly), hold the arm and pull the assembly to the cleaning position. Pivot the blade about 30° from the arm, lift the retaining spring, then slide the blade down the arm slightly and lift off the arm. Pull the two steel strips out of the upper part of the rubber filler blade, then detach the blade from the retaining clips, being careful not to bend the clips. Install by squeezing the new rubber filler blade into the retaining clips so that the clips engage the recesses. Slide the steel strips into the rubber filler blade again, being careful not to tear the rubber and that the strip is fully seated. When refitting onto the arm, make sure it passes through the small hole in the blade and that the retaining spring is fully engaged. Wiping coverage can be adjusted by loosening the nut on the tapered and slined shaft. Pull or pry off the arm and adjust the arm so that the area covered is uniform when the glass is wet. Replace nut and tighten, then operate wipers and make sure the blades do not strike the windshield frame.

Servicing Wiper Motor (Early Model)

Disconnect the right-hand connecting rod at the ball joints and remove, then disconnect the left-hand rod at the wiper shaft ball joint. Remove the motor securing screws, then pull the motor out

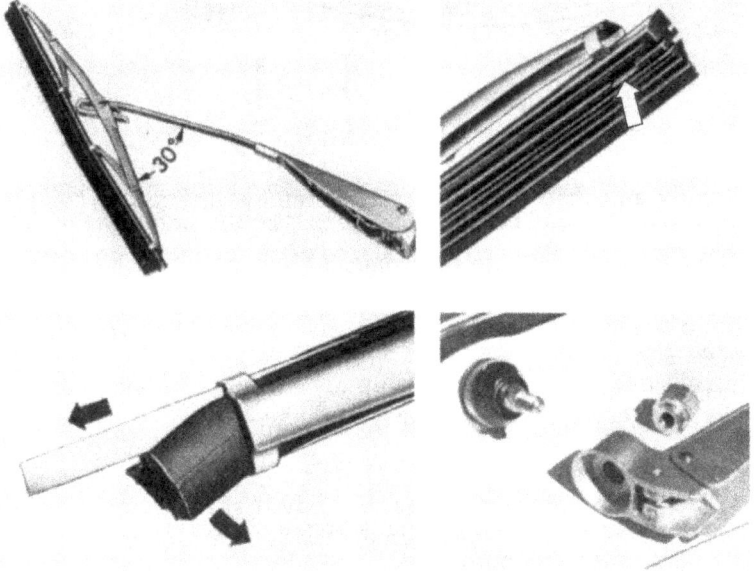

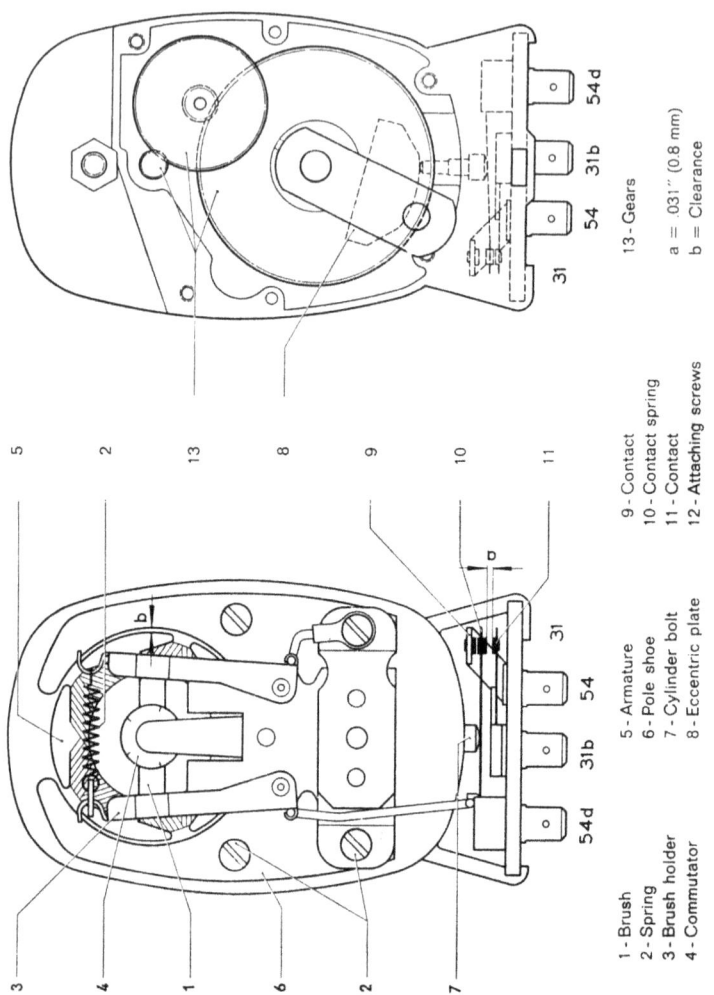

slightly and disconnect the cable. Remove the motor complete with the left-hand rod. Reverse the procedure to replace the unit. The motor brushes can be replaced after the motor has been removed and the cap has been unclipped or the screw removed. Unhook the brush holder spring, swing brush holders outward, then pull brushes out with long-nosed pliers and insert new brushes. Ensure that the brushes are tight in the holders and that the ends contact properly on the commutator.

Servicing Wiper Motor (Later Model)

The wiper motor may be serviced by first removing the entire wiper frame and linkage as an assembly. Start by disconnecting the battery ground strap, then loosen the clamping screws in the

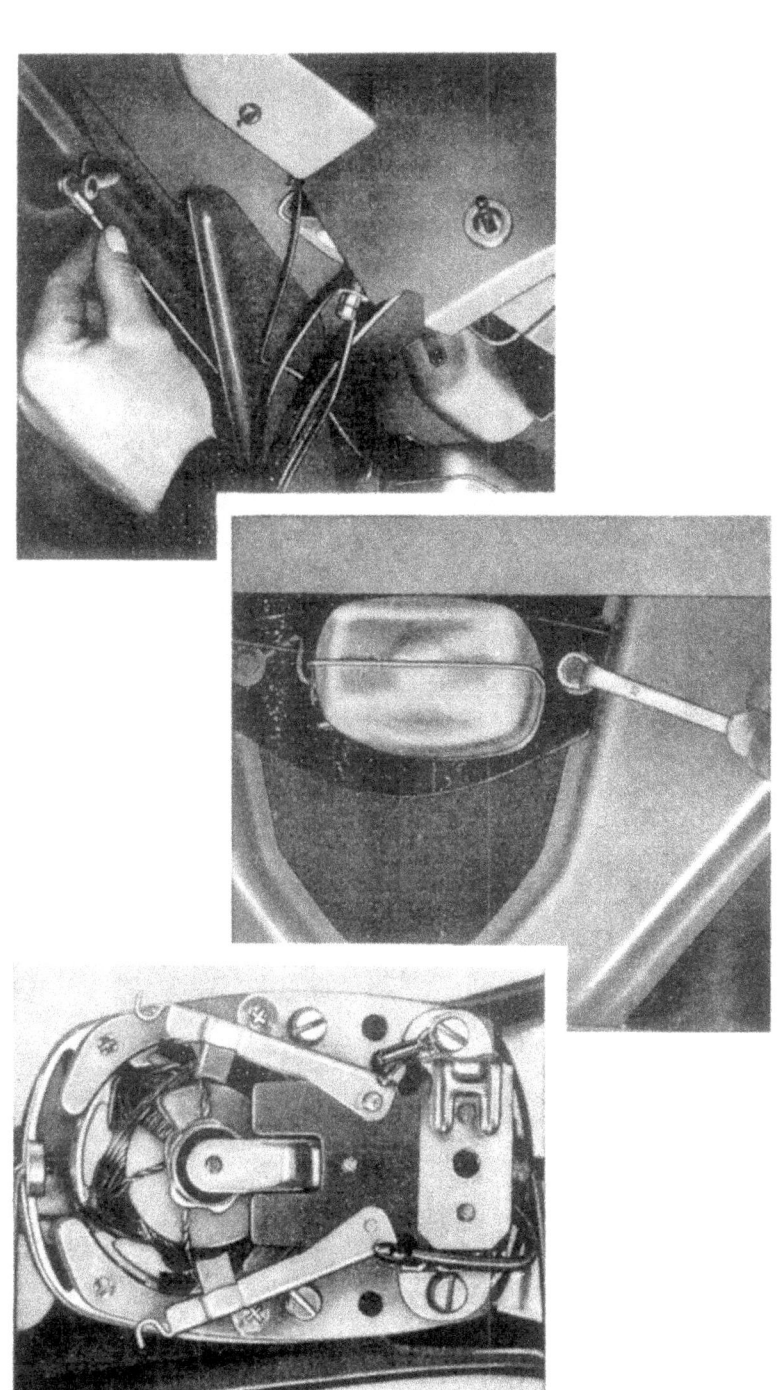

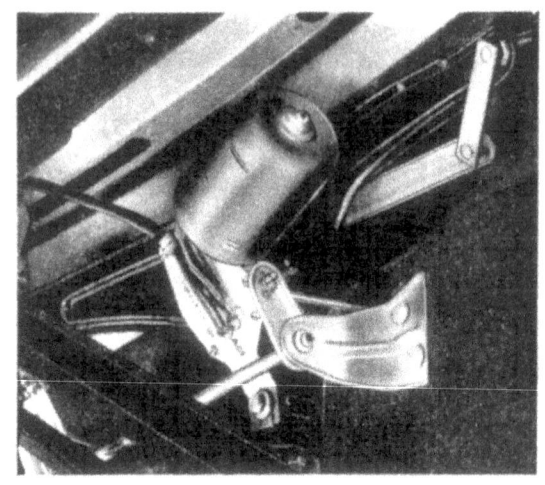

LATER MODEL WIPER MOTOR ASSEMBLY
(SEE PAGE 216 FOR EXPLODED VIEW)

USE SCREWDRIVER TO PRY APART LINKAGE

wiper arm brackets and remove the arm and blade assembly. Take off the wiper bearing hexagon nut with washers, removing the bearing sealing grommet if age cracked. Disconnect the cables from the wiper motor cable connectors, then remove body-to-frame mounting screws and remove frame from under dashboard. Remove the motor from the frame and linkage by first taking off the lock washer and spring washer from the driving shaft, then disconnect the driving link. Loosen the wiper shaft securing nut, then remove one motor securing nut and remove the motor from the frame. Replace the motor, then replace the frame under the dashboard and move the frame in the elongated hole so that the wiper spindles are vertical to the windshield. Make sure that the seals and washers are in the correct order, then finally make sure that the power cables are properly connected and the ground strap on the windshield frame securing screw is making good contact. Both rods are of different lengths, and must be replaced side-for-side.

While the wiper motor frame is removed, the wiper motor bearings can be renewed if necessary by first unhooking the spring between the frame and the connecting rod. Take off the lock and spring washers at the bearings, remove the drive link and connecting rod, inner seal and washer, then unscrew the retaining nut and remove the wiper bearing and washer. When installing the bearings, make sure the pressed lug on the wiper frame engages the groove on the wiper bearing. Check the plastic bushes in the linkage for wear, and if necessary, renew the complete linkage. Replace the complete linkage with the hollow side of the linkage facing toward the frame and the angled end of the driving link toward the right hand wiper bearing. **Renew the** bearing sealing grommet if age-cracked.

As with any electric motor, the brushes are subject to wear. If motor fails, check brushes and replace if necessary, then make sure that the commutator slots are free of carbon (clean with a soft cloth and benzine), and the area is free of oil or grease. Fine polishing cloth should be used only if burn marks are found. The later motor has 3 carbon brushes.

Windshield Washer Tank (Early Models)

To operate, press the rubber bellows on the tank. To fill (preferably with a solution of 3 parts water and 1 part cleaner-antifreeze of methylated spirits), screw the plastic ring off the container and remove the bellows. About 1 quart of liquid will fill the container, and if used in the above ratio, should keep the water from freezing, down to a temperature of $-12°C$. ($5°F$.). Remove tank by removing screws retaining tank and disconnecting hoses. Be sure to bleed off liquid before removing hoses.

Windshield Washer Tank (Later Models)

To pressurize the windshield washer system, first remove the cover and cap, then fill the container with about 1 quart of water, to which has been added one of the popular cleaner-antifreeze solutions (or pure spirit). A solution of 1-to-3 will keep the water from freezing down to a temperature of —12°C. (5°F.). Tighten the filling cap, then pressurize the system with a common tire air hose, being careful not to exceed 35 psi (the instrument panel valve could be ruptured with too much pressure). Remove tank by removing the right front trim panel screws, remove panel, then remove screws retaining tank bracket. Be sure to bleed off air pressure before disconnecting hoses. To replace, reverse the removal procedure.

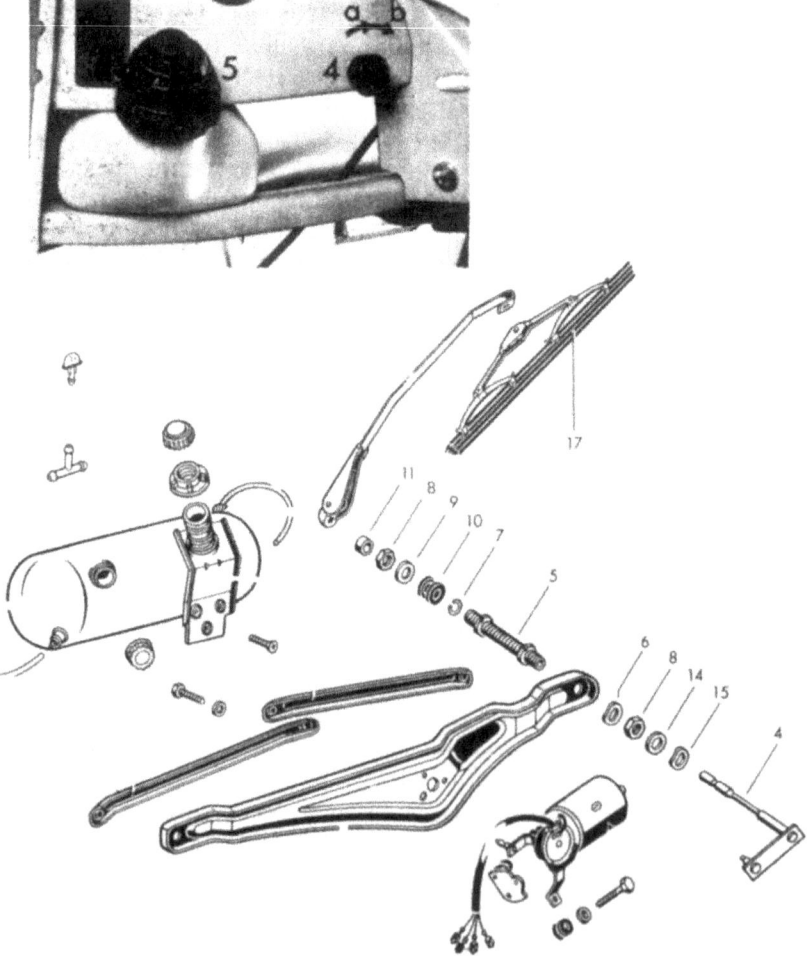

Windshield Washer Spray Jets

Two spray jets are used to squirt water on the window for cleaning purposes. Either jet can be aimed with a pin or piece of fine wire so that the jets of water strike the window uniformly. Simply insert the wire in the hole and position it as necessary. To remove a jet and rubber seal, press it upwards out of the hole in the cowl panel. After installation, check that the rubber seal is properly seated, and the jet is tight. All connectors are pulled off the hose for removal.

Windshield Wiper Motor Trouble Checking

Symptoms	Cause	Remedy
Windshield wiper motor operates too slowly, cuts out or comes to a standstill	a - Brushes worn b - Brush tension spring too weak or annealed c - Brush levers not free on their pivots d - Commutator dirty e - Joints of windshield wiper linkages devoid of grease	a - Replace brushes b - Replace tension spring c - Free the brush levers d - Clean the commutator e - Throughly lubricate all joints with universal grease
Motor squeaks when running. Runs slowly. Armature burnt.	a - Windshield wiper linkage joints dry b - Armature rubbing on pole shoe	a - Lubricate with universal grease b - Check armature for ease of movement, loosen four screws and re-align pole shoe
Motor will not start or will not stop	a - Pole shoe out of line and touching armature due to being dropped or struck on motor cap b - Armature burnt by winding or ground short circuit. Cause: Overloading	a - Check armature for ease of movement, loosen four screws and re-align pole shoe b - Replace motor

Ignition Switch Steering Column Lock and Buzzer

As standard equipment, the ignition/starter switch locks the steering wheel so it cannot be turned. Remove by first disconnecting the battery ground strap, then turn the key to "Fahrt." Remove the cables to the turn signal switch and the steering/ignition lock, then remove the turn signal switch. Unscrew the canceling ring and remove the steering wheel (see "Steering chapter), then remove the spring. Remove the circlip and washer over the steering/ignition lock rubber mounting, then loosen the steering column cover. Push the cover upwards and disconnect the ground cable. Pull out the column tube upward through the rubber mounting of the steering/ignition lock. Unscrew the steering/ignition lock securing screws and remove the lock from the carrier. To remove the lock, unscrew the steering column bracket, then use a piece of bent steel wire to depress the lock cylinder spring from below through the opening (see arrow) and pull the lock cylinder out with the key.

When installing, be sure there is a gap of .08 to .12" between the turn signal switch and the lower edge of the steering wheel hub when securing the switch to the column tube. Connect the ground cable to the column tube by bending the tongue over. Connect the cable to the turn signal switch and the steering/ignition lock (see the wiring diagram for 1968 and later and the "Steering" chapter).

On 1970 models with an ignition key buzzer that operates when the front door is opened, use the previous procedure to remove the steering column lock, then unplug the connector from the housing. Reverse the procedure to replace the connector. The buzzer is located behind the dashboard, and may be unbolted for removal. The wire leading to the ignition switch

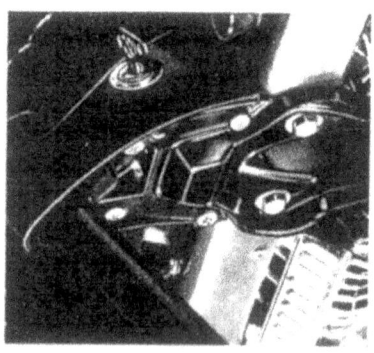

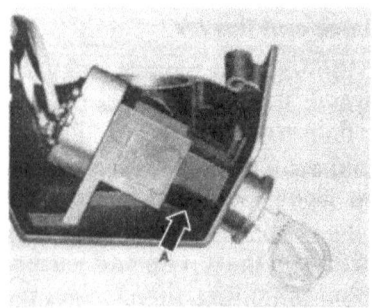

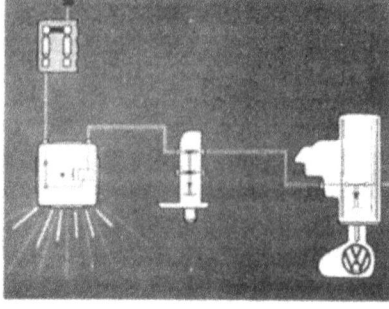

is the ground for the unit. The power comes from terminal 30 on the fuse box, and a front door switch has been added to operate both the buzzer and the cab light. Use a screwdriver to remove the door switch.

Heated Rear Window

As standard equipment on 1969 and later models, the rear window has been laced with heating wires of an electric defogger and defroster. The toggle switch on the dashboard to the right of the steering column is serviced the same as the other switches, from under the dashboard. Should the rear window need replacement, disconnect the wires at the top of the rear lift-up door first. The switch and rear window are connected through the wire harness, and the other rear window terminal is grounded.

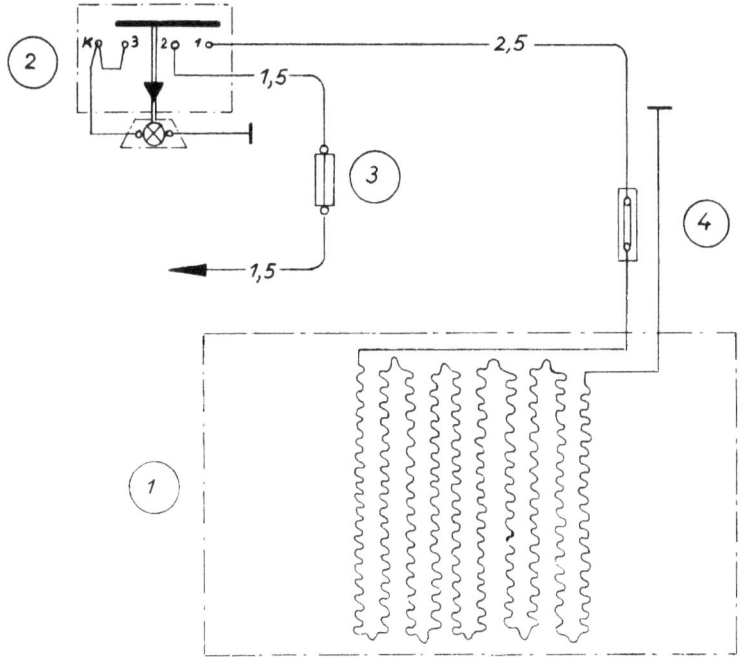

1 HEATED REAR WINDOW
2 PUSH-PULL SWITCH
3 FUSE HOLDER
4 TERMINAL BLOCK

Wiring Diagrams

Prior To 1960
(For U.S. Version)

Key to Part Designations

A	- Battery		M^2	- Parking Light, right
B	- Starting Motor		N	- Ignition Distributor
C	- Generator		O	- Ignition Coil
D	- Ignition Switch		P^1	- Spark Plug Connector for Cylinder 1
E	- Windshield Wiper Switch		P^2	- Spark Plug Connector for Cylinder 2
F	- Lighting Switch		P^3	- Spark Plug Connector for Cylinder 3
G^2	- Direction Indicator Switch		P^4	- Spark Plug Connector for Cylinder 4
H^1	- Horn Button		Q^1	- Spark Plug for Cylinder 1
H^2	- Horn		Q^2	- Spark Plug for Cylinder 2
J^1	- Dimmer Switch		Q^3	- Spark Plug for Cylinder 3
J^2	- Indicator Flasher Relay		Q^4	- Spark Plug for Cylinder 4
J^3	- Stop Light Switch		S	- Fuse Box
J^4	- Oil Pressure Switch		T^1	- Cable Connector single
J^5	- Switch for Interior Light		T^2	- Cable Connector 5 point
K^1	- Headlamp Warning Light		U^1	- Direction Indicator, left front
K^2	- Generator and Cooling Warning Light		U^2	- Direction Indicator, right front
K^3	- Direction Indicator Warning Light		W	- Windshield Wiper Motor
K^4	- Oil Pressure Warning Light		X^1	- Stop/Tail/Indicator Light, left
K^5	- Speedometer Light		X^2	- Stop/Tail/Indicator Light, right
L^3	- Two-Filament Bulb, left		Y^1	- Interior Light, front
L^4	- Two-Filament Bulb, right		Y^2	- Interior Light, rear
M^1	- Parking Light, left		Z	- License Plate Light

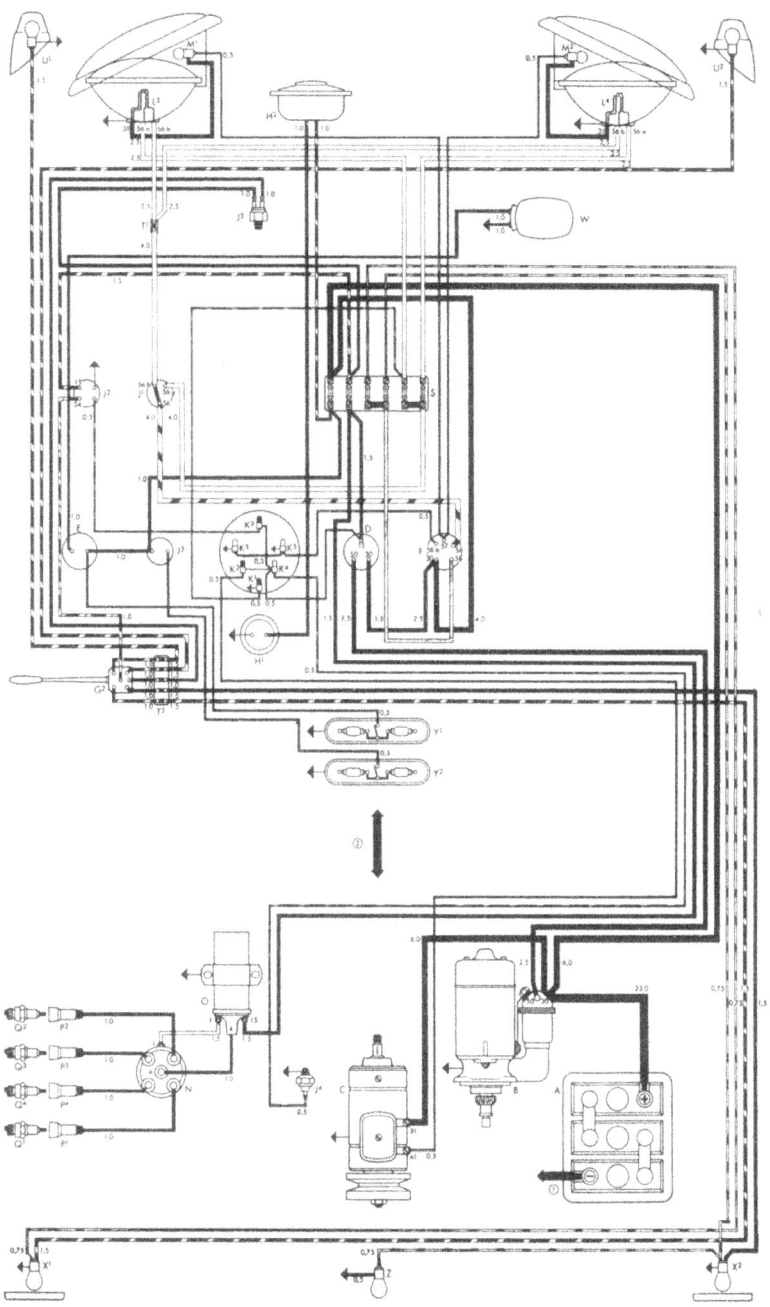

Key to Wiring Diagram
Type 2 USA Version

(Prior To 1968)

A - Battery
B - Starter
C - Generator
D - Starter/ignition switch
E - Windshield wiper switch
F - Lighting switch
G - Turn indicator switch
H - Horn
H^1 - Horn button
J - Flasher relay
J^1 - Emergency light relay
J^2 - Dimmer switch
J^3 - Stop light switch
J^4 - Oil pressure switch
J^5 - Fuel gauge sender unit
J^6 - Emergency light switch
J^7 - Interior light switch
K^1 - High beam warning light
K^2 - Generator & cooling warning light
K^3 - Turn indicator warning light
K^4 - Oil pressure warning light
K^5 - Speedometer light
K^6 - Fuel gauge light
K^7 - Clock light
L^1 - Sealed-Beam unit, left
L^2 - Sealed-Beam unit, right
M^1 - Parking light, left
M^2 - Parking light, right
N - Distributor

O - Coil
O^1 - Automatic choke
P^1 - Spark plug connector for cylinder No. 1
P^2 - Spark plug connector for cylinder No. 2
P^3 - Spark plug connector for cylinder No. 3
P^4 - Spark plug connector for cylinder No. 4
Q^1 - Spark plug for cylinder No. 1
Q^2 - Spark plug for cylinder No. 2
Q^3 - Spark plug for cylinder No. 3
Q^4 - Spark plug for cylinder No. 4
R - Radio
R^1 - Aerial
R^2 - Connection for rear loudspeaker
   (Only Models 241—244 and 251)
S - Fuse box
T - Cable connector
T^1 - Cable connector
U^1 - Turn indicator, front left
U^2 - Turn indicator, front right
W - Windshield wiper motor
X^1 - Stop/tail/indicator light, rear left
X^2 - Stop/tail/indicator light, rear right
Y - Front interior light
Y^1 - Rear interior light
Z - License plate light

① - Ground strap from battery to body
② - Ground strap from transmission to body
③ - Windshield wiper motor ground connection

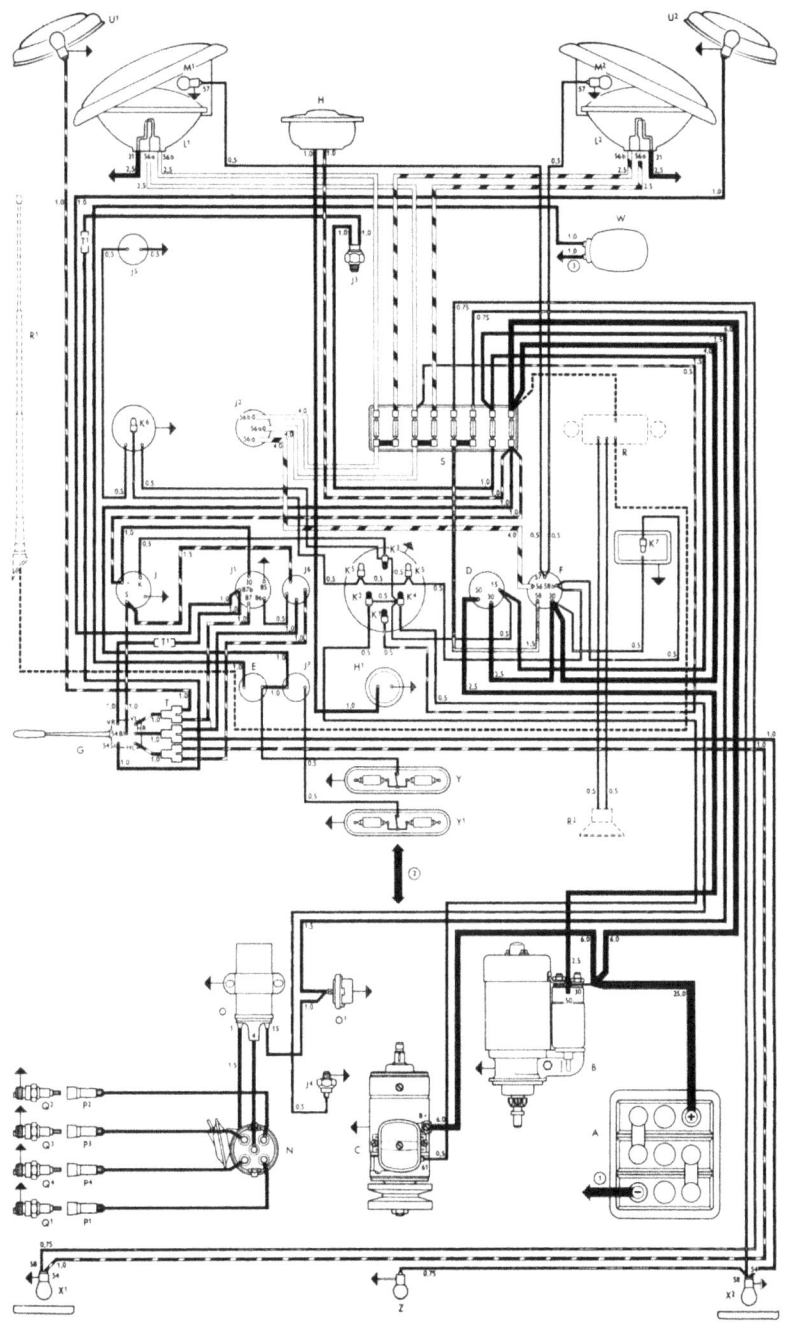

Wiring Diagram VW Transporter US Version

1968 AND LATER

A - Battery
B - Starter
C - Generator
C^1 - Regulator
D - Ignition/starter switch
E - Windshield wiper switch
F - Lighting switch
G - Turn signal switch and hand dimmer
H - Horn
H^1 - Horn button
J - Emergency light relay
J^1 - Brake light switch (2×)
J^2 - Oil pressure switch
J^3 - Fuel gauge sender unit
J^4 - Warning switch for brakes
J^5 - Emergency light switch
J^6 - Interior light switch
J^7 - Dimmer relay
J^9 - Back-up light switch
K^1 - High beam warning lamp
K^2 - Generator and fan warning lamp
K^3 - Turn signal warning lamp
K^4 - Oil pressure warning lamp
K^5 - Speedometer light bulb
K^6 - Fuel gauge light bulb
K^7 - Clock light bulb
K^8 - Emergency light warning lamp
K^9 - Brake system warning lamp
L^1 - Sealed beam unit, left
L^2 - Sealed beam unit, right
M^1 - Parking light, left
M^2 - Parking light, right
N - Distributor
O - Ignition coil

O^1 - Automatic choke
O^2 - Electro-magnetic pilot jet
P^1 - Spark plug connector, No. 1 cylinder
P^2 - Spark plug connector, No. 2 cylinder
P^3 - Spark plug connector, No. 3 cylinder
P^4 - Spark plug connector, No. 4 cylinder
Q^1 - Spark plug for No.1 cylinder
Q^2 - Spark plug for No. 2 cylinder
Q^3 - Spark plug for No. 3 cylinder
Q^4 - Spark plug for No. 4 cylinder
R - Radio
R^1 - Aerial connection
R^2 - Rear loudspeaker connection
S - Fuse box
S^1 - Back-up light fuse
T^1 - Cable connector, single
U^1 - Turn signal, front left
U^2 - Turn signal, front right
W - Windshield wiper motor
X^1 - Brake, turn signal and tail light, left
X^2 - Brake, turn signal and tail light, right
Y - Interior light, front
Y^1 - Interior light, rear
Z - License plate light
Z^1 - Back-up light, left
Z^2 - Back-up light, right

① - Battery to body ground strap
② - Transmission to body ground strap
③ - Windshield wiper motor ground connection

Black dotted lines = Optional extras
All fuses: 8 amps.

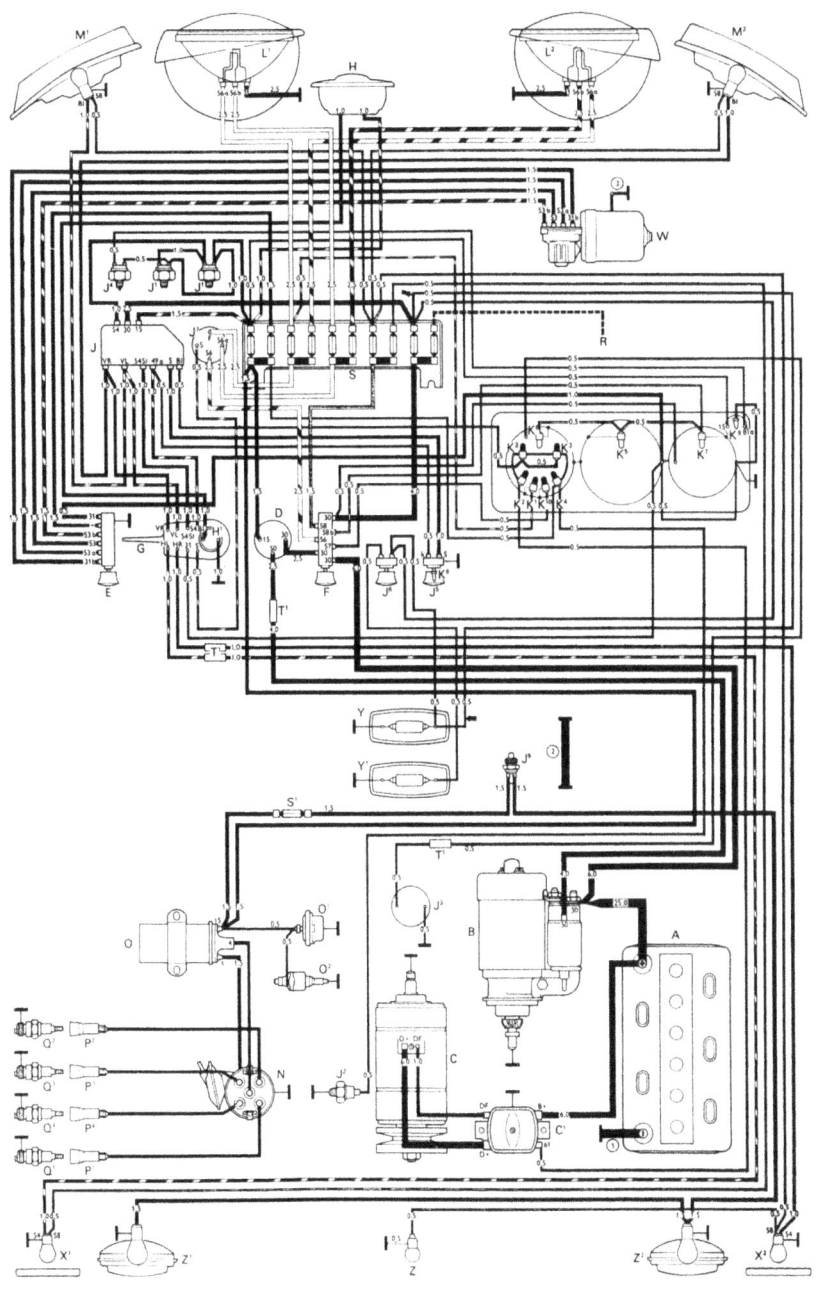

Clutch

The clutch is a conventional single plate, dry disc type with release bearing located in the transmission case. It requires no servicing. Maintenance consists of adjustment of clutch pedal free travel to insure that clutch is not dragging and is engaging fully. This free travel is from .4 to .8 inch.

1 - Release lock nut on the threaded cable end.

2 - Adjust clutch clearance by turning the adjusting nut. Depress clutch pedal several times and recheck pedal free-play.

3 - When the correct adjustment has been reached, hold adjusting nut in position and tighten lock nut.

4 - Grease clutch cable adjusting nut with Universal Grease.

Occasionally it will be found necessary to replace a clutch release cable, especially after a prolonged bad weather driving period when road salt, etc. may cause accelerated wear at the ball nut end of the cable.

To replace, place van on floor stands, disconnect the ball nut end at the clutch operating lever on the transmission case, then take rubber boot off cable sleeve. Under the floor, remove inspection cover and detach cable from pedal linkage, slide off the rubber boot and withdraw cable from conduit. In installing a new cable

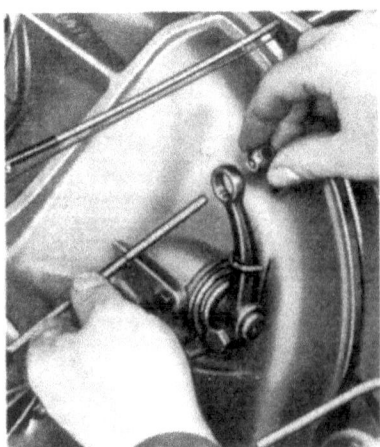
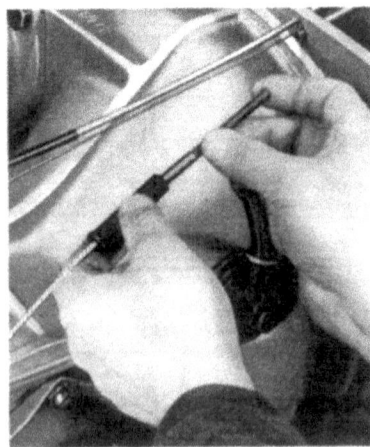

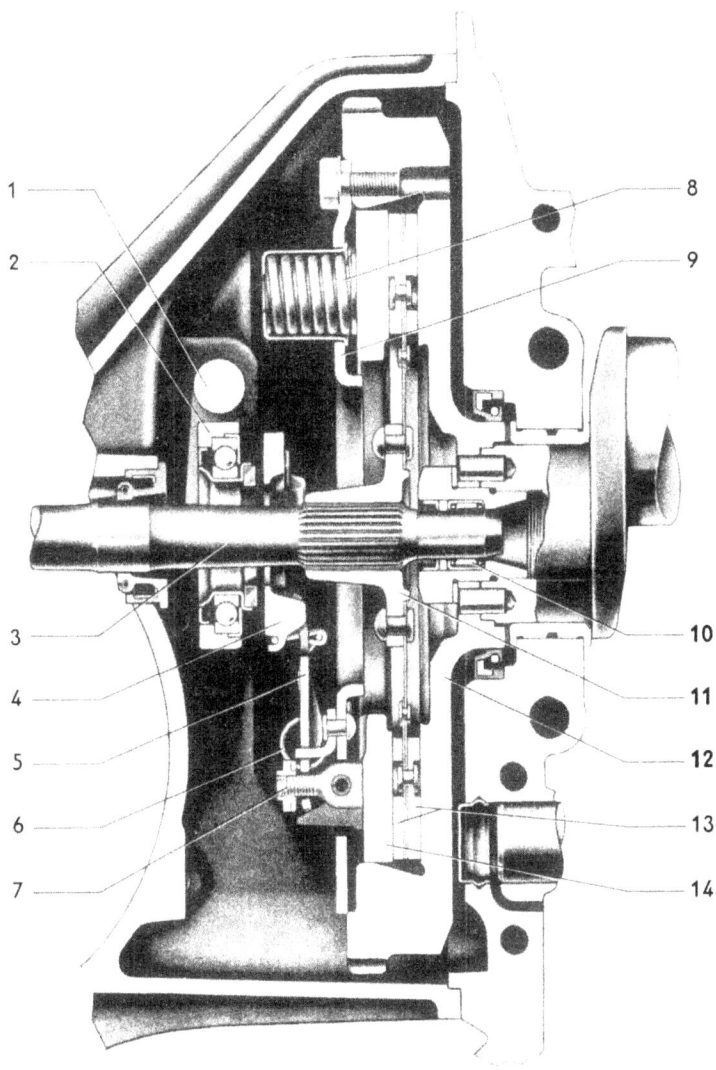

CLUTCH

1 - Operating shaft
2 - Ball thrust bearing
3 - Main drive shaft
4 - Release plate
5 - Release lever
6 - Release lever spring
7 - Bolt and special nut
8 - Thrust spring
9 - Cover
10 - Needle bearing for gland nut
11 - Driven plate (disc)
12 - Flywheel
13 - Lining (facing)
14 - Pressure plate

check the threads at the transmission end and grease them with Universal grease. Make sure the two rubber boots make a good seal and grease the nut before taking it up.

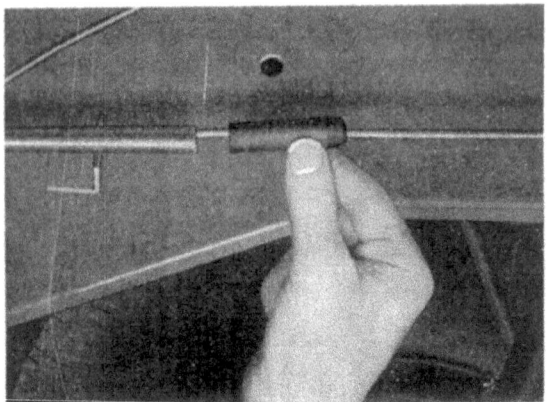

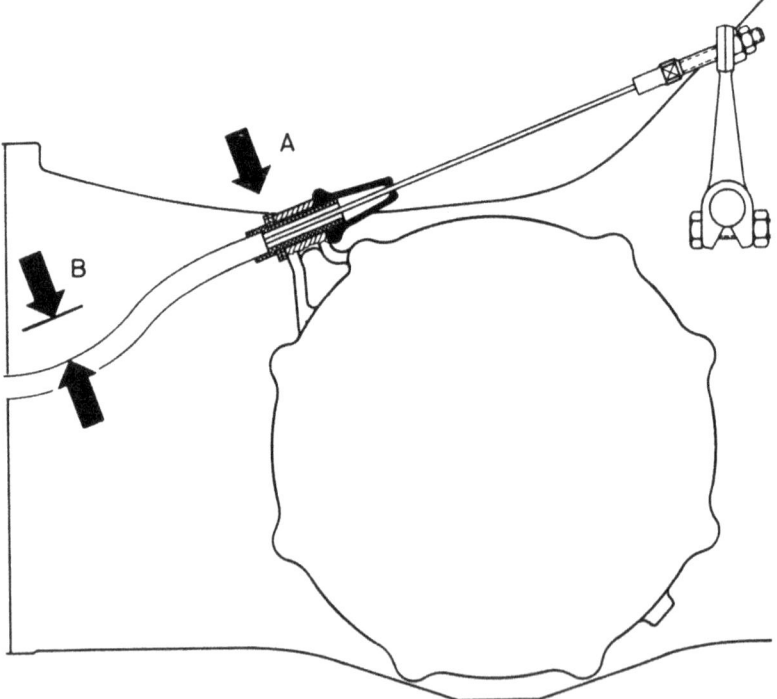

The clutch cable sleeve should bend as shown in the diagram about 13/16 inch to 1 and 3/16 inches. This tension is obtained by inserting washers at **A**.

Note: Re-adjust clutch pedal free travel after installing a new cable.

To remove the clutch, first mark the clutch and flywheel so replacement is simplified. Loosen the clutch cover securing bolts evenly and diagonally, giving each bolt one or two turns at a time to prevent distortion from the thrust spring pressure. When all bolts are removed, take out pressure plate and disc. To renew the release bearing, remove the retaining springs with a screwdriver as shown. See "Engine Removal—Refitting" for clutch and release bearing replacement.

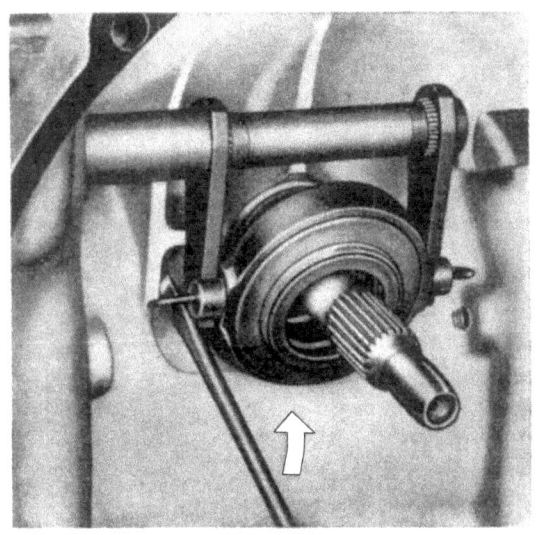

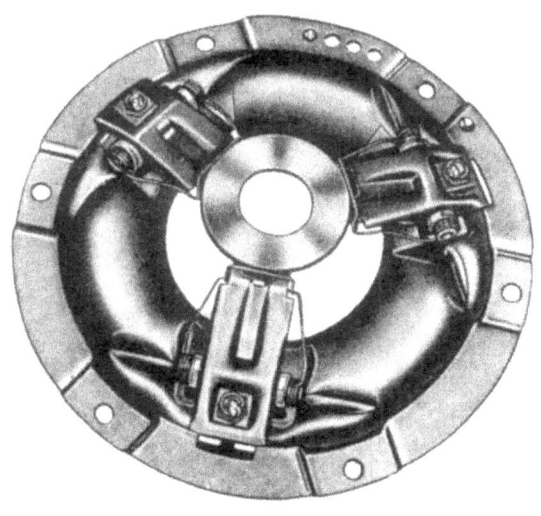

Note: Nine thrust springs are used on the 200 mm diameter clutch used on 1962 models and later. In 1968 a three-fingered diaphragm design was adopted. Removal and installation procedures remain the same. Any further repair on the clutch system should be handled by a VW dealership service department. Only a genuine VW replacement disc is recommended should the old one be worn or oily, causing slippage or chatter.

Clutch trouble shooting

Symptom	Cause	Remedy
1 - Noise	a - Needle bearing in flywheel gland nut worn	a - *Renew gland nut and fill with 0.2 cc universal grease*
	b - Driven plate fouling pressure plate	b - *Renew or straighten driven plate*
	c - Weak release lever springs or unequal tension	c - *Renew springs*
	d - Release bearing defective	d - *Fit new bearing*
2 - Chatter or grabbing	a - Transmission case not tightly mounted	a - Tighten mounting bolts and nuts
	b - Sag of cable guide tube too slight or excessive	b - Correct the sag to 1"–1.8" (25-45 mm)
	c - Uneven contact of pressure plate, or worn	c - *Renew or regrind pressure plate*
	d - Release plate not running true	d - *Adjust or replace release plate*
	e - Unequal tension of thrust springs	e - *Renew thrust springs*
	f - Cushion segments excessively or unequally set	f - *Reset cushion segments or replace clutch driven plate*
3 - Dragging or incomplete release	a - Excessive pedal free-play	a - Adjust clutch clearance: .4"–.8" (10–20 mm) at clutch pedal
	b - Sag of cable guide tube too great	b - Correct the sag to 1"–1.8" (25-45 mm)
	c - Driven plate not running true	c - *Straighten or replace driven plate*
	d - Cushion segments excessively or unequally set	d - *Reset cushion segments or replace clutch driven plate*
	e - Plate linings broken	e - *Install new linings or replace clutch driven plate*
	f - Main drive shaft not running true with gland nut (Installation tolerances)	f - *It is sometimes sufficient to loosen the engine mounting bolts, move the engine slightly and retighten the bolts. Otherwise check gland nut. If the thread is damaged or there is excessive play between inner and outer thread the gland nut cannot be centered correctly*
	g - Needle bearing in gland nut defective or insufficiently greased	g - *Replace gland nut or grease needle bearing with 0.2 cc universal grease*
	h - Splines on main drive shaft or clutch driven plate dirty or burred	h - *Clean splines. Remove burr*
	i - Sticky clutch linings	i - *Wash the linings with fuel*
	k - Felt ring in gland nut tight on main drive shaft	k - *Lubricate felt ring or replace the gland nut by one which has a better fitting felt ring*
	l - Stiffness in the pedal cluster, clutch cable and the operating shaft	l - Grease the parts thoroughly with universal grease
4 - Slipping	a - Lack of pedal free-play due to lining wear	a - Adjust clutch clearance .4"–.8" (10–20 mm) at clutch pedal
	b - Grease or oil on clutch linings	b - *Replace clutch linings. Replace engine or transmission oil seal if necessary*

Operations shown in italics should be carried out by an authorized VW workshop

Transmission-Rear Axle

The Volkswagen transmission, (Figs. 128,129), mounts in a yoke at rear of car with the engine bolted to its bell housing in the back. It is really a transaxle, since the housing contains both differential and transmission gears with a common oil supply. Power flow is from the engine through the clutch forward via transmission driveshaft over the rear axle and into one of four driving gears of the transmission. This gear meshes with one of four driven gears and power goes backward up to the pinion which drives the differential ring gear. The ring gear drives the carrier which contains the axis for two spider gears. The spider gears mesh with the side gears which drive the rear axles via fulcrum plates (universal joints). In cars built since May, 1959 (Engine No. 5,000,001) each of the four forward transmission gears is fully synchronized by means of cone-type clutches, (Fig. 130) that bring the two rotating members to the same speed before engagement. Actually the four helically cut driven gears are in constant mesh with their counterparts on output shaft and shifting locks the gear to the shaft it is riding on, first and second gears to the output shaft, and third and fourth gears to input shaft.

The transmission gear ratios are as follows:

CHASSIS #469447 to 614 455	CHASSIS #614 456 & LATER
First .... 3.80 to 1	First .... 3.80 to 1
Second .... 2.06 to 1	Second .... 2.06 to 1
Third .... 1.32 to 1	Third .... 1.22 to 1
Fourth .... 0.89 to 1	Fourth .... 0.82 to 1
Reverse .... 3.88 to 1	Reverse .... 3.88 to 1

Reduction gears in malleable iron cases are provided on the outer ends of the half axles. The reduction drive gears are splined to the half axle shafts, ratio 1.39:1 for the 1200 engine, 1.26:1 for the 1500 engine.

Shifting is accomplished via the gearshift lever to the shifting rod which runs under floorboards mounted on guides (Fig. 131), to a coupling connecting to the transmission shift rod. The transmission shift rod ends in a finger. Moving the gear shift lever rotates the finger so that it engages one of the hooks at the end of each of three shifting rails, one for first and second, one for third and fourth, and one for reverse. Each shift rail

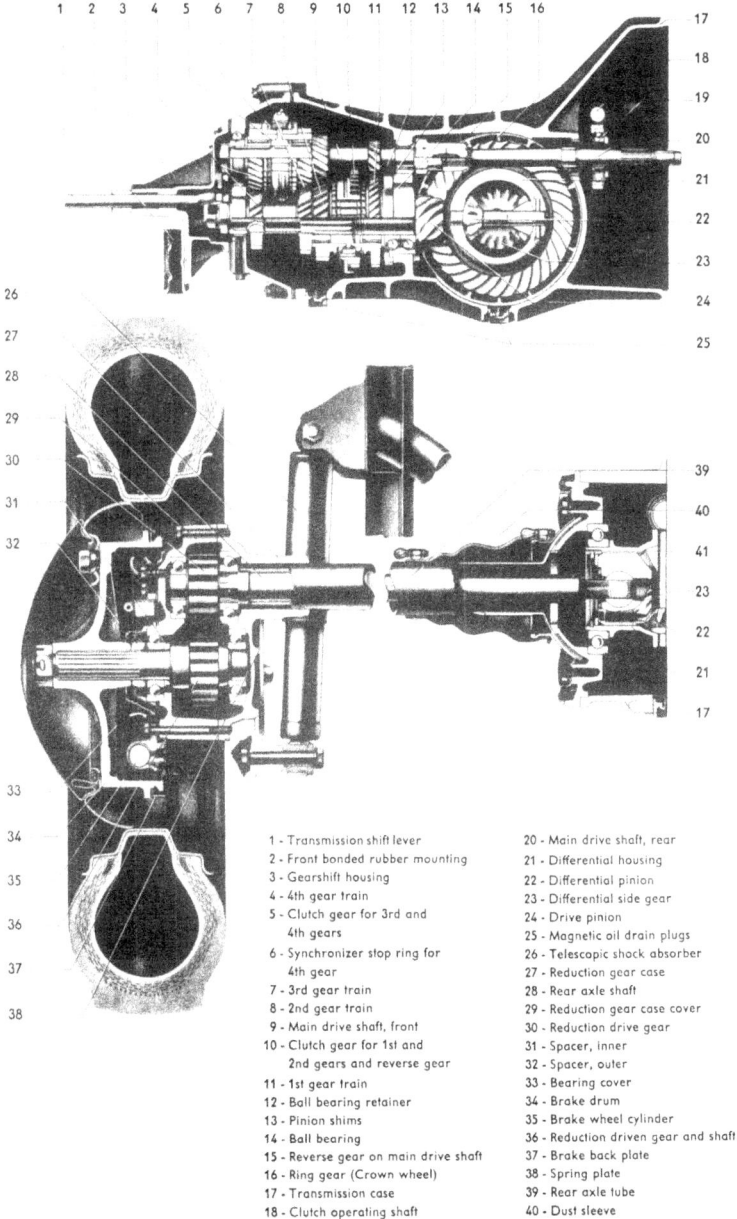

1 - Transmission shift lever
2 - Front bonded rubber mounting
3 - Gearshift housing
4 - 4th gear train
5 - Clutch gear for 3rd and 4th gears
6 - Synchronizer stop ring for 4th gear
7 - 3rd gear train
8 - 2nd gear train
9 - Main drive shaft, front
10 - Clutch gear for 1st and 2nd gears and reverse gear
11 - 1st gear train
12 - Ball bearing retainer
13 - Pinion shims
14 - Ball bearing
15 - Reverse gear on main drive shaft
16 - Ring gear (Crown wheel)
17 - Transmission case
18 - Clutch operating shaft
19 - Clutch release bearing
20 - Main drive shaft, rear
21 - Differential housing
22 - Differential pinion
23 - Differential side gear
24 - Drive pinion
25 - Magnetic oil drain plugs
26 - Telescopic shock absorber
27 - Reduction gear case
28 - Rear axle shaft
29 - Reduction gear case cover
30 - Reduction drive gear
31 - Spacer, inner
32 - Spacer, outer
33 - Bearing cover
34 - Brake drum
35 - Brake wheel cylinder
36 - Reduction driven gear and shaft
37 - Brake back plate
38 - Spring plate
39 - Rear axle tube
40 - Dust sleeve
41 - Axle tube retainer

233

goes into the transmission and attaches to a selector fork. Each selector fork rides in a groove in the outer circumference of a clutch gear that it moves back and forth to connect one of the four transmission gears to its splined shaft. Detents interlocking

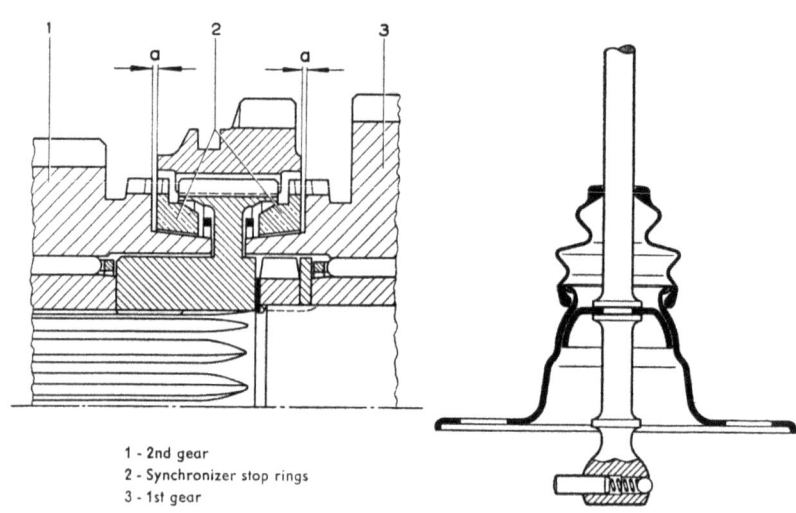

1 - 2nd gear
2 - Synchronizer stop rings
3 - 1st gear

FIG. 130   FIG. 131

FIG. 132

the shifting rails in the transmission case prevent the finger from shifting more than one gear at a time, which would be disastrous.

The transaxle is about the most complicated part of the car and its repair requires training and specialized tools and equipment. It is thus best left to the skilled mechanics of the authorized Volkswagen dealer. We will however, quickly run through the important parts of the transaxle.

Full Synchromesh Transmission

The fully synchronized transmission introduced with the 40 hp engine is tunnel shaped compared to its predecessor which was split down the middle. The rear axles, (Fig. 132), can be removed by first taking off the rear axle tube retainer without disassembling the whole transmission.

To remove the transmission/axle as an assembly, follow this procedure: Prior to raising the vehicle, loosen the rear axle shaft nuts. This is most important since an accident could occur if these nuts were removed when the vehicle is on a hoist. Raise vehicle and remove engine if it will prove too bulky for the lift or trolley jack to be used. If necessary, pull off brake drums complete with their wheel. Unbolt the lower shock absorber mount and spring plates, (Fig. 133), and disconnect the shifting rod coupling by removing the rear screw and shifting gears to release rod, (Fig. 134). The brake and clutch hoses and cables must be disconnected. Remove the stud nuts at the front rubber

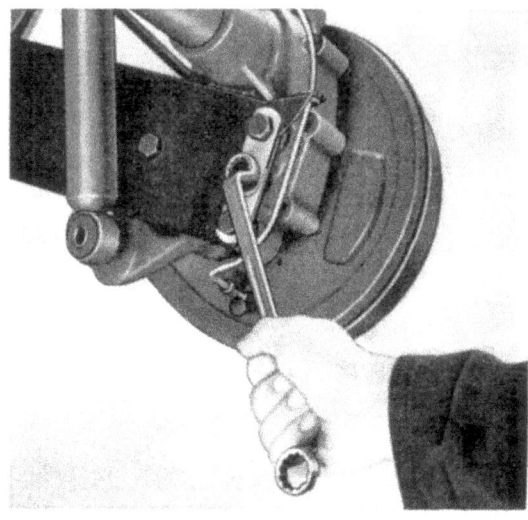

FIG. 133

mounting of the transmission case, (Fig. 135), and support the transmission with the trolley jack.

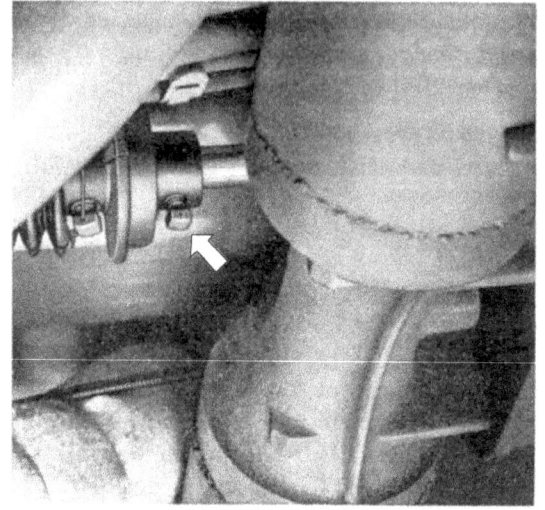

FIG. 134

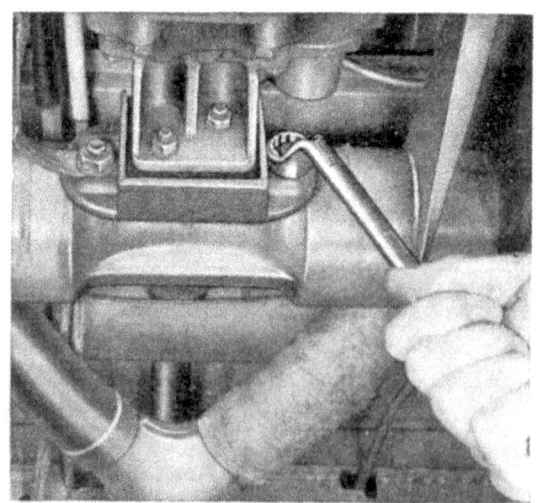

FIG. 135

FIG. 136

FIG. 137

Remove the bolts at the transmission carrier, (Fig. 136), then remove the whole transmission toward the rear with the trolley jack or equivalent, (Fig. 137). Reverse the removal procedure to install transmission, first greasing the transmission carrier mounting bolts and tightening, then tightening the nuts of the mounting plate at the front of the transmission case. Be sure the points of the shifting rod coupling screws are correctly bedded in their recesses, then secure screws individually with wire looped around the rod. Screw in the spring plate mounting bolts loosely, and align the holes on the spring plate and the reduction gear case with a pilot. Placing a clamp over the brake drum and spring plate can help prevent cross-threading of the mounting bolts. Torque the spring plate mounting bolts to 72—87 ft. lb. in the order indicated, (Fig. 137A). Use new lock plates and bend tabs up after bolts are tightened.

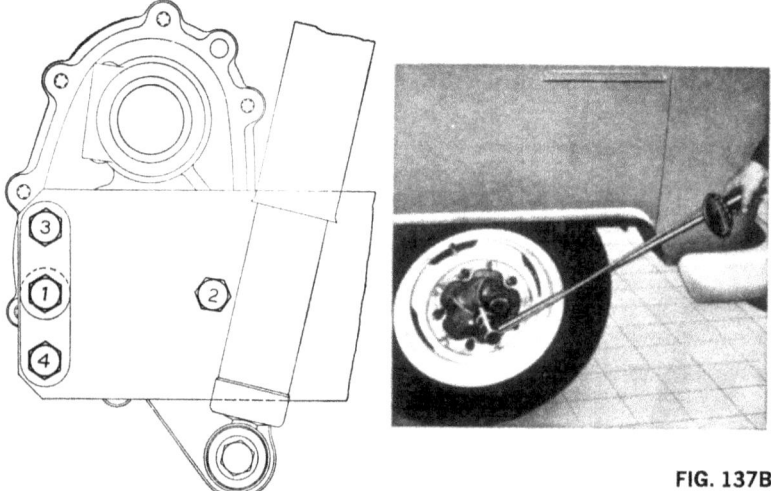

FIG. 137B

FIG. 137A

Check the splines on the brake drums. Renew the brake drum if the splines are worn or damaged, and coat lightly with graphite grease before installing. Lower the vehicle to the ground, then use a torque wrench to tighten the rear axle nuts to 216 ft. lb. (Fig. 137B). If the cotter pin cannot be inserted, turn the nut on to the next hole.

The rear wheel bearings and gears, (Fig. 138), are lubed both from the transmission and the transmission oil used to fill the reduction gear case. An oil seal keeps the lubricant where it

1 - Gasket	5 - Ball bearing	9 - Oil seal
2 - Reduction gear shaft	6 - Washer (VW 1200 Transporter only)	10 - Oil deflector
3 - Brake back plate	7 - Gasket	11 - Bearing cover
4 - Inner spacer	8 - Outer spacer	12 - Cover retaining screw

FIG. 138

belongs and an oil slinger, (Fig. 139), in the rear brake drum functions just in case the oil seal doesn't. The replacement rear axle rubber boots are of the split type so that the whole works doesn't have to be reassembled to replace them. Replace the boots when they show any damage from age, wear, or contact with oil, fuel, and salt. They are slotted for easy removal or replacement, and should be replaced with the flange located horizontally toward the rear of the vehicle. Prior to inserting the screws, coat the mating surfaces with VW sealing compound D-1a, then finger tighten the screws. Lower the vehicle so the complete weight is on the wheels, then tighten the dust sleeve screws and retaining clips but do not overtighten and check that the dust sleeves are not distorted or strained, no matter what position the axle shafts are in (raise the vehicle once more to check). See the sections dealing with the brakes, clutch and engine for remaining procedures.

This completes the procedure that may be accomplished with ordinary hand tools and general mechanical skill. The following procedures to disassemble the complete transaxle should be left up to the skilled technicians of a VW dealership, who have the special tools for the job. The transaxle is disassembled in the following order: Remove starting motor and drain oil from transmission and reduction gear cases. Remove wheel brake parts and back plates, then remove reduction gear cases. Remove

VW Transporter 1200   VW Transporter 1500

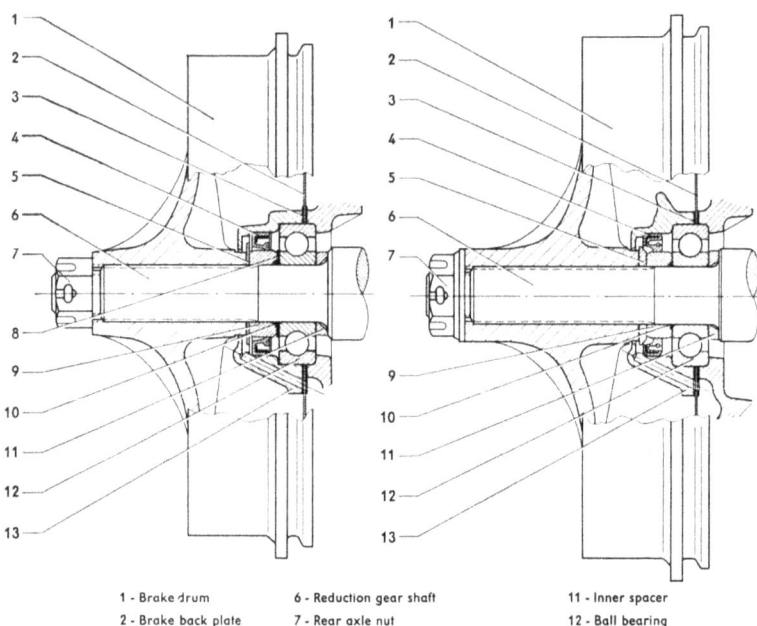

1 - Brake drum	6 - Reduction gear shaft	11 - Inner spacer
2 - Brake back plate	7 - Rear axle nut	12 - Ball bearing
3 - Gaskets	8 - Washer (VW Transporter 1200 only)	13 - Bearing cover
4 - Oil seal	9 - Outer spacer	
5 - Oil deflector	10 - Gasket	

FIG. 139

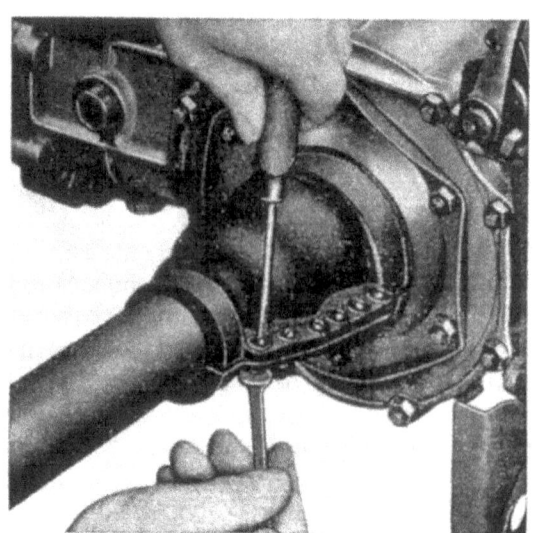

FIG. 140

FIG. 141

FIG. 142

FIG. 143

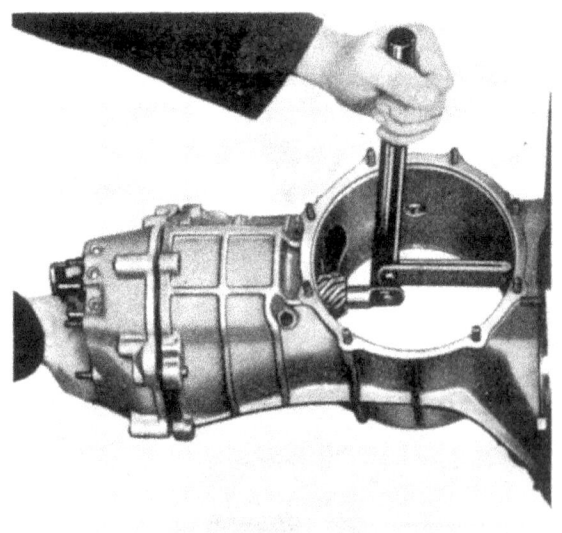

FIG. 144

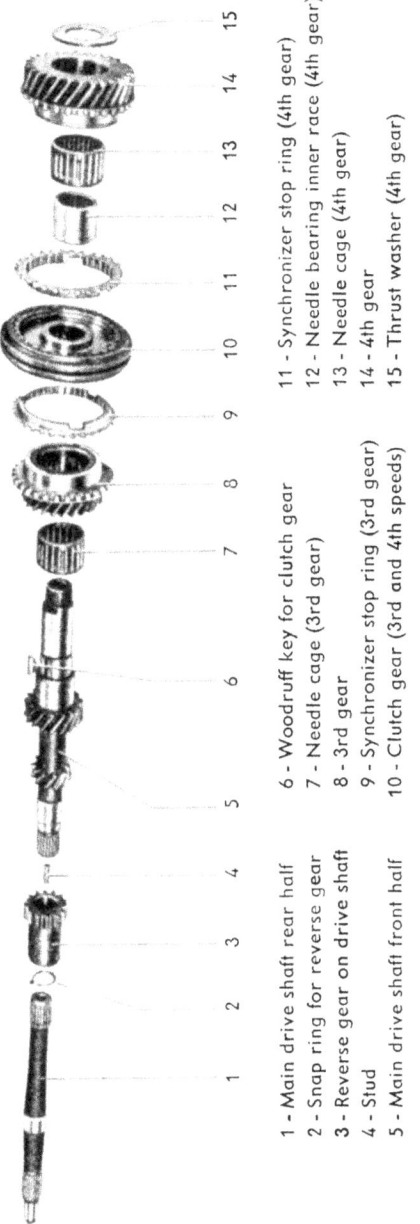

1 - Main drive shaft rear half
2 - Snap ring for reverse gear
3 - Reverse gear on drive shaft
4 - Stud
5 - Main drive shaft front half
6 - Woodruff key for clutch gear
7 - Needle cage (3rd gear)
8 - 3rd gear
9 - Synchronizer stop ring (3rd gear)
10 - Clutch gear (3rd and 4th speeds)
11 - Synchronizer stop ring (4th gear)
12 - Needle bearing inner race (4th gear)
13 - Needle cage (4th gear)
14 - 4th gear
15 - Thrust washer (4th gear)

FIG. 145

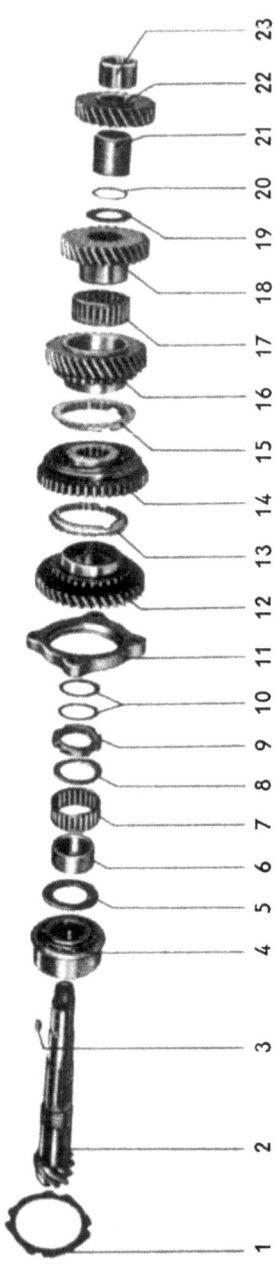

1 - Shim
2 - Drive Pinion
3 - Woodruff key for 4th gear
4 - Ball bearing
5 - Thrust washer for 1st gear
6 - Needle bearing inner race (1st gear)
7 - Needle cage (1st gear)
8 - Thrust washer for needle bearing (1st gear)
9 - Round nut
10 - Shims, end play 1st gear
11 - Ball bearing retainer
12 - 1st gear
13 - Synchronizer stop ring (1st gear)
14 - Clutch gear for 1st and 2nd gears, and reverse gear
15 - Synchronizer stop ring (2nd gear)
16 - 2nd gear
17 - Needle cage (2nd gear)
18 - 3rd gear
19 - Concave washer
20 - Shims for concave washer.
21 - Spacer sleeve
22 - 4th gear
23 - Inner race, needle bearing in gear carrier

FIG. 146

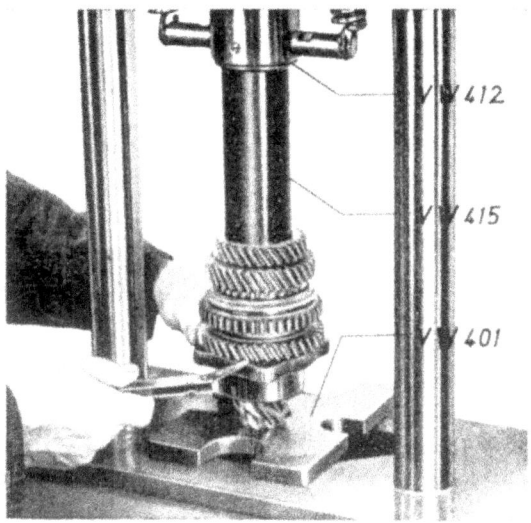

FIG. 147

rear axle tubes and shafts, gearshift housing, differential and rear main drive shaft. Remove transmission gear carrier, then remove reverse drive gear and reverse gear shaft. Remove main drive shaft and drive pinion from gear carrier, and lastly remove selector shafts and detent balls and springs.

The gearshift housing at the front of the transmission is easily unbolted. When assembling, its bolts are torqued to 14 ft. lb. The gear carrier stud nuts are unscrewed to remove the gear carrier, and are retightened to 14 ft. lb. The final drive cover stud nuts are removed to take off the final drive cover, (Fig. 141), and upon retightening are torqued to 22 ft. lb. The final drive cover, (Fig. 142), requires a puller to remove.

When pressing out differential, note the thickness and arrangement of the differential shims to facilitate reassembly. After loosening reverse gear retaining ring, slide reverse gear rearward and unscrew rear section of main driveshaft, (Fig. 143). Reverse gear can now be removed. After removing screws of pinion bearing retainer, transmission is pushed forward out of case with special tool, (Fig 144). Note thickness of pinion shims to facilitate assembly. Fig. 145, shows exploded view of main drive shaft or input shaft and Fig. 146, shows drive pinion shaft or output shaft. The disassembly of both of these require special tools such as hydraulic press and fixtures, (Fig. 147).

The differential, (Fig. 148), is similar in action to that of other cars, but requires many special tools to set up. The biggest difference in construction being the unique universal joints which

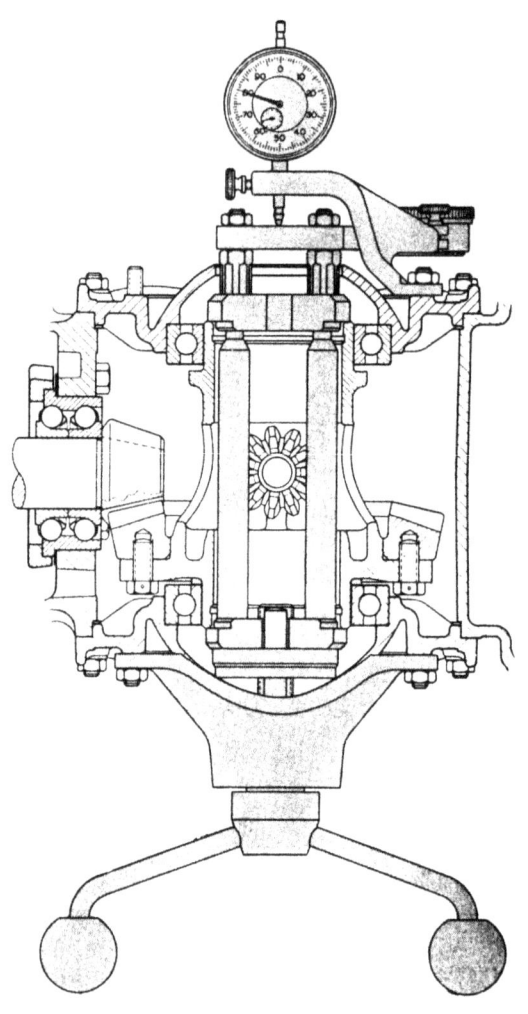

FIG. 148

are necessary because of the swinging rear axles. They consist of: the flattened inner ends of the rear axle shafts, (Fig. 149), and the hollowed out side gears which nestle the fulcrum plates against the axle flats. For minimum wear and noise the pinion is adjusted fore and aft by means of shims and the ring gear is adjustable sideways also by means of shims, (Fig. 150).

Special tools are required to make these adjustments.

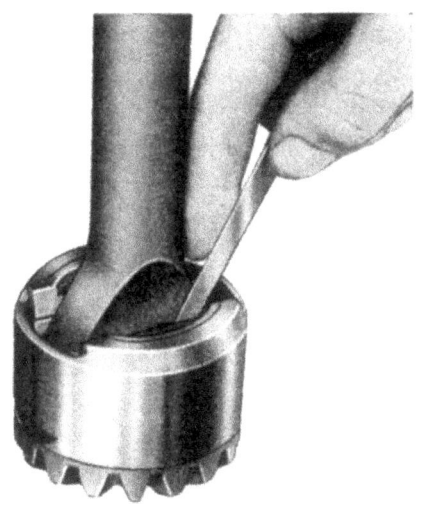

FIG. 149

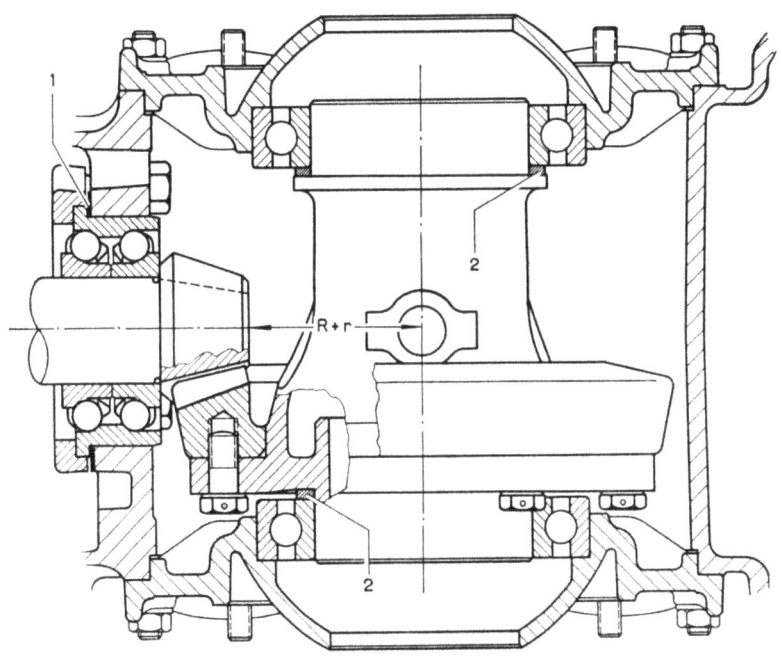

1 - Pinion shims
2 - Shims S_1 (ring gear side) and S_2 for the differential

FIG. 150

Pre-1960 Transmission

In the older transmission, that is, the type with only 2nd, 3rd and 4th gears synchronized, the case is made in halves which are machined together. The two halves are assembled without gaskets, only a thin coating of sealing compound.

Fig. 151 shows the transmission with one half removed. When taking the transmission apart, the arrangement of differential bearing shims should be carefully noted. These shims determine the correct amount of preloading of the differential ball bearings. (When a new case is being fitted, it has to be carefully measured to determine amount of shims for correct preloading.)

Figs. 152 and 153 show the components of the main shaft and the pinion shaft. All parts should be carefully checked against the factory wear tolerances. Worn parts should be replaced. Also carefully inspect synchronizing units. Worn synchronizer rings should be replaced at this stage. Prematurely worn synchronizer rings usually point to an incorrectly adjusted or dragging clutch.

The top shaft is supported in two ball bearings and the lower shaft is carried in a double row angular contact bearing and a roller bearing near the pinion end.

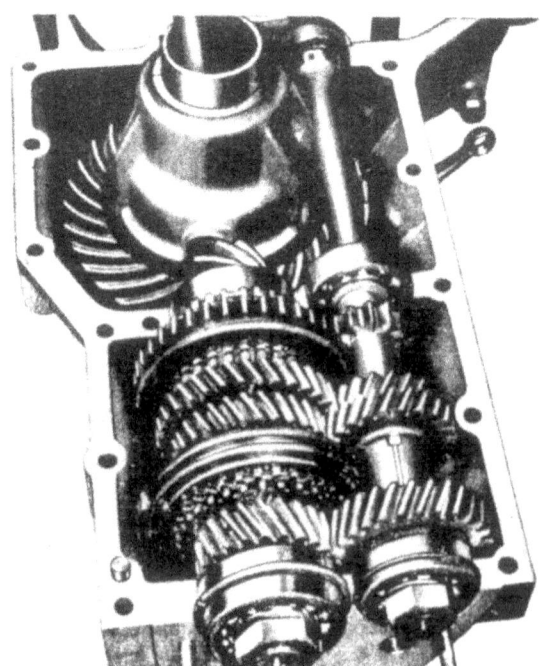

FIG. 151

TRANMISSION-REAR AXLE
Early Model

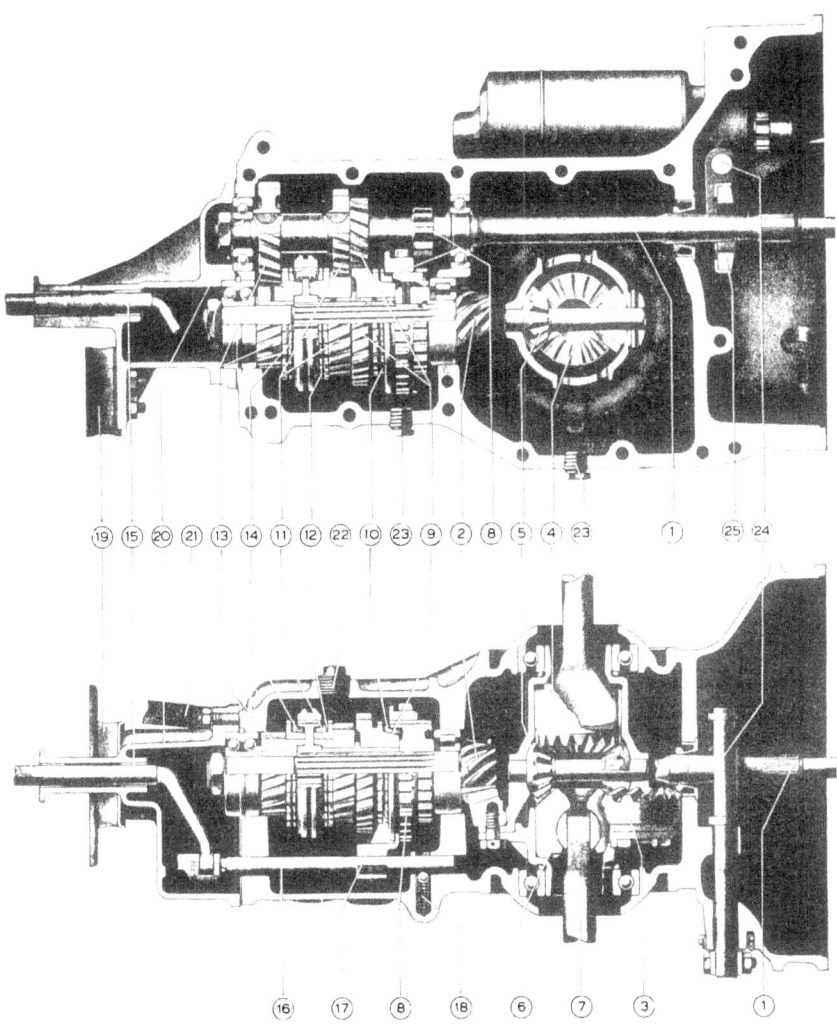

1-Main drive shaft
2-Drive pinion
3-Ring gear
4-Differential side gear
5-Differential pinion
6-Fulcrum plate
7-Axle shaft
8-1st gear train
9-2nd gear train
10-Synchronizer ring
11-3d gear train
12-Synchronizer ring
13-4th gear train
14-Synchronizer ring
15-Shifting rod
16-Shift rail
17-Selector fork
18-Detent spring and ball
19-Flexible mounting
20-Shift housing
21-Ground strap
22-Oil filler plug
23-Oil drain plug
24-Clutch release bearing shaft
25-Release bearing

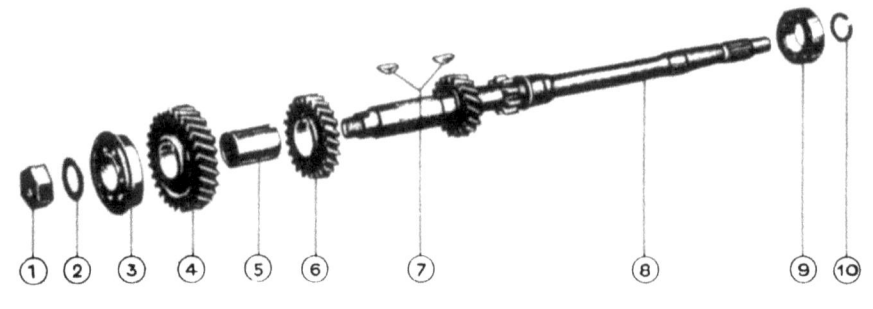

1-Hex. nut
2-Lock washer
3-Ball bearing
4-4th gear
5-Spacer
6-3d gear
7-Keys
8-Main shaft
9-Ball bearing
10-Retaining ring

FIG. 152

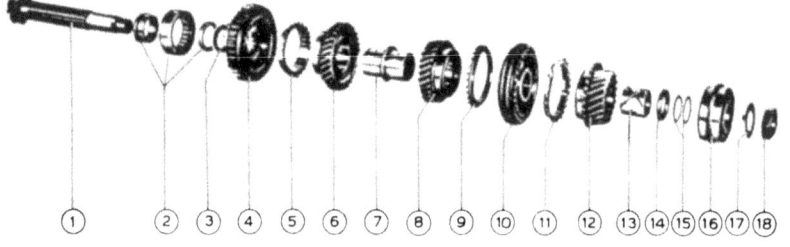

1-Pinion shaft
2-Roller bearing
3-Shim
4-Synchro sleeve and 1st gear
5-Synchronizer ring (2nd gear)
6-2nd gear
7-Bushing
8-3d gear
9-Synchronizer ring (3d gear)
10-Syn. hub and sleeve (3d and 4th gears)
11-Synchronizer ring (4th gear)
12-4th gear
13-Bush
14-Friction washer
15-Shims
16-Double row ball bearing
17-Lock plate
18-Nut

FIG. 153

Fig. 154 shows the layout of the front bearings. These bearings are located laterally by the outer ring in the groove on one end and by the gearshift housing at the other end. The outer races of above mentioned bearings are installed with a pre-load of .0008-.0043 in. through the expedient of selective fitting of paper gaskets between transmission case and gearshift housing (Fig. 154). In the case of the lower ball bearing, distance C (which includes the gasket) should be slightly smaller (by .008-.0043 in.) than distance D (the amount outer race of bearing protrudes). Both bearing outer races are mounted at the same pre-load and before measuring distances D and E as indicated, the shafts should be tapped backwards with a soft hammer. Measuring should be done with an accurate depth micrometer (Fig. 155).

Fig. 156 shows interlocking system of the selector shafts. This arrangement prevents accidental engagement of two pairs of gears at the same time. When disassembling shift rails, prevent detent balls jumping out by covering the holes.

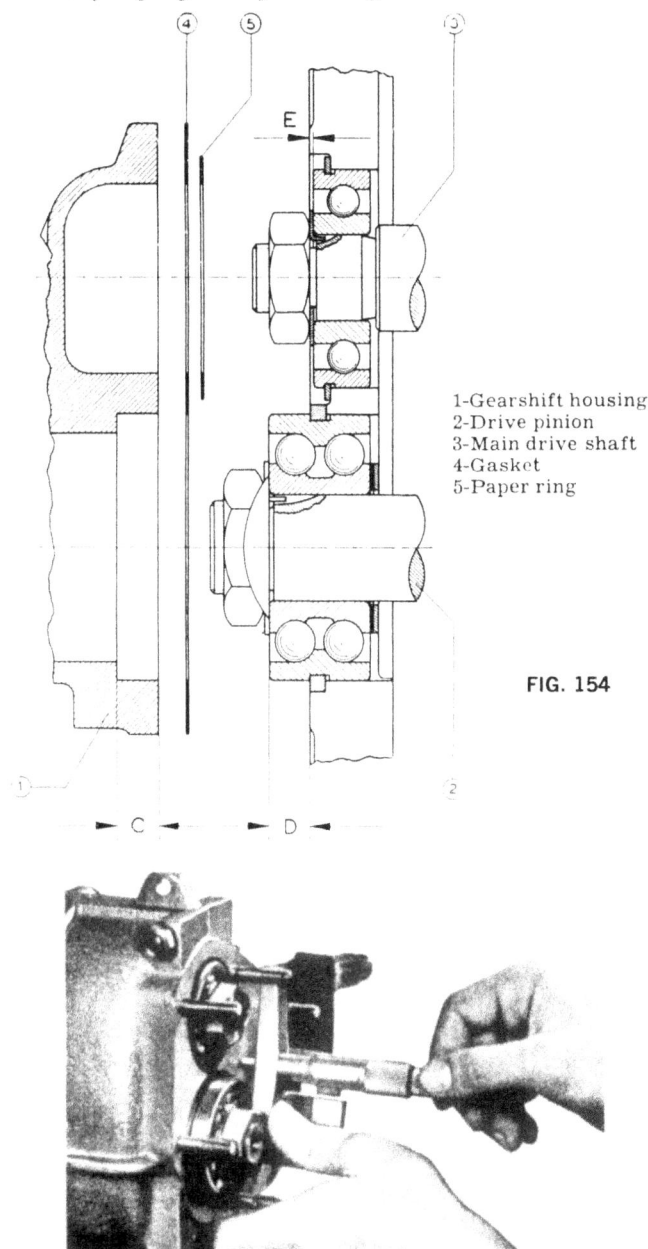

1-Gearshift housing
2-Drive pinion
3-Main drive shaft
4-Gasket
5-Paper ring

FIG. 154

FIG. 155

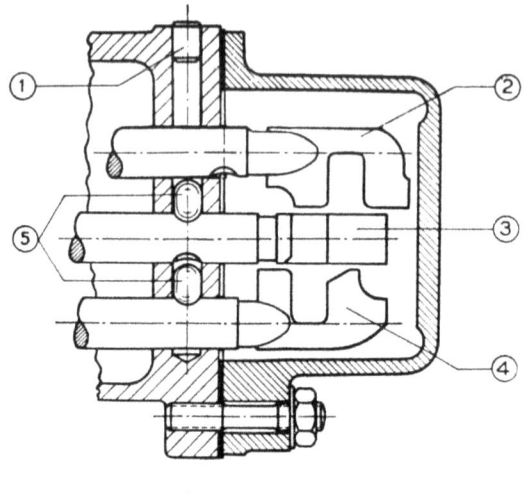

1-Plug
2-Shift rail (reverse)
3-Shift rail (1st and 2nd)
4-Shift rail (3d and 4th)
5-Interlock plungers

FIG. 156

Servicing Rear Wheel Outer Bearing Or Seal

With the vehicle raised and the complete wheel brake assembly (including cylinder) removed, take out the cover retaining screws and remove the cover and oil seal. Remove the brake back plate and take off the outer spacer as well as the gasket and washer between the spacer and ball bearing. Use an extractor such as VW 241 with thrust pad VW 202k to remove the bearing, then take out the inner spacer.

Install by reversing the procedure, first checking the ball bearing, outer spacer and oil seal for rust, wear, unevenness, scores or cracks, and renewing as necessary. Replace the two gaskets, then coat the spacer and oil seal with oil. Be sure the components are absolutely clean, then press the oil seal into the cover to a depth of .185 to .197 in. with tool VW 230 or equivalent. Be sure the oil drain passage is clean and the oil deflector has been placed in the cover prior to installing the oil seal. Install the cover on the wheel so the oil drain passage points downwards as shown by arrow. If renewing cover screws, use only quality specification "10K", then torque screws to 40—43 ft. lb. Use procedure in the brake section to complete the repair. Check brake drum splines for wear; if worn, replace drum.

Servicing Reduction Gear

Remove reduction gear by first removing case screws, then tapping off cover and gasket. Remove the snap ring from the rear axle shaft (see exploded view), then extract outer ball bearing from the rear axle shaft with a puller such as Special Tools VW 202 and VW 202a. Remove reduction drive gear and driven gear and shaft. Use Special Tools VW 241a and VW 202k or equivalent to extract inner ball bearing from rear axle shaft. Use Special Tools VW 421a and VW 435 or equivalent to extract the inner ball bearing from reduction gear shaft. If the ball bear-

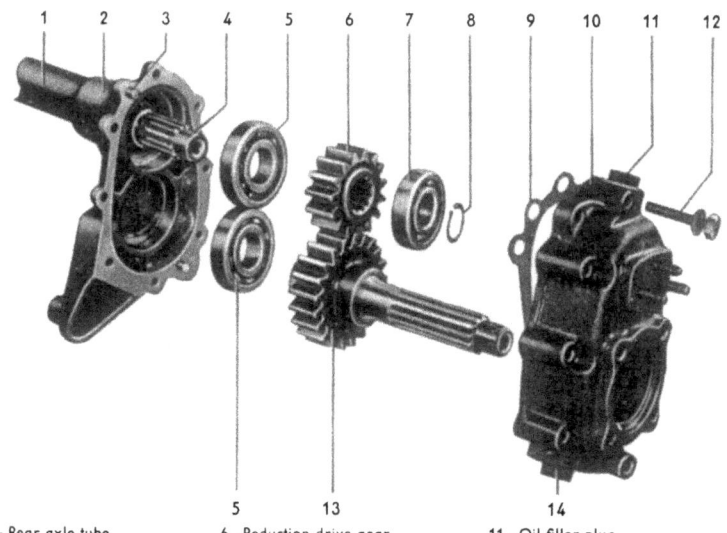

1 - Rear axle tube
2 - Reduction gear case
3 - Dowel pin
4 - Rear axle shaft
5 - Ball bearing
6 - Reduction drive gear
7 - Ball bearing
8 - Snap ring
9 - Gasket
10 - Reduction gear case cover
11 - Oil filler plug
12 - Reduction gear case screw
13 - Reduction driven gear and shaft
14 - Oil drain plug

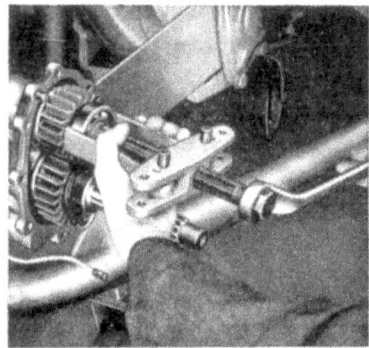

ing is too tight on the shaft, use Special Tools VW 241a in conjunction with VW 202k and VW 435 (or equivalent).

The reduction gear is installed after checking all gears and bearings for wear, damage and cleanliness, and removing old gasketing from the reduction gear case jointing faces. Renew parts as necessary. Use the drift Special Tool VW 240a or equivalent to drive the inner ball bearing of the rear axle shaft into the reduction gear case. Use the sleeve Special Tool 244b or equivalent to drive the outer ball bearing of the rear axle shaft into position. Use the installing device VW 690 or equivalent to slide into place until the snap ring can be located. Check the tension of the snap ring, replacing if necessary.

Place a new gasket between the reduction gear case jointing faces, then securely tighten the case screws. After assembling the rear wheel bearings and brakes, using instructions found elsewhere, fill the reduction gear cases and check the transmission oil level as described in "Lubrication".

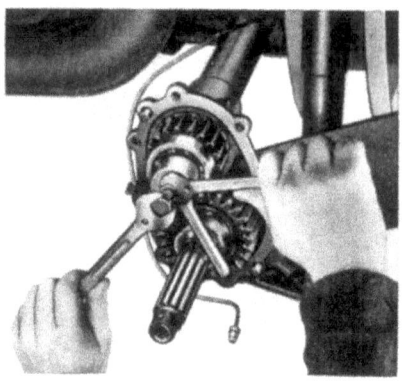

Servicing Gearshift Lever (Early and Later Models)

Remove cab floor mat, then remove screws attaching the gearshift lever ball housing to the floor. Remove the gearshift lever, ball housing, rubber boot and spring as a single unit. Turn the spring to remove it from the ball and pin. Remove the stop plate, then clean off all components and check the rubber boot for cracks. Check the lever collar, stop plate, and ball socket in the shifting rod for wear. Check that the locating pin on the lever is secure, and the spring in the steel ball still has tension. Replace any parts as necessary. Reverse the procedure to install, making sure that the turned-up edge of the stop plate is on the right hand side (looking at it in the direction of travel). Grease all moving parts (including shifting rod guide) with universal grease, then fit the lever ball housing so that the lever is vertical and the locating pin engages in the slot provided in the ball socket. The stop plate should seat in the hollow flange of the ball housing.

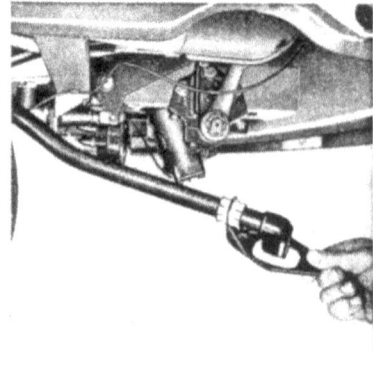

After tightening mounting bolts, check the position of the gearshift lever by engaging the gears. Correct if necessary.

Servicing Front Gearshift Rod

With vehicle raised and handbrake released, remove the gearshift lever and cover plate under the cab. Remove the lock wire at the front shift rod coupling and remove the front screw, then detach the handbrake cables from the handbrake lever and pull the shift rod and guide toward the front. Slip the guide off the shift rod. Install by reversing the procedure, first checking the shift rod guide and rod for wear and alignment, and replacing parts as necessary. Lubricate the shift rod bearing points and guide with universal grease, then connect the shift rod coupling and secure with wire. Prior to operating vehicle, adjust handbrake and check handbrake operation.

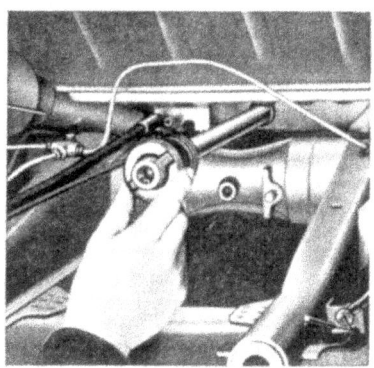
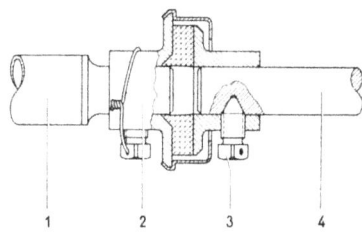

1 - Shifting rod
2 - Coupling
3 - Screw
4 - Transmission shift rod

Servicing Rear Gearshift Rod

With vehicle raised, transmission and engine removed, and lock wire of the front shift rod coupling removed, remove the rear screw from the coupling. Pull the shift rod towards the rear and remove the front rubber boot from the protection sleeve. Take out the rear shift rod coupling, then remove the rear rubber boot and bushes from the shift rod. Install by reversing the procedure, checking the bushes, rubber boots and shift rod for wear and distortion. The recesses for the coupling screws must be in line to avoid difficulty with gear shifting. Lubricate bushes with universal grease after sliding onto shift rod, then install the shift rod and push the rubber boots onto the protection sleeve. Fit the shift rod coupling, secure with wire, bleed and adjust brake system, then road-test the vehicle.

Rear Suspension

The Volkswagen's rear suspension consists of two solid, separate torsion bars controlling two trailing arms, one of each to each rear wheel. Each trailing arm (or torsion arm) trails downward and rearward to the rear wheel from the torsion bar housing on the chassis. As the rear wheels on the swing axles move up and down, they also move forward, toeing in slightly. The trailing arms are flat spring plates that flex slightly to allow for this movement.

Torsion Bar Adjustment

The trailing arms are adjustable on their torsion bars, primarily to allow for sag after a number of years. To remove torsion bar, take trailing arm from rear axle so wheel can be swung down and back out of the way. Remove screws that attach spring plate hub cover and take off cover, (Fig. 178). Withdraw outer rubber bushing from the spring plate hub, then release the tension on the spring plate with a tire iron, (Fig. 179). Pull off the spring plate and the inner rubber bushing from the spring plate hub, then remove the torsion bar from the frame cross tube, (Fig. 180). If the torsion bar is broken, pull the remaining piece out with a tube which has been opened up to a conical shape or remove the other torsion bar and push piece out with a long rod.

When installing, note the following. Grease both sets of splines and use powdered graphite on rubber cushions to prevent squeaking. Install cushion so that wider part is upward, (Fig. 181). Use jack under spring plate to twist torsion bar to

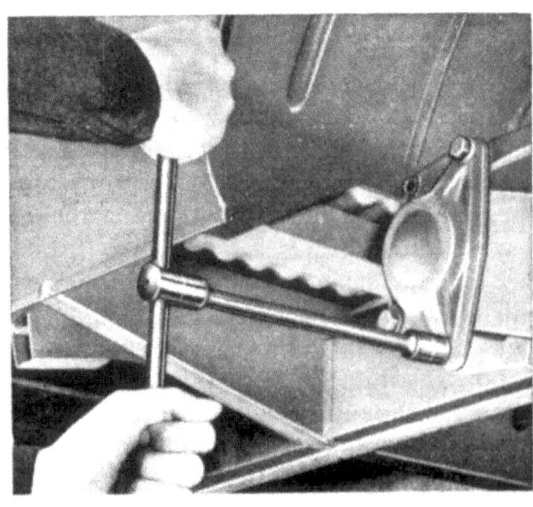

FIG. 178

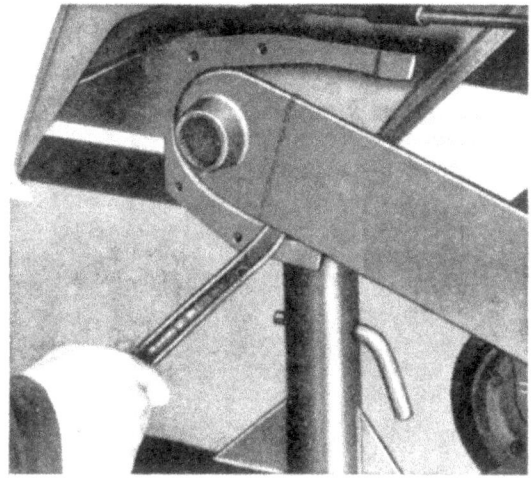

FIG. 179

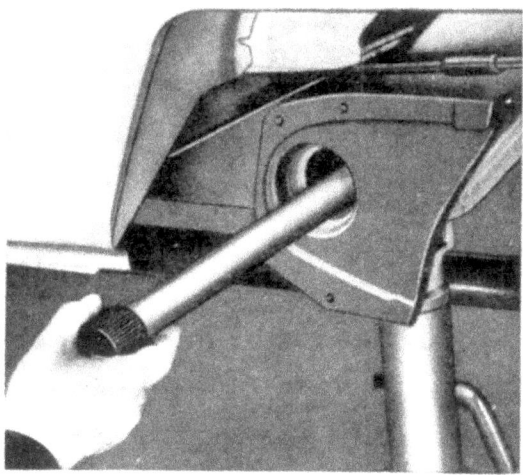

FIG. 180

the point where it can be pushed back in over the lower stop, (Fig. 182).

Using a tool such as that shown, press in the spring plate and inner rubber bushing. Be sure to support the thrust screw on the complete spring plate hub to prevent distortion, (Fig. 183). It is advisable to first screw in two tapered guide pins of local manufacture (about 2" long and installed diagonally), to guide in the hub cover, then tighten two of the cover bolts in the other diagonally placed holes. Remove the guide pins and replace the remaining two bolts, tightening all bolts to 22 ft. lb.

Before measuring any suspension angles, check that the car is level, using Special Tool VW 245a (protractor) on one of the

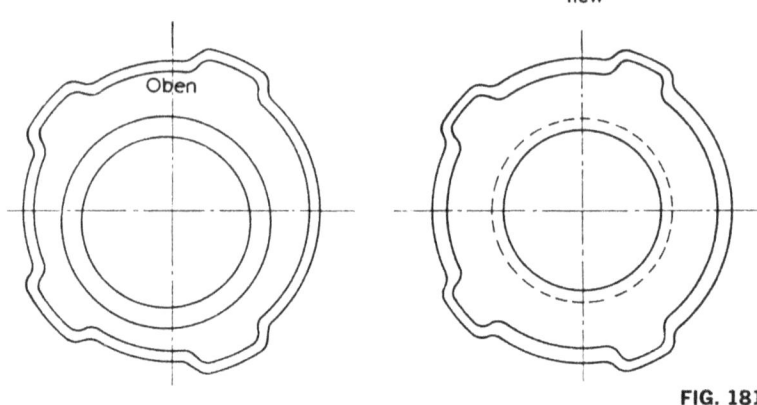

FIG. 181

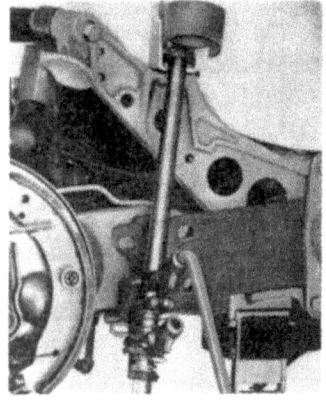

FIG. 182

FIG. 183

frame side members, (Fig. 184.)

Spring plates are adjusted by measuring their angle of inclination with protractor VW 245a, (Fig. 185). The rear axle must be separated from the spring plate and supported separately, with the spring plate in an unloaded condition and hanging freely. The angle should be 20° ± 30′. The inner ends of the torsion bars have 44 splines and the outer ends have 48 splines to allow a Vernier effect for minute adjustments. If the inner end of the bar is turned by one spline, the adjustment is altered by 8° 10′. If the spring plate is displaced by one spline, the adjustment is altered by 7° 30′, thus allowing a minimum spring plate inclination adjustment of 0° 40′ when splines are moved in opposite directions.

 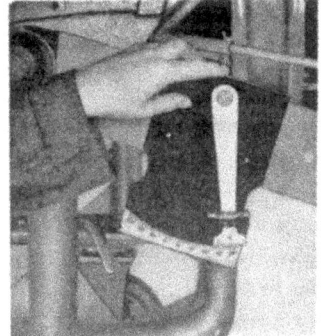

FIG. 184   FIG. 185

Since the inner and outer ends of each torsion bar have a different number of splines, there is no danger of replacing them incorrectly. However, the torsion bars are prestressed and the left torsion bar should not be placed on the right side of the vehicle and vice versa. They are marked R and L.

Rear Wheel Camber and Toe-Out

With the spring plate correctly adjusted, the camber of the rear wheels should be 4° 30′ ± 30′, vehicle unloaded, with a maximum difference between rear wheels of 20′ camber. The camber is measured by rolling the car until two of the wheel bolts are vertically aligned and then use the protractor on two bolt heads, (Fig. 186). This allowance should be adhered to since it affects the handling of the vehicle.

If, when bolting the rear axle back onto the spring plate, the mounting holes are aligned with a pilot, the rear wheels should be correctly repositioned for toe-out. Correct toe-out of the rear wheels is —20′ ± 15′, with a maximum of 10′ toe-out or toe-in for either one wheel.

FIG. 186

Double Joint Rear Axle

To improve the handling qualities in windy weather and help to smooth out the ride on rough roads for all Transporter models, a new rear suspension design has been incorporated. This uses diagonal trailing arms in addition to the regular trailing arms, with double-joint rear axles connecting the suspension to the transmission/differential.

This whole combination works as follows: The individually-mounted rear wheels no longer swing in an arc as they go over a bump or into a chuckhole, with the differential as the center. Now the wheels are set at a slightly negative camber, which is best for good roadholding, and they go slightly more negative under load or cornering weight transfer. Toe-in also increases as the wheel moves upward. The lateral forces are thus taken up by the diagonal trailing links and transferred directly to the frame (they are pivoted inboard at the torsion bar housing and trail outward and rearward, connecting to the rear axles just inside the wheels. In all, the vehicle loading thus does not effect much change in rear wheel track, camber, and toe-in.

The longitudinal forces are still transferred to the cross tube by the trailing links. The drive shafts, which had to absorb the lateral movements previously, are now equipped with two universal joints, one on the transmission case and the other at the wheel. The universal joints are of the constant velocity sliding type, and up to an inch of axial play can be absorbed. The shafts are simply connected to flanges at both ends, simplifying the whole suspension and transmission service procedure. The rear

FIG. D-2

bearings are permanently lubricated (as are the constant velocity universal joints), so no longer share a common oil supply with the transmission (Fig. D-2).

The power flow is from the flange on the differential (naturally the differential has been redesigned) to the outer housing of the joint, from here via balls to the joint hub and then via splines to the drive shaft. At the other end of the drive shaft the power is transferred in the reverse order to the rear wheel shafts. All movements taking place between joint flange on differential and wheel shafts are compensated for by the constant velocity joints. The grooves in which the balls move inside the joint are arranged in such a way that, together with the torque effective on the shaft, all variations in length are taken up by the joints and the shaft remains in the correct position (Fig. D-3).

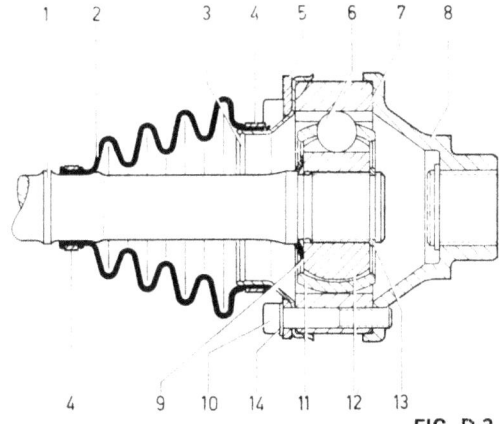

1 - Drive shaft
2 - Rubber seal
3 - Cap
4 - Hose clip
5 - Plate
6 - Ball
7 - Outer housing
8 - Flange
9 - Dished washer
10 - Socket head screw
11 - Ball cage
12 - Joint hub
13 - Circlip
14 - Lock washer

FIG. D-3

Rear Suspension

Depending on service to be performed, all or part of this procedure may be used. Before raising car, be sure to remove the hub cap, loosen the wheel bolts, then remove the cotter pin from the slotted nut on the end of the shaft and loosen the nut. This last item is important since an accident could be caused if nut were to be loosened or tightened while the car is raised. Remove rear axles by unscrewing socket head screws at both ends, then tilt shafts downward and remove. Prevent entry of dirt by covering velocity joints with plastic caps or a substitute (Fig. D-6). Screw slotted nut off end of shaft and pull brake drum off, then detach brake line and handbrake cable. Remove screws holding bearing cover and backplate and take cover and backplate off. Use a chisel to mark both the top and bottom position of the

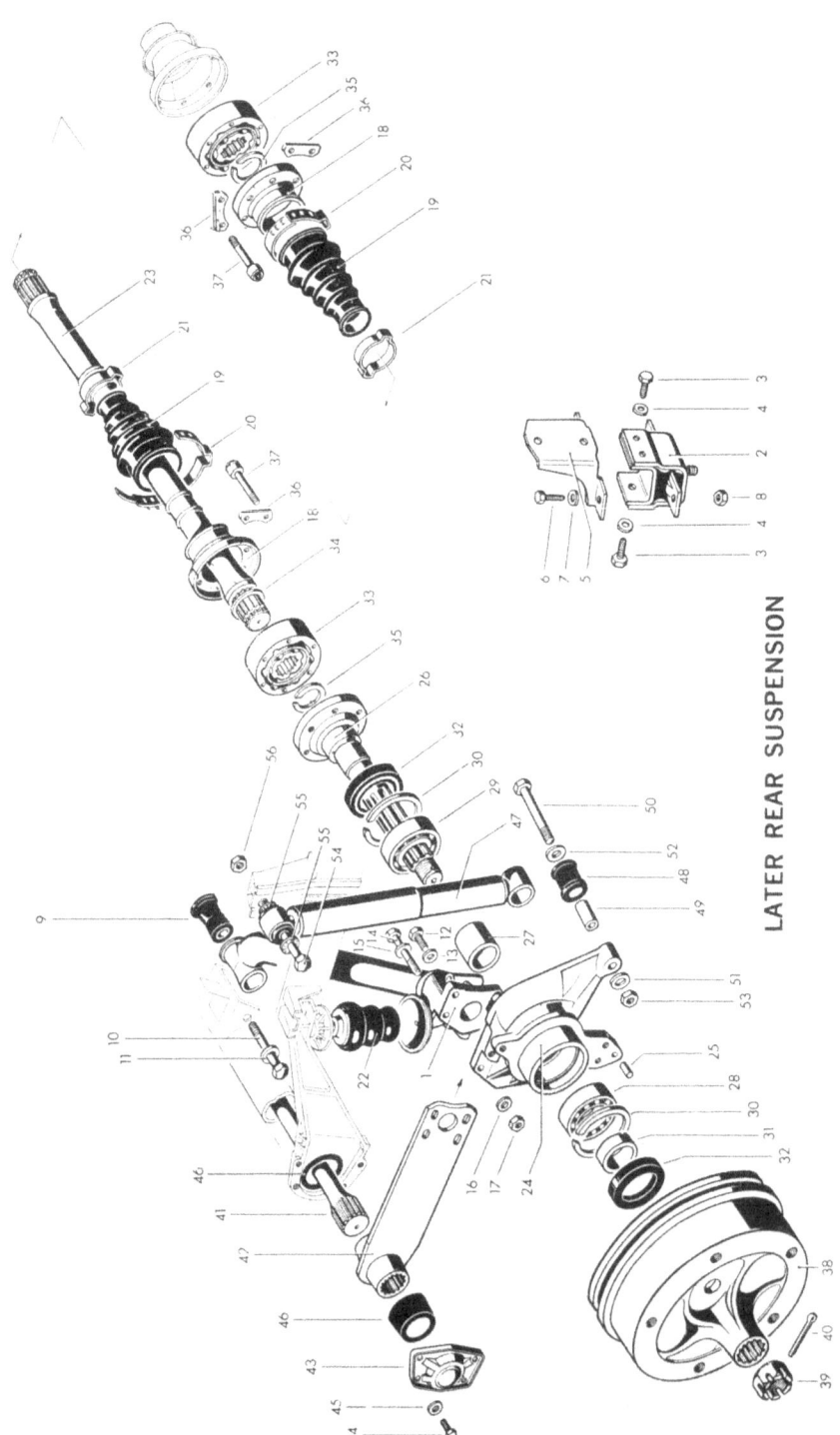

spring plate and the diagonal arm (Fig. D-7).

Remove the lower shock absorber screw, then the screws and nut securing the diagonal arm on the spring plate. Remove the socket head screw holding the diagonal arm to the bracket, then take off the arm (Fig. D-8). Lift spring plate off the lower stop with a tire iron (Fig. D-9), then remove spring plate hub cover, rubber bushing, and release tension on the spring plate with a tire iron. Remove spring plate and inner rubber bushing, then pull the torsion bar out. If the torsion bar is broken, pull the remaining piece out with a metal tube which has been opened up to a conical shape or remove the other torsion bar and push piece out with a long rod.

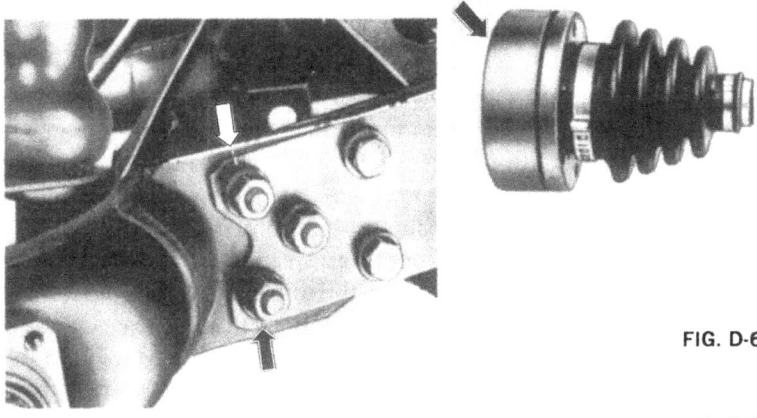

FIG. D-6

FIG. D-8

FIG. D-7

FIG. D-9 **FIG. D-10**

To service the rear wheel bearings, clamp the diagonal arm in a vise and knock out the shaft with a rubber mallet. Remove the spacer ring, the roller bearing inner ring, then the spacer. Knock out the outer ring with a drift and lever the inner oil seal out with a tire iron (Fig. D-10). Remove the circlip (Fig. D-11) and pull the bearing out, then press the bonded rubber bush out of the arm (Fig. D-12). Press the oil seal out of the cover. Before beginning assembly, inspect the bearings, oil seals, circlip, rubber bush, spacer rings, sleeve and rear wheel shaft for wear and damage. Install bearing by first pressing in the bonded rubber bush (Fig. D-13), then driving the ball bearing in as far as it will go and install circlip (Fig. D-14). Drive the oil seal in, then pack the bearing housing in the arm with so much lithium grease (about 60 grams), that the spacer sleeve can just be pushed in. Drive in the roller bearing outer ring, then the shaft together with the inner spacer ring. Drive in the inner ring of the roller bearing,

FIG. D-11 **FIG. D-12**

FIG. D-13 **FIG. D-14**

being sure to support the wheel shaft flange when knocking the ring in. Press the oil seal into the cover. Then grease the outer seal lightly with lithium grease and install it.

The rear suspension is installed after checking the torsion bar, rubber bush, spring plate, and diagonal arm for wear and damage. If the torsion bar should have its protective paint damaged, touch up the spot with paint to avoid fatigue fractures due to corrosion. If the bar has to be replaced, be sure the new bar is stressed in the correct direction. The left bar has an "L" stamped on the end face, the right bar has an "R", and they must not be interchanged. Grease the torsion bar splines before inserting, then coat the inner rubber mounting bush with talcum powder. DO NOT substitute anything else for talcum powder as this substance helps hold the rubber bush stationary (it will twist internally). The rubber bush must be mounted so the wording "Oben" is at the top (Fig. D-15). Install spring plate and outer bush. Adjust torsion bar as outlined previously, however, the camber setting is now $+10'$ to $1°$, vehicle unloaded, with a maximum difference between left and right wheels of 20' camber. The toe-in angle for both is 10 to 5', with a maximum toe-out of 10' and a maximum toe-in of 5' for either wheel.

Continue assembling parts by installing spring plate bearing cover with two diagonally placed screws, using longer screws if necessary. Place the flange of the diagonal arm between the spring plate leaves (Fig. D-16). Lift the spring plate up to the lower stop using the car's jack, then tighten the cover securing screws (Fig. D-17). Install the remaining cover securing screws, then replace the two long screws (if used) with the proper screws, finally torquing all screws to specifications. Attach the diagonal arm to the frame with the socket head screw and tighten the screw. Lock the socket head screw into place by peening the bracket collar into one of the grooves in the screw with a dull chisel.

Align the chisel marks on the spring plate and diagonal arm,

FIG. D-15

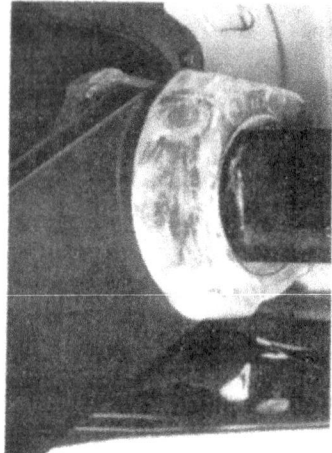

FIG. D-16

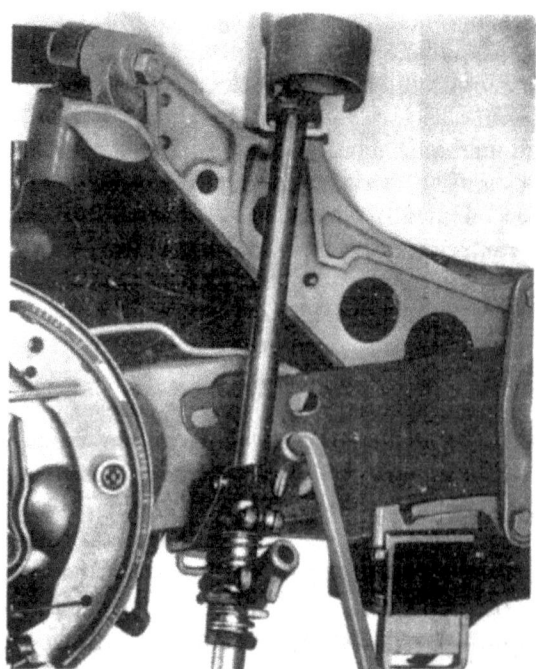

FIG. D-17

or if either part has been renewed, check the position of the rear wheels on an axle alignment stand after assembly is complete, correcting as necessary. In this case, the spring plate should be evenly centered on the diagonal arm during assembly. Torque nuts and screws to 87 ft. lb. after either procedure.

Install the backplate and bearing cover on the diagonal arm and torque the screws to 36. ft. lb., then connect the brake line and the handbrake cable. Grease the joints lightly and install the drive shaft (remove cover), making sure the flanges are perfectly clean and grease-free. Use new lock washers and torque to specifications. Install the brake drum and screw on the slotted nut (do not tighten). Replace the wheel, LOWER the car to the ground, then torque the slotted nut to 217 ft. lb. and fit the cotter pin. If the cotter pin cannot be inserted, turn on to the next hole. Bleed the braking system. Check the rear axle nuts for tightness after the first 300 miles.

Removing Constant Velocity Joints

Remove socket head screws and tilt drive shaft down to remove it from vehicle, then loosen the dust seal clips and slide back dust seal. Remove circlip from the ball hub, then use a drift to drive off cap.

Note: Do not tilt the ball hub more than 20° in the joint outer part with the protective cap removed since balls can fall out.

Slide the outer part with balls on to the ball hub, then press the drive shaft out of the ball hub, being sure to support the hub. Remove the dished washer.

Disassembling Constant Velocity Joints

Press the ball hub and ball cage out of the outer ring, then press the balls out of cage. If disassembling more than one joint at a time, be sure not to mix parts since balls, and ball hub along with outer ring, are matched sets. Finally, tip the ball hub out of the ball cage via the grooves.

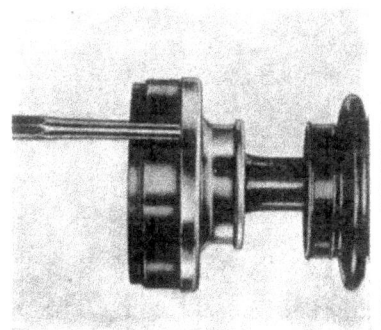

Assembling Constant Velocity Joints

Check the outer ring, ball hub, ball cage and balls for wear and radial play in the joints. Excessive play will cause load-change noise, and joint should be replaced. Clean components and insert ball hub along both grooves in the ball cage (in any position), then press balls into cage.

Insert ball hub into outer ring. Hub and outer ring are a matched pair. Make sure that the chamfer on the inside diameter of the ball hub (splines) points to the contact shoulder on the drive shaft. Also make sure that the chamfer on the hub points to the larger diameter of the outer ring. Place hub-ball-cage assembly upright into the joint piece, making sure that a wide ball groove **a** (see illustration) on the joint piece is always together with a narrow ball groove **b** on one side after pivoting the hub into position in the outer ring.

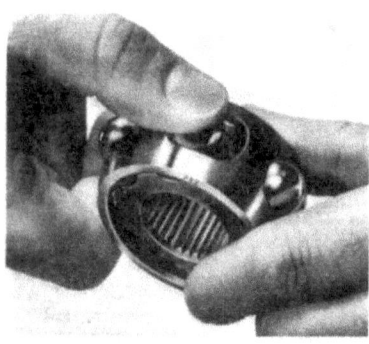 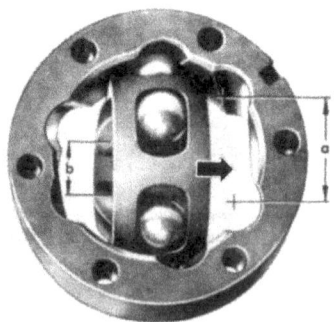

As the ball hub with cage and balls is pivoted into the outer ring, be sure the hub is pivoted out of the cage (arrows) until the balls fit into the clearance caused by the races. Press the cage firmly (arrow) until the hub snaps completely into position. Finally, check the joint for proper operation by making sure the ball hub can be moved back and forth by hand over the complete range of movement.

Installing Constant Velocity Joints

Inspect dished washer, protection cap, constant velocity joint, rubber boot, and drive shaft for damage or wear, replacing as necessary. Place new hose clips on the drive shaft, and if possible, use a sleeve over the splines to slip the rubber boot onto the shaft. Place the cap into position (but do not connect the rubber boot yet) and place the dished washer on the shaft. Use a press (as illustrated) to press the joint onto the drive shaft,

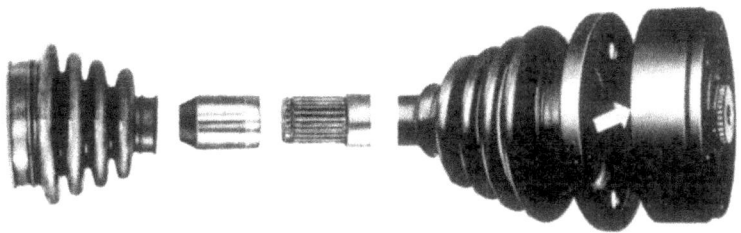

making sure the large diameter of the outer part of the joint points to the cap (see arrow in illustration). Be sure to place drive shaft on the lateral support of the press. Press a new circlip into the groove, then squeeze the circlip all around with water-pump pliers until the circlip is completely into the groove. Tap cap into place with a hammer.

To lubricate the joint, use lithium grease with MoS^2 additive. Place 60 grams between the outer part of the joint, the protective cap, and the rubber boot. Press another 30 grams from the front into the open joint, but make certain that the contact surfaces between the joint, cap and rubber boot are free of grease.

Fit the rubber boot into position, fit the hose clips and tighten, then squeeze the rubber boot by hand to force grease into the velocity joint from behind. Finally, place the drive shaft into position in the vehicle, making sure flanges are clean. Install socket head screws with new lock washers and tighten to the torque shown in the chart.

Modifications To Transmission

Along with the redesign of the rear suspension, the transmission was changed to do away with the need for reduction gears on the outer axles and accommodate the double-joint axles. Gear ratios are: First 3.80:1, Second 2.06:1; Third 1.26:1; Fourth 0.82:1; and Reverse 3.61:1. The ring and pinion gear ratio of the differential is 5.375:1.

On the 1968 transmission, three clamping plates were used to hold the double taper roller bearing for the drive pinion. On the 1969 transmission (Chassis No. 219 000 001) a retaining ring is

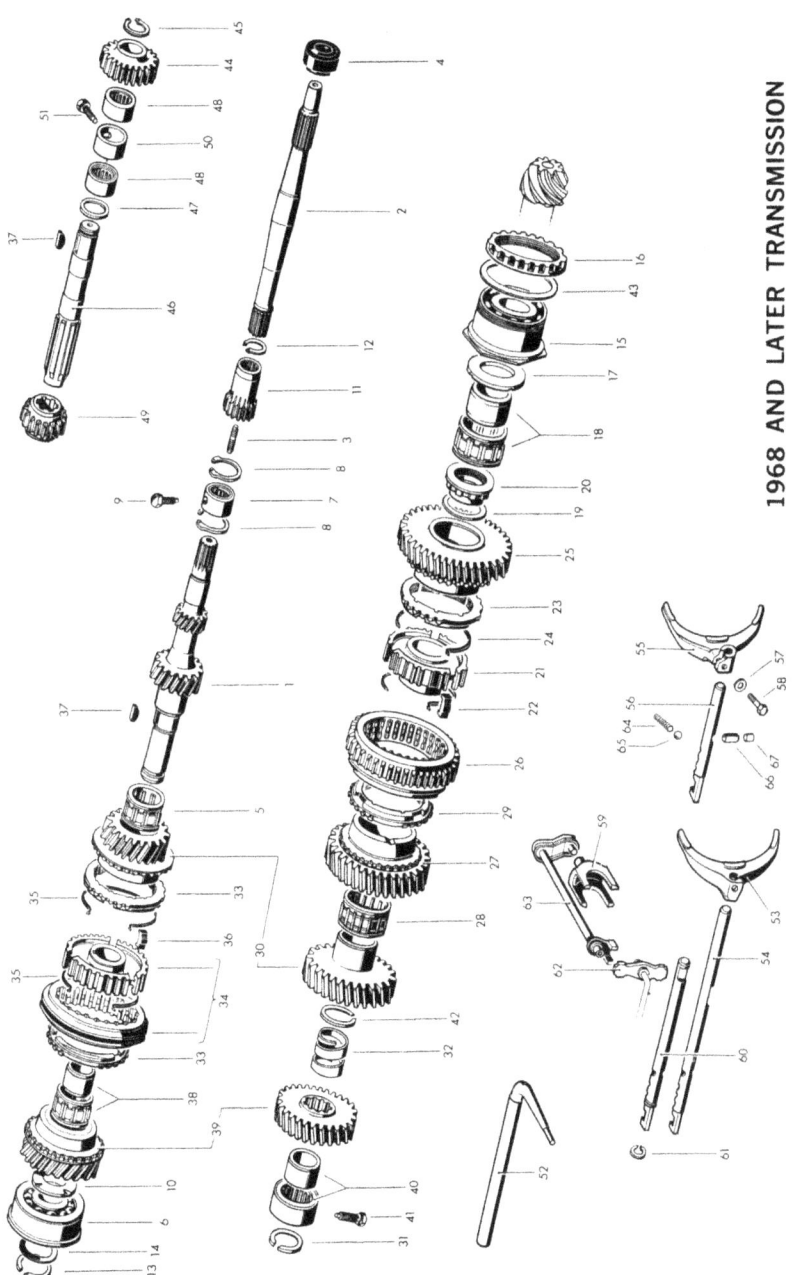

used in the place of the clamping plates. The bearing outer ring has been provided with flats which rest against appropriately shaped flats in the housing and prevent the bearing from turning when the retaining ring is being loosened or tightened. The shim has been relocated on the other side of the housing wall between the bearing shoulder and the housing.

Differential

Along with the double-joint axle, the differential has been redesigned for 1968 and later vehicles. The inner end of the axle no longer pivots within the transmission case, but is bolted directly to the differential flange through a constant velocity universal joint. If differential service needs to be performed, this very exacting procedure should be left up to the skilled mechanics of an authorized Volkswagen dealer. However, we shall run through the service procedure.

On the early 1968 transmission, the differential bearing preload and backlash between the ring gear and the pinion is adjusted with shims. Bolt-on final drive covers are used on the 1968 transmission. Beginning with the later 1968 transmission,

EARLY 1968 DIFFERENTIAL

No.	Designation	Qty.	Note when removing	Note when installing
1	Differential	1	see disassembling and assembling differential	
2	Cover/final drive	2	pull out with VW 771/22	
3	Outer ring/taper roller bearing	2	press out with 401, 459/1, 408	press in with 401, 459/1, 473, 408
4	Oil seal	2	press out with 401, 459/1, 473, 408	in with 401, 442, 408
5	O ring	2		fit new
6	Shim S 1	×	note thickness	measure
7	Shim S 2	×	note thickness	measure
8	Nut M 8 x 1,25	12		tighten to 3.0 mkg
9	Washer/spring washer	16		
10	Flange	2	lever off	drive on
11	Spacer ring	2		fit new if play at flange
12	Circlip	2		fit new
13	Cap	2		fit new
14	Bracket	1		

EARLY 1968 DIFFERENTIAL

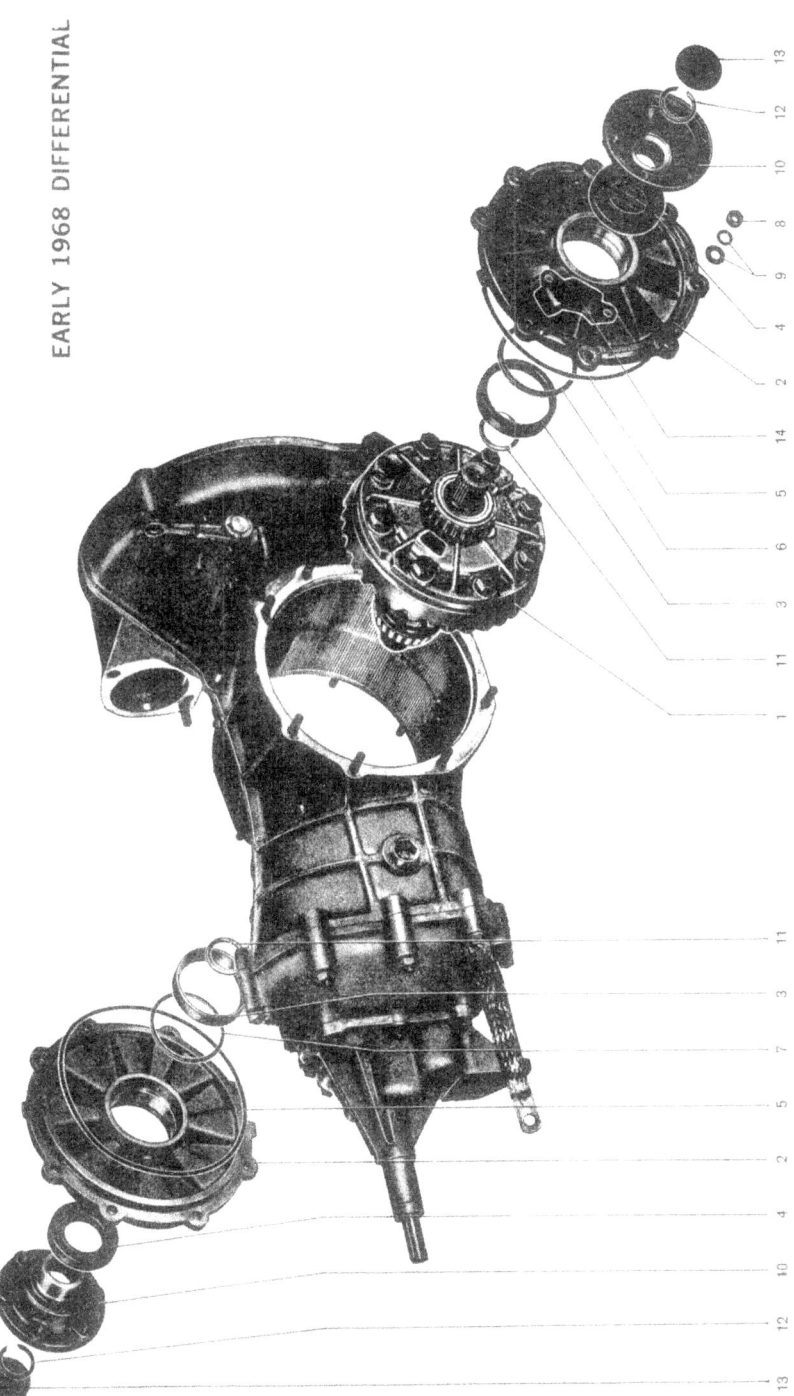

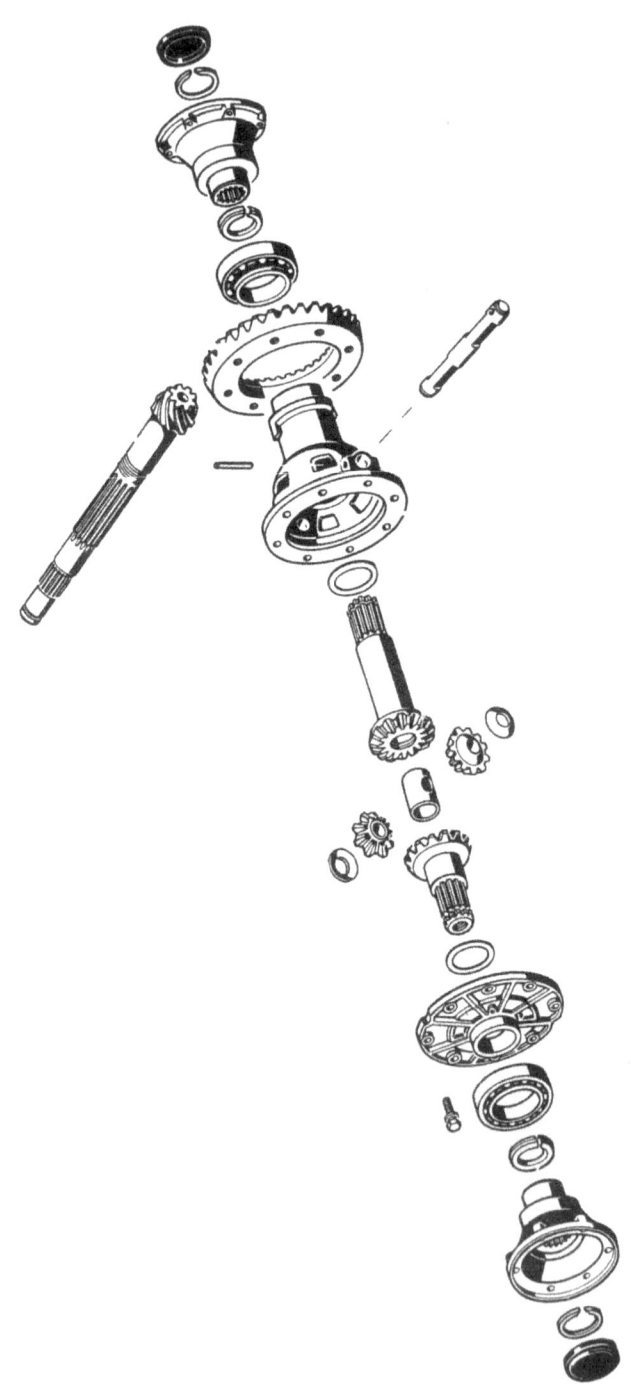

the differential bearings are installed in threaded adjusting rings and adjustment for differential bearing preload and backlash is made by screwing the rings in to a certain depth.

Servicing Differential (Early 1968 Model)

This procedure may only be used in the case where the differential is to be removed from the transmission case and then replaced WITHOUT DISASSEMBLY. Should parts need to be replaced, there will be the problem of adjusting gear backlash. This type of adjustment, along with other internal transmission repairs, should ONLY be done by a Volkswagen dealership service department, since they have the experienced personnel and the special tools so necessary to do the job.

With transmission suitably mounted on a stand (Special Tool VW 307), oil drained and starter motor removed, pierce the right cap (13) (direction of vehicle travel) in the flange (10) with a screwdriver and lever out. Remove the circlip (12) and lever off flange (10). Do not remove cover for the final drive at this stage, but instead turn over transmission and allow spacer ring (11) to fall out. Remove the left cap (13), circlip (12), flange (10) and turn transmission over once more to remove spacer ring (11). Turn over once again and remove the stud nuts holding the left final drive cover (2). Pull the cover off with multipurpose tool VW 771/22 or equivalent.

Use a shop press to remove the oil seal from the final drive cover with Special Tools VW 401, 408 and 473. Use the press to remove the bearing outer ring with Special Tools VW 401, 459/1, 473 and 408. Be sure to keep the covers, bearing outer rings, spacer rings and shims side-for-side and in the correct relationship. Be sure to mark parts upon removal to prevent any later mixup.

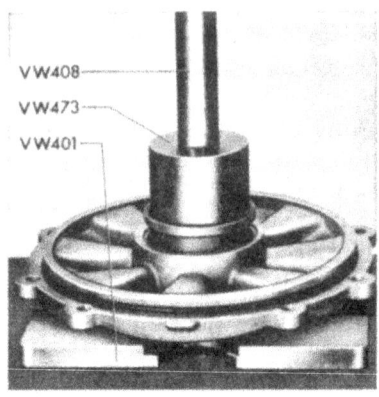 

Remove the shims (6) from the bearing outer ring or from cover, then remove the O-ring from cover. VW service practice is to always renew the oil seals and O-rings. Lift out differential, then remove the right final drive cover. Check the bearings and differential. If either the bearings or differential show signs of wear or damage and need to be replaced, it would be best to turn the remainder of the procedure over to a VW dealership service department, since the differential ring gear and the pinion will have to be adjusted.

To install the differential, replace the shims in the final drive covers and press bearing outer rings in with Special Tools VW 473, 408, 401 and 459/1. Coat the oil seals lightly with oil and press them fully home into the covers with Special Tools VW 401, 442, and 408. Install O-rings and oil them lightly also. Install the right cover and tighten the nuts to 22 ft. lb.

Replace the differential complete with the bearings into the housing and oil the bearings with hypoid oil. Install the cover on the ring gear side and tighten the nuts to 22 ft. lb. Insert the spacer washers, slide flanges on and secure with new circlips. If necessary, lift the differential side gear and press the flange down at the same time with Puller VW 201 and an M 10 stud (or equivalent device). This will squeeze the wavy spacer washer together until the circlip fits into the groove properly. Use Special Tool VW 244 b to drive the new caps into the flanges.

Servicing Differential (1968 Model and Later)

This procedure may only be used in the case where the differential and bearings are to be removed from the transmission case and then replaced WITHOUT DISASSEMBLY. Should parts need to be replaced, there will be the problem of adjusting gear backlash. This type of adjustment, along with other internal transmission repairs, should ONLY be done by a Volkswagen dealership service department, since they have the experienced personnel and the special tools so necessary to do the job.

Before beginning repair work, be sure to mark both of the adjuster rings both for depth in the transmission case and side-for-side OR measure exactly the installation depth of both (using a straight-edge and dial gauge combination to measure the depth of the outer circumference of the bearing ring) and record the values. If possible, measure this depth with Special Tool VW 382/7. Also, slacken the right adjuster ring (2) (after recording depth measurement), in order to release pressure on the transmission case as otherwise the clutch housing cannot be taken off.

1968 AND LATER DIFFERENTIAL

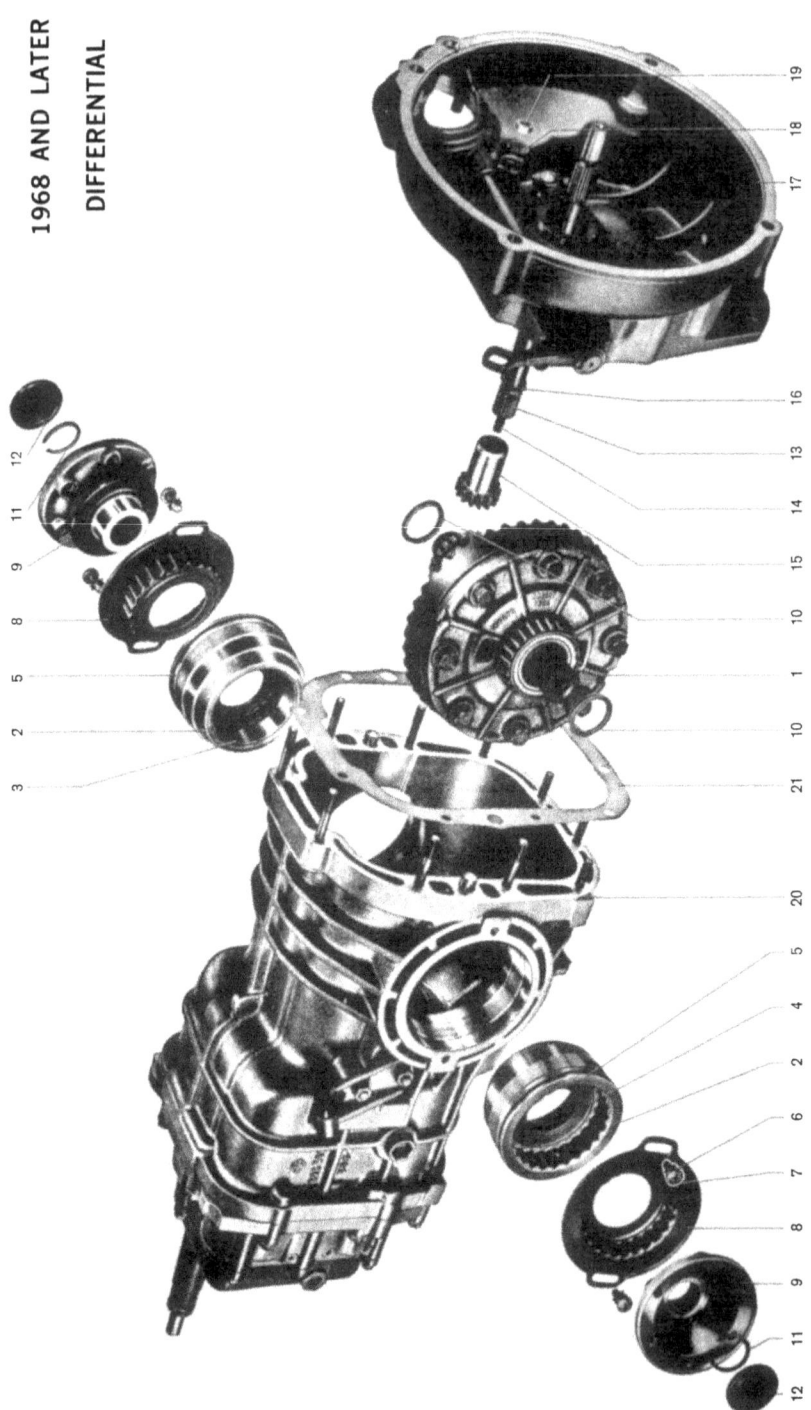

280

1968 AND LATER DIFFERENTIAL

No.	Designation	Qty.	Note when: disassembling	Note when: assembling	Remarks
1	Differential	1	see disassembling and assembling differential		
2	Adjuster ring/ final drive	2	screw out and in with VW 381/15		
3	Outer ring/taper roller bearing	2	press out with VW 472/1	press in with VW 401, 472/1 and 408	
4	Oil seal	2	press out with VW 473	press in with VW 472/1	
5	O ring	2		fit new	
6	Lock washer B 7	4			
7	Screw M 7	4		tighten to 1 mkg	
8	Lock plate	2			
9	Flange	2	lever off	drive on	
10	Spacer washer	2	fit new washer if there is play at flange		
11	Circlip	2		fit new	
12	Cap	2	pierce and lever out	drive in with VW 244 b	
13	Drive shaft, rear part	1		screw together and back off one spline	
14	Stud M 7	1	use only stud with broken thread		
15	Reverse gear	1			
16	Circlip	1		fit new	
17	Clutch housing	1			
18	Spring washer B 8	10			
19	Nut M 8	10		tighten to 2 mkg	
20	Transmission case	1			
21	Gasket	1		fit new	

Be sure to mark both adjuster rings and other parts side-for-side to aid reassembly.

If possible, mount the transmission in a holder and drain the oil. Pierce the cap (12) in joint flange (9) with a screwdriver and lever out cap, then remove the circlip (11) with circlip pliers and pry off flange (9) with two levers. Remove the screws (7) holding the lock plates (8) for the adjuster rings (2) and remove plates, then remove the nuts (19) holding the clutch housing (17). Use a rubber mallet to knock the clutch housing off its dowels, then remove circlip (16) from the rear part of the drive shaft (13) and

remove the drive shaft. Unscrew the adjuster rings (2) with socket VW 381/15 and ratchet, then remove adjuster rings.

Remove differential and ring gear (1) from the transmission case, then remove spacer washers and mark side-for-side. Use Special Tools VW 401, 473/1 and 408 to press oil seals from the adjuster rings. Use Special Tools VW 401, 459/1, 472/1 and 408 to press bearing outer rings from adjuster rings. Remove O-rings (5) from adjuster rings. Check the spacer washers, bearings and differential for damage or wear. VW service procedure is to renew the oil seals and O-rings as a matter of course.

If the differential or bearings show signs of damage or wear and need repair, it would be best to turn the remainder of the

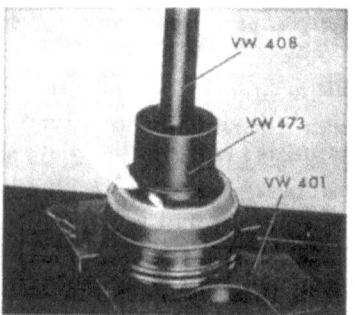 

procedure over to a VW dealership service department, since the differential ring gear and drive pinion will have to be adjusted.

To install the differential, place the differential in the transmission case with the correct spacer washers side-for-side. Be sure the differential is not inserted backwards. Press bearing outer rings into the adjuster rings using Special Tools VW 401, 472/1 and 408 until the bearing rings are fully bottomed. Use Special Tools VW 401, 472/1 and 408 to install the O-ring and oil seal. Install the adjuster ring that has been fully removed first, leaving the right-hand ring loose until the clutch housing has been installed. Coat threads of rings with lithium grease with MoS^2 additive. Install both adjuster rings to the marks made when removing them or to the depth measured. If the latter method is used, keep Special Tool VW 382/7 in contact with the adjuster rings while screwing them in.

Screw together front and rear parts of the drive shaft, back off one spline, then slide the reverse gear on and install a new circlip. Use a new gasket when installing the clutch housing. Tighten the nuts. Coat the machined surfaces of the adjuster

rings with a preservative such as underseal, then install locking plates for adjuster rings by tightening both screws. Install the spacer washers, slide flanges on, then fit new circlips. Drive in a new cap (12) with Special Tool VW 244b.

Note: Should it be impossible to fit the circlip, lift the differential side gear and simultaneously press down the joint flange with a fabricated tool such as that shown. Use an M 10 bolt. This will squeeze the wavy spacer ring together.

Tightening Torques

Location	Designation	Thread	Class	lb. ft.	mkg
Clutch housing	Temperature switch	M 14 x 1.5	GD-ZuA 14	18	2.5
Transmission case	Selector switch	M 14 x 1.5	GD-ZuA 14	18	2.5
Gearshift housing	Neutral safety switch	M 14 x 1.5	GD-ZuA 14	18	2.5
Converter / drive plate	12-point socket head screw	M 8 x 1.25	8 G	18	2.5
Gearbox / transmission case	Retaining ring	M 80 x 1	Cq 35	101–115	14–16
Lock plate / retaining ring	Tapping screw	4.8	Cq 5 K	7.0	1.0
Gear carrier / transmission case	Hex. nut	M 8 x 1.25	6 G	14	2.0
Lock plate / bearing ring	Fillister head screw	M 7 x 1.25	6 S	7.0	1.0
Gearshift housing / transmission case	Hex. nut	M 7 x 1	6 G	11	1.5
Converter housing / transmission case	Hex. nut	M 8 x 1.25	6 G	14	2.0
Cover / transmission case	Fillister head screw	M 7 x 1.25	6 G	7.0	1.0
Bonded rubber mounting / converter housing	Hex. nut	M 8 x 1.25	6 G	14	2.0
Transmission mounting / bonded rubber mounting	Hex. nut	M 8 x 1.25	6 G	14	2.0
Shift fork / shift rod	Hex. head screw	M 8 x 1.25	C 45 KN	18	2.5
Bearing lock screw	Hex. head screw	M 8 x 1.25	5 S	7.0	1.0
Pinion	Round nut	M 35 x 1.5	Cq 35	130–145	18–20
Ring gear	Hex. head screw	M 10 x 1.5	10 K	32	4.5
Gearshift housing / bonded rubber mounting	Hex. nut	M 10 x 1.5	8 G	25	3.5
One-way clutch support tube / converter housing	Socket head screw	M 6 x 1	10 K	11.0	1.5
Clutch / clutch carrier plate	12-point socket head screw	M 6 x 1	10 K	11	1.5
ATF feed pipe / transmission	Union	M 12 x 1.5		7.0	1.0
ATF return pipe / transmission	Union	M 14 x 1.5		22–29	3–4
Clamp screw / clutch lever	Hex. head screw	M 8 x 1.25	8 G	18	2.5
Constant velocity joint / flange	Socket head screw	M 8 x 1.25	10 K	25	3.5
Brake drum / rear axle shaft	Slotted nut	M 24 x 1.5	C 45 KV	217	30
Diagonal arm / spring plate	Hex. head screw	M 12 x 1.5	10 K	87	12
Diagonal arm / frame mount	Fitted screw	M 14 x 1.5	C 45	87	12
Spring plate cover / frame cross tube	Hex. head screw	M 10 x 1.5	8 G	22	3.0
Shock absorber / frame arm	Hex. head screw	M 12 x 1.5	6 G	44	6.0
Shock absorber / bearing housing	Hex. head screw	M 12 x 1.5	8 G	51	7.0
Transmission mount / frame fork	Fitted screw	M 18 x 1.5	8 G	167	23

Front Axle

The front axle is properly two parallel tubes which are set across the front of the chassis and attached by anchor plates and side bolts. Inside the tubes, multi-leaf torsion bars are anchored at the center. Parallel trailing torsion arms at either end are connected by divided knuckle pins which form a swivel for Elliot type steering knuckles (stub axles). Tubular shock absorbers control bounce and rebound.

The whole assembly forms a parallelogram which is quite sturdy. It is important that greasing operations be carried out with the front end jacked up or with the van on a chassis hoist inasmuch as the van's weight should not be on the wheels during this process.

Torsion Arm Link Pin Adjustment

Inspect condition of the torsion arm link pin by allowing the wheel to hang free and rocking it to check for end play between torsion arms and link. If play is present, keep vehicle's front end off ground and back off on pinch bolts at the torsion arm eyes. Grease torsion arm link pins thoroughly prior to any adjustments, turning the pins in both directions to remove old grease and dirt. Adjust by tightening the link pins fully, back off about ⅛th of a turn, then re-tighten carefully until resistance is first felt due to the shouldered end of the pin being pulled up. This will allow free movement between the torsion bars and the knuckle pins without any perceptable slackness. If there is no more possible adjustment, the shims are worn and must be replaced. Tighten the pinch bolts at the torsion arms eyes, then have the suspension toe-in checked and corrected if necessary.

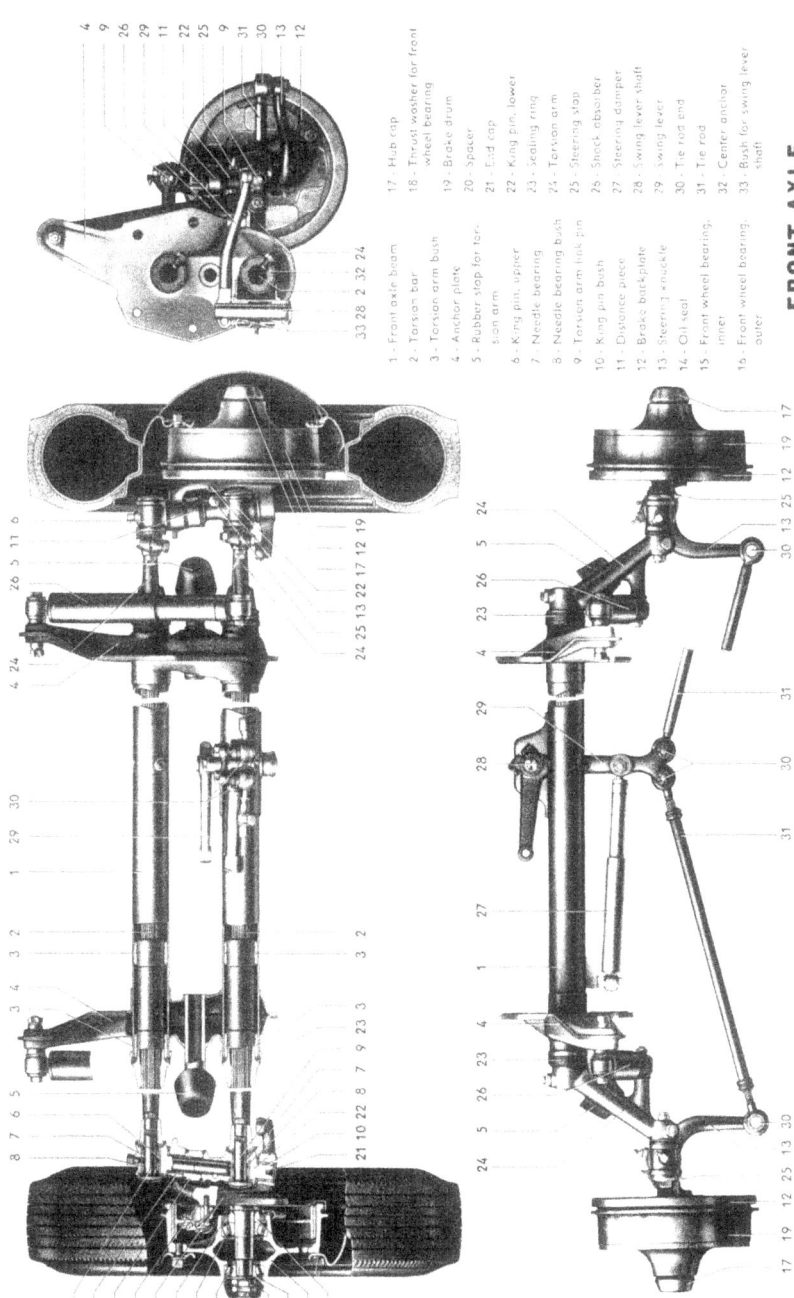

FRONT AXLE

1 - Front axle beam
2 - Torsion bar
3 - Torsion arm bush
4 - Anchor plate
5 - Rubber stop for torsion arm
6 - King pin, upper
7 - Needle bearing
8 - Needle bearing bush
9 - Torsion arm link pin
10 - King pin bush
11 - Distance piece
12 - Brake backplate
13 - Steering knuckle
14 - Oil seal
15 - Front wheel bearing, inner
16 - Front wheel bearing, outer
17 - Hub cap
18 - Thrust washer for front wheel bearing
19 - Brake drum
20 - Spacer
21 - End cap
22 - King pin, lower
23 - Sealing ring
24 - Torsion arm
25 - Steering stop
26 - Shock absorber
27 - Steering damper
28 - Swing lever shaft
29 - Swing lever
30 - Tie rod end
31 - Tie rod
32 - Center anchor
33 - Bush for swing lever shaft

Front Wheel Bearings

Improper clearances lead to destruction of bearings and races, therefore it is mandatory to maintain correct adjustment of the front wheel bearings. With the grease cup removed, (VW tool 637 is handy) insert the blade of a screwdriver between the drum and the outer thrust washer. If the washer can just be moved but no play can be felt by rocking the brake drum, adjustment is correct.

To remove excess play after prying up the noses of the lock plate, hold the adjusting nut with one 27mm wrench while loosening the locking nut with another. Tighten inner nut to some 21 ft. lb., then loosen until washer can just about be moved with a screwdriver and drum cannot be rocked. Hold inner nut exactly in this position, place a new lock washer on shaft, then tighten lock nut to 50 ft. lb. without changing clearance. Check bearing play once more, then secure nuts by bending lock washer up on one side and down on the other. Make sure the brake drum revolves freely in both directions with no noticeable axial play.

Servicing Tie Rod Ends

The tie rod ends shoud be replaced if they have too much play between the ball studs and sockets. If the springs in the tie rod ends are suspected to be too weak, the tie rod ends should be replaced as a trial. With the vehicle raised and the front wheels removed, remove the nuts on the tie rod ends, then press out tie rod ends and remove the tie rods. Prior to installation, check the tie rods for bending and damage; renew rather than trying to bend into shape. Either replace the whole rod or the individual tie rod ends, and always replace a tie rod end with damaged ball stud thread. Tilt both tie rod ends as far as possible to the front or rear so that they are properly aligned with each other. Tighten the castellated nuts on the tie rod ends, being sure not to damage the rubber dust caps nor to press out any grease. Each tie rod end should have about 5 grams of grease and damaged dust caps must be replaced. Tighten the castellated nuts on the tie rod ends, then check toe-in and adjust if necessary. Secure the nuts with cotter pins and lubricate the tie rod ends.

1968 And Later Models

Ball joints, the dust seals of which are damaged, should be renewed only if excessively worn, otherwise it is sufficient to clean them in a cleaning solvent and grease them until they are free from dirt.   Maintenance-free ball joints connect the torsion arms to the steering knuckles. They are pressed into the torsion arms and bolted to the steering knuckles. The upper joints engage in eccentric bushes with which front wheel camber can be adjusted.

Removing and Installing Front Axle

The front axle need only be removed if the axle beam itself is damaged and has to be replaced. All other repairs and adjustments can be carried out with the axle installed.

If it is suspected that the axle beam is bent or distorted due to accident, the beam can be checked by placing a straight edge in the axle tube. Do not attempt to straighten damaged axle beams.

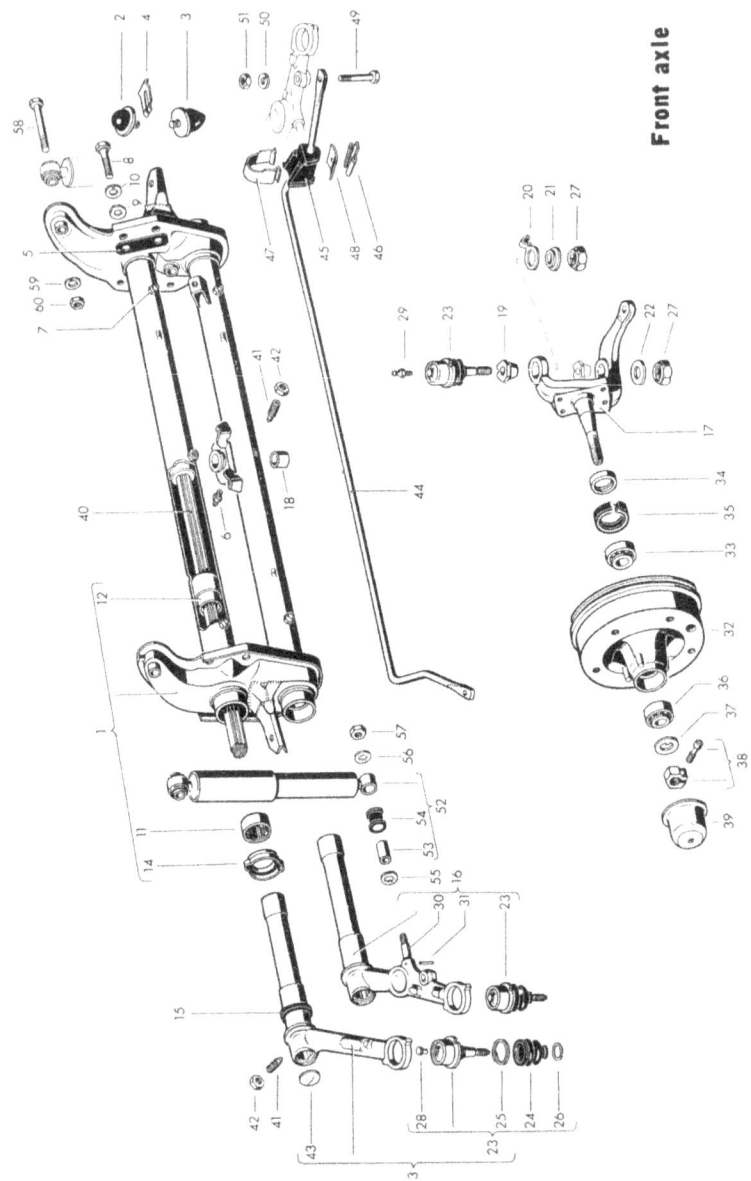

Removal

1 — Loosen wheel bolts, raise car and remove front wheels. Pull fuel hose off and plug it. Remove fuel tank. Loosen clip on steering column tube, pull flat connector for horn cable off the steering column and then pull column off coupling flange complete with steering wheel. Remove cotter pin from speedometer cable in left front wheel and pull cable out of steering knuckle. Disconnect brake hoses at brackets and plug them with bleeder valve dust caps. Detach steering damper from bracket on axle beam. (Figure A-11). Press long tie rod end off with VW266h or similar tool after bending up lock plates and removing nuts. Take tie rod and steering damper out (Figure A-12). Remove two body bolts (Figure A-13). Loosen four axle securing screws on frame head. Position floor jack to receive on it, remove screws and take axle off.

FIG. A-11

FIG. A-12

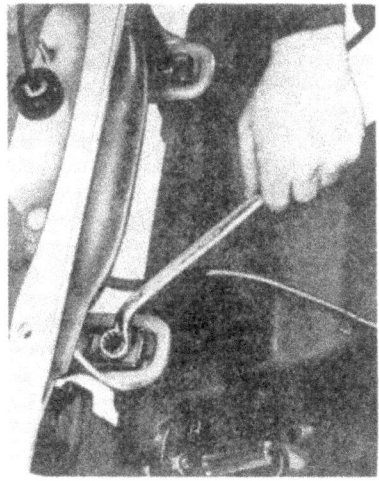

FIG. A-13

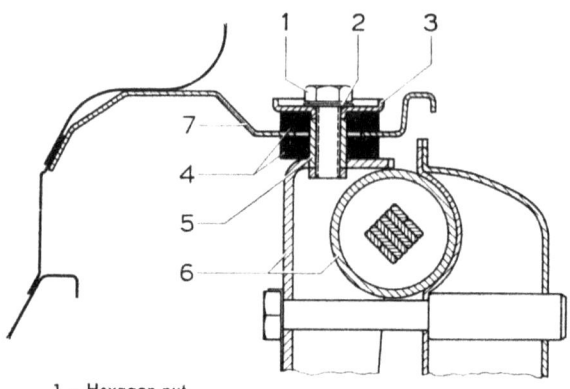

1 – Hexagon nut
2 – Lock washer
3 – Washer for spacer
4 – Rubber packing piece
5 – Threaded bush
6 – Front axle
7 – Body

FIG. A-14

FIG. A-15

Installation

Note the following points:

1 — Place a rubber packing piece on each of the threaded bushes on the front axle.
2 — Use new spring washers for the securing screws.
3 — Tighten the front axle securing screws to 5 mkg (36 ft. lbs.).
4 — Tighten the body bolts on front axle to 2.0 mkg (14 ft. lbs.). Do not forget rubber packing pieces, washers for spacer and spring washers (Figure A-14).
5 — Tighten tie rod end nuts and secure with cotter pins.
6 — Install the steering damper bolt in the front axle bracket.

Use a new lock plate. Tighten bolt to 2.5 - 3.0 mkg (18-22 ft. lbs.) and secure it. The lock plate should be fitted so that the opening of the "U" shape points to the front and the short angled surface is on the bracket.

7 — Center the steering gear with the aid of the marking ring on the worm spindle and place column on column coupling with the steering wheel spoke horizontal. Secure steering column clamp screw with a new lock plate (Figure A-15).

8 — Take care that the brake hoses are not twisted on installation.

9 — Bleed brake system and adjust brakes.

10 — Check toe-in and camber.

FIG. A-16

FIG. A-17

Front Wheels Bearings
Removal

Loosen the lug bolts, raise car and remove front wheels. Remove cotter pin from speedometer cable in left front wheel and pull cable out of steering knuckle.

Remove hub cap (Figure A-16).

Loosen screw in clamp nut and remove clamp nut (Figure A-17).

Important: The left steering knuckle has a left-hand thread.

Remove bearing thrust washer and brake drum. Press inner bearing and oil seal out of brake drum on a press, with VW 412, VW 446 and VW 447 c adapters. Press out outer race of outer bearing, using VW 412, VW 446, VW 447 d, VW 401 and VW 402 adapters.

Note: Thrust washers VW 447 c and VW 447 d must be installed in the brake drum so that the lugs engage in the grooves in the hub (Figure A-18).

Installation

Note the following points:

1 — Thoroughly clean brake drum, hub, bearings, brake mechanism, back plate and steering knuckle in a suitable cleaning solvent. Dust and material rubbed off the brake linings have a grinding action and must not be allowed to enter the bearings and seatings.

2 — Check the wheel bolt threads in the drum and the condition of the friction surface.

3 — Check accuracy of drum dimensions.

4 — Check bearings for wear and damage and fit new bearings if necessary.

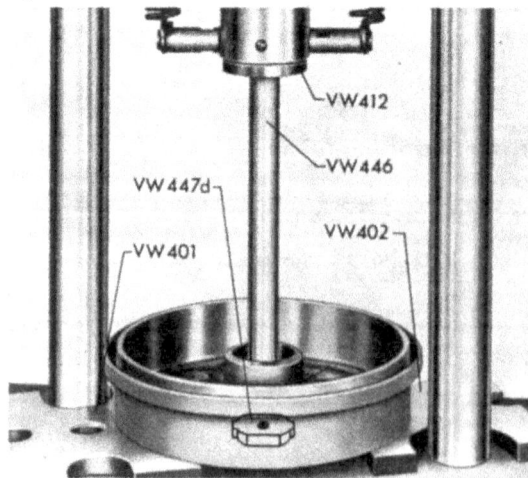

FIG. A-18

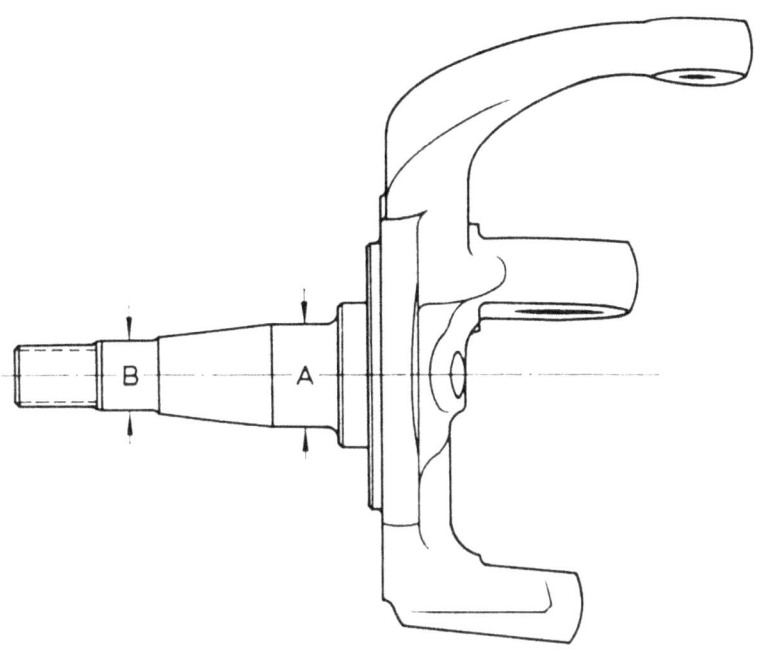

Inner bearing seat A	=	$\dfrac{26.98 \text{ mm diameter}}{26{,}97 \text{ mm diameter}}$
	=	$\dfrac{1.0622 \text{ in. diameter}}{1.0618 \text{ in. diameter}}$
Taper roller bearing inside diameter	=	$\dfrac{27.00 \text{ mm}}{26.99 \text{ mm}}$
Outer bearing seat B	=	$\dfrac{17.46 \text{ mm diameter}}{17.45 \text{ mm diameter}}$
	=	$\dfrac{.6874 \text{ in. diameter}}{.6870 \text{ in. diameter}}$
Taper roller bearing inside diameter	=	$\dfrac{17.47 \text{ mm}}{17.46 \text{ mm}}$

FIG. A-19

5 — Check bearing seats for size and for signs of seizure (Figure A-19).

6 — Press outer race of inner bearing in on a press, using VW 432, VW 411 and VW 401. Install cage and inner race.

7 — Check condition of oil seal and press it in on a press, using VW 432, VW 411 and VW 401. Ensure that the oil seal goes in without tilting.

8 — Press outer race of outer bearing in on a press, using VW 432 and VW 411.

9 — Lubricate bearings with lithium grease of the correct specification. Press grease into the cages and between the rollers and lightly grease bearing seats. Fill hub of drum with grease but leave hub cap free from grease.

Important: Only good quality grease should be used. Do not mix different brands and types of grease as this can be harmful. The amount of grease required for each wheel is about 50 grams.

10 — Install brake drum and push inner race of outer bearing on to stub axle, using sleeve VW 244 c.

11 — Be sure that the thrust washer is fitted properly. Otherwise the bearing adjustment will be incorrect.

12 — Adjust bearings in accordance with the instructions given below.

Checking and Adjusting Front Wheel Bearings

Taper roller bearings are used for the front wheels. The instructions for the adjustment of the front wheel bearings must followed closely. Incorrect adjustment can damage or destroy the bearings in a very short time.

To Check

Lift front of vehicle. Check that drum turns freely. The brake linings must not rub. Pull hub cap off and check bearing play as follows:

1 — Unscrew one wheel bolt and screw in the threaded pin of dial gauge bracket VW 769.

2 — Set bracket so that the dial gauge pin of dial gauge bracket VW 769.

2 — Set bracket so that the dial gauge pin touches the clamp nut.

3 — Move wheel in and out firmly and read off axial play (Figure A-20). The axial play must be between .03 - .12 mm (.001 - .005 in.). If the dial gauge shows the play not to be within the limits, readjust bearings.

Note: Near the upper adjusting limits, an axial movement can be clearly felt. This movement is permissible, and does not mean that the bearings must be readjusted. Only if front axle noises are unusual is it necessary to readjust the bearings. In such a case, work to as near the lower limit as possible (.03 - .06 mm).

To Adjust

Loosen screw in clamp nut. Tighten clamp nut to a torque of 1.5 mkg (11 ft. lbs.). The wheel must be turned while doing this

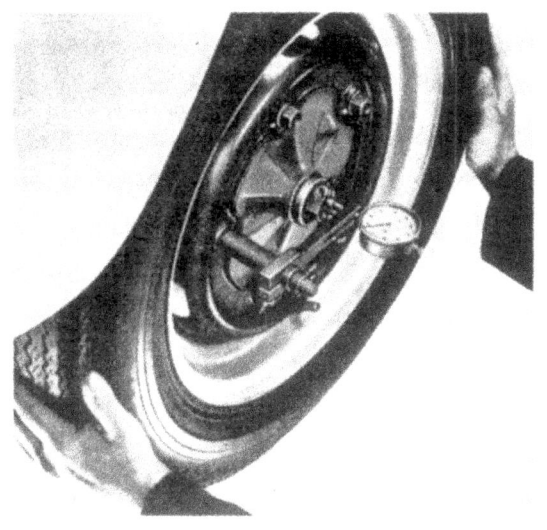

FIG. A-20

FIG. A-21

FIG. A-22

so that the bearing rollers contact the shoulder of the inner race. Slacken clamp nut off until the axial play is between 0.03 and 0.12 mm when the wheel is moved firmly in and out. Tighten clamp nut screw to 1 mkg (7 ft. lbs.) (Figure A-22). Check adjustment again. Install hub cap after making sure that it is free from grease.

Fitting New Shock Absorber Pin in Torsion Arm

For cases where it is necessary to fit a new shock absorber mounting pin in the torsion arm, an oversize pin is supplied as a replacement part. When installing this pin, the hole in the torsion arm must be bored out and reamed.

Removal

1 — Remove torsion arm.
2 — Drive dowel pin out.
3 — Pull old pin out.

To remove a broken pin, center punch the remaining part and drill a 3 mm (.118") pilot hole in it. Then drill the rest out with a 10.75 mm (.423") drill. The broken part will usually come out on its own accord with the last few turns of the drill.

Installation

1 — Drill out the hole in the torsion arm with a 12.3 mm (.484") drill and ream it out with a 12.5 P8 (12.455 - 12.482 mm) diameter reamer. If a reamer of this size is not available, the oversize pin can be ground to fit the drilled-out hole. An interference fit of 0.01 - 0.05 mm (.0004 - .002") must be obtained.
2 — Press the oversize pin in until it projects 45.0 - 45.5 mm (b). Drill a 4.0 - 4.08 mm hole in the oversize pin (d) (Figure A-23).
3 — Drive dowel pin in.

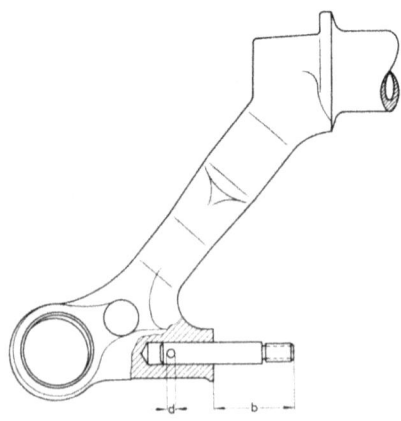

FIG. A-23

Shock Absorbers

Maintenance attention to shock absorbers is limited to inspection for leakage and for failure. If the vehicle bottoms excessively on rough roads or can be set in motion for two or three bounces by rocking, the shock absorbers require replacement. Minimal leaks of fluid if performance is satisfactory are not harmful inasmuch as a self-contained reservoir holds an amount of fluid equal to the portion in use. Excessive leakage will result in loss of shock action, of course. There is no provision for replacement of fluid. The entire unit must be replaced.

Do not confuse the front and rear shock absorbers when replacing. **Front shocks are painted black, rear shocks are gray.**

Remove front shocks by raising the vehicle and removing the nut on the torsion arm stud and the bolt on the front axle and plate, then pull off the shock absorber. Renew shock absorber complete with bushes, check attaching bolt and torsion arm stud for wear. Tighten nuts so they bear securely against the metal insert in the bush, otherwise premature wear and rattling during operation will set in. Use the same procedure to renew the rear shock absorbers, noting that the rear units are painted grey.

Adjustable (Koni) Shock Absorbers

Where roads are especially rough, the vehicle can be outfitted with reinforced adjustable shock absorbers manufactured by Koni and sold at VW dealerships. These have the advantage of not being greatly affected by tropical heat, sustained high loading, and stone damage. Various models of these shock absorbers can be installed to protect delicate loads being carried in the vehicle. Adjust the Koni shock absorbers for the particular vehicle as shown in the chart, but do not try to change the setting for a softer ride since there could be detrimental effects on the vehicle. Adjust the setting by fully compressing the shock absorber and turn larger tube to the left until the adjusting dog engages in the slot in the bottom valve. Turn the shock absorber from the zero position (left stop) the prescribed amount to the right in the direction of the arrow marked "heavy".

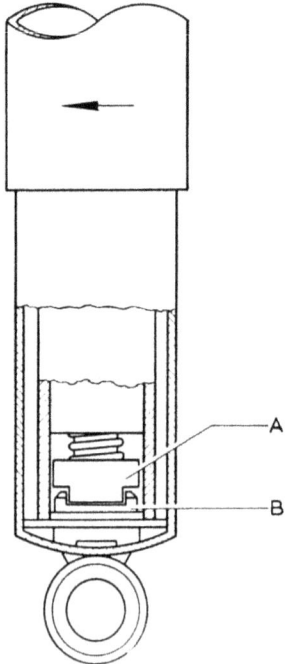

A - Adjusting dog
B - Bottom valve

Type	front	rear
Ambulance Micro Bus	0	½ turn
Kombi Delivery Van Pick-up	½	1—1½ turns

Steering

A ZF (Model 532) steering gear utilizing the worm and peg principle assures smooth, firm control on the VW Transporter.

The forward position of the driver calls for a different system of links and levers than that found in the passenger car, but the steering has the same feel of immediate response without heaviness that characterizes the latter vehicle. Keeping the gear case topped with the correct weight of oil (see Lubrication Chart) and inspection of all connections are the primary responsibilities of maintenance. Reference to the adjacent diagrams will clarify the function of each part of the system. End play and backlash are independently adjustable. The end play is corrected by insertion or removal of shims at the adjuster flange (see photo). Excessive backlash can be removed by setting the steering in the straight ahead position, loosening the lock nut and turning the adjusting screw until a slight drag is felt in the mid-range of the lock-to-lock travel. Do not set the adjustment so that steering is stiff. This will cause accelerated wear on the mechanism.

NOTE: VW Ross steering is fitted to some units. It is not adjusted in the same manner as the ZF and ATE, and some parts are not interchangeable. Adjustment procedure is for the ZF and ATE only. Refer to your VW dealer's service department.

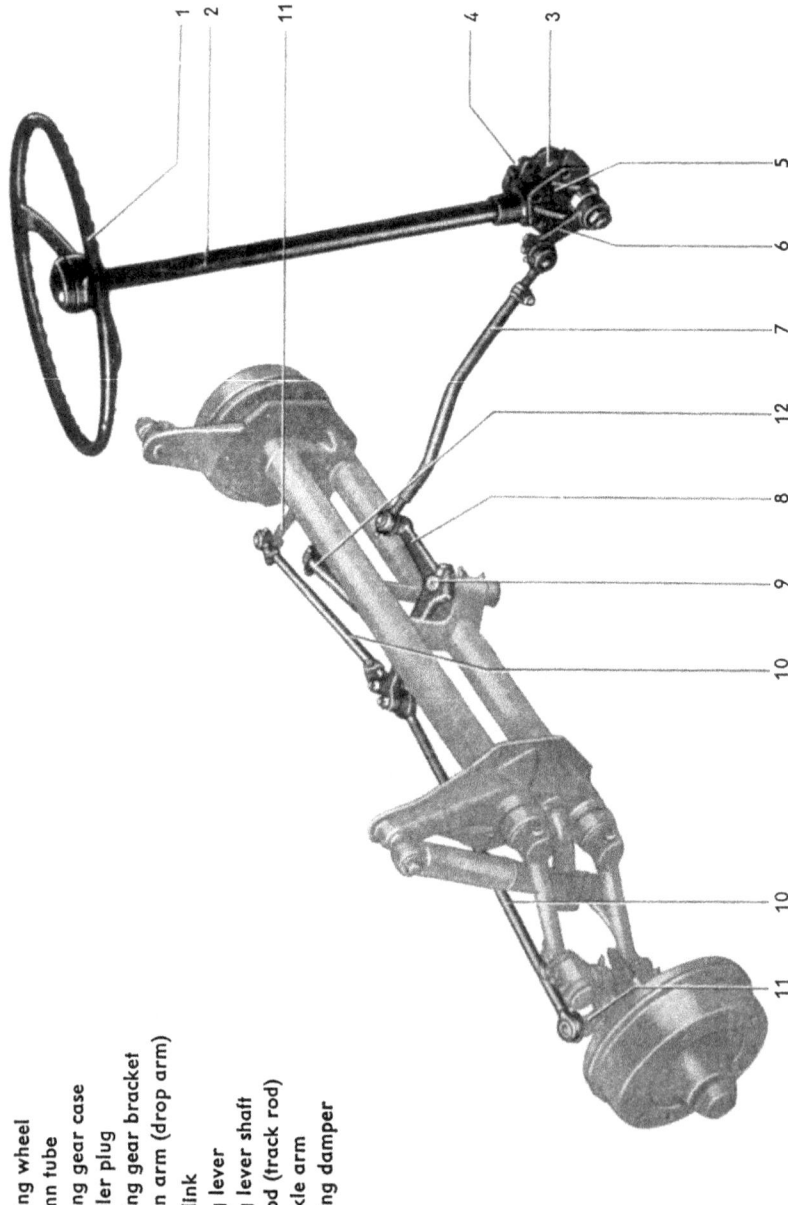

1 - Steering wheel
2 - Column tube
3 - Steering gear case
4 - Oil filler plug
5 - Steering gear bracket
6 - Pitman arm (drop arm)
7 - Draglink
8 - Swing lever
9 - Swing lever shaft
10 - Tie rod (track rod)
11 - Knuckle arm
12 - Steering damper

Steering Gear Adjustment

Jack up the front of the vehicle (support the front axle), then remove the cover plate under the pedal assembly. Disconnect the draglink from the pitman arm, using a puller if necessary. Disconnect the horn cable from the horn button and detach the cable clip, then remove the cable as the first step of adjusting the steering column end play. Remove the adjuster flange and add or subtract shims, then replace the flange and turn the steering gear from one end position to the other with the steering wheel. Insufficient end play is indicated by steering stiffness, excessive end play results in axial movement when turning the steering wheel. Use the following shims: ATE type, .05 & .30 mm; ZF type, .30, .15, .125 and .10 mm. Insert the end cover with the guide tube and tighten the bolts. Make sure the steering is functioning correctly after adjusting it by checking that the bolts in the adjuster flange are evenly tightened. Finally, install the horn cable clip and bend up the ends against the bolts. Connect the horn cable.

The backlash between the stud and the worm is adjusted after the steering is set to the approximate straight-ahead position by halving the total lock-to-lock turns of the steering wheel (2.4). Loosen the locknut on the adjusting screw, then turn the adjusting screw clockwise until a slight drag is felt in the mid-position range of the steering movement. Tighten the locknut and turn the steering wheel from lock to lock. A slight drag should be felt in the mid-position range. Do not set the adjustment excessively stiff to improve steering conditions, since this will impair the action and shorten the life of the steering gear. Check the remainder of the system to find the trouble.

Install the draglink and adjust it if necessary. Fill the steering gear from underneath with a ½ pint of SAE 90 hypoid oil. Check the vehicle for correct toe-in, then adjust if necessary.

Servicing Steering Damper

When the steering wheel becomes "shaky" after one of the wheels has gone over a bump, the steering damper is probably worn and should be renewed. With the vehicle raised, detach the damper from the bracket and swing lever, replace with a new damper, then install with a new lock plate.

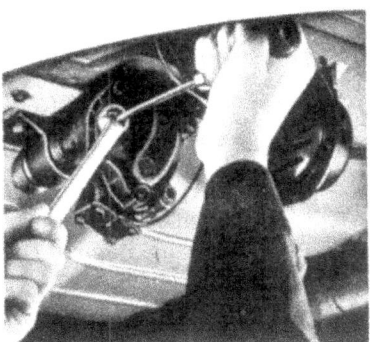

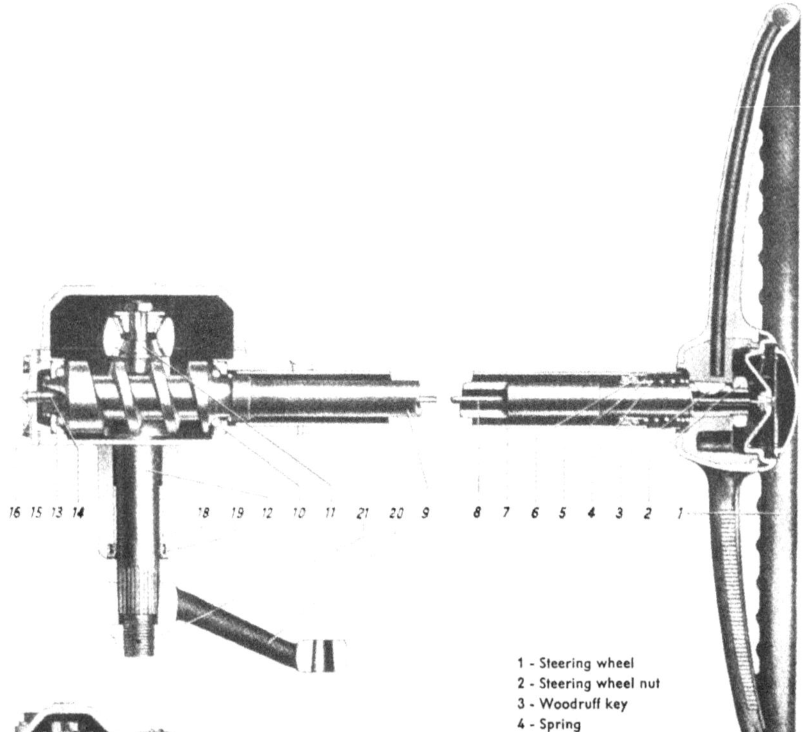

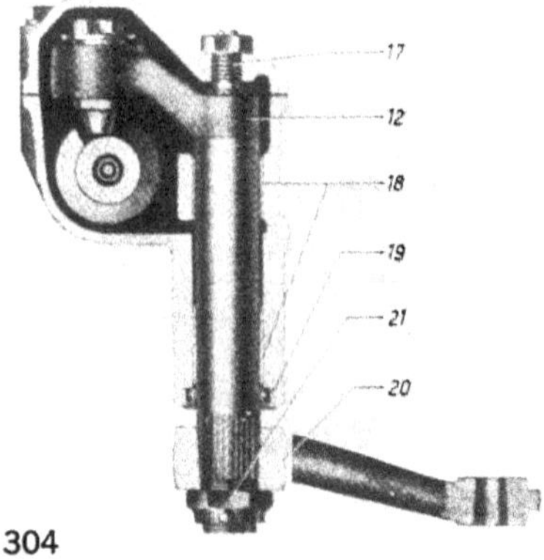

1 - Steering wheel
2 - Steering wheel nut
3 - Woodruff key
4 - Spring
5 - Expander ring
6 - Ball bearing assembly
7 - Tube
8 - Horn button cable
9 - Steering column and cam
10 - Ball bearing, upper
11 - Timken bearing
12 - Lever shaft
13 - Ball bearing, lower
14 - Horn cable retainer tube
15 - Shims
16 - Adjuster flange
17 - Adjuster screw
18 - Lever shaft bushes
19 - Oil seal
20 - Pitman arm (drop arm)
21 - Castle nut

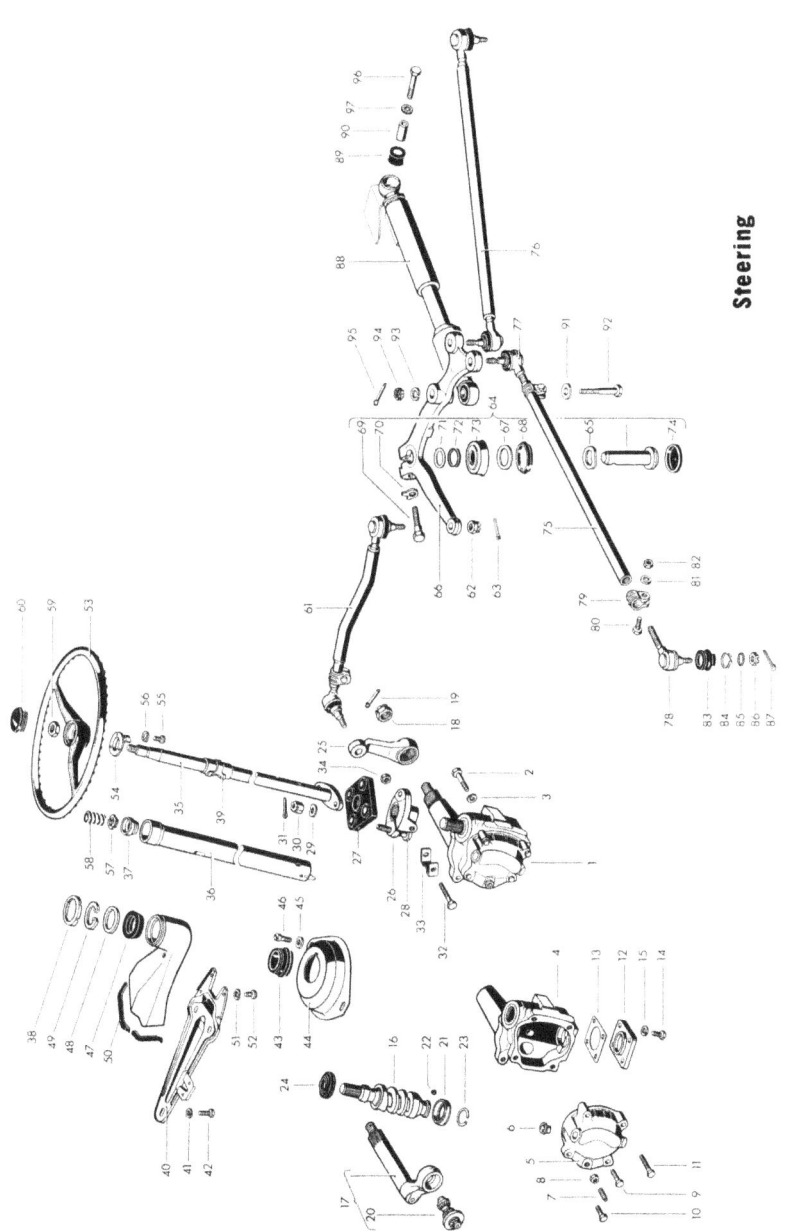

Steering Wheel

To remove the steering wheel, first place the road wheels exactly straight-ahead (preferably drive straight forward and stop), disconnect the battery ground cable, then remove the horn button cover by twisting a screwdriver between it and the horn ring. Disconnect the horn ground cable, remove button, then remove the direction indicator switch. Loosen the steering wheel nut until its face is slightly above the column top end, then mark the column and steering wheel so both can be aligned upon reassembly. Remove indicator cancelling switch from below, then try to remove steering wheel straight up. If it cannot be removed, use a puller bar (VW 202p), hooks (VW 202d), thrust pad (VW 202k) and a puller spindle (VW 202). Place the puller so as to avoid damaging the steering column. When installing, check the Woodruff key for wear in the keyway milled in the steering column, replacing the key if necessary. Tighten the steering wheel nut to a torque of 18 to 22 ft. lb.

Collapsible Steering Column Bracket

On 1970 and later vehicles, the upper steering column is mounted with a mounting bracket (A) with a predetermined location to collapse in the center (arrow) when sufficient force is exerted, such as in a front-end collision. Also, a support (B) has been added at the side. It is mounted between the break-away screw attachment of the mounting bracket at the instrument panel and an L-shaped piece at the fresh air control box. The insert illustration shows the screw attachment using plastic-coated washers (C) which will disconnect only when impact forces are exerted on the vehicle's front end or the steering wheel by the driver's chest. This will allow the mounting bracket to fold upward or downward, and the support (B) to deflect to the side. It will be necessary to replace the complete bracket following an accident, and the complete steering system should be examined. This whole procedure should be left to the service department of an authorized VW dealership.

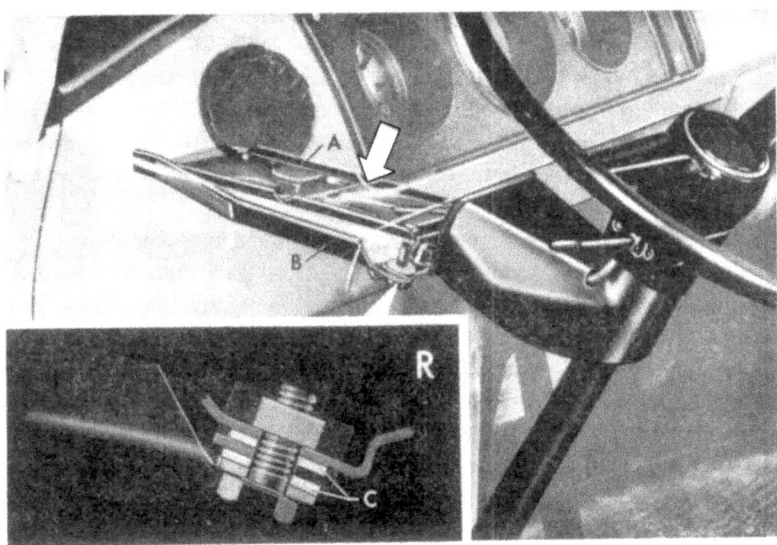

Steering Geometry & Alignment

The correct functioning of all parts of the steering and wheel alignment factors is of utmost importance in the steering and riding qualities of VW Transporters. These adjustments are not ordinarily carried out except in VW garages and alignment shops having the equipment necessary. However, for the owner who may find himself in an area where correct specifications are not universally known, the following material will be of assistance.

The camber, kingpin inclination, caster, toe-in of the front wheels, toe-out and camber of rear wheels are all related. If any one becomes altered from factory specifications, excessive tire wear, hard steering, shimmy, tramp, wander or poor road holding may result.

Toe-in for front wheels under maximum load should be 2 to 5 mm, (.08" to .2"). This value is achieved by setting the toe-in at 0 mm (with a tolerance of plus or minus 1 mm) with the vehicle ready for the road but unladen and without driver.

Camber for front wheels is set at 0° 40' (plus or minus 30') with wheels straight ahead. It is not adjustable but may be out of agreement because of incorrect installation of shims in the torsion arm link pins. NOTE: Correcting improper camber due to bent components by changing link pin shims is not admissible.

Wheel angularity. There is a difference of 2° 30' in the angularity of the outside wheel and the inside wheel when turned to a 20° lock both right and left. (The wheel at the outside of the curve will be at **less** of an angle than the inside wheel). This measurement should be measured at the outer wheel and should be true within plus or minus 30'.

Caster angle is 0° when measured at the front axle tubes. The inclination of these tubes should be taken at each end of the tubes with a protractor-level. Setting of rear axle torsion bars can affect caster and steering, so these should be checked.

Rear Wheel Camber is measured with vehicle unladen and is changed by adjusting torsion bars in their splines (see rear suspension section).

Correct camber for Delivery Van, Kombi, Microbus and Pickup is 4°30' (plus or minus 30'). For Ambulance 3° (plus or minus 30') and for the Fire Truck 4°30' (plus or minus 20'). Maximum permissible difference between camber on both wheels is 20'.

Rear Wheel Toe-out should not exceed .5 mm to 4 mm (.02" to .16").

All measurements should be taken with tires inflated to correct pressure and with vehicle ready for the road minus driver.

Steering Troubles and Their Remedies

Trouble	Cause	Remedy
Steering Stiff Steering uniformly stiff in all positions of road wheels, plus absence of self-centering action	a - Steering gear incorrectly adjusted	a - Check adjustment of steering gear. Adjust column end-float and stud-backlash as detailed. Check oil level. Replace worn parts as necessary
	b - Steering king pins too stiff, possible seized	b - To check, raise vehicle and detach tie rods. Try to free stiff king pins by thoroughly lubricating. If necessary, recondition or renew worn or seized parts
	c - Swing lever shaft stiff, possibly seized	c - To check, raise vehicle, detach tie rods and draglink from swing lever. Try to free swing lever shaft by lubricating thoroughly. If necessary remove front axle and recondition or replace shaft bushes, renew swing lever shaft.
Although sufficiently light in action, steering fails to center after cornering	a - Incorrect adjustment of front wheels	a - Check front wheel alignment (caster, camber, toe-in) and correct as detailed
	b - Steering knuckle arms bent	b - Remove steering knuckles and check with gauge VW 258 c. Bent steering knuckles must be renewed and not straightened.
Steering Slack Backlash in steering gear	a - Steering gear incorrectly adjusted	a - Check adjustment of steering gear. Correct as detailed
	b - Worm, stud or taper roller bearing worn	b - Dismantle steering gear. Replace worn parts
Slackness in tie rod or draglink ends	Excessive wear in rod or link ends	Replace worn parts
Slackness in front suspension	Excessive bearing wear (torsion arms, link pins, knuckle pins, steering knuckles and front wheel bearings)	Check adjustment of link pins and front wheel bearings. If necessary, readjust. Replace parts showing excessive wear

BRAKE SYSTEM

The front brakes are of the two leading shoe variety while a leading shoe and a trailing shoe are fitted to each of the rear wheels. The difference in the arrangements is reflected in adjustment nut location. The front wheels have an upper and a lower nut while rear wheels have both nuts at the top of the drum. Condition of the lining can be determined by inspection through the elongated hole in the brake drum. When thickness remaining is less than 2.5mm (.1") the lining should be replaced.

NOTE: Front and rear wheel brake cylinders are not inter-interchangeable. Front: 1" dia., rear .87" dia.
Front and rear lining widths are different. Front: 2", rear: 1.6".
Aluminum rivets should never be used in replacing lining. VW factory rivets are recommended.

Brake Adjustment

It is necessary periodically to adjust the brakes because of lining wear. Too much pedal travel is a clue that the clearance between drum and shoe is excessive. Adjustment is made at top and bottom nuts on each wheel through a hole suitably placed in the wheel with the car jacked up so that wheels can rotate freely.

Prior to adjustment depress the brake pedal several times to make sure that the shoes are centralized in the drums. Then, take a large screwdriver and, having rotated the wheel so that the

1200 Model

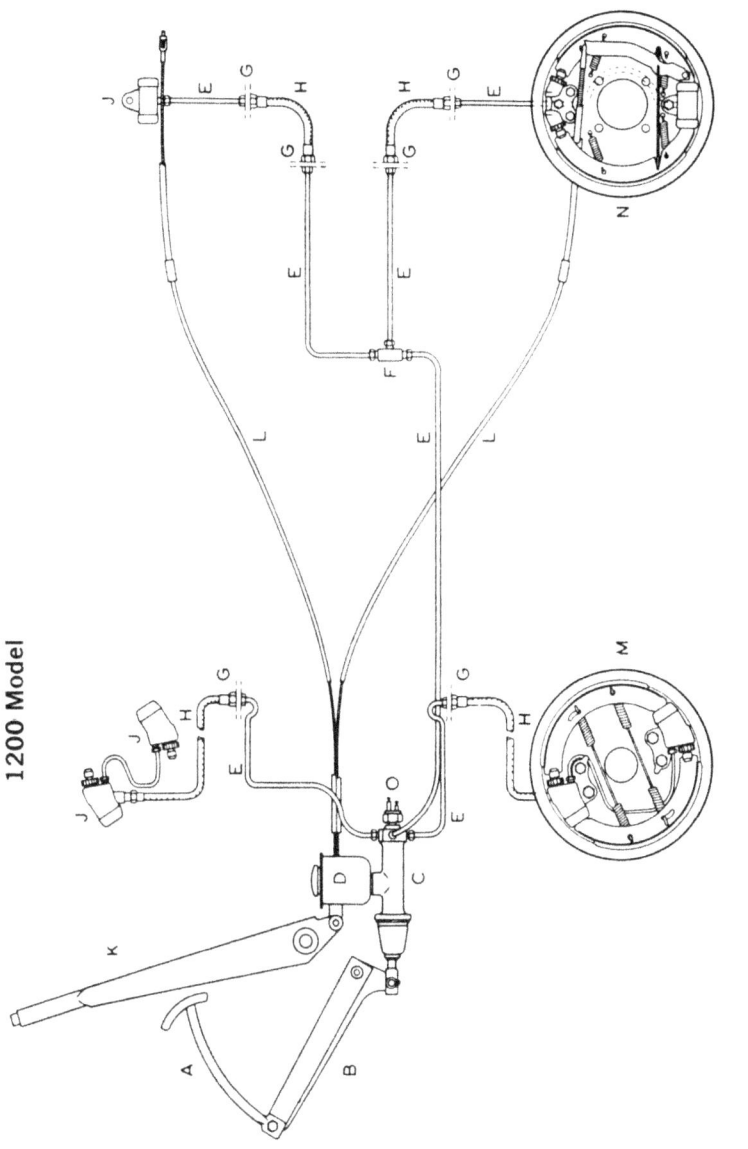

Diagrammatic view of complete hydraulic brake system

A - Brake pedal
B - Operating lever
C - Master cylinder
D - Fluid reservoir
E - Hydraulic lines
F - Three-way connection
G - Brake hose brackets
H - Brake hose
J - Wheel cylinder
K - Hand brake lever
L - Cable conduit tubes
M - Front wheel brake
N - Rear wheel brake
O - Stop light switch

	1200 Model	1500 Model
Master cylinder		
Diameter	22.2 mm	22.2 mm
Stroke	30 mm	36 mm
Brake drum diameter	230 mm	250 mm
Brake lining width		
Front	50 mm	55 mm
Rear	40 mm	45 mm
Lining thickness	5 mm	5 mm
Brake shoe support	angled	straight
Wheel cylinder diameter		
Front	25.4 mm	25.4 mm
Rear	22.2 mm	22.2 mm

1500 Model

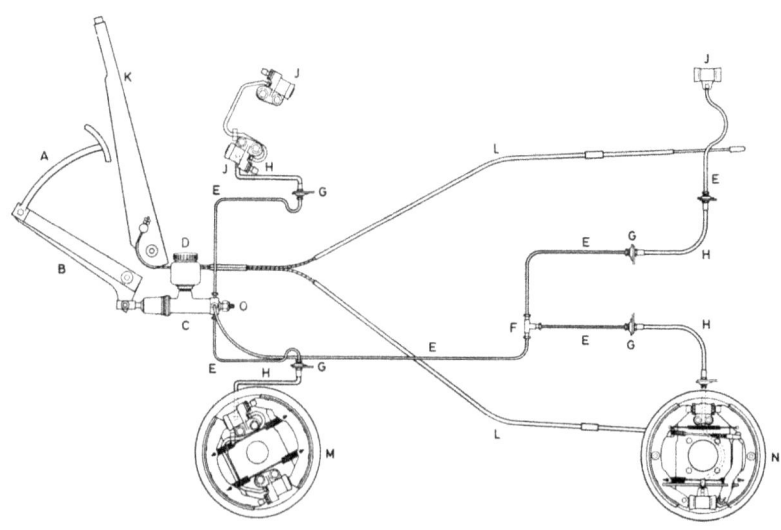

Layout of brake system

A - Push rod
B - Brake pedal
C - Master cylinder
D - Reservoir
E - Brake line
F - Three-way union
G - Hose bracket
H - Brake hose
I - Wheel cylinder
K - Handbrake lever
L - Cable guide tube
M - Front wheel brake
N - Rear wheel brake
O - Stop light switch

access hole is opposite an adjusting nut, turn the nut (using the screwdriver as a lever) until a light drag is felt when the wheel is turned by hand. Back off nut 3 or 4 teeth until wheel rotates freely. Repeat the process on the other adjusting nut. You will note that the bottom nut rotates in an opposite direction from the top to tighten.

Adjusting Handbrake

(Early Models)

With Transporter supported on stands:
1. Remove cover plate under pedal linkage.
2. Back off locknuts at front end of crake cables and tighten adjusting nuts to a degree that will allow the rear wheels to turn freely with handbrake off.
3. Pull handbrake up two notches and make sure rear wheels react in the same amount. At the fourth notch it should be impossible to turn the wheels by hand.
4. Tighten locknuts.

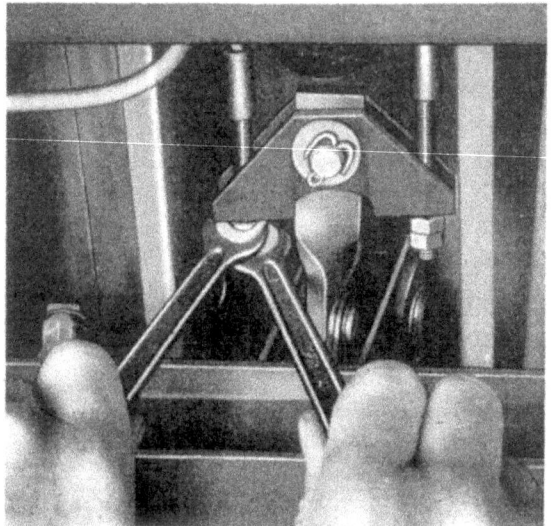

On models prior to 1968, the handbrake is operated by simply pulling back on the lever (22). The handbrake is released by pulling the lever back, pressing the locking button, then allowing the lever to spring forward. On 1968 and later models, pull the handle (9 on picture in the Instrument Panel section of the Electrical Chapter) straight

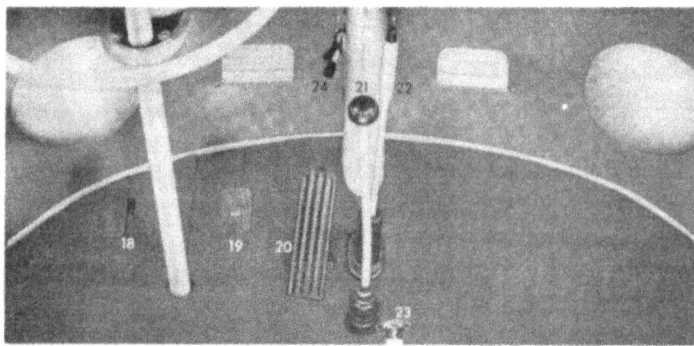

out to set; then turn handle clockwise and push in to release. Adjustment on both models is accomplished by first lifting the vehicle so at least the rear wheels are free to rotate. Slip up the rubber boot at the base of the handbrake lever (on the floor), then loosen the locknuts on the front ends of the brake cables, holding the shaft with a screwdriver. Tighten adjusting nuts so the rear wheels still turn freely with the handbrake off. Apply the handbrake 2 notches and check that the braking effort is the same at both rear wheels. Apply the handbrake 2 notches more (a total of 4), and ensure that the back wheels cannot be revolved. If vehicle is equipped with a compensating lever, make sure it is horizontal after the handbrake is applied. Tighten the locknuts, then slip the boot down into position. Road test the vehicle.

Important: When renewing the rear brake shoes, check and adjust the handbrake so the shoes do not drag. Since the handbrake has been tightened while the old brake shoes have worn, the new shoes will most likely be held outward even while handbrake is fully released.

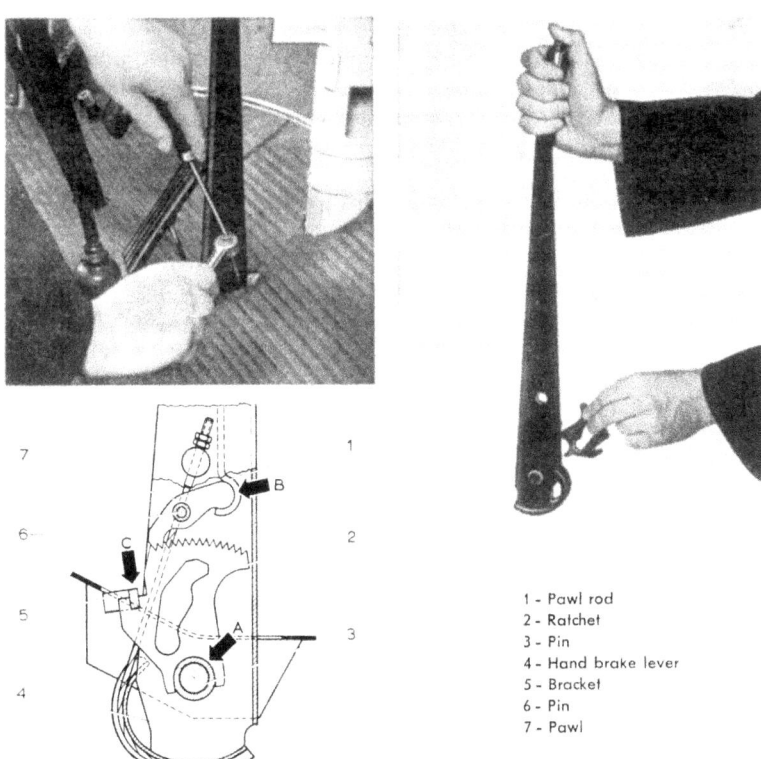

1 - Pawl rod
2 - Ratchet
3 - Pin
4 - Hand brake lever
5 - Bracket
6 - Pin
7 - Pawl

Handbrake Servicing (Prior To 1968)

Push lever boot upwards and remove from lever, then remove the lock and adjusting nuts from ends of brake cables. Remove cover plate under pedal cluster, then pull brake cables from mounting. Remove accelerator lever spring and pull push rod from accelerator lever. Remove spring clip from other side of handbrake lever pin with a screwdriver, then remove pin from mounting. Remove the handbrake lever from the bottom, then press the button and remove the ratchet. Clean and grease lever components, then reassemble, adjust and check brake operation under road conditions.

Handbrake Servicing (1968 And Later)

Remove rubber floor mat, then pull rubber boot up and off adjusting mechanism. Remove the lock and the adjusting nuts from the cable ends. Remove the circlip from the lever pin, then remove the pin. The whole mechanism may be removed by removing the bolts holding the bracket to the dashboard, or the unit may be disassembled by knocking out the pin holding the handle to the ratchet bar, removing the handle and bushings, then twisting up on the spring holding the ratchet pawl and removing the pawl. Unscrew the ratchet bar from the loopscrew and remove the ratchet bar, then remove the circlip from the pin holding the loopscrew in place. Remove the pin, loopscrew, and the handbrake lever. Remove the bolts holding the bracket to the dashboard, then remove the screws holding the facing plate to the bracket. To assemble, reverse the order of disassembly, then adjust the handbrake and test the system on the road.

Handbrake Cable Servicing (Early And Later Models)

To remove the handbrake cable, remove the lever boot and lock and adjusting nuts from the cable ends. Remove the cover plate under the pedal cluster, then pull the cable from the mounting. Remove the rear wheel and brake drum, then the brake shoes. Detach the cable clip off the back plate, then pull the cable and guide hose from the back plate and guide tube. Install the replacement cable in reverse order, noting the following: Clean the cable and guide tube, then make sure the length of the new cable is correct (cable length has changed as a result of changes made in the vehicle's rear track width). Use universal grease to lubricate the whole length of the cable. Finally, adjust the handbrake and check the operation under road conditions.

Order for Bleeding Brakes

After any disconnection of a hydraulic line it is necessary to bleed the system until it is certain that all air is forced from lines. The bleeding is to be carried out at individual wheel cylinders in this order: (Vehicle viewed from driver's seat) 1: Right rear, 2: Left rear, 3: Right front, 4: Left front.

Have one man pump the brakes and check the master cylinder fluid level while the other bleeds the system. Remove bleeder valve dust cap and attach bleeder hose to the valve. Submerge free end of hose in a clean glass container partially filled with brake fluid. If possible, keep the end of the hose above the level of the bleeder valve. With a wrench, loosen the bleeder valve about one turn, then have the brake pedal depressed quickly and allowed to return slowly, continuing this action until the fluid runs out of the bleeder hose in a continuous stream, clean and without air bubbles. Keep a continuous check on the amount of fluid in the master cylinder reservoir, since otherwise air will be drawn in and **all** wheel cylinders will have to be rebled. When the fluid does come out free of bubbles, keep the brake pedal in a fully depressed position and quickly close the bleeder valve. Repeat the operation on each wheel in sequence, finally tightening and replacing the dust cap on each bleeder valve. Never reuse old fluid removed from the brake system or fluid from a can that has been opened and stored for over six months, since moisture from the air will have blended with the fluid. This water will naturally cause such problems as pitting and corrosion of the cylinders and rusting-through of the brake lines, both of which will lead to leakage.

Front Brake

Front Brake Drum Servicing

On the left-hand front wheel, remove the cotter pin holding the speedometer drive cable, then pull off the grease cap, bend back the lock washer and remove the nuts with two open-end wrenches. Remove the thrust washer and slacken the brake shoes from behind the wheel. **Note:** There is a left-hand thread on the left-hand spindle.

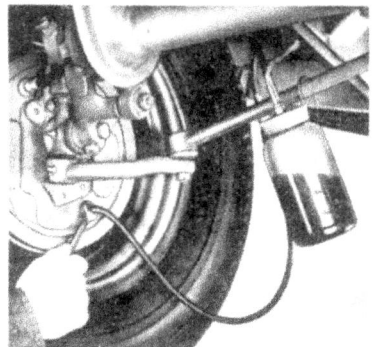

On the 1200 Transporter:

	Normal size	Turning size for 0.5 mm oversize brake linings	Wear limit
Inside dia.	230.2 + 0.3 mm	231.2 + 0.3 mm	231.7 mm
Wall thickness	6.4 — 6.0 mm		5.4 mm
Taper	max. 0.1 mm		
Run-out	max. 0.25 mm		

The braking surface must not be more than 0.25 mm out-of-round.

On the 1500 Transporter:

	Normal size	Turning size for 0.5 mm oversize brake linings	Wear limit
Inside dia.	250 + 0.2 mm	251 + 0.2 mm	251.5 mm
Wall thickness	6.5 — 6.15 mm		5.5 mm
Taper	max. 0.1 mm		
Run-out	max. 0.25 mm		

If drum will not come away from spindle with hand pressure, use a puller ring attached to the drum with the wheel bolts.

Brake drums should be checked for condition of braking surface (wear and cracks) and all components (except brake shoes) cleaned with solvent. If shoes are being renewed, it should be considered mandatory to turn drums so shoes and drums meet parallel to each other. Use chart to check the front drum tolerances. Be sure to pack the wheel bearings with high-quality wheel bearing grease and do not mix different brands. Be sure to clean bearing housing inside drum, races and wheel bearing, then replace with all fresh grease. Press about 250 g into the cage and between the rollers, replace the brake drum, then adjust the wheel bearings.

1200 Model (230 mm)

1 - Brake back plate
2 - Brake shoes
3 - Brake linings
4 - Return springs
5 - Anchor block with brake cylinder
6 - Adjusting nut
7 - Bridge pipe

To remove front brake shoes, pry shoe away from backing plate at top to disengage from adjusting screw, taking care not to damage the leaf spring of the adjustment device. Then unhook return springs from their slotted holes. In re-installing, make sure

1500 Model (250 mm)

1 - Brake back plate
2 - Brake shoes
3 - Brake linings
4 - Return springs
5 - Anchor block with brake cylinder
6 - Adjusting nuts
7 - Bridge pipe

1200 Model (230 mm)   1500 Model (250 mm)

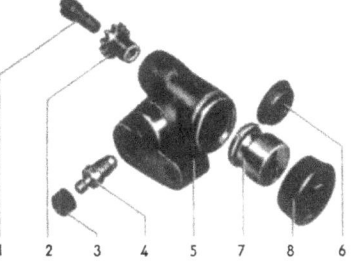

1 - Adjuster nut	4 - Bleeder valve	7 - Piston
2 - Adjuster screw	5 - Cylinder body	8 - Boot
3 - Dust cap	6 - Cup	

1 - Adjusting screw	4 - Bleeder valve	7 - Piston
2 - Adjusting nut	5 - Cylinder body	8 - Boot
3 - Dust cap	6 - Cup	

that correct width shoe is used (see Note). First connect the return springs so they do not chafe the spacer or the wheel cylinder tube. The springs are hooked in position from the inside of the webs and the lower spring should be hooked at one end only. Install rear shoe first; cylinder end before adjusting end, repeat with front shoe.

Wheel cylinders may now be removed by unscrewing four bolts. Prior to installing the brake drum, make sure the shaft seal is in good condition, then adjust the wheel bearings correctly. Tighten wheel cylinder bolts to 40—44 ft. lb. Adjust the brakes and bleed the complete system as described elsewhere in this chapter. Road test the vehicle to ensure proper brake operation.

Rear Brake

Note: Loosen or tighten the axle shaft nuts with the vehicle on the ground, **not** while the vehicle is on a lift. The amount of torque necessary could cause the car to shift on a lift, possibly causing a serious accident. If possible, remove and grease wheel bolts to prevent bolts from rusting and freezing into place. Such an occurrence can prove frustrating, especially when a tire needs to be changed by the roadside. **Do** leave the wheel on the brake drum during brake repairs, including turning the drum; first, however, torque all bolts diametrically opposite in turn to 80—94 ft. lb. This will prevent drum warpage and pulsating brakes.

Remove the brake drum nut and drum (first turn the brake adjusting nuts to slacken the brake shoes, then use either a 3 ft. long breaker bar or an impact wrench to remove the shaft nut and the drum). Re-

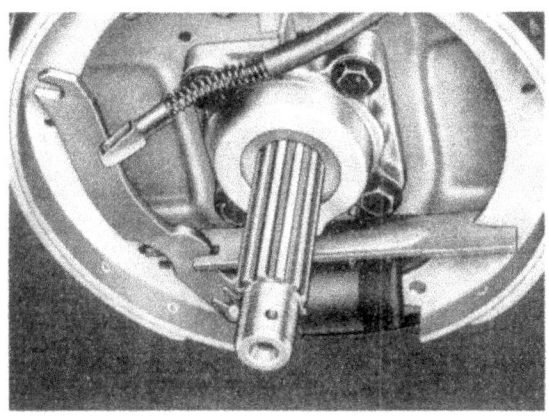

move oil deflector, then unhook the handbrake cable. Remove the shoe hold-down spring seats, springs and pins, then unhook the upper brake shoe return spring. Hold both shoes at the top and simultaneously unhook them from the anchor, then allow upper ends to come together so the shoes, lower return spring, brake shoe lever, push bar and clip may be removed as a unit. Spread the shoes to remove the push bar, then unhook the lower return spring. Detach the brake lever from the brake shoe by removing the circlip from the anchor pin.

Brake drums should be checked for condition of braking surface (wear and cracks) and all components (except brake shoes) cleaned with solvent. If shoes are being renewed, it should be considered

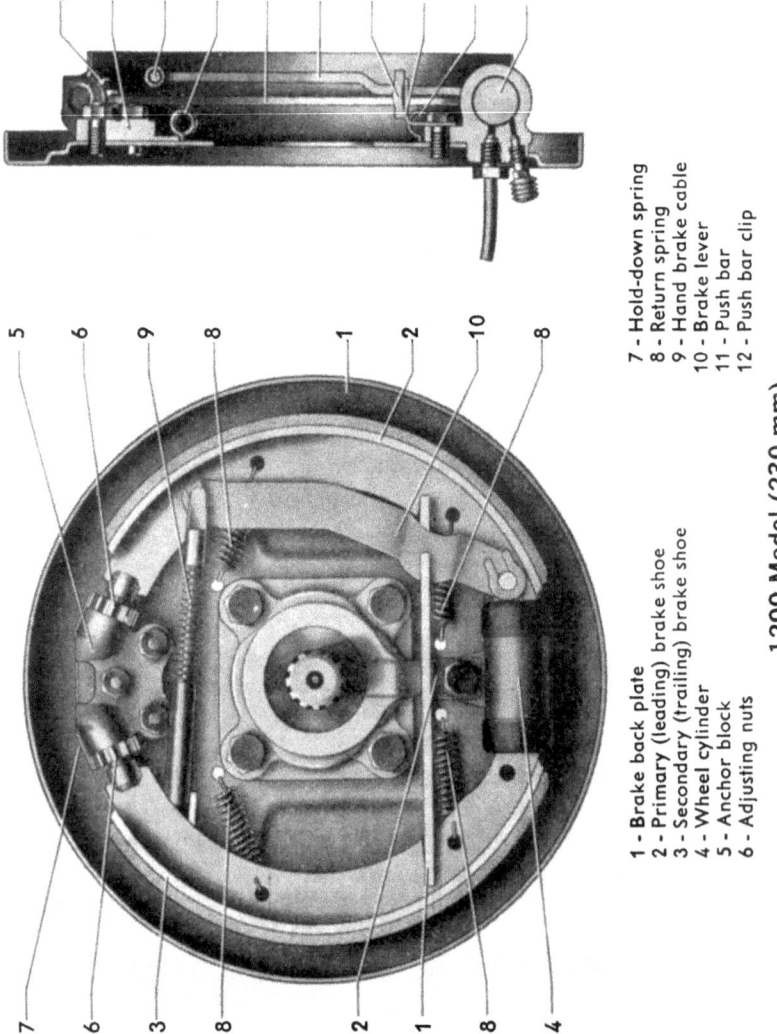

1 - Brake back plate
2 - Primary (leading) brake shoe
3 - Secondary (trailing) brake shoe
4 - Wheel cylinder
5 - Anchor block
6 - Adjusting nuts
7 - Hold-down spring
8 - Return spring
9 - Hand brake cable
10 - Brake lever
11 - Push bar
12 - Push bar clip

1200 Model (230 mm)

mandatory to turn drums so shoes and drums meet parallel to each other. Use chart to check the front drum tolerances. Be sure to pack the wheel bearings with high-quality wheel bearing grease and do not mix different brands. Be sure to clean bearing housing inside drum, races and wheel bearing.

Wheel cylinders may now be removed by removing one screw. Make sure replacement brake shoes are of the same type of lining material and the same width as the shoes on the other wheel on the same axle. Install brake shoes with brake lever, push bar, return springs and clip, then connect brake cable. Hook in upper return spring, then install brake shoe retaining spring, spring seat and pin. Tighten wheel cylinder screw to 40—44 ft. lb. and axle shaft nut to 216 ft. lb., then insert cotter pin. Turn nut further to insert pin if necessary. Bleed hydraulic brakes and adjust foot and handbrakes, being sure to replace the bleeder valve dust caps. Finally, road test the vehicle to ensure proper brake operation.

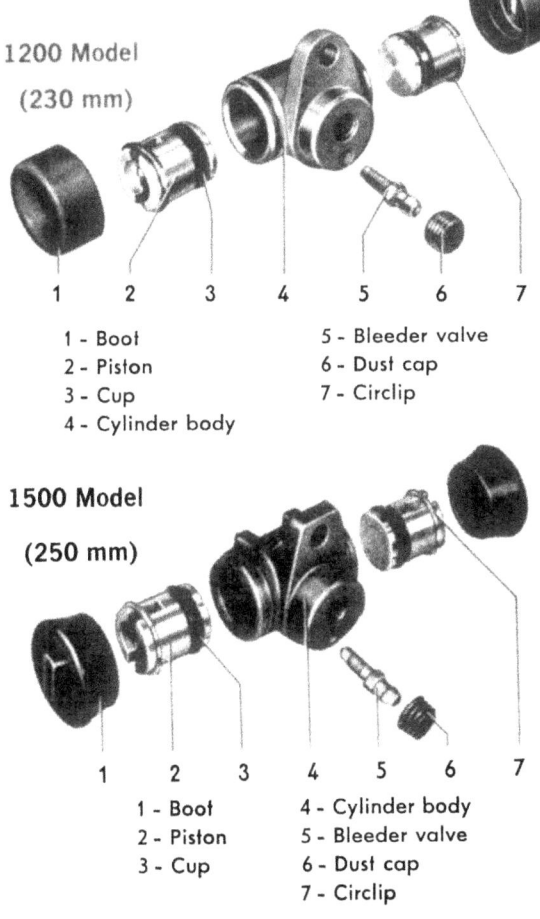

1200 Model
(230 mm)

1 - Boot
2 - Piston
3 - Cup
4 - Cylinder body
5 - Bleeder valve
6 - Dust cap
7 - Circlip

1500 Model
(250 mm)

1 - Boot
2 - Piston
3 - Cup
4 - Cylinder body
5 - Bleeder valve
6 - Dust cap
7 - Circlip

1500 Model (250 mm)

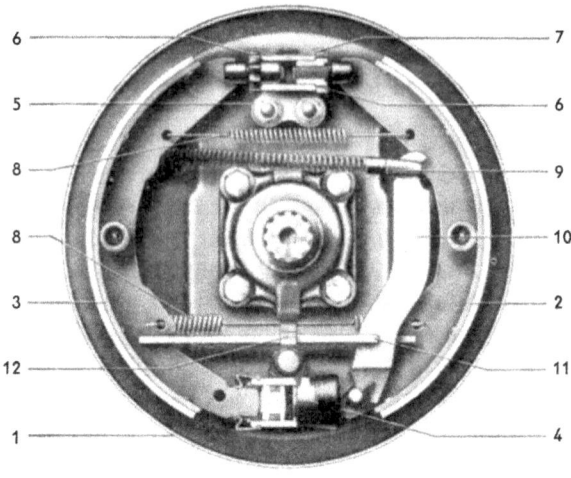
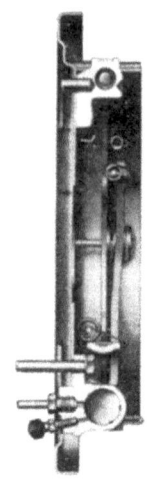

1 - Brake back plate
2 - Primary (leading) brake shoe
3 - Secondary (trailing) brake shoe
4 - Wheel cylinder
5 - Anchor block
6 - Adjusting nuts
7 - Adjusting nut spring
8 - Return spring
9 - Hand brake cable
10 - Brake lever
11 - Push bar
12 - Push bar clip

Wheel Cylinders

Repair (Front and Rear)

Remove rubber boot(s), pull out piston(s), then remove cup(s) from piston(s). Screw out bleeder valve. To assemble the cylinder, first clean all parts in denatured alcohol or brake fluid. Other fluids destroy rubber parts and may leave a deposit, so should not be used. Examine all parts for wear while drying, especially making sure the sliding surfaces of the piston(s) and cylinder are smooth and not scored. A cylinder hone may be used to slightly true the cylinder. DO NOT over-hone. Check the fit of the dry piston(s) in the dry cylinder bore. The piston(s) must slide through the bore without binding and not be worn unevenly or be out of round. If not, replace the complete cylinder with new or factory overhauled parts. Also replace the cylinder complete if piston(s) are so loose that they wallow excessively. Fit new cup(s) of the correct size, making sure parts are from a genuine VW repair kit. Install parts after coating the bore and cup(s) with genuine VW Brake Fluid.

Note: Through the years, production changes have been incorporated for more braking area and easier inspection and adjustment. The width of the rear brake shoes has been increased, and the diameter of the rear wheel brake cylinder has been rduced to provide quicker action. All brake drums now have 4 holes, the back plates having 2 inspection holes and 2 adjusting holes each. These changes have also necessitated modifications to the bearing housings, rear axle shafts, wheel discs, hub caps and trim rings.

Brake Master Cylinder

The hydraulic brake master cylinder is located under the floor adjacent to the pedal linkage. A removable plate protects it from damage. The accompanying exploded view portrays the various components. It is important that only Lockheed or VW brake fluid be used in this system and, should it be disassembled and cleaned, never use gasoline, kerosene or solvent. Wash all parts only in clean brake fluid.

It is important that the vent hole in the cover remain unobstructed at all times to prevent the formation of a vacuum in the reservoir. Be particularly careful when painting the chassis, if such an operation is necessary. When filling the reservoir, check the vent and be sure that the cover itself is absolutely free from dirt or foreign matter which might contaminate the fluid and clog tiny orifices. Fill the reservoir to within ¾ of an inch of the upper edge.

Differences in temperature cause expansion and contraction of brake fluid in cylinders and lines. For this reason a by-pass port has been incorporated in front of the main rubber cup. If it is clogged or covered by incorrect position of the cup, brakes will drag as a result of pressure built up in the system. Clean fluid and exact adjustment of the piston pushrod length guard against this condition.

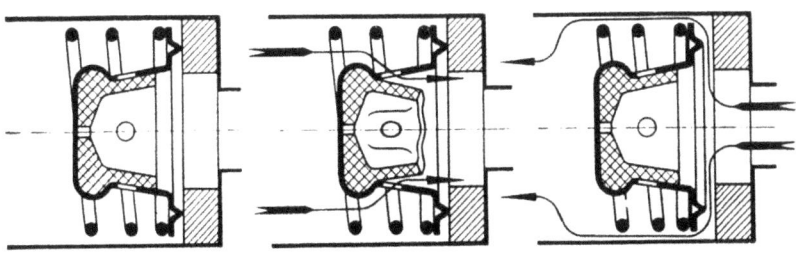

Released position   Braking position   Return position

1200 Model (30 mm stroke)

Another part fitted to control the fluid movement already described is the double-acting check valve. If a vacuum occurs in the brake system, the check valve reacts to the slightest change and permits the necessary quantity of fluid to flow from the reservoir through the cylinder pressure chamber into the system. The valve is also lifted from its seat by excessive pressure in the system so that the surplus fluid can return to the reservoir. When braking, the fluid flows past the check valve into the brake lines and returns freely when the pedal is released. The check valve is fitted with a small spring which maintains a slight pressure in the system. This ensures that the system is absolutely full and the force exerted at the brake pedal transferred to the complete brake system without delay.

1500 Model (36 mm stroke)

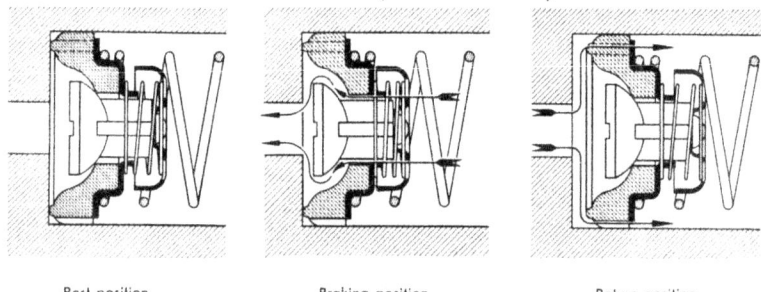

Rest position   Braking position   Return position

Dimension **a** in the diagram regulates clearance S which is critical to within 1mm (0.04"). **a** should be 2 21/64 inches to 2 23/64 inches. The stop plate may have to be bent to allow this clearance (see arrow in photo).

Note: If occasion arises to replace the master cylinder, the correct replacement will have a diameter of 22.2 mm, (0.874").

1200 Model (30 mm stroke)

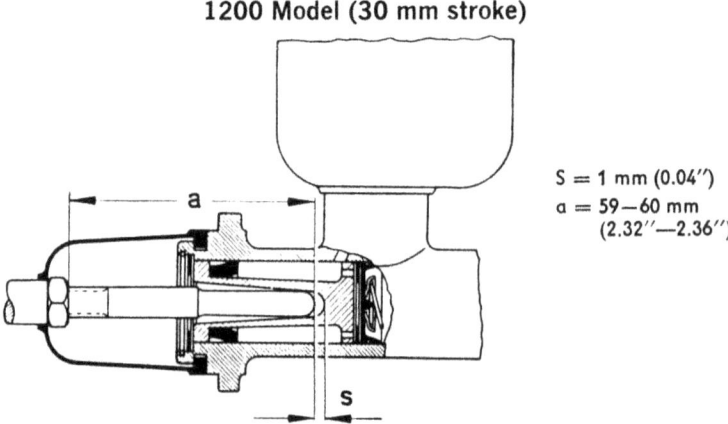

$S = 1$ mm (0.04")
$a = 59-60$ mm
  (2.32"—2.36")

1500 Model (36 mm stroke)

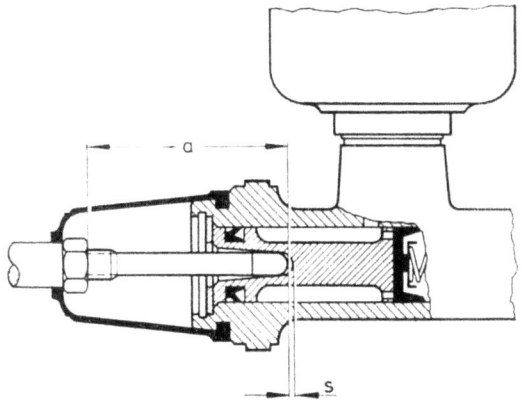

$a = 69.5$—70.5 mm (2.735—$2.774''$)
$S = 1$ mm ($.040''$)

Master Cylinder Removal

Remove bolts holding plate to underside of cab, then remove plate to gain access to master cylinder. Remove lower reservoir tank hose (if so equipped) and drain fluid from upper reservoir tank. Dis-

1200 Model (30 mm stroke)

1 - Cover
2 - Gland nut and strainer
3 - Fluid reservoir
4 - Gasket
5 - Master cylinder body
6 - Stop light switch
7 - Piston stop plate
8 - Lock wire
9 - Boot
10 - Check valve seat
11 - Check valve
12 - Piston return spring
13 - Main Piston cup
14 - Piston washer
15 - Piston
16 - Secondary piston cup
17 - Push rod
18 - Push rod clevis end

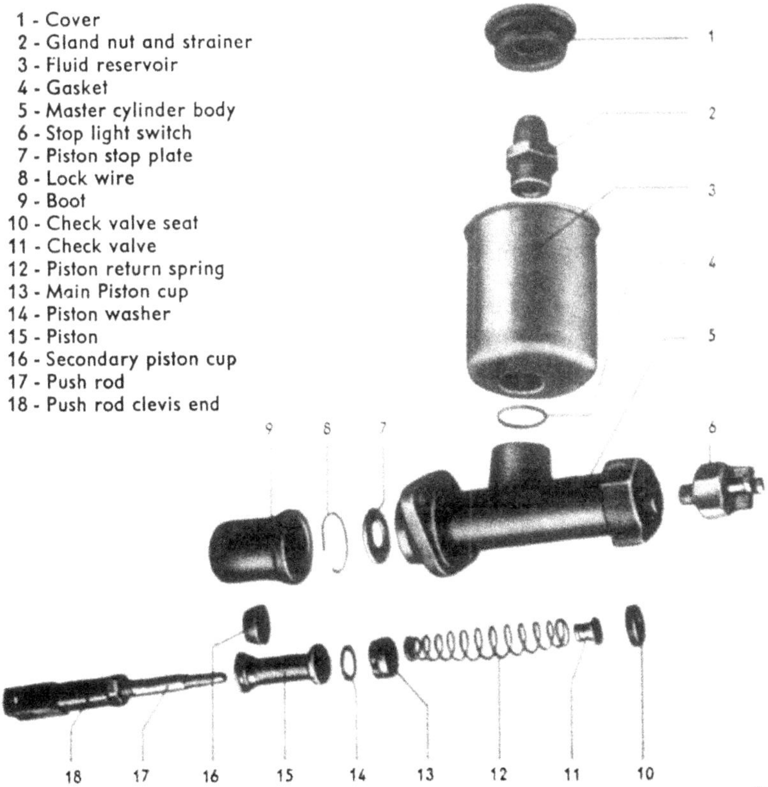

1500 Model (36 mm stroke)

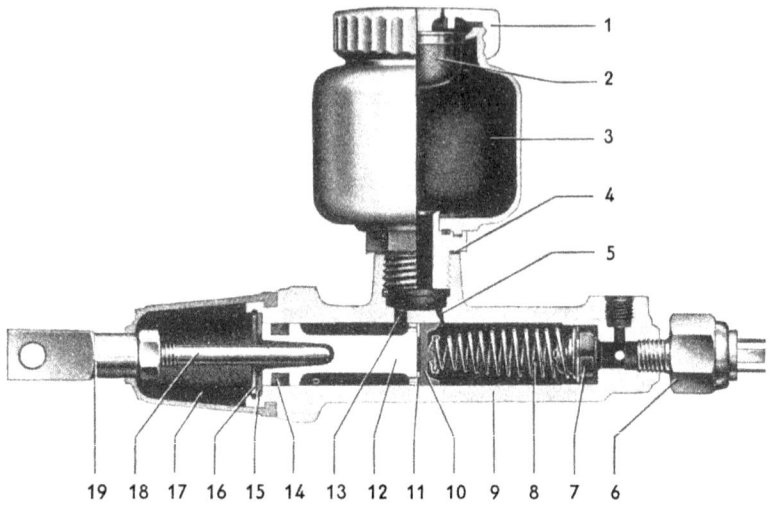

1 - Cover
2 - Filter
3 - Reservoir
4 - Gasket
5 - By-pass port
6 - Stop light switch
7 - Check valve
8 - Spring
9 - Cylinder body
10 - Primary cup
11 - Piston washer
12 - Piston
13 - Intake port
14 - Secondary cup
15 - Stop washer
16 - Lock ring
17 - Boot
18 - Push rod
19 - Clevis

connect all stoplight cables from switches. Disconnect brake lines and plug with bleeder valve caps. Either bend up lock plate of clevis pin in master cylinder operating rod or remove cotter pin and washer, then remove clevis pin. Remove the mounting bolts and withdraw the master cylinder, fluid reservoir and push rod toward the rear.

To install, reverse the order of the removal procedure, noting the following: First, check the length of the push rod against the accompanying illustrations: It must either conform to these measurements, or if a later model, conform to the length of the rod when it was originally removed. If fitting a new push rod, transfer this measurement to the new rod. Install the master cylinder complete with the reservoir and push rod, making sure the boot is properly located. A new lock plate or cotter pin (as necessary) must always be fitted on the push rod pin. After replacing the master cylinder, adjust the stop plate by tapping it until there is a clearance of .04 in. (1 mm.) between the tip of the push rod and the recess in the piston. Make sure the vent hole in the upper reservoir cap is open, and fill the brake system with fresh, high-quality brake fluid. Bleed the brake system, check the system for leaks, and check the brakes on the road. Make sure the brake lights work, along with the warning system.

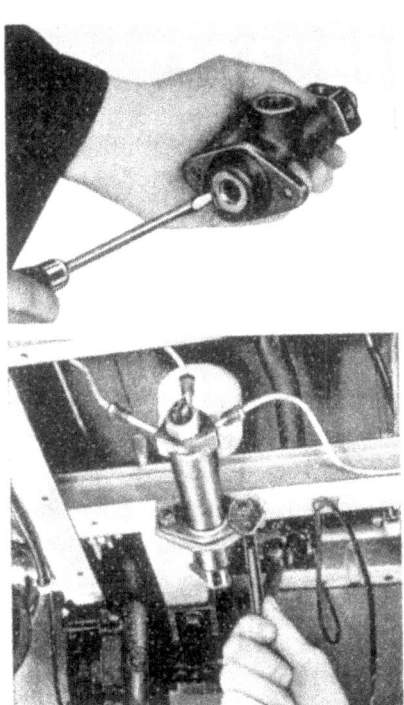

Single Circuit Master Cylinder Repair

Pull out push rod, empty fluid reservoir, remove and disassemble it, then remove the rubber boot. Remove the lock ring, then take out the piston stop plate and the piston. Remove the piston washer, main cup, return spring with seat and check valve. Screw off the stop light switch.

To assemble the master cylinder, first clean all parts in denatured alcohol or brake fluid. Other fluids destroy rubber parts, and also should not be used since they may leave a deposit. Examine all parts for wear while drying, especially making sure the intake and bypass ports are open and free from burrs. Check the fit of the piston in the cylinder bore. If it is too loose, ("falls" to the bottom when fitted dry), replace the complete master cylinder with a new or factory rebuilt unit. Otherwise, it is best to use a VW-manufactured repair kit. Always renew the two rubber cups, noting the diameter of the master cylinder. Install the check valve and spring with the washer, then install the main cup and washer. Coat the piston and cylinder bore with Genuine VW Brake Cylinder Paste and install with the secondary cup, then insert the stop plate. Insert lock ring and check that it is seated correctly. Place a gasket between the fluid reservoir and the master cylinder, then install the reservoilr. Make sure the vent hole in the fluid reservoir cover is clear.

Tandem Master Cylinder

The dual brake system uses a tandem master cylinder and a brake fluid reservoir divided into two chambers. In the eventuality of leakage from one of the circuits, the other will remain intact, allowing safe stopping with the remaining brakes. Basically, the design of the master cylinder is similar to two single-circuit master cylinders fitted one behind the other. One of the circuits actuates the front wheel brakes and the other the rear wheel brakes. This divides the systems into individual sections, each able to work separately from the other.

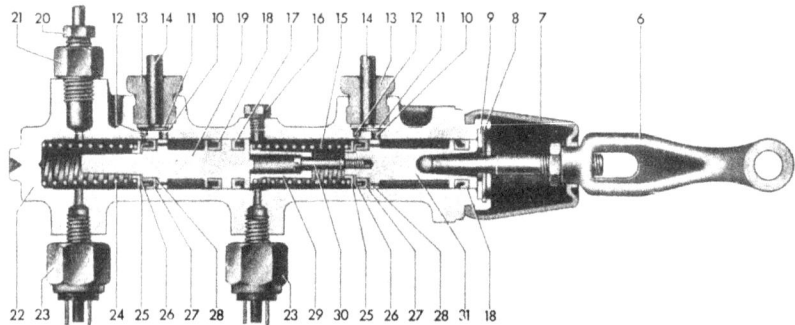

6 - Push rod
7 - Boot
8 - Spring ring
9 - Stop ring
10 - Feed port
11 - Sealing plug washer
12 - Campensating port
13 - Sealing plug
14 - Feed line
15 - Rear brake circuit piston spring
16 - Stop screw and seal
17 - Seal
18 - Secondary cup
19 - Front brake circuit piston
20 - Brake line union nut
21 - Residual pressure valve
22 - Master cylinder housing
23 - Brake light switch
24 - Front brake circuit piston spring
25 - Spring plate
26 - Support ring
27 - Primary cup
28 - Cup washer
29 - Stop sleeve
30 - Stroke limiting screw
31 - Rear brake circuit piston

Should a leak occur in the front brake circuit, both master cylinder pistons and the brake fluid between the pistons are pushed forward until the front brake circuit piston bears against the forward end of the master cylinder housing. It is then possible for pressure to increase in the rear brake circuit pressure chamber.

Should the leak instead occur in the rear brake circuit, the rear brake circuit piston is pushed forward until it comes to bear against the stop sleeve. As the brake pedal is depressed further, mechanical force is transferred to the front brake circuit through the rear brake circuit piston. This causes the hydraulic pressure to be built up in the front brake circuit.

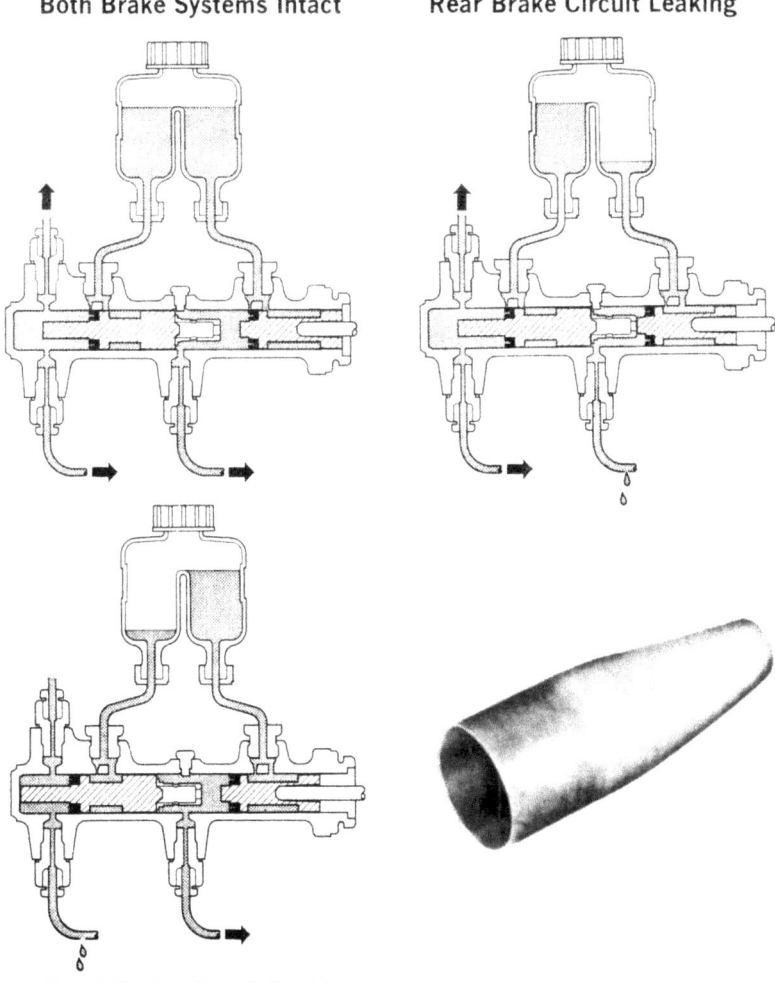

Both Brake Systems Intact

Rear Brake Circuit Leaking

Front Brake Circuit Leaking

In the event of failure of one brake circuit, the driver will notice the increase of brake pedal travel and the lessened effectiveness of the brakes. On most models shipped to America there is also a dashboard-mounted warning system to visually indicate there has been a failure of one of the brake circuits. This system includes a warning device in the master cylinder, a switch, and a push-button warning light mounted in the dashboard.

On a master cylinder in which the pressure of one of the two circuits has fallen, there will be unequal pressure, causing one of the pistons in the warning device to move one way or the other and pressing in the switch pin to close an electrical circuit and illuminate the dashboard warning light. With an intact brake system the pressures of all chambers are equalized, thus keeping the pistons in one position. The push button allows the driver to check the electrical circuit.

The lower brake fluid reservoir is divided into two compartments, although there is only one filler opening. The upper fluid reservoir should be filled to the upper edge of the securing strap. Be sure to use the best quality brake fluid and never reuse old brake fluid. One brake line carries the fluid down to the reservoir on top of the tandem master brake cylinder.

To take the place of the check valve used on the single cylinder, residual pressure valves are used, one in each connection on the tandem master cylinder (two front brake lines and one rear up to 1970 model, then one front and one rear after that). This unit functions so that a low residual pressure remains in the brake system, thus the force applied at the brake pedal is transferred directly to the various parts of the brake system with no lost motion.

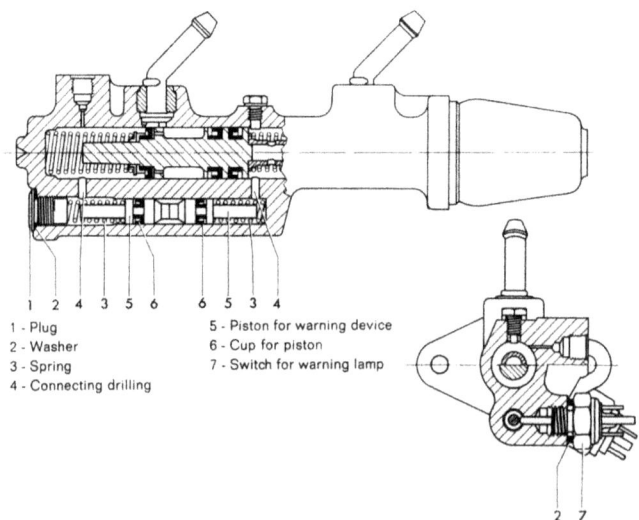

1 - Plug
2 - Washer
3 - Spring
4 - Connecting drilling
5 - Piston for warning device
6 - Cup for piston
7 - Switch for warning lamp

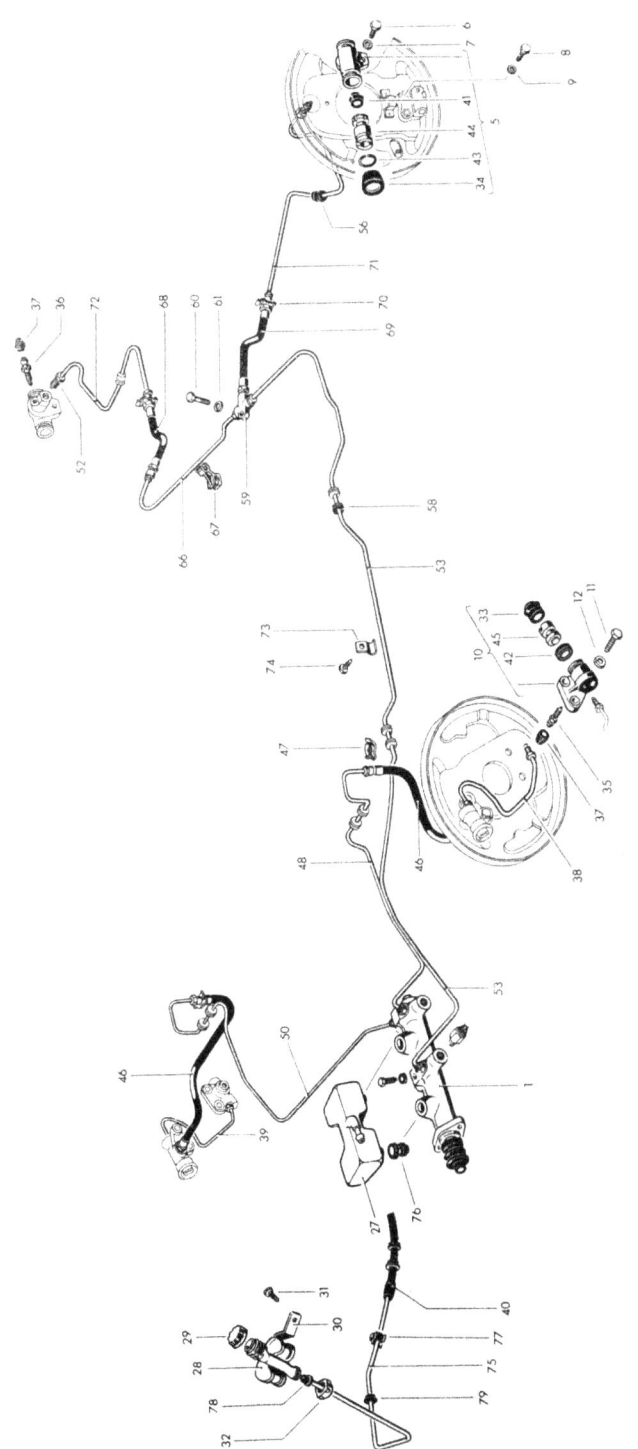

Brake cylinders — Lines

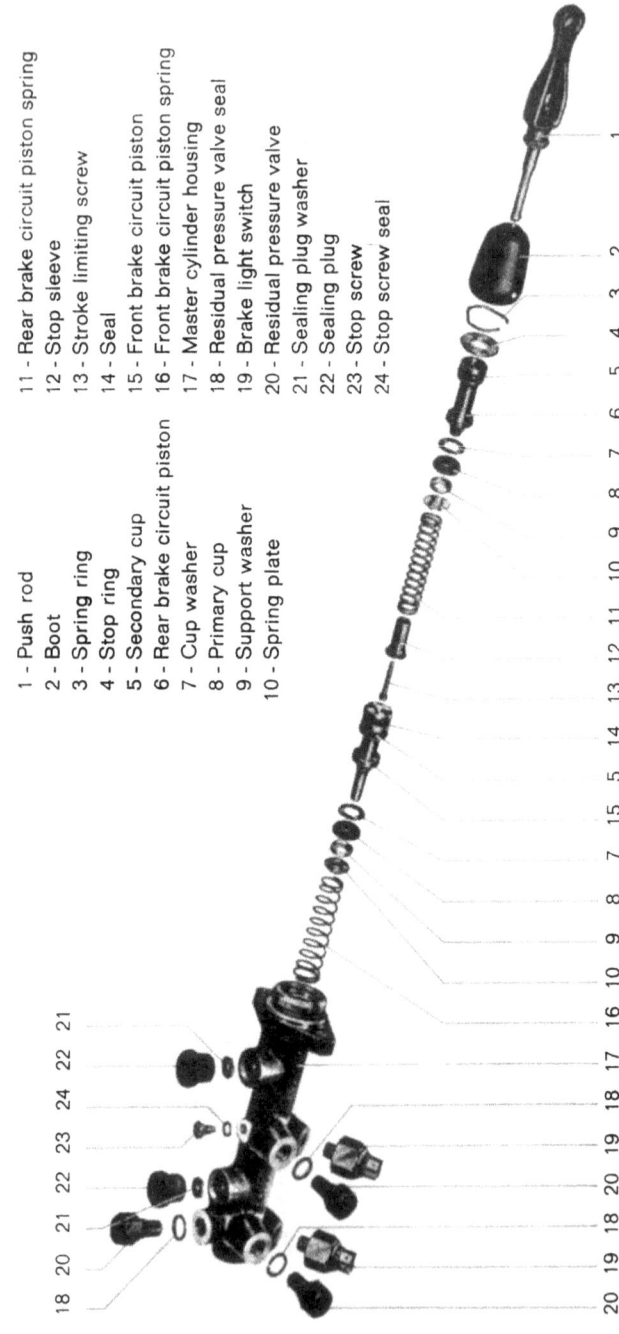

1 - Push rod
2 - Boot
3 - Spring ring
4 - Stop ring
5 - Secondary cup
6 - Rear brake circuit piston
7 - Cup washer
8 - Primary cup
9 - Support washer
10 - Spring plate
11 - Rear brake circuit piston spring
12 - Stop sleeve
13 - Stroke limiting screw
14 - Seal
15 - Front brake circuit piston
16 - Front brake circuit piston spring
17 - Master cylinder housing
18 - Residual pressure valve seal
19 - Brake light switch
20 - Residual pressure valve
21 - Sealing plug washer
22 - Sealing plug
23 - Stop screw
24 - Stop screw seal

334

Tandem Master Cylinder Repair

To disassemble, remove the boot and unscrew the stop screw. Remove the sprirng ring for the stop ring, then remove the internal parts. Finally, unscrew the residual pressure valves and the brake light switch.

To assemble, first clean all parts in alcohol or brake fluid, then check for wear. Make sure the compensating ports are not blocked and are free of burrs. Clean and dry the pistons, then make sure each is a suction fit in the cylinder. All the cups are of the same shape and size, (with the exception of the secondary cup for the rear brake circuit) and so are interchangeable. The various names given the cups are only to explain their function. Reverse the removal procedure to assemble the master cylinder, coat the cylinder bore and pistons with Genuine VW Brake Cylinder Paste, and upend the housing to make assembly easier (parts will fall off the piston otherwise). Before installing the stop screws and sealing ring, make sure the piston for the front brake circuit is not covering the hole. If it is, use the push rod to push the parts further in as the stop screw is turned down. Torque the residual pressure valve and the brake light switch to 11—14 ft. lb., then install the protective breather cap with the breather hole DOWN. A fitting sleeve, as illustrated, must be used to install the secondary cup of the front braking system, and is helpful when installing the other cups. Make the fitting sleeve from flexible plastic material, for example a section cut from a plastic household bleach bottle. If only part of the braking system was repaired or disconnected, it is sufficient to bleed only the brake circuit which was repaired. Otherwise, start with the front brake circuit.

Wheels and Tires

The Transporter uses 7.00—14 6 PR tubeless tires mounted on 5 JK x 14 wheel discs with drop center rims (Fig. 217). Starting with the 1968 models, all vehicles **other** than the Station Wagon use 7.00—14 8 PR tubeless tires. For the life of the tires, and the best road holding and resistance to side winds, tire pressure should be regularly checked and maintained. With up to a $^3/_4$ payload, and especially when travelling on bumpy roads, the factory recommended pressures are 28 front and 33 rear for pre-1968 models. With a full load, increase rear tire pressure to 40 psi. Use either 36 psi or 41 psi (fully loaded) for rear tires on 1968 and later models. For long, high speed trips, the tire pressures should be increased by 3 psi at both the front and rear for all years and models. Keep the spare tire at 44 psi and release pressure as necessary after mounting. Tire pressure should be adjusted with cold tires; never let air out of tires after a fast drive because heat build-up will give a false reading. Fig. 218 shows the effect of over and under inflation. Generally, a slight loss in pressure is harmful because of excessive internal friction and heat build-up, but tires can be considerably over inflated before bruising becomes a problem.

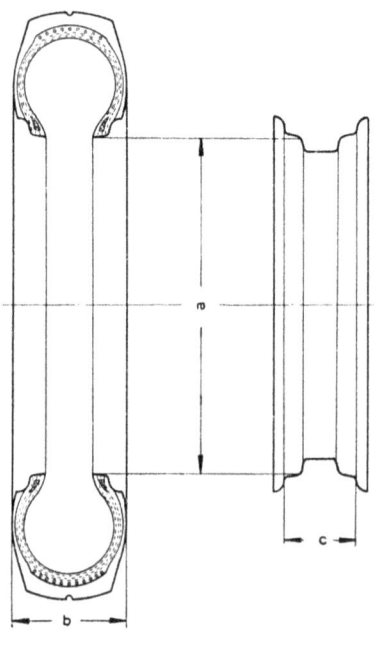

a = 14   b = 7.00"   c = 5JK   **FIG. 217**

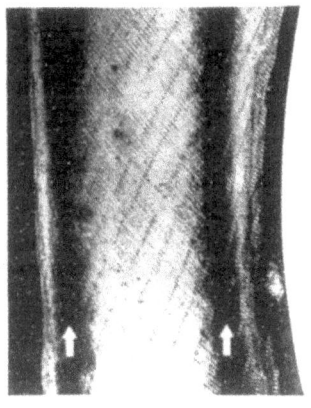

Dark stripes inside the tire are the first sign of under-inflation.

Stepped or heel and toe wear indicates over-loading or, if combined with excessive wear of the tread outer edges, under-inflation.

FIG. 218

Fig. 219, shows air seal formed by correctly mounted tire and valve.

Tire rotation has been dropped from the Volkswagen maintenance plan because the tires are so large for the weight of the car, that without half trying, you can get 40,000 miles to a set of tires. Tire rotation however will give even better mileage because each wheel position produces a different amount and kind of wear. You may wish to rotate tires according to Fig. 220, but rotation method doesn't really matter as long as tires are rotated the same way each time and at uniform intervals.

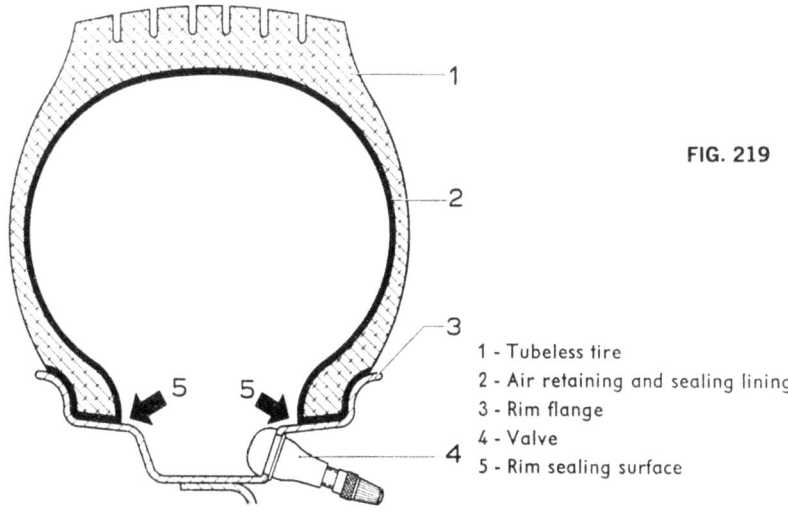

FIG. 219

1 - Tubeless tire
2 - Air retaining and sealing lining
3 - Rim flange
4 - Valve
5 - Rim sealing surface

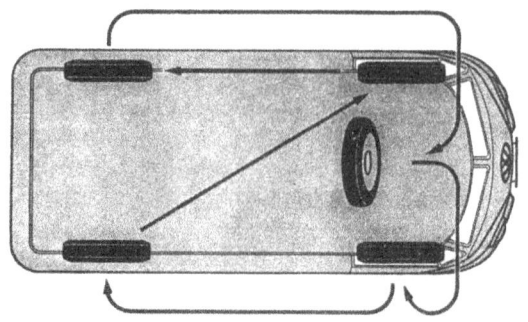

FIG. 220

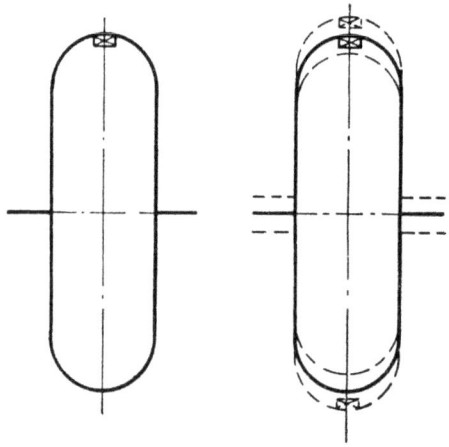

FIG. 221

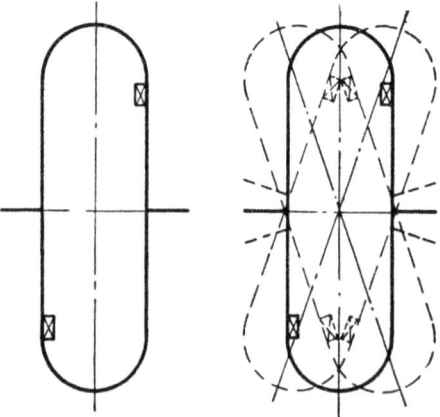

FIG. 222

Tire Inspection

The tires should be frequently checked but always during Maintenance Service for correct inflation and undue signs of wear as well as for cracks, grease, cuts, and bruises. Flints and stones that are embedded in the tire should be removed.

Note: Care should be taken when using a simple tire gage for a prolonged period. After a certain time of use, such tire gages are subject to variations. Although the readings obtained often depart only slightly from the real pressure in the tube, the detrimental over or underinflation may lead to abnormal tire wear. Therefore, it is absolutely necessary to regularly check the tire gage for accuracy.

The tightness of the valve cores can easily be checked by moistening a finger and placing it on the valve opening. Renew leaky valve cores.

Abnormal Tire Wear

Following are the causes for abnormal tire wear:
Underinflation or overinflation
Poor driving habits
Overloading the vehicle
Bad road conditions
Improper wheel adjustments

SERVICE DIAGNOSIS OF ABNORMAL TIRE WEAR

TYPE OF WEAR	CAUSE
Wear at the sides of the tread.	Underinflation.
Wear at the center of the tread.	Overinflation.
Spotty or irregular wear (gouges and waves).	Wheel assembly static and dynamic unbalance.
	Lateral wheel run-out.
	Excessive play in wheel bearings or at king pin.
Lightly worn spots at the center of the tread (cups).	Wheel and tire static unbalance.
	Radial wheel run out.
Flat spots at the center of the tread.	Violent brake application. Brake drum out of round. Check brakes!
Heel and toe wear (saw-tooth effect with one end of each tread block worn more than the other) leading to cracks in the fabric structure which becomes visible outside in the long run.	Typical for overloading. Check inside of tire casing for cracks.
a. Side wear.	a. Incorrect camber. Continual driving on steeply cambered (high-crowned) roads.

b. Feather edge of rubber on one side of the tread blocks.

b. Wheels toe-in or toe-out excessively. If the rear wheels are concerned, check adjustment of spring plate and effect of shock absorbers.

c. Rounding and roughening of the tread at the outside shoulder of the tire.

c. Caused by high speed driving on curves, called cornering wear.

Underinflation

An underinflated tire will be subjected to excessive flexing of the side walls and resultant heat. Underinflation can be determined by wear at the sides of the tread. Two black stripes will first form inside the tire casing. They will lead to damage of the fabric structure. If the tires are further operated with insufficient air pressure, the plies in the side walls will separate so that the tires are ruined. The underinflated tire contacts the road along the sides, where the tread is subjected to greater wear than in the center.

Overinflation

Overinflated tires cannot absorb shocks and abnormal wear will occur at the center of the tread, making the tires susceptible to bruises and breaks.

Driving Habits

The average speeds of automotive vehicles have gone up considerably in the course of the past decade. The tire wear increases rapidly with the speed. High-speed operation causes much more rapid tire wear because of the high temperature and greater amount of scuffing and rapid flexing to which the tires are subjected. Fast acceleration, sudden severe brake application, turning corners and rounding curves too fast or sharply will additionally contribute to increased and uneven tire wear. The reasons for increased tire wear when applying the brakes are clear, but it should be borne in mind that unequally or improperly adjusted brakes or differences in the quality of the brake shoe linings may lead to abnormal wear of some tires. Eccentric brake drums may also be the cause for unequal tire wear.

Overloading the Car

Tires interpose a cushion between the road and the car wheels. The compressibility of the air in the tube allows the tires to absorb shocks resulting from irregularities in the road. It is the interrelation of air pressure, air volume and load that determines the correct tire size. Each tire size has to cope with a certain continuous load at a given inflation pressure. A temporary overloading is common in the operation of a motor vehicle; a fact which has been taken into account in designing the tires. Continuous overloading, however, has a detrimental effect on the tire structure.

This wear results in a saw-tooth effect with one end of each tread block worn more than the other.

With the tire continuously overloaded, the fabric structure inside the tire will crack. After some time of operation, the cracks appear outside in the tire walls.

Road Surface

The tire life largely depends on the condition of the surface. To contribute to safe driving, antiskid material is now used to cover the roads. This provides frictional contact between the wheels and the road so that good traction is secured. This will make the tires subject to increased wear.

On steeply cambered roads (high crowned roads), the tires have to resist a side force which the driver attempts to compensate by applying a certain force on the steering wheel toward the center of the road so that the tires drag at an angle to the direction of vehicle movement.

Even a slight departure from the correct toe-in adjustment is very detrimental to the tire life under such conditions. If the toe-in is excessive, the tire towards the nearer curbstone wears more rapidly. If the toe-in adjustment is too low, the wheel toward the center of the road wears faster. This wear is usually distinguished by side wear and feather edges of rubber that appear on one side of the tread design.

A faster wear on steeply cambered (high crowned) roads must be taken into consideration, even if the toe-in adjustment is correct, but such wear will not be confined to one tire.

Misaligned Wheels

There are also several types of wear which can be attributed to wheel misalignment. In each case of abnormal tire wear, it is strongly recommended to check the following:

    Front axle track
    Track with steering at full lock
    Position and track of the rear wheels
    Position of both axles in relation to one another
    Wheel base on both sides
    Camber
    Spring plate adjustment
    Shock absorber operation

Misaligned wheels cause part of the tread rubber to be

scraped off; this is indicated by feather edging of the tread and side wear.

A chassis that has been involved in an accident should in all cases be checked for proper alignment to assure a perfect track of wheels.

Wheel and Tire Balancing

The wheel and tire assembly balance must be maintained to insure good riding qualities and best steering performance of the car. A statically unbalanced condition of a wheel and tire assembly is indicated by an up and down hopping or pounding action (Fig. 221). The wheel wobbles or shimmies if it is dynamically out of balance (Fig. 222). The faster a car the more important is a perfect wheel and tire balance.

It is generally not necessary to balance new wheels and tires. They are statically balanced during the course of production. Any remaining unbalance is so negligible that it does not affect the driving qualities of the Volkswagen. The wall of the tire is marked by either a single or double dot. The valve is supposed to be situated at this location during mounting so as to counteract the remaining unbalance.

Wheel balance is the first item to check after the tire has been repaired, retreaded or recapped. Should it not be possible to have repaired tires balanced both statically and dynamically put the wheel on the rear axle.

Under these circumstances fast driving should be avoided.

Heater and Controls
EARLY MODELS

Air warmed by the heat dissipated by the engine is used to make the cab comfortable in cold weather. A double-walled junction box prevents the possibility of exhaust fumes from entering the vehicle, but leaks or rusted-through points could cause such unpleasant results. So it is wise to check this portion of the system before the onset of winter or when it is expected that the heater will be used. If there is a complaint of unpleasant fumes in the cab it can be caused by dirty engine cooling fins or a dirty oil cooler. A dirty engine also operates at a higher temperature, therefore keeping it clean is important in two ways. Lack of heat can be attributed to faulty control linkage, a failure in the thermostat controlling the cooling air throttle ring or leakage in body ducts.

The junction box is removed with the exhaust pipe in this fashion:
1. Remove nuts from exhaust flange.
2. Remove slotted screw at bottom of junction box.
3. Remove cotter pin and unhook connector rod from the heat control flap (arrow in illustration).

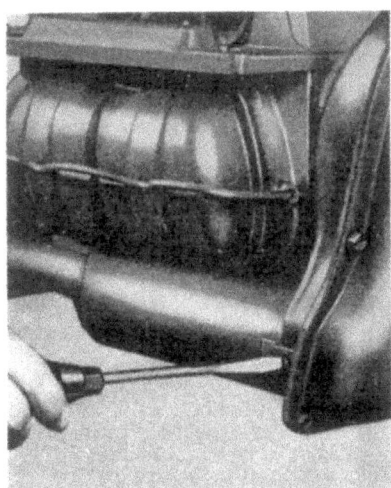

When replacing, lubricate moving portions with graphite and grease (VW-A 070).

Servicing Heater Control Cable

With the vehicle jacked up, release the nut of the clamp with 9mm and 10mm open end wrenches to avoid breakage of cable through twisting, then disconnect cable from clamp, remove rubber grommet from conduit tube and slide it off cable. It is now possible to withdraw the cable after releasing the threaded cap by grasping the knob and pulley.

To install a new cable:
1. Be sure to grease the cable, threaded sleeve and thread with Universal Grease.
2. The longer end of the heating control cable must be inserted into the right hand conduit tube (as seen from the driving position).
3. Before installing the control knob unit, turn it anti-clockwise until the stop can be felt, then turn it clockwise three turns.
4. Insert the control knob unit, taking care that the guide nose enters the slot in the threaded sleeve. It is correctly installed if the threaded sleeve does not protrude above the conduit tube.

The heat control valve and the control flap at the rear of the heating channel should open and close simultaneously and move freely. Adjust the cable so that the valve is fully closed with the heater control knob at full "on" and fully opened with the knob at the closed position.

Servicing Control Knob:
1. With cable withdrawn and knob pulled out of base, remove the cable pin with a drift and take off the control knob unit.
2. Screw off the threaded sleeve, then drive out the grooved pin and withdraw the knob from the spindle. Remove the threaded cap and spring washer.
3. To assemble, reverse the disassembly procedure, cleaning

parts and lubricating with universal grease.
4. Be careful when driving the grooved pin in to avoid damaging the knob.

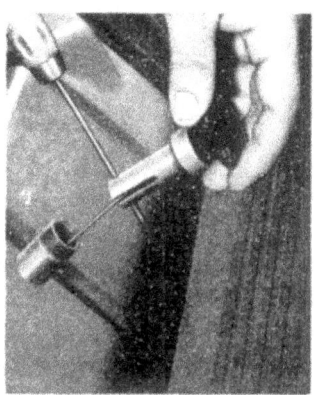 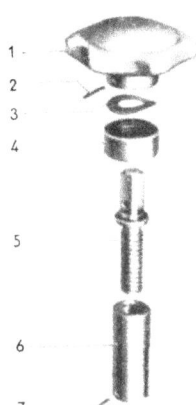

1 - Knob
2 - Grooved pin
3 - Spring washer
4 - Threaded cap
5 - Spindle
6 - Threaded sleeve
7 - Cable pin

LATER MODELS

Heater Control Box

Part of the air sucked in by the fan to cool the engine is diverted in the fan housing to the two heat exchangers surrounding the exhaust pipes. This heated air is then forced into the heater control box where a flap controls the flow of air into the interior of the vehicle. Should exhaust fumes enter the vehicle along with the heated air, check the heater box and exhaust pipe for leaks and repair immediately. Adjust the flap for opening and closing as previously described.

Disassemble by removing the locking washer for the heater flap operating lever, then removing the lever. Bend up the metal tabs on the heater control box, then hook the box off upwards. When assembling, reverse the order, checking the control flaps for proper contact all around. Also replace any broken off metal tabs with screws. Lubricate all bearing points with high melting point graphite grease. Use lithium grease rather than universal grease to lubricate the heater control cable and the moving parts of the control knob.

Heating Control Levers

To control the heating for either the left or right side of the vehicle, move the desired heating control lever from the down position (off) upward until the desired flow is achieved. To adjust the control, first

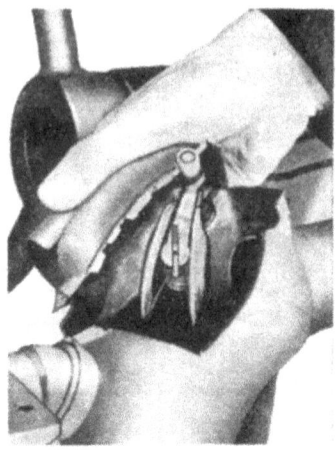 

loosen the nut on the clamping bush pin at the heat exchanger under the engine, then with the lever at the full off position and the cable fully extended but straight, tighten the nut on the clamp. Operate the flaps a few times to check the operation of the heater. Both the pin and the nut should be held with wrenches (9 and 10 mm) to avoid damaging the cable.

To adjust a loose heating control lever, fit two wrenches to the nuts on the ends of the shaft and loosen or tighten as desired. To renew the control cable and housing, first disconnect the cable as described previously, then from under the dashboard, unscrew the nut from the shaft holding the heating operating lever. Remove the white plastic plugs from the levers affected, using pliers to squeeze the plugs if necessary. Use the pliers to pull out the spring clips, then remove the knobs with attached levers from the driver's side of the dashboard. Slip the levers and plastic friction separator from the shaft, then unclip the spring-clip from the end of the cable and remove the solid cable end.

Remove the front trim panel screws and the trim panel, then the plate underneath the cab to provide access to the cable and housing. Use universal grease to lubricate the replacement cable, routing cable and cover carefully to prevent kinks. Reverse the procedure to replace cable, then tighten the nut on the clamping bush pin at the heater junction box (after making the previously described adjustment), then adjust the tension on the heating control lever mounting nut.

Heat Distributing Controls.

On the large, vertical tube that extends from the floor to the underside of the dashboard is a lever that controls the distribution of the warmed air in the driver's compartment. Move the lever down for defrosting the windshield, up for heating the legroom. In cold climates,

EXHAUST SYSTEM

HEATING

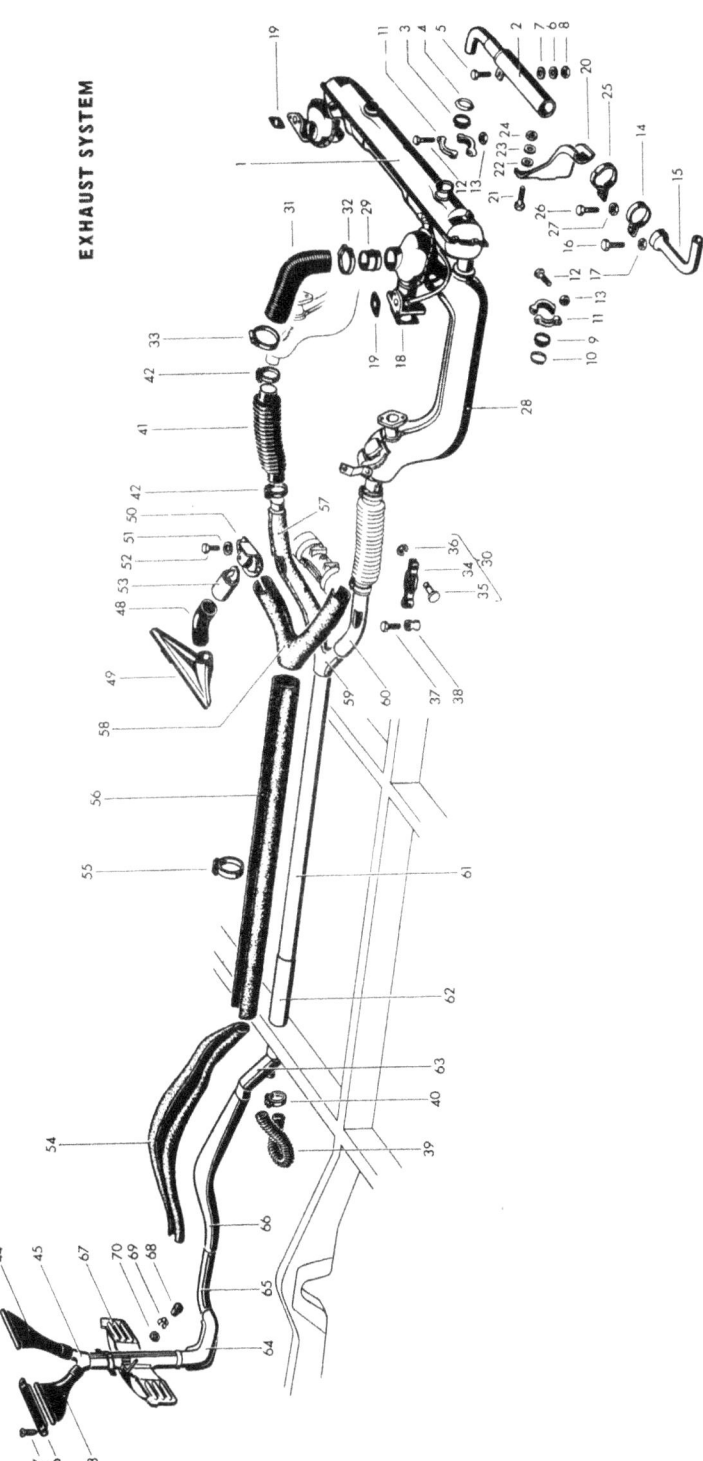

it is suggested that the air first be distributed to the defroster vents on the bottom edge of the windshield, with all other vents kept closed. Once the windshield is reasonably clear, the air distribution lever can be pulled up to allow warm air into the front legroom through outlets located beneath the dashboard. Should this lever become loose, bend it slightly with pliers. To replace the whole regulator and ducts, remove the screws holding both front trim panels in place, fold back the rubber mat, and remove the screws keeping the tubing sections in place. Reverse the procedure to replace the regulator and ducts.

A control knob at the front of the driver's seat allows warm air to enter the passenger compartment from the slots on the floor in front of the middle seat. Pulling up on the knob increases the flow from the outlet. Adjust this control from beneath the vehicle by pushing the knob all the way down, removing the plate underneath the cab, then loosening the nut on the clamping bush pin (holding the pin with another wrench so the cable is not bent). Hold the flap lever so the flap is fully closed, then retighten the nut. Knob, cable and cable housing renewal can be accomplished after disconnecting the cable as described. Be sure to use universal grease to lubricate the replacement cable.

Some station wagon models also have two vents under the rear bench seat. The levers are moved inward to allow warm air to flow. These levers may be bent with pliers should they become loose. To remove the units, remove the trimming for the seat frame, then unscrew the mounting screws holding the outlets in place. Pull off the duct and plug the tube.

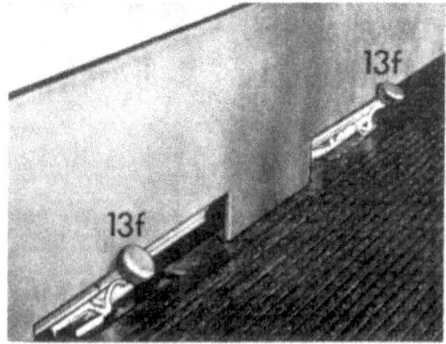

Ventilation

Fresh air is taken in by a vent above the windshield and is distributed through the cab and cargo or passenger space by a duct located in the overhead. The flow of air is regulated by a throttle which can be located in five positions. The controlling lever is situated on the left hand side of the duct channel. The distribution is controlled by a handle at the bottom of the chanel. An explanation of all parts is covered by a diagram. The throttle is fully open when the lever is in the farthest forward position and the flow decreases as it is pulled toward the rear. The distribution control handle in transverse position causes all the air to be ducted into the cab. In driving position, the cargo space is ventilated. In oblique position, both compartments are ventilated.

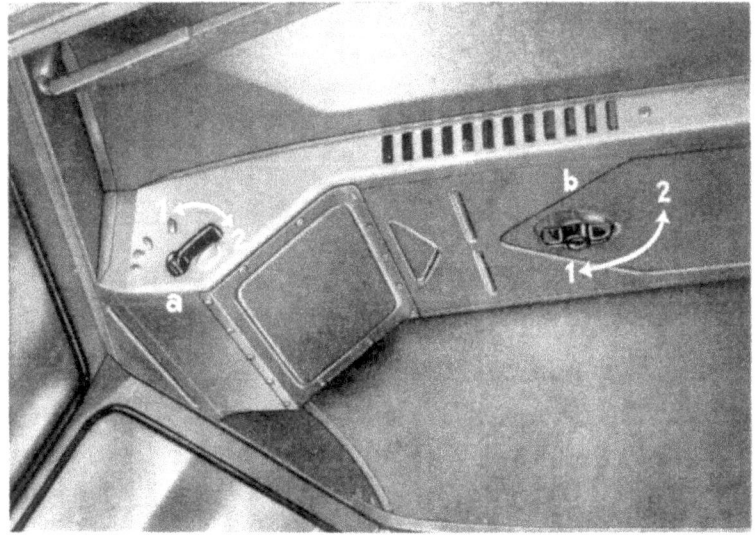

a - Fresh air
   regulator
   lever
   1 - On
   2 - Off

b - Fresh air
   distribution
   1 - Cab
   2 - Cargo
      room or
      passenger
      compart-
      ment

Remove cover plate (26) to service both front and back controls and flaps. Front shaft is drawn to the left after being loosened. Remove the handle and pull shaft to the right to remove. On both controls,

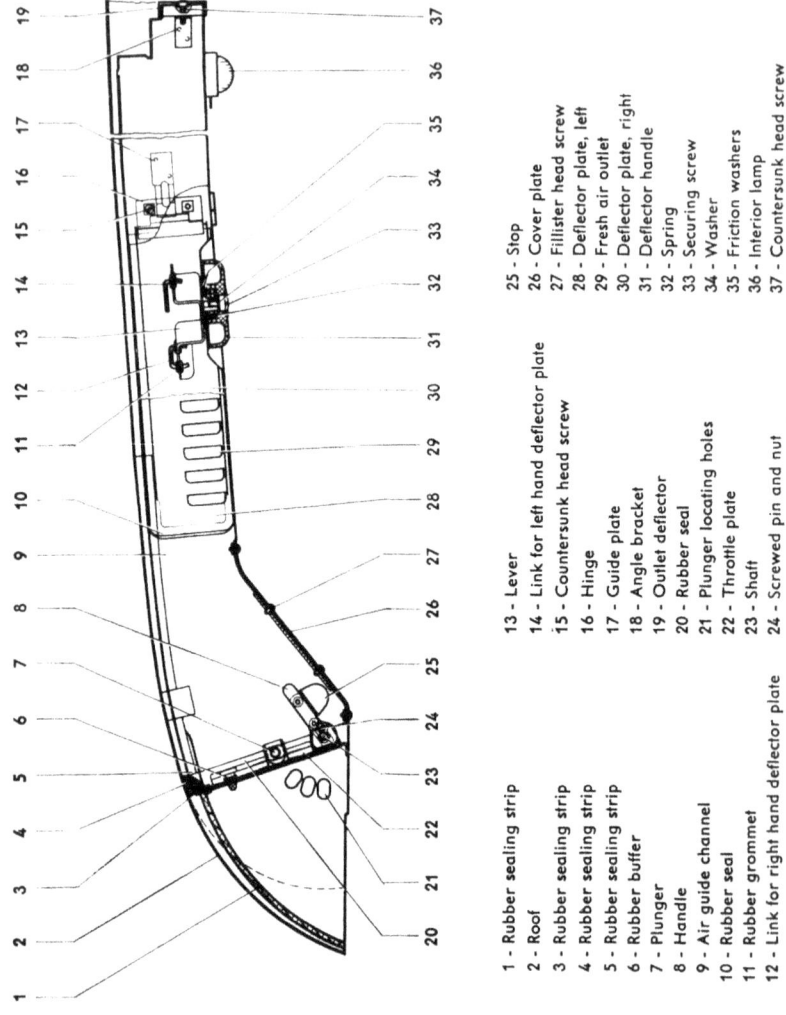

1 - Rubber sealing strip
2 - Roof
3 - Rubber sealing strip
4 - Rubber sealing strip
5 - Rubber sealing strip
6 - Rubber buffer
7 - Plunger
8 - Handle
9 - Air guide channel
10 - Rubber seal
11 - Rubber grommet
12 - Link for right hand deflector plate
13 - Lever
14 - Link for left hand deflector plate
15 - Countersunk head screw
16 - Hinge
17 - Guide plate
18 - Angle bracket
19 - Outlet deflector
20 - Rubber seal
21 - Plunger locating holes
22 - Throttle plate
23 - Shaft
24 - Screwed pin and nut
25 - Stop
26 - Cover plate
27 - Fillister head screw
28 - Deflector plate, left
29 - Fresh air outlet
30 - Deflector plate, right
31 - Deflector handle
32 - Spring
33 - Securing screw
34 - Washer
35 - Friction washers
36 - Interior lamp
37 - Countersunk head screw

check the condition and security of the rubber seals and plugs, then replace as necessary. On the front control, install new seals by cementing in the duct with suitable adhesive or replacing the flap. On the rear control, replace by inserting the deflector plates into the air duct and checking that the rear hinges (16) engage in the guides (17) fixed in the duct. While one man maneuvers the deflector plates another man can check the position of the hinges by looking through the air outlets in the cargo area.

Ventilation System (Later Models)

Fresh outside air enters the vehicle through inlets at the bottom edge of the windshield, and is discharged into the cab through adjustable vents on both sides of the dashboard. On the deluxe Station Wagon, two ventilation ducts on the front doors take air to two additional adjustable discharge vents located on the partitions behind the front seats. Two motor-driven fans power the system on some models, each fan being located under the dashboard just ahead of the front doors.

The controls for the ventilator system and the individual air ducts are incorporated into the blue operating levers mounted in the dashboard. A switch on the instrument panel turns on the fan motors. Moving the control lever from the closed position operates the linkage to open the flap, allowing fresh air to enter the ventilator system. Air flow can be pointed in any desired direction by turning the discharge vents. Each discharge vent also has a flap to adjust the volume of air being discharged.

To adjust a ventilator control, use pliers to turn the linkage connector located under the dashboard, lengthening or shortening the rod. Should a control lever itself be either out of adjustment or need to be serviced, fit two wrenches to the nuts on the ends of the shaft and loosen, unscrew or tighten as desired. The linkage rods are removed after the spring-clips are unsnapped. Remove the lever knobs by squeezing the white plastic plugs with pliers so they can be pulled out, then pull out the spring clips with the pliers. Remove the knobs with their attached levers from the driver's side of the dashboard. Slip the lower lever sections and plastic friction separator from the shaft. All four levers and the mounting are replaced as a unit should any part prove faulty. In this case, remove the cables and the heater control levers, then unscrew the unit. Be sure to adjust the linkages after replacing.

To remove the vent fan, disconnect the battery ground strap, then remove the plastic shrouding, exposing the fan motor ground wire and the two connectors. Disconnect these wires, then remove the screw holding the motor to the shroud. If motor is not working, replace as

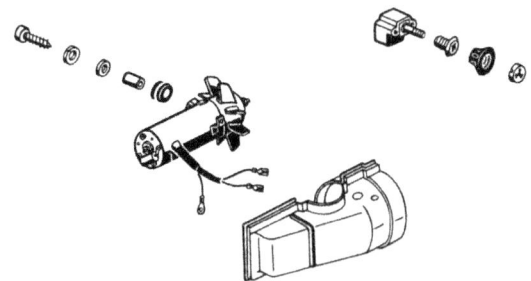

a complete unit. To replace, reverse the removal procedure, being sure to locate the motor so the fan blades clear the plastic shrouding.

The adjustable discharge vents can be easily serviced by pulling out vent with fingers or by inserting a thin screwdriver blade between the adjustable portion and the surround and prying out the vent. The surround can then be removed.

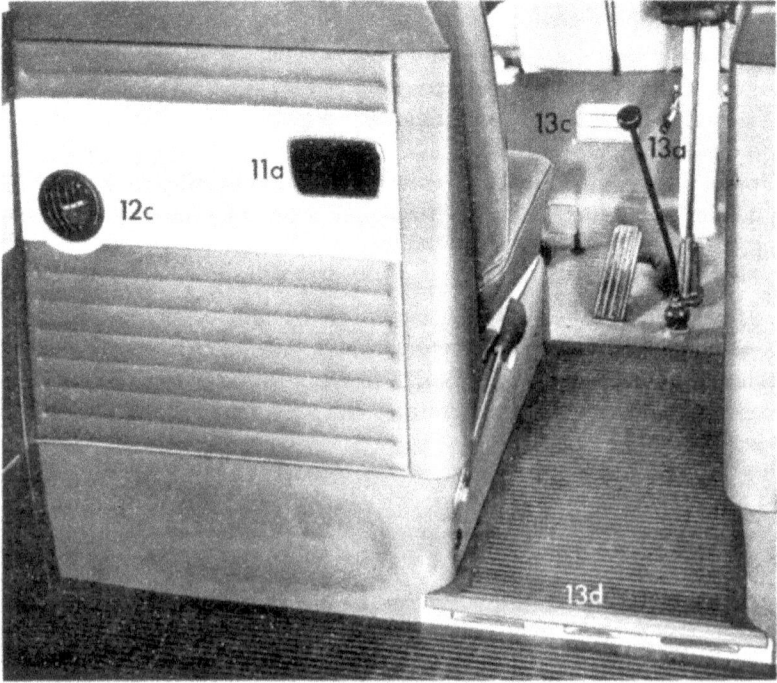

Body

Attaching Seat Belts

Before it bcame mandatory that seat belts be added to the rear seats, the VW Transporters came equipped with anchor points that could be used for installing the belts, provided that VW belts were used. These anchor points are illustrated, and are each capped with a plastic screw which must be removed before the anchor bolt may be screwed into the threaded hole. No nut is needed, providing a simple installation procedure. Remove the rear floor mats to reveal the anchor points behind the center seats and behind the rear seat. A third mounting point is provided by each of the outer seats for installing combination lap/shoulder belts.

Sliding Door

Press outside handle downward to open then slide back all the way until the hook catches it at the back frame. Pushing the handle downward and pushing the door forward until it latches will close it, and then the handle must be pulled upward to bring the sliding door flush with the rear panel. To open the door from the inside, push the inner handle forward (A or D), then push the door back until it catches. Door must be push-closed from the outside. Always make sure the sliding door is completely closed when the vehicle is moving, and either lock the door from the outside with the key or from the inside by pressing the small catch (C or E) forward.

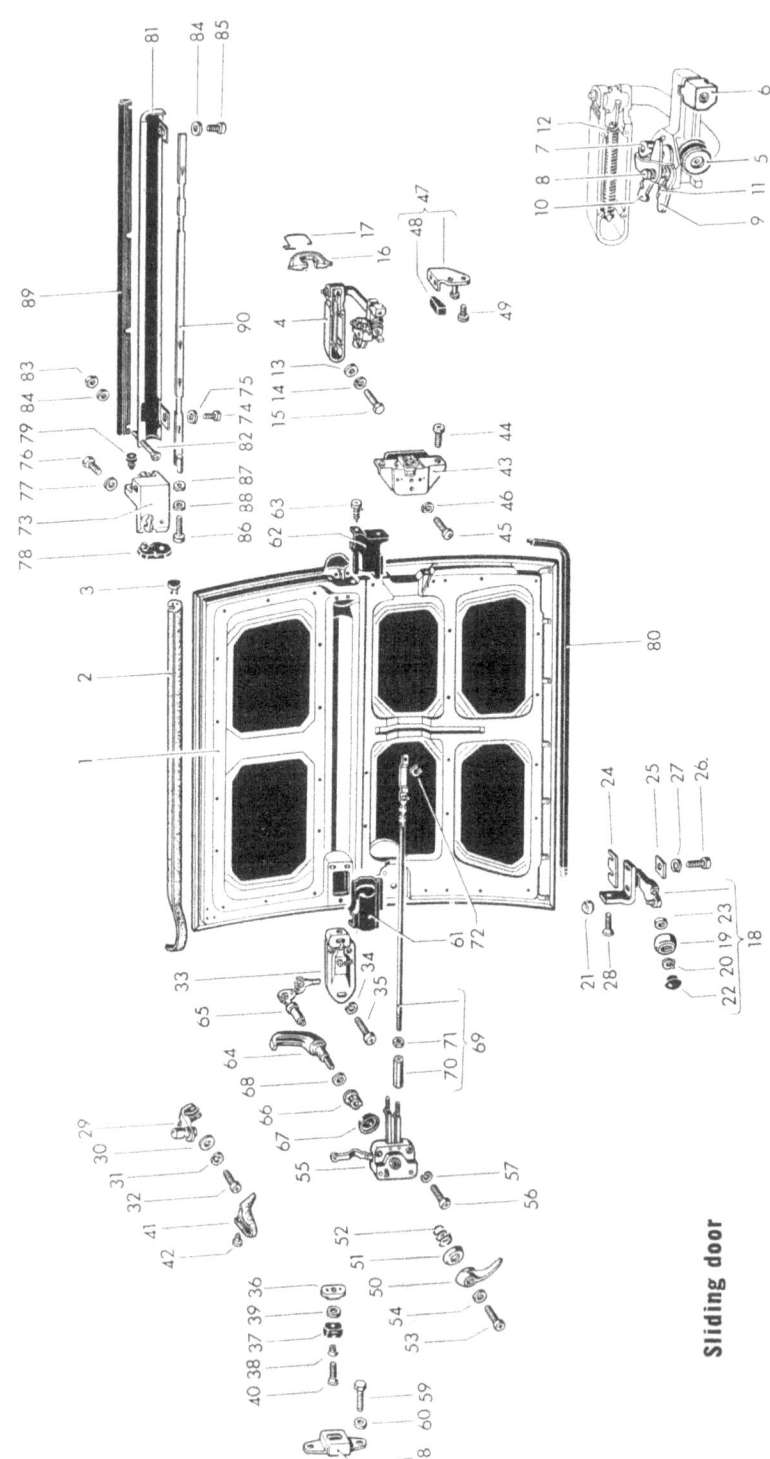

It is best to treat this door gently because of the complicated and expensive mechanism used to hold it in place. Parts in the rear mechanism may be replaced by first removing the plastic cover screws (63), then the cover (62). Remove the screws (15) holding the swing mechanism (4) in place, and remove the mechanism from the rear, supporting the door with blocks if necessary. Determine which parts need to be renewed or take the assembly with you when purchasing parts at the VW dealership.

Servicing Front Doors (1968 and Later)

Each front door is equipped with a roll-down window and a vent window. Four and a half turns are required to open or close the roll-down window. To remove both side windows, first note the angles of the handles, then press the escutcheons for the window crank and inner handle against the trim panel and knock out the retaining pins with a punch. Remove the crank, handle, and both escutcheons. On later models with safety door handle and window winder, either pull the winder plastic cover up or if necessary, place a piece of cardboard between the handle and the trim panel, then pry up on the plastic cover by placing a screwdriver between the cardboard and the cover. Unscrew Phillips head screw and remove handle.

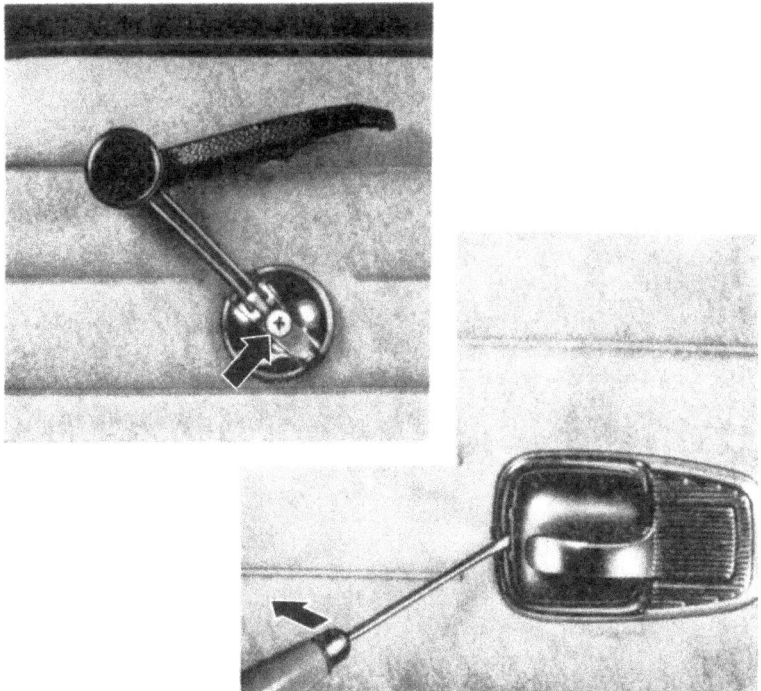

The safety inner door handle may be removed by first prying up on the trim plate with a screwdriver, then removing the Phillips head screw that will be revealed along with the escutcheon. Carefully remove the trim panel. The panel on models with the safety door handle and window winder is also hooked on the arm rest support on the door inner panel with the arm rest retaining plate. Pull trim panel away slightly, then lift it clear. Remove screws holding ventilation duct if so equipped.

Press retaining ring off check strap pin and take pin out, then remove four screws from the window lifter channel. Push window upwards and wedge into place. Remove five screws in window lifter and one screw for vent wing. Press window lifter towards outer panel and take it out downwards. Pull window glass down, then tilt it slightly and remove it from door. It may be necessary to remove the window trim molding with weatherstrip, and the best way to do this is to press the trim molding clips out from the rear. Remove the slot seal on the door inner panel.

To remove the vent wing window with its frame, unscrew the Phillips head screw in the upper window frame and hexagon head screw near the remote control lock on the inner

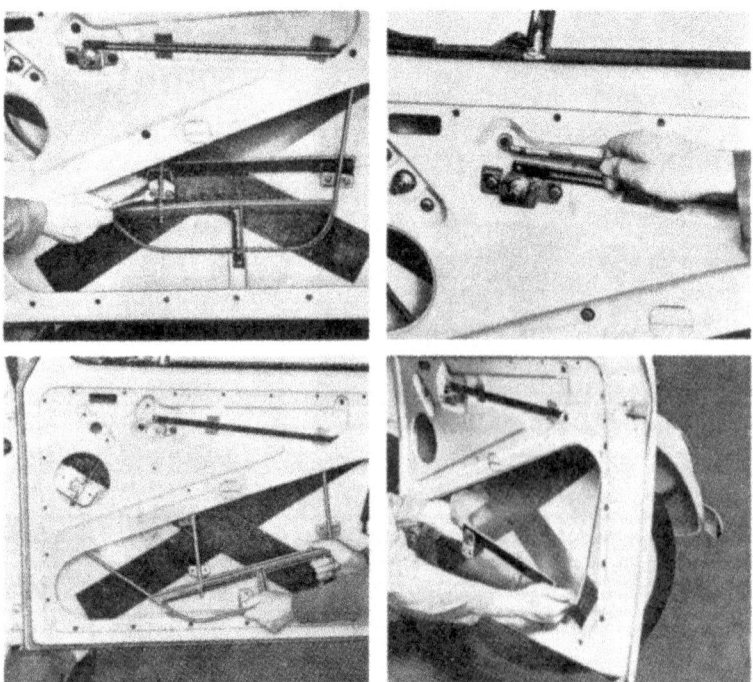

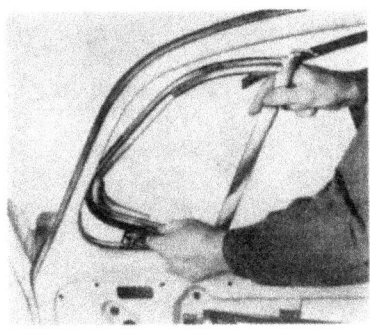
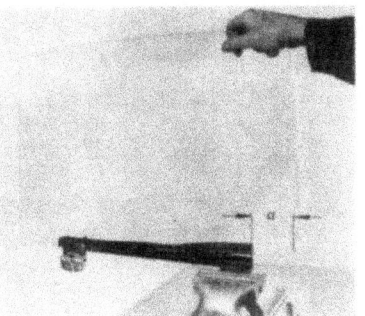

panel, then remove the front window guide channel with vent wing frame.

To install windows, first install the lifter channel (if it was removed) at a distance of about $a = 3.15$ in. from the straight guide edge. Use universal grease to lightly coat the lifter cable, then check that the damping strips on the door are secure and that the drain holes at the bottom of the doors are clear. Install the glass run channel with vent wing frame, then insert the window into the glass run channel from below and slide it upwards. Replace lifter and attach it to inner panel. If lifter cannot be pushed through the front window guide channel near the remote control lock, lift the vent wing slightly.

Remove wedge from window and push downward. Attach lifter channel loosely to window lifter on each side, then operate window a few times to center. Finally, tighten screws in window lifter channel. Replace plastic sheet (or a new sheet) onto inner door panel with universal adhesive D12. Replace rubber buffers, conical springs with large ends toward the trim panel, and finally the trim panel. Replace the crank and handle at the correct angles respectively, then check that all parts operate (repeat check several times). Replace ventilator duct if such was removed.

Striker Plate Adjustment

The latch and striker plate operate to both hold the door shut safely (including a safety catch to hold the door when it isn't completely closed) and prevent the housing from rattling. Projecting from the latch housing are the safety catch on the end and the latch bolt on the underside. As the door is closed, the latch bolt first engages the safety notch on the striker plate. This will hold the door closed even though it is not fully shut. If the door is pulled to sufficiently, the latch bolt will

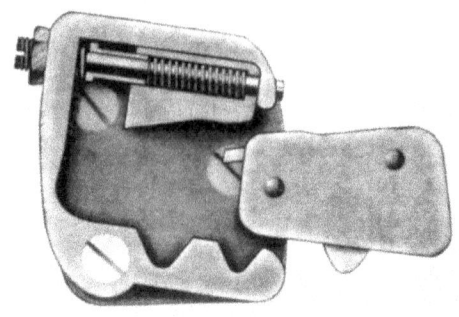 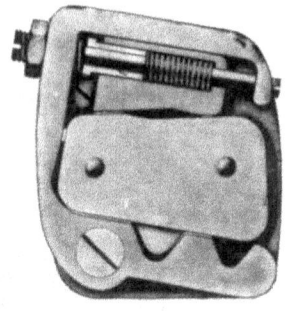

engage the second, inner notch. At this time the safety catch strikes the inner surface of the striker plate and is pushed back into the housing, locking the latch and preventing the door from inadvertently opening.

Rattles between the striker plate and housing are prevented by an adjustable plastic wedge. This wedge presses the latch bolt against the right-hand flank of the inner notch, and the housing against the bearing surface of the striker plate. The following adjustment will correct those functions that are defective.

Unscrew the striker plate screws and remove the plate. First check that the door is properly fitted by checking that the gap between the top of the door and the edge of the roof, and between the edge of the door and the side panel of the body are about equal. Make sure that the door is flush with the side panel of the body, the waistline moldings of the door and body are in line, and the door does not rub at either the top or bottom. If any of these items are incorrect, adjust the door by loosening the hinges and repositioning.

To check that the lock is functioning correctly, first make sure the top and bottom surfaces of the latch housing are perfectly flat, with no worn edges for the latch bolt and the safety catch. Make sure the latch bolt retracts completely into the housing

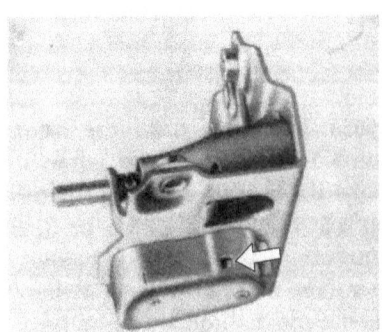 

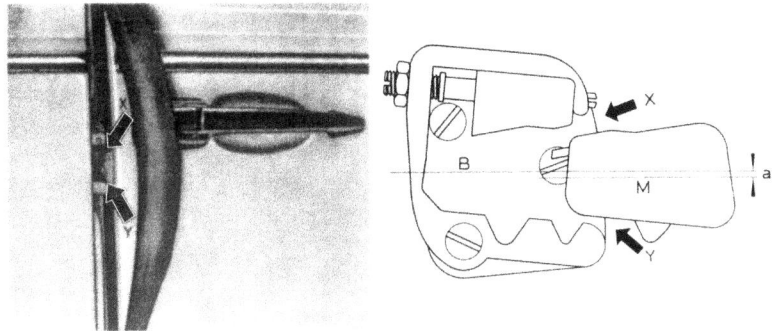

when the door handle is pulled. If not, this could make it difficult to either open or close the door. Adjust or replace mechanism as necessary.

Check that the striker plate has not been worn down on the bearing surfaces **A** and **B**. If so, renew the striker plate. Check that the plastic wedge is not scored or worn due to the latch housing being damaged, and renew the wedge if necessary. Replace the striker plate, lightly tightening the screws, then loosen the locknut on the wedge adjusting screw and turn the screw to the right until the stop bush contacts the striker plate housing to give the wedge a maximum amount of freeplay.

Adjust the striker plate sideways until the door and rear quarter panel are flush with one another. Push the door weatherstrip to one side with the door nearly shut as illustrated, then check that the space between the latch housing **M** and the striker plate is greater at the top **X** than at the bottom **Y**. When the door closes, the latch should strike the bearing edge of the striker plate, lifting the door about .08 in., **a**. Once the striker plate is satisfactorily adjusted, check that the latch bears on the striker plate correctly by opening and closing the door several times. Spreading a thin coat of lubricant on the bearing surface and observing whether it is distributed will help. If the latch apparently does not bear evenly, the striker plate is tilted and will have to be adjusted. Finally, make sure the striker plate securing screws are completely tightened.

The plastic wedge is held on an adjustable shaft with a stop so the wedge is kept from deflecting when the body is subject to torsional stress and road shocks. Adjusting the screw (shaft) positions the stop so that the wedge cannot move out of place when the door is closed. First (if the instructions preceding these were followed), the adjusting screw should be fully over to the

striker plate housing. Otherwise, hold the adjusting screw **3** with a screwdriver while loosening the lock nut, then turn the screw to the right until the stop bush contacts the striker plate housing. Now start turning the adjusting screw counterclockwise, intermittently shutting the door between adjustments of a few turns or less, until the wedge **4** creates resistance (closing pressure) when opening the fully closed door. Should the resistance be too great, or the door spring back to the safety position when it is being closed, turn the screw in clockwise and check again. Finally, hold the adjusting screw with a screwdriver and tighten the lock nut, then lubricate the contact surfaces with MoS^2 paste or vaseline. If the striker plate was renewed, it may settle in a bit, necessitating readjustment of the wedge after a short time.

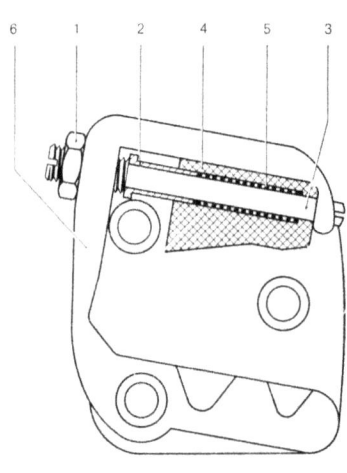
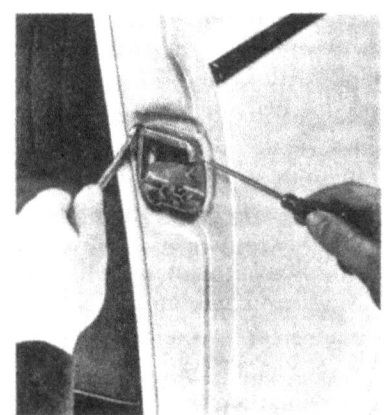

1 - Lock nut
2 - Stop
3 - Adjusting screw
4 - Plastic wedge
5 - Spring
6 - Body of striker plate

Seat Adjustments And Removal (Early Models)

Only the driver's seat has adjustments. Lift the lever at the right front side of the seat frame and position the seat forward or backward as desired. Make sure the seat is locked into position following adjustment so it will not shift while driving or braking. To remove seat, simply hold handle up while sliding seat forward off the runners. Adjust the backrest angle by evenly turning the two adjusting screws (A) in or out. Remove the passenger's seat by tilting it forward and lifting it from the catches.

On models with seats in the cargo space, remove the seats with the wrench in the tool kit. Unscrew the nuts from underneath, then remove the seat. The center seat may be reversed upon replacement so it faces rearward, if desired.

Seat Adjustments And Removal (Later Models)

The driver's seat has full position and back rest angle adjustments, while the passenger's seat can be adjusted to two positions. On the driver's seat, lift the lever (D) on the front left side of the seat frame and position the seat as wanted. Make sure the lever is returned to a locked position so the seat will not shift while driving or braking. The back rest is adjusted by turning wheel (E). There is no provision for tilting the back rest forward. Passenger seat adjustment is accomplished by lifting up the seat front until the backrest becomes detached (F) from the partition. Lift the seat and fit it into the other adjustment notch, lift the front again to allow the catch to fit into the mounting in the partition, then lower the seat front and check that the back rest is secure.

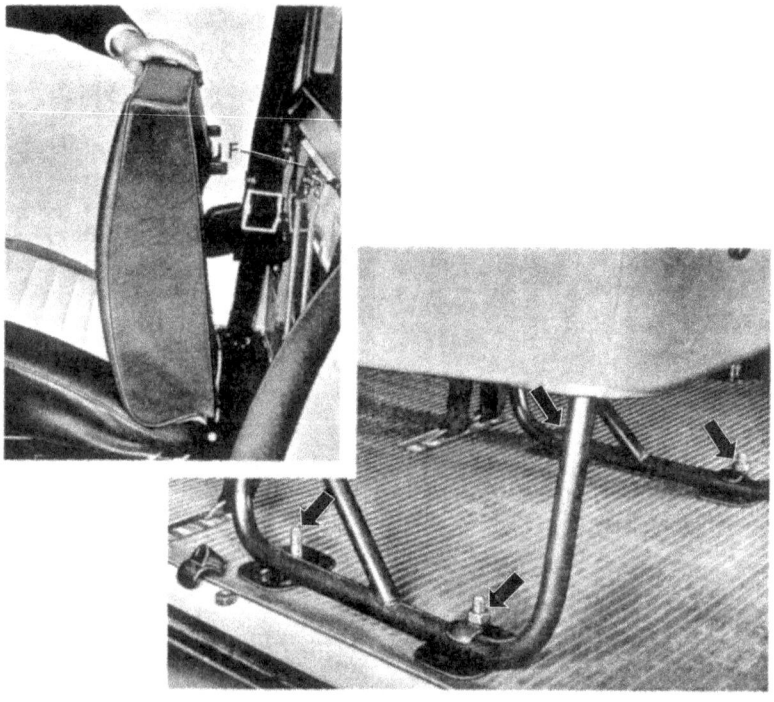

On models with seats in the cargo space, remove the seats by unclipping the side trimming from the seat frame, use the wrench in the tool kit to unscrew the nuts, and remove the mounting supports and seats. Remove the mounting plates and turn the bolts 90° in either direction to remove them. The rear heater outlet unit may be unscrewed, the hose pulled off, and the outlet plugged. Reverse the procedure to replace the seats. The center seat may be reversed so it faces rearward, if desired. The divided section of the center seat may be tilted forward by pulling up on the catch knob built into the side of the back rest.

Ashtrays

On the early models, press the ashtrays up from below. On later models, remove the front ashtray by pressing the leaf spring downward while pulling out the ashtray. The passenger compartment ashtrays are removed by lifting them out of the lower portion of the retaining frame. Install by inserting ash tray first at the top where the leaf spring is located, then push ash tray into the retaining frame.

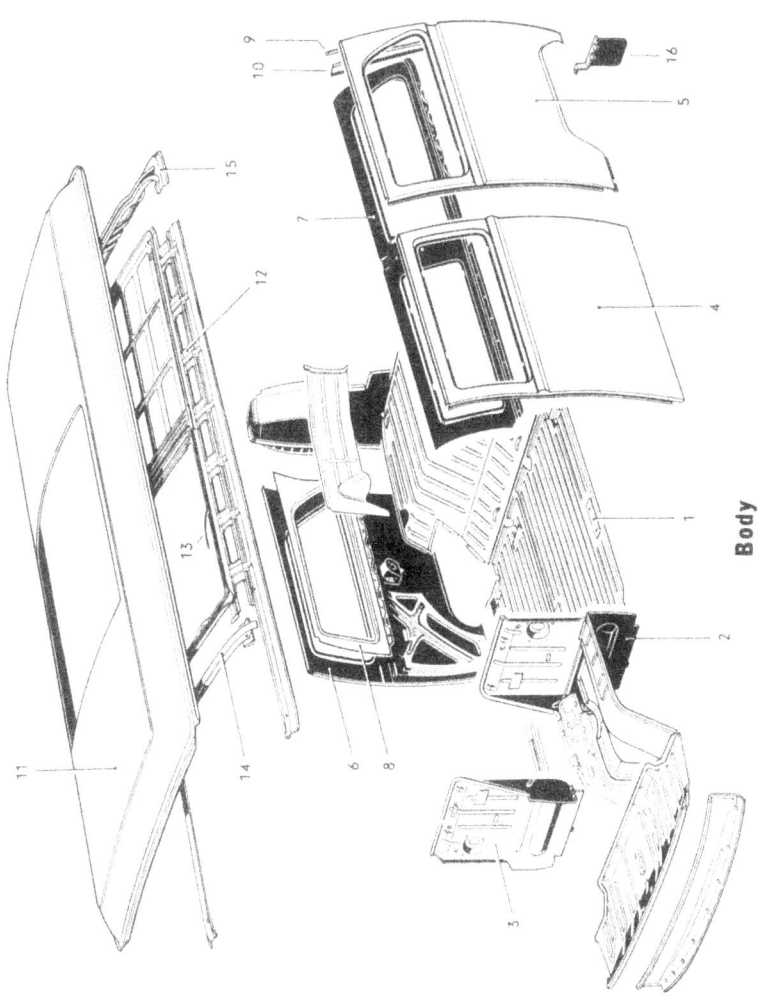

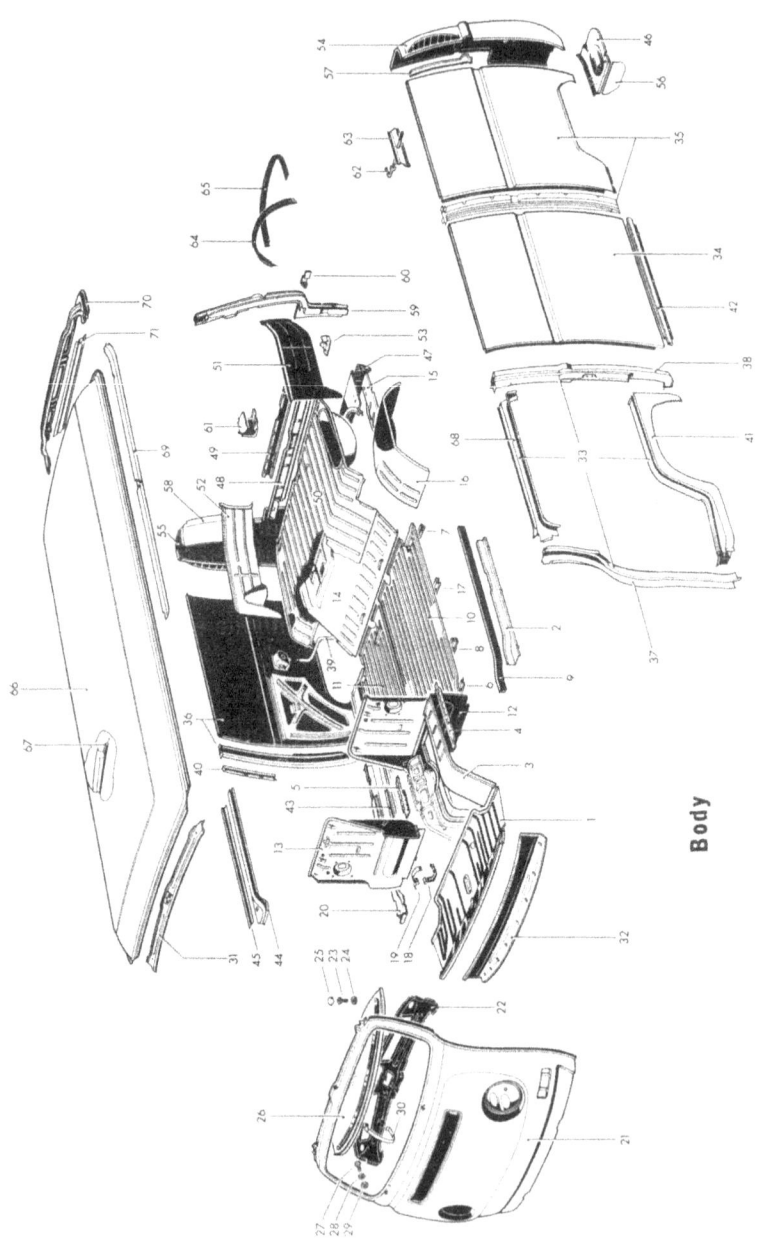

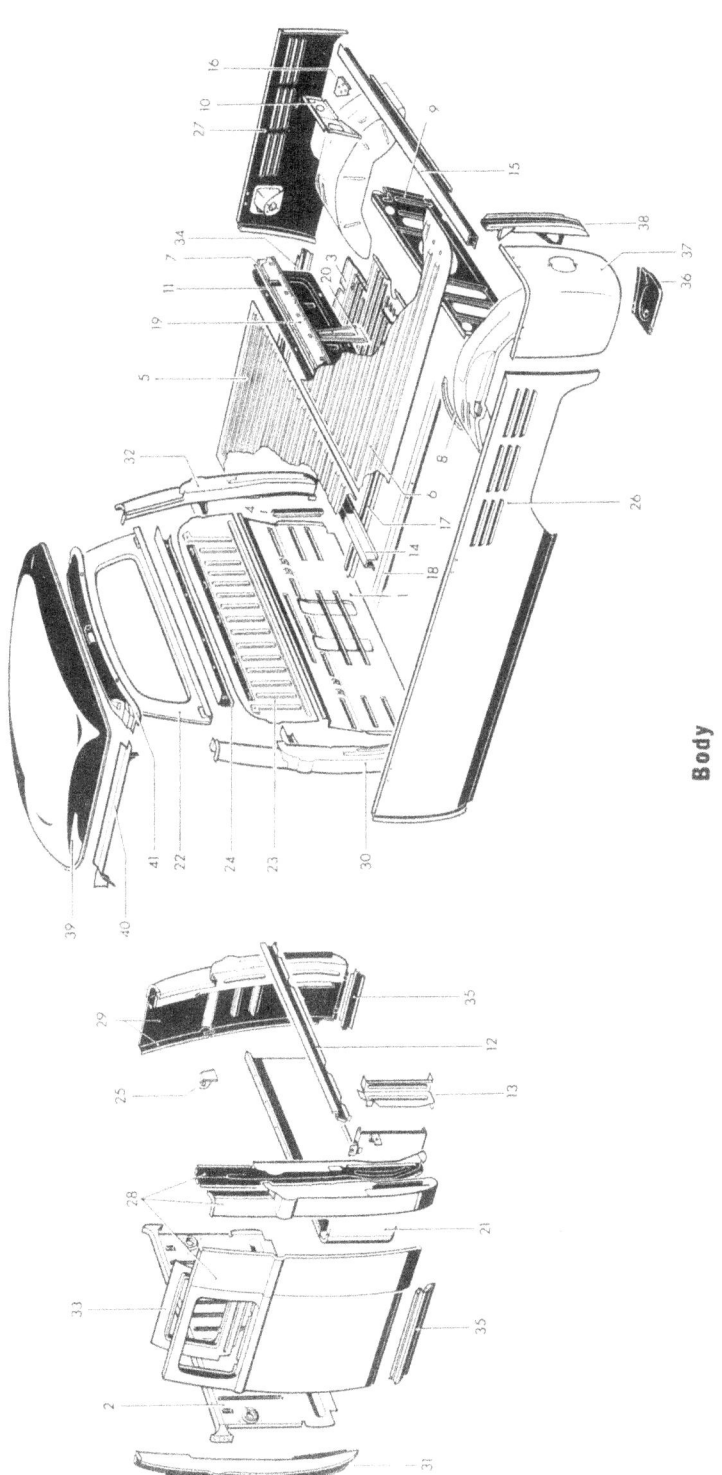

Body

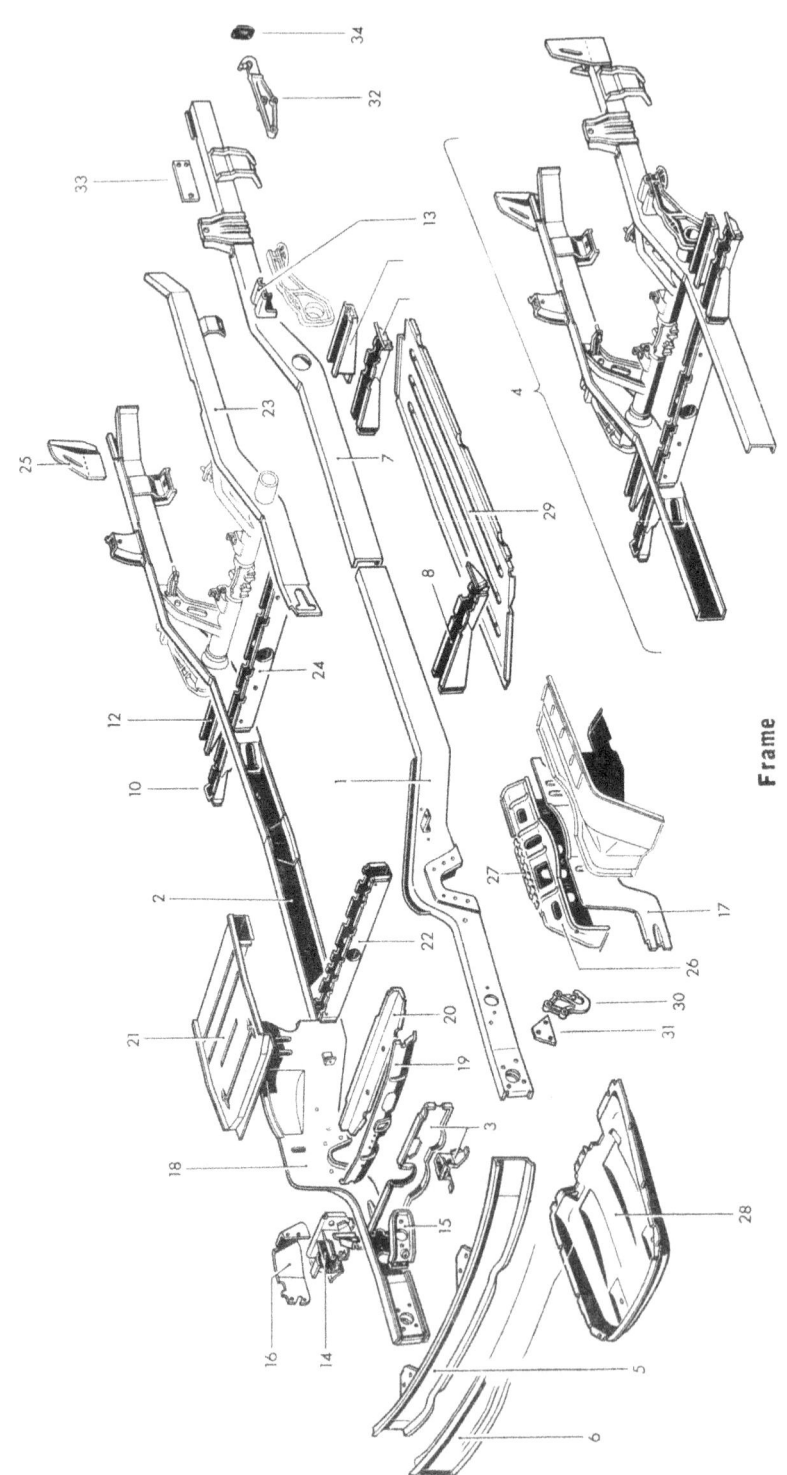

Cleaning

Bodywork

Although everyone has their favorite methods of cleaning their car, Volkswagen has a few suggestions that they apply to their vehicles. First and foremost is the warning that the **vehicle should never be washed, waxed, or polished in the sunshine,** and that before waxing or polishing, the vehicle must be washed and dried thoroughly. A wash-and-wax solution may be applied **after** a thorough washing and drying rather than waxing in the normal way. This easier method involves putting the solution in a bucket of water and applying it to the paint, then wiping dry. This type of wax will come off with the next car wash, however, and will only protect the vehicle if it is applied every two or three weeks when the car is washed.

Spots

Every car tends to collect some sort of spots on the paintwork that can eventually cause permanent stains if not removed. Tar and oil stains are specially penetrating, so should be removed as soon as possible. Insects should also be washed off quickly as they can cause stains if left on too long. Certain solutions are sold that safely remove both hardened tar and insects from the paintwork. Trees are also a source of sticky saps that will spot the paintwork, and these should be quickly removed with car shampoo. In all cases, the car should be washed (or, preferably, shampooed) with a chamois, then wiped dry and waxed following any such spot removal.

Chrome, Glass And Rubber

Parts other than the body panels can be preserved and cared for quite easily with the modern array of cleaning products. A chrome cleaner that also protects the parts in winter weather is well worth the cost. A good glass cleaner, used with a chamois reserved for just the windows, should help to keep the glass free of streaks when it rains. A chamois that is also used on the painted body panels will pick up particles from polishes and paint cleaners, and these will be left on the glass. Wiper blades should also be cleaned at this time, and blades that have been dry for a long period of time should be removed and scrubbed lengthwise with a hard brush and alcohol or strong detergent solution. These blades need cleaning to remove accumulated tar splashes, insects and oil deposits. Replace blades that have become hard, cracked or inflexible.

Other rubber parts such as gaskets and weatherstrips must

remain supple to seal the joint. To retain the original flexibility of the rubber, either coat with a silicone spray or rub in glycerine or talcum powder from time to time.

Sunroof

On the plastic sunroof material used up until 1968, clean regularly with a mild soap solution and lukewarm water or any normal plastic cleaner. On a very dirty roof, use a hard brush to help remove dirt from the grained surface, but be careful not to scratch the paint along the edges. To remove stubborn spots, use a cloth moistened with benzine, then rinse well with a lukewarm soap solution. **Caution:** Never try to remove spots with paint thinner, chlorine-based spot removers, or similar solutions as these will damage the material.

For fabric sunroofs, brush with a soft brush only to remove dust and dirt, wash only with clear water. If soap is required to remove spots, clean the entire roof to avoid "circling." Tar or oil can be removed by careful application of gasoline but remember any treatment with organic chemicals can damage the waterproofing and the weather resistant qualities of the fabric.

Upholstery

Seats, headlining, side trim panels and other artificial leather upholstery can best be cleaned with a dry foam upholstery cleaner and a soft brush or cloth, or may simply be wiped off with a damp cloth if just dusty. Use only a dry foam cleaner on the seats and backrests because the material is air-permeable and liquid cleaners would penetrate into the textile backing. After each cleaning, the surface should be rubbed dry with a soft cloth with particular care that the seams are dried.

Oil or grease spots can be treated with a soft cloth moistened in benzine. Turn the cloth several times and dry the area with a fresh cloth.

Shoe polish stains can be treated with benzine or turpentine as outlined above. Rust should be removed carefully with a weak solution of hydrochloric acid (1 part to 10 parts water) applied by moistening a cloth in the solution. Dab at the spots but do not spread them by rubbing. Do not soak the area and do not let the solution penetrate the seams of the upholstery or the metal of the vehicle. Use clear water to remove all traces of acid. Blood is best treated with only clear, lukewarm water, and dabbed with a soft cloth rather than rubbed.

To prevent the formation of mold and damp stains inside the vehicle while storing in a closed shelter for long periods, open the car doors and the garage doors occasionally.

Caring For Seat Belts

Check buckles, retractors and anchors from time to time to make sure they function correctly and that they haven't chafed the belt. To clean belts, wash on vehicle with mild detergent, then allow to dry in the shade before retracting. Never bleach or dye the belts since these chemicals may weaken webbing.

Emergency Procedures

Pushing

To start the car, when troubled by a low battery or faulty starter, have it pushed by a vehicle equipped with bumpers of an equal height. Place the gearshift in neutral, turn the ignition key to the **ON** position, then wait until the pushing vehicle has left the VW free rolling at a speed between 15 and 20 mph. Clutch and shift into third gear, then slowly let out the clutch and feed gas. Never attempt to start the vehicle by towing.

Towing

Under no circumstances should the bumpers be used for towing since they would probably bend. On pre-1968 models, attach a tow rope to the lower front axle tube as near as possible to the right-hand side member. Be sure to pass the rope over the stabilizer and then around the axle tube. If towing from the rear, attach the rope to the shock absorber bracket.

On 1968 and later vehicles, towing eyes are provided on the

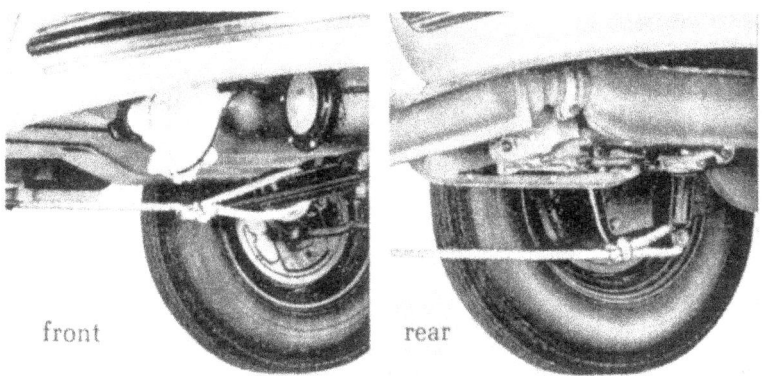

front   rear

right side underneath the front and rear bumpers to ease the attachment of a towrope.

Do not try to pull the vehicle up steep hills or out of deep mud or snow with these methods as strain may be put on the VW components. Never tow the vehicle to start it.

Rocking To Free From Snow Or Mud

It is often possible to free a mired vehicle by rocking it back and forth. Rock it as far back as possible, with one hand on the handbrake, and then hold it there with the handbrake while shifting into first gear. Release handbrake while letting up on the clutch and applying gas as needed. Rock the vehicle back and forth in this manner, building up momentum until it is either freed or further attempts become futile. Tarps, blankets, branches and other brush placed ahead of the rear wheels can sometimes provide the needed traction to rescue the vehicle. Should the vehicle be stuck on an incline, it is best to rock the vehicle in reverse or third gear only.

Changing Tires

Should an emergency roadside tire change be necessary, be sure to first turn on the **emergency blinker system.** All other precautions, such as placing flares or reflectors on the road several hundred feet to the rear of the vehicle at night, should be taken. Set the handbrake and block both the front and rear of a wheel on the opposite side to keep the vehicle from rolling (especially on an incline).

Use the jack bar and the wire hub puller to remove the hub cap by hooking the puller into the holes in the edge of the cap and levering against the wheel rim with the jack bar. With wheel still on the ground, loosen all the wheel bolts about one turn

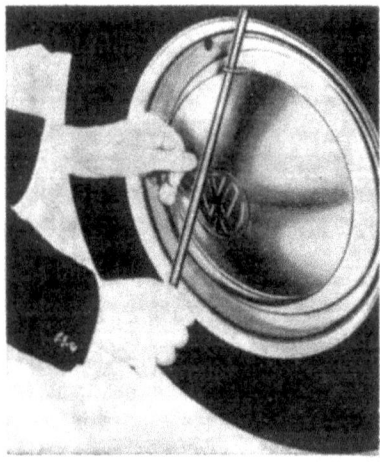
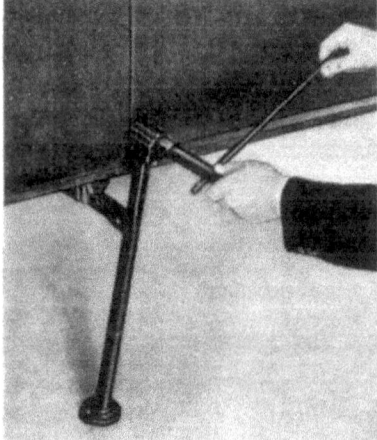

with the socket wrench and bar, then insert the jack into the square socket under the body. Turn the hexagon at the top of the jack until the base touches ground. Should the ground be so soft the base sinks down when the hexagon is turned with the socket wrench and bar, raise up the jack base and place a wooden block under it. Remove wheel bolts and wheel once it has completely cleared the ground.

Place spare wheel against drum and raise or lower the vehicle with the jack so the holes in the wheel are roughly aligned with the threaded holes in the drum. Screw one bolt finger-tight, then lift wheel to align it with the other holes in the brake drum and screw in the remaining bolts. Wheel should contact the drum all around, centered by the tapered bolt heads, prior to being lowered to the ground with the jack. Use the wrench and bar if necessary for this. Once the vehicle is on the ground and the jack has been removed, tighten the wheel bolts diagonally to as near the same torque as possible. If there is a torque wrench at hand, tighten the bolts to 87 ft. lb., tightening diagonally. This procedure is important both for safety and to prevent the drum from warping, causing pulsating brake application.

Replace the trim ring, then install the hub cap over it with a blow of the hand. Make sure the spare tire has the correct pressure (front, 28 psi; rear, 36 psi) before driving any long distances. Be sure to remove blocks from the opposite wheels, replace warning reflectors and tools, and turn off the emergency blinker system before driving off.

Warning Lights

The red warning light indicates loss of power from the generator or the loss of a fan belt. The green warning light indicates the loss of oil pressure. Should either of these lights come on while driving, stop and investigate immediately. If the fan belt is intact, the car may be driven to a service station. Otherwise, replace the fan belt before driving on. If the oil level dipstick shows there is oil in the engine, the vehicle may be driven to the nearest service station at reduced speed. If the turn signal flasher blinks at an increased rate, this is an indication that a road light bulb is burned out and should be replaced as soon as possible. See the engine or electrical sections for corrective measures.

Cold Weather Operation

Winter Tires

With the added hazards of snow and road ice, the tires become much more of a factor for safe operation of the VW. Tires that are worn are not only unlawful but become a greater hazard under poor weather conditions. Mud and snow tires with special heavy treads help traction considerably but should never be used only for the front wheels. The best solution is M+S tires with spikes fitted to all four wheels. These increase the safety margin even on hard snow and ice. State laws vary for use of spiked tires, so it is best to check. Be sure that the ply rating (PR) of the winter tires is not less than the original equipment.

On the VW, a tire pressure 3 psi higher than that specified for the tire concerned will improve operating characteristics. Spike-equipped M+S tires should not be operated at excessive speeds when new in order to give the spikes time to settle. Also, winter tires cannot be expected to have the same degree of adhesion on dry, wet or snow-free roads as a normal tire, and under these conditions will also wear rapidly, particularly at high speeds. To sum up, any type of M+S tire only has advantages when conditions are especially frigid, and the vehicle is driven at reduced speeds.

Snow Chains

For occasional operation on snowy or icy roads, snow chains are the best compromise. Only thin chains which do not protrude from the tire tread and inner side wall by more than $1/2$ in. (including tensioner) should be fitted, and then only to the rear wheels. Chains can be fitted both to regular and M+S tires, but should be removed when the vehicle is driven over long stretches of road which are free from snow since the chains serve no useful purpose, wear out quickly, and cause damage to the tires.

Door Locks

Should the vehicle be washed in winter, cover the door locks with tape so water does not enter the mechanism and freeze (or at least do not aim the water jet directly at the lock). Open a frozen lock by heating the key before inserting it (hold with pliers from tool kit and heat with a cigarette lighter). Squirt an anti-freeze solution or glycerine into the lock cylinder as soon as possible to prevent further freezing.

Useful Winter Accessories

Items that will aid driving under harsh winter conditions include a spray de-icing solution to melt ice from windows, a plastic scraper to remove snow and ice from windows and lights, and a small shovel to remove snow from the wheels should the vehicle become mired.

Engine Lubrication

Should the Transporter be operated for short distances and in city traffic during the winter, it is recommended that the oil be changed every 1,500 miles and SAE 20 W/20 oil be used. Should these winter temperatures average below 5°F., then use SAE 10 W oil. If the vehicle is driven only a few hundred miles a month under these conditions, it is advisable to have the oil changed every 6 to 8 weeks. Should the vehicle be operated regularly under arctic conditions of below —13°F., change the oil every 750 miles and use SAE 5 W oil. In either of these cases, avoid driving at high speeds for long periods when using SAE 10 W oil and the outside temperature is above 32°F., or if using SAE 5 W oil when the temperature is above 5°F.

Transmission Lubrication

Should the temperature stay below —13°F. for long periods, it is recommended that automatic transmission fluid (ATF) be used in the place of transmission oil. The vehicle should not be operated with this fluid when the temperature rises to about the freezing point. At this point the transmission should be refilled with SAE 80 or SAE 90 hypoid transmission oil.

Battery Care

In cold weather the battery tends to drop in capacity, and is also used much more to power the lighting system and the starter, all of which raises current consumption. Any battery that is not fully charged has only a fraction of its normal capacity when cold, and this may not be enough to start an engine containing thickened oil. Should the vehicle be operated only short distances in city traffic under these circumstances, it would be wise to have the battery charged from an external source occasionally.

Lubrication

Note: See section entitled COLD WEATHER OPERATION for additional lubrication information.

Oil Change

The oil should be changed every 3,000 miles, assuming the vehicle operates under normal conditions. This should be regarded as a constant rule, no matter how good the oil is, since any oil begins to break down after a period of service. The application of any oil additive will not change this process, and should be thought of as simply a waste of money. Use a branded HD oil "For Service MS", any brand, and if possible, stick to the same brand throughout your ownership of the vehicle. Use SAE 30 oil for general use and in hot climates.

With the engine warm, drain the engine oil by removing the plug in the oil strainer cover plate, then remove the cap nuts holding the cover plate in place and remove the complete strainer assembly. Clean the strainer and scrape off any gasket material that sticks. Remove magnetic ring (if so equipped) and wipe clean. Renew the gaskets and the copper washers under the cap nuts, then replace the assembly as illustrated and tighten down the cap nuts snugly. **Refill the engine with 5.3 U.S. pints (4.4 Imp. pints) of HD oil,** branded "For Service MS".

The classification of oil into various viscosity grades indicates its resistance to flow at a given temperature. All SAE grades cover a temperature range of about 60°F. and the two ranges of two neighboring grades overlap by some 30°F. Brief variations in temperature between seasons can therefore be disregarded.

For the same reason oils of different viscosities can be mixed when oil has to be added between oil changes and the viscosity of the oil in the engine no longer corresponds to the actual temperature.

1 - Oil drain plug
2 - Gasket
3 - Bottom plate
4 - Gasket
5 - Oil strainer
6 - Lock washer
7 - Nut

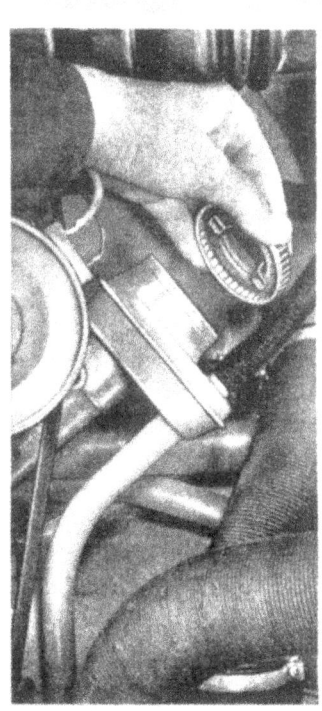

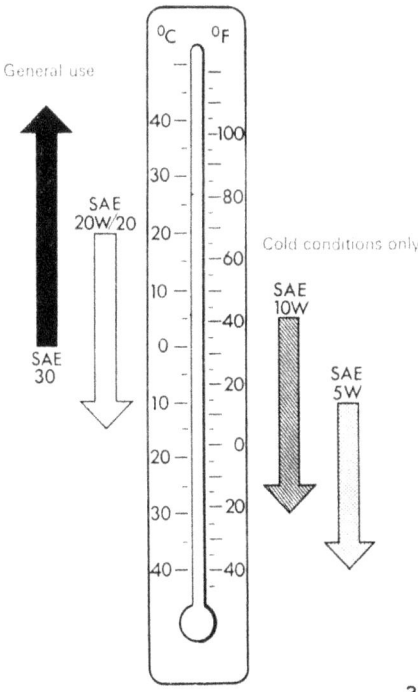

Temperature ranges of SAE grades

Transmission Oil Change

Hypoid oil of SAE 90 rating is used in the transmission-differential. The one filler plug (A) is used to check the level of the oil for the combined unit and to add new oil. The oil should be to the bottom edge of the filler hole. Check the oil level every 6,000 miles and check the transmission for leaks. The new oil sometimes runs into the transmission very slowly, and if it is poured in too fast, may overflow and give the impression that the housing is already full. Do not use any additives in the transmission.

Change the transmission hypoid oil every 30,000 miles by removing the magnetic drain plug (B) and draining off the old oil while it is still warm, then clean the plug thoroughly before replacing it. Put in 7.4 pints of good quality hypoid oil (use SAE 80 hypoid oil in arctic climates the year around), noting the above precaution about allowing the oil to flow in slowly enough so it is completely filled. It is essential to the silent running and service life of the transmission that the correct amount of oil is used.

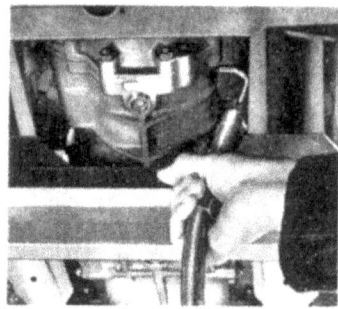
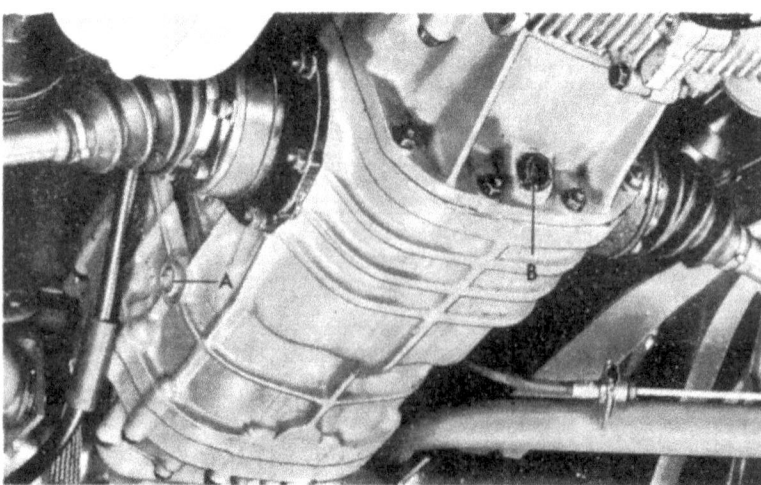

Note: On transmissions used between 1961 through 1967, remove both drain plugs simultaneously, drain oil and clean plugs, then fill transmission slowly with 5.3 pints of good quality SAE 90 hypoid oil at the 30,000 mile oil change. Also change the oil in the reduction gears at this time, putting in .53 pints of the same oil in each side.

Front Suspension (1961 Through 1967)

Note: Be sure to lift the front end off the ground prior to lubricating the front suspension since this assembly must be free of load.

Use lithium-based multi-purpose grease to lubricate the front suspension. Be sure to clean off all nipples and the grease gun

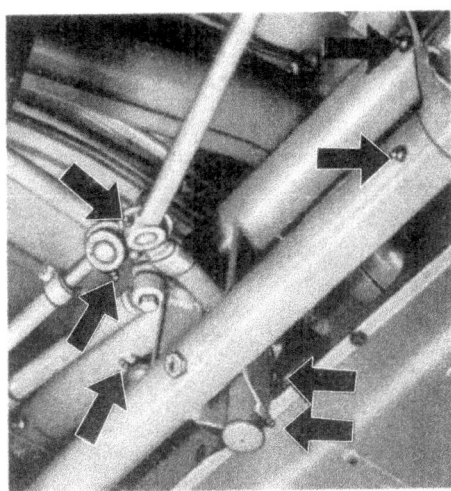

The number and the location of the lubrication points of the chassis can be gathered from the Lubrication Chart and the corresponding illustration.

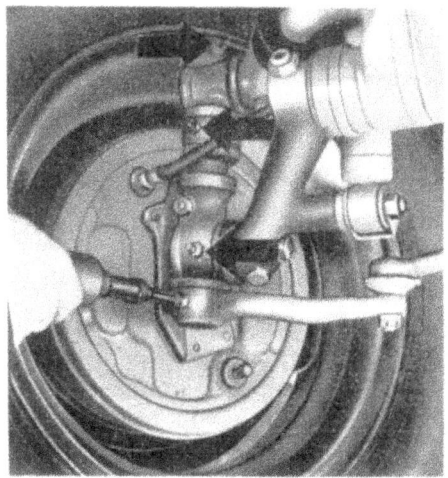
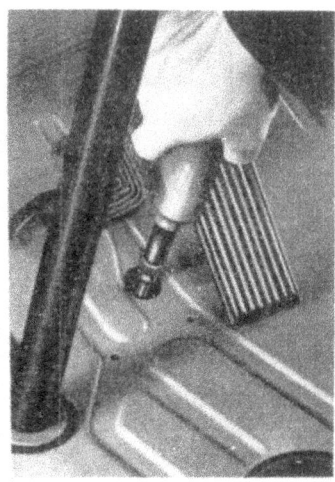

nozzle prior to greasing. Grease the four nipples on the axle tubes and the four on the king pins, then grease the swing lever shaft. Place gun on nipples and inject grease until fresh grease begins to come out of the bearing. Remove grease from tires and brake hoses. Grease these bearings once every 3,000 miles or at least twice a year. If the vehicle is to be mainly used on rough or graded roads, be sure to grease the king pins every 1,500 miles.

Front Suspension (1968 And Later)
Note: Be sure to lift the front end off the ground prior to lubricating the front suspension since this assembly must be free of load.

Use lithium-based multi-purpose grease to lubricate the front suspension. Be sure to clean off all nipples and the grease gun nozzle prior to greasing. Grease the four nipples on the axle tubes and the one for the swing lever shaft, injecting grease until fresh grease begins to come out of the bearing. Be sure to wipe off any grease and oil left on tires and brake hoses to prevent rapid deterioration of these parts. Grease these bearings once a year even if the vehicle is not driven 6,000 miles.

Distributor
Check the distributor breaker arm fiber block for grease, and if necessary, apply a small amount of cam grease.

Body
On bodies prior to the 1968 model, lubricate the door, rear flap and engine cover hinges every three months by cleaning the slots and applying a few drops of engine oil. Lubricate the lower guide and support rollers on vehicles with sliding doors, using a grease gun to lubricate the grease nipples on the rollers.

On 1968 and later models, lubricate the hinge on the rear door, the hinges and lock of the engine compartment lid, and the hinge for sliding door (see arrows) at the notches. On the door hinges, remove the plastic plug on top by prying up with a screwdriver and fill chamber with engine oil. This chamber should be checked at least once every three months, then the plug is pressed in and excess oil wiped off.

On all models, lubricate the striker plates of the doors and the support spring for the engine comparement lid with stick lubricant. Use graphite on all lock cylinders by dipping the key into the dry graphite, insert the key into the lock and move it back and forth several times.

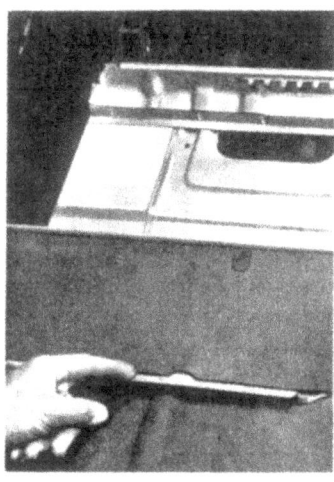

Driver's Seat

If the driver's seat becomes hard to adjust, remove seat by pushing it forward out of the runners. Wipe the runners free of residue both top and bottom, then grease the runners lightly both top and bottom.

Carburetor Linkage

Oil the linkage at the following locations: throttle valve shaft, choke valve shaft and fast idle cam, accelerator cable swivel pin, lever and connector rod for accelerator pump.

Oil Filler Plug

Oil Strainer
with cover

Oil Drain Plug
for crankcase

Magnetic Oil Drain Plugs
for rear axle and transmission

Oil Drain Plug
for reduction gears at rear wheels

LUBRICANTS

Lubricant	Lubrication points		Specifications		
			Temperature °C °F		
Engine oil (Trade-mark HD oil for spark ignition engines)	Engine, oil bath air cleaner door hinges, carburetor controls, felt in ignition distributor cam	M	above −30 −86		SAE 30
			up to 0 +32 −30 −86		SAE 20 or SAE 20 w
			below 0 +32		SAE 10 w
			below −25 −13		SAE 5 w
Transmission oil	Transmission case, reduction gear cases	G	above 0 +32		SAE 90
			below 0 +32		SAE 80
	Steering gear case	G	SAE 90		
Universal grease	Front axle, tie rod ends, steering arms, drag link, Brake cables, Ignition distributor cams, Door and lid locks	F	Anti-freeze, water-repellent grease		
Special grease	Front wheel bearings	W	Antifriction bearing grease		

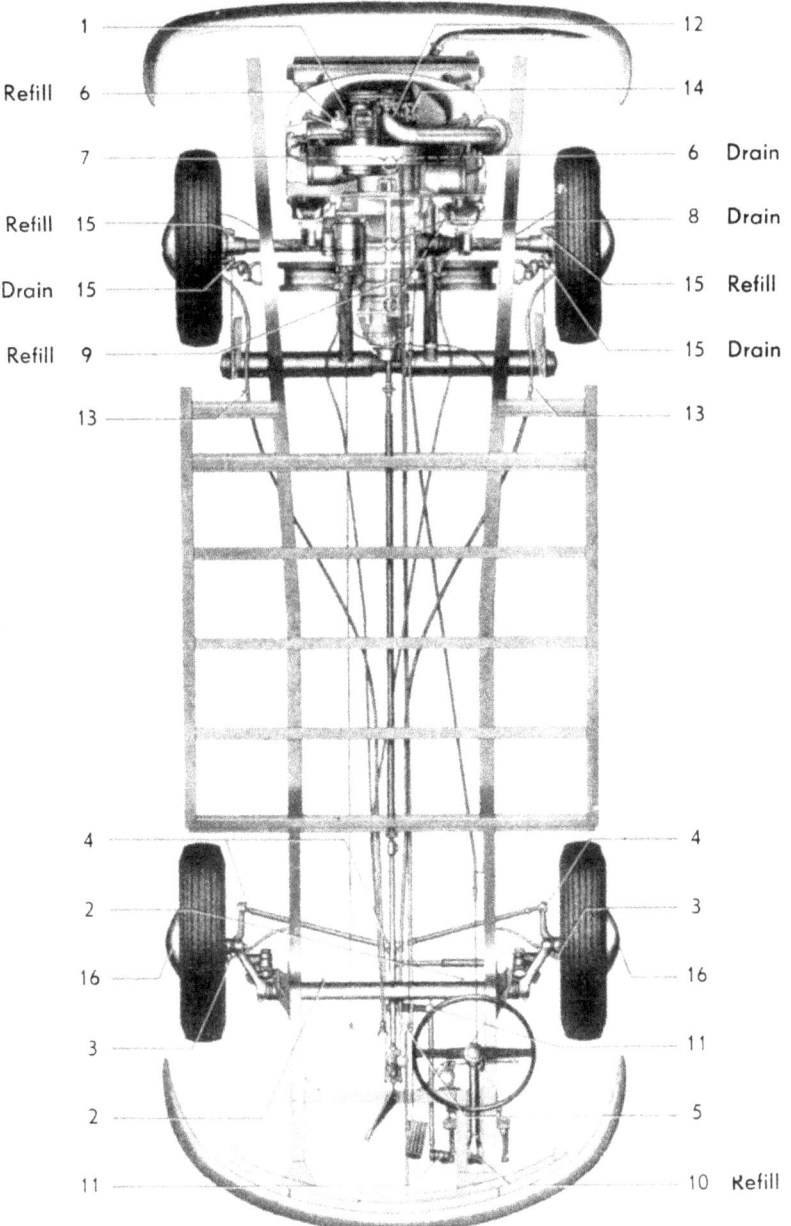

LUBRICATION CHART

km.Miles 500 300	2000 1200	4000 2400	No.	Lubrication points	Lubricant	Every	
			1	Engine: check oil level	M		
✓	✓	✓	2	Front axle tubes	F		
✓	✓	✓	3	King pins	F	2000 km.	
✓	✓	✓	4	Tie rod ends	F	1200 Miles	
✓	✓	✓	5	Steering arms	F		
✓	✓	✓		Door hinges	M		
✓	✓	✓	6	Engine: change oil	M		
✓	✓	✓	7	Engine: clean oil strainer			
✓	✓	✓		Clean magnetic oil drain plugs			
		✓	9	Transmission: check oil level	G		
✓		✓	10	Steering gear: check oil level	G	4000 km.	
✓		✓	11	Draglink	F	2400 Miles	
✓		✓	12	Carburetor controls	M		
✓		✓	13	Brake cables	F		
✓		✓	14	Breaker arm fiber block in ignition distributor	F		
✓		✓		Door and lid locks	F		
✓	✓		8	Transmission: change oil	G	12 000 km.	
✓	✓		15	Reduction gear case: change oil	G	7200 Miles	
			14	Felt in ignition distributor cam	M		
			16	Front wheel bearings	W	24 000 km.	14 400 Miles

Maintenance Chart

500 km / 300 miles	5000 km / 3000 miles	Operation	Every
		Check nuts and bolts on chassis, body, rear axle, front axle and steering for tightness	
		Check rear axle and engine for leaks	
		Check tire pressures and wheel mounting bolts for tightness	
		Check front wheel bearing play	
		Check fan belt	
		Clean fuel pump filter	
		Clean breaker points, grease distributor Check contact breaker points and timing	
		Check valve clearance	
		Check spark plugs and compression	
		Check exhaust system for damage	
		Check clutch pedal free-play	5000 km 3000 miles
		Check torsion arm link pins, tie rod ends and dust seals, steering damper mounting and toe-in	
		Check steering adjustment	
		Check tire wear, damage and pressure	
		Check hydraulic brake system for leakage and damage Check brake fluid level and adjustment of hand and foot brakes	
		Check thickness of brake linings through inspection hole	
		Check battery, electrical system and headlight alignment	
		Road test: Foot and hand brake operation, heating, idling adjustment	
		Clean, grease and adjust front wheel bearings	50 000 km 30 000 miles

Specifications and Data

Technical Data
VW 1200

Engine

Design	4-cycle, air-cooled, internal-combustion engine in unit with transmission and differential in rear of car
Number of cylinders	4
Arrangement of cylinders	Two pairs horizontally opposed
Bore	77 mm (3.031'')
Stroke	64 mm (2.520'')
Piston displacement	1192 cc (72.74 cu. ins.)
Compression ratio	7.0 : 1
Maximum performance (DIN)	34 bhp. at 3600 rpm.
(SAE, with air cleaner)	40 bhp. at 3900 rpm.
Maximum torque (DIN)	8.4 mkg 61 ft. lbs. at 2000 rpm.
(SAE, with air cleaner)	8.9 mkg 65 ft. lbs. at 2400 rpm.
Total weight, dry	approx. 110 kg (242 lbs.)
Crankcase	The magnesium casting alloy crankcase is built in two halves, the joint passing vertically through the centre lines of both the main bearings and the camshaft bearings
Cylinders	Individual cylinders cast from special grey cast iron, finned
Cylinder heads	Cast in pairs, of aluminium alloy, finned for air cooling
Valve seat inserts	Shrunk in position, made of sintered steel alloy
Valve guides	Shrunk in position, made of bronze
Spark plug thread	Cut in the cylinder head
Crankshaft	High quality steel forging, four plain bearings
Main bearings 1, 3, and 4	Sleeve-type bearings of aluminium alloy
Main bearing 2 (center)	Split shell bearing of aluminium alloy
Main bearings 1—3	55 mm dia.
Main bearing 4	40 mm dia.
Flywheel	Steel forging, with integral starter gear ring
Connecting rods	H section steel forgings
Connecting rod bearings	3-layer, steel-backed
Piston pin bearing	Pressed-in bronze bushing
Pistons	Of aluminium alloy with steel inserts
Piston pins	Fully floating, secured by circlips
Piston rings	2 compression rings 1 oil ring
Valve actuating mechanism	1 camshaft situated below crankshaft, valves operated via push rods, cam followers and rocker arms
Camshaft	Of grey cast iron, runs in three bearings machined direct in crankcase
Camshaft drive	By helical gears from the crankshaft
Valves	1 intake valve and 1 exhaust valve for each cylinder
Exhaust valve	Heat-resistant seating surface
Arrangement	Overhead
Clearance: Intake	0.20 mm (.008'') } up to a max. oil temperature of 50° C (122° F)
Exhaust	0.20 mm (.008'')
Valve springs	1 spring per valve
Valve timing with a valve clearance of 1 mm (.04''):	
Intake opens	6° before TDC.
Intake closes	35° 30' after BDC.
Exhaust opens	42° 30' before BDC.
Exhaust closes	3° after TDC.

Cooling system	Air cooling by fan on generator armature shaft
Fan drive	From crankshaft through V-belt
Ratio: crankshaft/generator	approx. 1 : 1.8
Cooling air intake	Thermostat-controlled
Amount of cooling air (Without heating air requirement)	500 liters (18 cubic feet) per second at 3600 engine rpm.
Lubrication	Pressure feed lubrication by gear pump
Oil cooling	Oil cooler situated in cooling air stream
Oil pressure control	By warning light
Ignition	Battery ignition
Ignition coil	Bosch TE 6 B 4 ⎫ VW 111 905 105 F ⎭ intermittently
Ignition distributor	Bosch ZV/PAU 4 R 5 mk ⎫ VW 113 905 205 B ⎭ intermittently
Spark timing	10° before TDC.
Firing order	1—4—3—2
Spark advance	By vacuum control
Breaker point gap	0.4 mm (.016″)
Spark plugs	14 mm thread, heat range 175 Bosch W 175 T 1 Beru 175/14 Champion L 85 or spark plugs of similar values from other manufacturers
Spark plug gap	0.6—0.7 mm (.024 to .028″)

Clutch

Design	Single disc, dry, KS 200 (Fichtel and Sachs)
Pedal free-play	10 to 20 mm (.4 to .8″)
Total lining area	363 sq. cm (60.4 sq. ins.)

Fuel System

Carburetor	Downdraft, SOLEX 28 PICT, with accelerator pump and automatic choke
Venturi	22.5 mm dia. integral
Main jet	122.5
Air correction jet	145 y (with emulsion tube)
Pilot jet	g 55
Pilot jet air bleed	2.0
Pump jet	0.5
Power fuel jet	1.0
Float needle valve	1.5
Float weight	5.7 grams (0.20 oz.), plastic material
Pump output	0.8—1.0 cc per stroke
Air cleaner	Oil-bath type with pre-heater tube
Fuel pump	Diaphragm type, mechanically operated
Feed pressure	maximum 0.2 kg/sq. cm (2.8 psi) at 3600 rpm.
Fuel delivery via float needle valve 1.5	minimum 300 cc/min. (.63 U. S. pints/min.) at 3600 rpm.
Fuel filter	Fuel filter in fuel pump

Ambulance

Fuel tap	Three-way tap with fuel reserve position

Transmission and Rear Axle

Type	4 speed transmission combined with differential in one housing
Transmission	4 forward gears, 1 reverse, 1st—4th gears constant mesh with helically cut teeth, cone type synchronisation and baulk rings
Ratios	1st speed 3.80 : 1
	2nd speed 2.06 : 1
	3rd speed 1.22 : 1
	4th speed 0.82 : 1
	Reverse 3.88 : 1
Gearshift control	Remote control shift linkage with ball-type lever in center of frame
Rear axle	Spiral toothed bevel gears with bevel gear differential and swing axle shafts
Ratio	4.125 : 1
Rear wheel drive	Reduction gears
Ratio	1.39 : 1

Chassis

Frame	2 ⊏-shaped side members connected by 6 cross members and welded to body floor plates
Wheel suspension front	Independent with two trailing links on each side
rear	Independent, swing axle with trailing links
Springing: front	2 full width, transverse, laminated torsion bars
rear	1 round transverse torsion bar on each side
Rear torsion bar setting unloaded	$20 \pm 30'$ spring plate angle
Ambulance	$25° \pm 20'$
Fire truck	$21° 30' \pm 20'$
Shock absorbers:	
front and rear	Double acting, telescopic
Steering	Ross steering gear with draglink in center of axle, divided tie-rod and steering damper
Ratio in straight-ahead position	15.1
Turns of steering wheel, lock to lock	2.8
Wheel setting, front	
a) at permissible total weight:	
Track on ground, front	1370 mm (54")
Toe-in	2—5 mm (.08—.20")
Camber	0°
King pin inclination	4° 20'
Caster (axle tubes)	0°
Caster	16 mm (.63")
b) unladen (without driver)	
Toe-in	0 ± 1 mm ($0 \pm .04"$)
Camber	$0° 40' \pm 30'$
Maximum wheel angle: inner	32°
outer	24°
Wheels	Steel disc with drop-center rims $4^1/_2$ K × 15
Tires	6.40—15
Dynamic rolling radius	328 mm (22.9")
Tire pressures	front 2 kg/sq. cm (28 psi)
	rear 2.3 kg/sq. cm (33 psi)
	Ambulance: front and rear 1.8 kg/sq. cm (26 psi)
Brakes: Footbrake	four wheel hydraulic (Ate) two leading shoe at front, single at rear
Handbrake	mechanical, acting on rear wheels
Effective lining area	approx. 836 sq. cm (130 sq. ins.)
Lubrication	Individual points

Body

Models 21, 22, 23, 24, 25 and 28:

Type .... Forward control, all steel box body of welded pressings. Side and cross members welded to the floor plates form a frame to which axles, engine and controls are attached

Driver's cab .... Full width of body, separated from load compartment up to waistline by a partition

Model 21:

Partition extended to roof by a fiberboard panel with a window
Engine compartment .... Box shaped in rear, full width of body, accessible through flap in rear panel
Load or passenger compartment .... Located between axles. Extends from cab to rear panel with stepped portion over engine. Access through wing doors in side and flap in rear panel

Models 23, 24, 25 and 28:

Space over engine serves as luggage compartment

Doors:
  Cab doors:
    Clear width .... 980 mm (36.6")
    Clear height .... 1140 mm (44.9")
    Opening angle .... 110°
  Wing doors:
    Clear width .... 1170 mm (46.1")
    Clear height .... 1200 mm (47.2")
    Opening angle .... 180°
Flaps:
  Engine compartment flap .... In lower part of rear panel, hinged at top, locked with square key
  Load compartment flap .... Over engine compartment flap with window, hinged at top, locked with door key

Models 24 and 25:

Sliding roof .... Golde
  Roof opening .... 940 mm wide (37.00")
                              1360 mm long (53.5")
Windows:
  Windshield .... V-type with center bar, inclined at 32°
  Cab door windows .... Vent wings with clamps, sliding windows which can be secured in four positions
  Type of glass .... Safety glass, windshield with clear vision zone in front of driver
  Windshield wiper .... Electric with two wiper arms
  Rear window:
    Height .... 265 mm (10.4")
    Width .... 660 mm (26.0")
    Glass .... Safety glass

Additional on Models 22, 23 and 28:

Passenger compartment side windows Three on each side, the rear ones being hinged
  Height .... 360 mm (14.2")
  Width .... 470 mm (18.5")
  Glass .... Safety glass

Additional on Models 24 and 25:

Windows all round	Side panel, rear panel and rear side windows being hinged
Glass type	Safety glass
Skylights	In edge of roof
Glass type	Tinted, heat-absorbing

All Models:

Seats:

Cab	Adjustable driving seat with adjustable backrest, and two seater bench seat which hinges forward complete with backrest

Models 22 and 24, (23 on request):

Passenger space	Two removable seat benches for three passenger each. The back of the front seat bench is divided to allow easy entrance for the rear seat passengers by folding it down at the door

Models 25 and 28:

Passenger space	two-seater bench at front, three-seater bench at rear

All Models:

Instrument panel	Extending over the entire width of the vehicle
Instrument unit	In front of the steering column. It consists of speedometer, mileage recorder and warning lights for headlights, generator charging, oil pressure and direction indicators, rheostat-controlled lighting
Fuel gauge	Electric, situated on left of speedometer
Ignition switch	Combined steering ignition lock with non-repeat device on steering column
Direction indicators	Operated by switch below the steering wheel
Space for radio	With grille in center of instrument panel

Interior trim:
   Cab:

Partition and floor plates	Covered with insulating material to prevent heat losses
Floor	Covered with rubber mats
Partition and doors	Provided with trim panels
Miscellaneous	Two sun visors. Outside driving mirrors on both sides Parcel shelf under instrument panel screwed to the front panel Flexible grab handle in front of passenger seat

On Models 24 and 25:

Inside driving mirror, clock. (outside mirror on drivers side only)

Models 21 and 23:

Load compartment	No fittings

Models 22, 24, 25 and 28:

Passenger space:

Floor	Covered with rubber mats
Cab partition, side panels and doors	With leatherette trimming
Roof and window frames	Lined with cloth

All Models:

Ventilation	Fresh air ventilation via an air duct in the center of the cab roof. Outlets allow ventilation of cab and cargo or passenger space
Regulation	By throttle plate which can be fixed in four positions
Heating	Fresh air heating with control in cab and two defroster vents at windshield

Additional on Models 22, 24, 25 and 28:

Heating	Duct with outlets underneath the rear seat bench

All Models:

Heating control	Fine regulation by rotary knob

Miscellaneous:

Bumpers	Front and rear, wrapped round body corners
Spare wheel	Behind seat back in cab
Fuel tank	In engine compartment
Filler tube	Under lockable lid in right-hand side panel
Tool kit and accessories	Underneath passenger's seat bench

Model 26 (Pick-Up):

Design	The self-supporting all-steel body with forward-control cab is welded to the underframe
Cab	Throughout the width of the car, equipped with rear view window. Doors, windows, seats, instrument panel, interior trim and heating are the same as in the cab of the Model 21

Double cab Pick-Up:

Cab	Extended to rear, with removable three-seater bench seat, accessible through side door
Ventilation	Fresh air regulation as in Model 21, but with shorter air guide channel

Model 26:

Platform	Consisting of corrugated sheet steel and protecting slats of hardwood. Hinged tail and side boards
Hoops (on request)	Bolted in position, with canvas cover
Additional load space (locker)	Underneath the platform, between the axles, fully enclosed, lockable
Engine compartment	Below platform at rear, accessible through a lid in the rear panel

Miscellaneous:

Bumper	Front and rear, wrapped round body corners
Spare wheel	In locker, under load platform
Fuel tank	Between locker and engine compartment
Tools and accessories	Below the passenger's seat bench

Model 27 (Ambulance):

Design	As Model 22
Cab	As Model 22
Partition	Extended to roof with glass, with sliding window
Ambulance compartment	Low-level load surface at front, stretcher table at rear. Accessible through side doors and large rear flap
Engine compartment	As Model 22

Doors:
    Cab .... As Model 21
    Ambulance compartment .... Double side door with retractable step
        Width .... 1170 mm (46″)
        Height .... 1190 mm (46.8″)
Windows .... As on Model 22, but without rear window
Flaps:
    Engine compartment .... As on Model 22
    Rear panel .... Above engine compartment flap, hinged at the bottom edge, handle with lock
Seats:
    Cab .... Same as on Model 21
    Ambulance compartment .... Removable seat at the front, sliding in runners. Another seat in front of the right-hand stretcher.
                                                Folding emergency seat on partition panel.
                                                Two stretchers according to DIN 13025
Instrument panel .... As on Model 21, but equipped with three-way fuel tap
Interior trim:
    Cab .... As on Model 21, but roof and doors lined with leatherette
    Ambulance compartment:
        Floor and rear panel .... Linoleum-covered
        Side panels and roof .... Trimmed with leatherette
        Other equipment .... Lockable cupboard, drawers, shelf and grab handles
        Heating .... As on Model 22, but with different outlet in ambulance compartment
        Ventilation .... As on Model 22, but equipped with two blowers for ventilation with vehicle stationary, amount of air delivered can be regulated in 2 stages
Miscellaneous:
    Bumper .... Front and rear, wrapped round body corners
    Spare wheel .... In cab behind seat back
    Tools and accessories .... Underneath the driver's seat bench
    Fuel tank .... In engine compartment

Electrical System

All Models:

Electrical system .... 6 V with voltage regulation
Battery .... 6 V 77 Ah
Generator .... Bosch LJ/REG 180/6/2500 L 3 } intermittently
                                     VW 113 903 021 C
Regulator .... on generator
    Type .... Bosch RS/TAA/180/6/4 } intermittently
                                     VW 113 905 805 C
Cut-in speed .... 1800—1850 generator rpm.
Starter .... Bosch EEF 0.5/6 L 1 } intermittently
                                     VW 113 911 021 A

Lighting

Two headlamps .... with asymmetric low beams and built-in parking lamp, adjustable
    Lamp diameter .... 180 mm (7″)
    Headlamp bulbs .... 45/40 Watts
    Parking bulbs .... 4 Watts each

Two tail/stop/indicator lamps	In twin compartment housings
Twin-filament bulbs:	
Tail lamps	5 Watts each
Stop lamps	18 Watts each
One license plate lamp	mounted in engine compartment flap
License plate lamp bulb	10 Watts
All warning lamp bulbs	1.2 Watts each
Speedometer lighting	indirect and rheostat controlled
Two bulbs	1.2 Watts each
Turn indicator lamps, front	above headlamp
rear	in upper compartment of rear lamps
Ball type bulbs	18 Watts

Models 21, 22, 23, 24, 25 and 28:

Interior lights	in cab and in load or passenger compartment

Model 26

Interior light	in cab

Modell 27

One interior light	in cab
Two interior lights	in ambulance compartment
Sundries	Spotlight with built-in mirror and switch, illuminated Red Cross sign, reversing lamp and buzzer with two press buttons in ambulance compartment

All Models:

All interior lights with two bulbs	5 Watts
Fuses	8 point fuse box on front panel below parcel shelf

Dimensions and Weights

Outer dimensions	Delivery Van Kombi Micro Bus Ambulance	De Luxe Micro Bus	Pick-Up Pick-Up with double cabin Pick-Up with enlarged platform	Pick-Up with enlarged wooden platform
Wheelbase	2400 mm (94.5")	2400 mm (94.5")	2400 mm (94.5")	2400 mm (94.5")
Track: front	1370 mm (53.9")	1370 mm (53.9")	1370 mm (53.9")	1370 mm (53.9")
rear	1360 mm (53.5")	1360 mm (53.5")	1360 mm (53.5")	1360 mm (53.5")
Length without bumper guards	4280 mm (168.5")		4290 mm (168.9")	4300 mm (169.3")
with bumper guards	4290 mm (168.9")	4300 mm (169.3")	4300 mm (169.3")	4300 mm (169.3")
Width	1750 mm (68.9")	1800 mm (70.9")	1750[2] mm (68.9")	1980 mm (78.0")
Height, unladen	1940[1] mm (76.4")	1940 mm (76.4")	1920[3] mm (75.6")	1920 mm (75.6")
Ground clearance, laden	240 mm (9.4")	240 mm (9.4")	240 mm (9.4")	240 mm (9.4")
Angle of approach	21°	21°	21°	21°
Angle of departure	20°	20°	20°	20°
Smallest turning circle approx.	12 m (39')	12 m (39')	12 m (39')	12 m (39')
Smallest tracking circle approx.	11.2 m (37')	11.2 m (37')	11.2 m (37')	11.2 m (37')

[1]) Ambulance with blue light: 2170 mm (85.4")   [2]) Pick-Up with enlarged platform: 2020 mm (79.5")
[3]) With cover: 2210 mm (87.0")

Load compartment dimensions	Delivery Van Kombi	Load compartment dimensions	Pick-Up	Pick-Up with double cabin	Pick-Up with enlarged platform	Pick-Up with enlarged wooden platform
Mean length	2700 mm (106.3")	Inside length	2600 mm (102.4")	1755 mm (69.1")	2600 mm (102.4")	2720 mm (107.1")
Mean width	1500 mm (59.1")	Inside width	1570 mm (61.8")	1570 mm (61.8")	1910 mm (75.2")	1850 mm (72.8")
Mean height	1350 mm (53.1")	Inside height	375 mm (14.8")	375 mm (14.8")	375 mm (14.8")	400 mm (15.7")
Load space approx.	4.8 cu. m (170 cu. ft.)	Platform	4.2 sq. m (45 sq. ft.)	2.75 sq. m (31 sq. ft.)	5.04 sq. m (55 sq. ft.)	5 sq. m (54 sq. ft.)
Height of load platform above ground (unlad.) front	500 mm (19.7")	Load space	1.55 cu. m (54.8 cu. ft.)	1.0 cu. m (35.3 cu. ft.)	1.9 cu. m (67.1 cu. ft.)	2.0 cu. m (70.7 cu. ft.)
rear	980 mm (38.6")	Height of platform above ground (unladen)	980 mm (38.6")	980 mm (38.6")	980 mm (38.6")	980 mm (38.6")

Luggage Space	Micro Bus	Locker under platform		Pick-Up Pick-Up with enlarged platform Pick-Up with enlarged wooden platform
Mean length	700 mm (27.6")	Length		1200 mm (47.2")
Mean width	1450 mm (57.1")	Width		1600 mm (63.0")
Mean height	800 mm (31.5")	Height		340 mm (13.4")
Load space	0.8 cu. m (28 cu. ft.)	Load area		1.9 sq. m (20 sq. ft.)
		Load space		0.65 cu. m (23 cu. ft.)
Height of load platform above ground (unladen)	980 mm (38.6")	Height of load area above ground (unladen)		500 mm (19.7")

Weights	Delivery Van	Kombi	Micro Bus	Pick-Up without tarpaulin	Pick-Up with tarpaulin
Unladen weight	1035 kg[1] (2282 lbs)	1120 kg[2] (2469 lbs)	1125 kg (2480 lbs)	1065 kg[1] (2348 lbs)	1100 kg[1] (2425 lbs)
Payload	830 kg (1830 lbs)	745 kg (1643 lbs)	740 kg (1632 lbs)	800 kg (1764 lbs)	765 kg (1687 lbs)
Permissible total weight	1865 kg (4112 lbs)	1865 kg (4112 lbs)	1865 kg (4112 lbs)	1865 kg (4112 lbs)	1865 kg (4112 lbs)
Permissible front axle load	950 kg (2094 lbs)	950 kg (2094 lbs)	950 kg (2094 lbs)	950 kg (2094 lbs)	950 kg (2094 lbs)
Permissible rear axle load	1015 kg (2238 lbs)	1015 kg (2238 lbs)	1015 kg (2238 lbs)	1015 kg (2238 lbs)	1015 kg (2238 lbs)

[1]) with driver   [2]) with driver and seats

Weights	Double Cab Pick-Up without tarpaulin	Double Cab Pick-Up with tarpaulin	Pick-Up with enlarged platform	Pick-Up with enlarged wooden platform	Ambulance Standard model	Ambulance DIN model
Unladen weight	1110 kg* (2448 lbs)	1135 kg* (2502 lbs)	1115 kg* (2458 lbs)	1130 kg* (2490 lbs)	1225 kg (2701 lbs)	1265 kg (2788 lbs)
Payload	755 kg (1664 lbs)	730 kg (1610 lbs)	750 kg (1654 lbs)	735 kg (1622 lbs)	640 kg (1411 lbs)	600 kg (1322 lbs)
Permissible total weight	1865 kg (4112 lbs)	1865 kg (4112 lbs)	1865 kg (4112 lbs)	1865 kg (4112 lbs)	1865 kg (4112 lbs)	1865 kg (4112 lbs)
Permissible front axle load	950 kg (2094 lbs)	950 kg (2094 lbs)	950 kg (2094 lbs)	950 kg (2094 lbs)	950 kg (2094 lbs)	950 kg (2094 lbs)
Permissible rear axle load	1015 kg (2238 lbs)	1015 kg (2238 lbs)	1015 kg (2238 lbs)	1015 kg (2238 lbs)	1015 kg (2238 lbs)	1015 kg (2238 lbs)

* with driver

Capacities

Fuel tank .... 40 liters, (10.5 U. S. gals.; 8.8 Imp. gals.) including 5 liters (1.3 U. S. gals.; 1.1 Imp. gals.) reserve
Crankcase .... 2.5 liters (5.3 U. S. pints; 4.4 Imp. pints)
Refill quantity: 2.5 liters
Transmission case .... 3.0 liters (6.3 U. S. pints; 5.3 Imp. pints)
Refill quantity: 2.5 liters (5.3 U. S. pints; 4.4 Imp. pints)
Reduction gear case .... 0.25 liter (0.5 U. S. pint; 0.4 Imp. pint)
Steering .... 0.25 liter (0.5 U. S. pint; 0.4 Imp. pint)
Brake .... 0.3 liter (0.6 U. S. pint; 0.5 Imp. pint)
Oil bath air cleaner .... approx. 0.25 liter (0.5 U. S. pint; 0.4 Imp. pint), fill to indicated level

Performance

Output .... 34 bhp. at 3600 rpm. (40 SAE bhp. at 3900 rpm.)
Maximum torque .... 8.4 mkg (61 ft. lbs.) at 2000 rpm.
Maximum speed .... 95 kph. (60 mph.) at 3620 rpm.
  Pick-Up with tarpaulin,
  Pick-Up with enlarged platform   } 90 kph. (56 mph.) at 3430 rpm.
  Pick-Up with enlarged wooden platform
Mean piston speed at top speed .... 7.7 m/s (1516 ft./min.)
  Pick-Up with tarpaulin
  Pick-Up with enlarged platform   } 7.3 m/s (1437 ft./min.)
  Pick-Up with enlarged wooden platform

Speeds at 3600 engine rpm.

1st gear	approx.	20 kph. (12 mph.)
2nd gear	approx.	38 kph. (23 mph.)
3rd gear	approx.	64 kph. (40 mph.)
4th gear	approx.	94 kph. (58 mph.)
Reverse	approx.	20 kph. (12 mph.)
Mean piston speed		7.68 m/s (1512 ft./min.)

Hill climbing ability on good roads, fully laden:

1st gear	approx.	26 % (15°)
2nd gear	approx.	13.5% (7.5°)
3rd gear	approx.	7 % (4.5°)
4th gear	approx.	4 % (2.5°)

Fuel Consumption

Average consumption according to DIN 70030

        9.2 liters per 100 km
       26.0 miles per U. S. gallon
       31.0 miles per Imp. gallon

Pick-Up with tarpaulin } 9.5 liters per 100 km
Pick-Up with enlarged platform 25.0 miles per U. S. gallon
Pick-Up with enlarged wooden platform 30.0 miles per Imp. gallon

Fuel .... 86 Octane

Oil consumption .... approx. 0.5—1.4 liters per 1000 km
                                      1.7—4.8 U. S. pts. per 1000 miles
                                      1.4—4.0 Imp. pts. per 1000 miles

Technical Data
(VW 1500 Transporter)

As for the VW 1200 Transporter with the following variations:

Engine

Bore .... 83 mm (3.27")
Stroke .... 69 mm (2.72")
Capacity .... 1493 cc (91.10 cu. ins.)
Compression ratio .... 7.8 : 1
Maximum output, DIN .... 42 bhp. at 3800 rpm.
   SAE, with air cleaner .... 50 bhp. at 3900 rpm.
Maximum torque, DIN .... 9.7 mkg (70.16 ft. lbs.) at 2200 rpm.
   SAE, with air cleaner .... 9.7 mkg (70.16 ft. lbs.) at 2400 rpm.
Valve clearance: inlet .... 0.30 mm (.012") up to a maximum oil temperature
               exhaust .... 0.30 mm (.012") of 50° C (122° F)
Valve timing with a valve clearance
of 1 mm (.040"):
   Intake opens .... 7° 30' before TDC.
   Intake closes .... 37° after BDC.
   Exhaust opens .... 44° 30' before BDC.
   Exhaust closes .... 4° after TDC.
Cooling system
   Crankshaft/generator ratio .... 1 : 1.9
   Air output .... approx. 550 liters (19.6 cu. ft.) per second at 3800 rpm.
   (Without heating air requirement)

Fuel System

Carburetor .... Downdraft SOLEX 28 PICT with accelerator pump and automatic choke
   Venturi .... 22.5 mm dia. integral
   Main jet 115
   Air correction jet .... 145 y (with emulsion tube)
   Pilot jet with electro-magnetic
      cut-off valve .... g 45
   Pilot jet air bleed 1.55
   Pump jet 0.5
   Power fuel jet 0.7
   Float needle valve 1.5
   Float weight .... 5.7 g (Plastic)
   Pump output .... approx. 1.2—1.3 cc per stroke (.73—.79 cu. ins.)
Fuel pump:
   Fuel delivery via 1.5 float needle valve. minimum 400 cc/min. (24 cu. ins.) at 3800 rpm.

Transmission and Rear Axle Drive

Rear axle drive .... via reduction gears
   Ratio .... 1.26 : 1

Chassis

Wheel setting:
  Front track, on ground .... 1375 mm (54.1″)
Brakes:
  Effective lining area .... 1028 sq. cm (159.2 sq. ins.)

Electrical System

Generator .... Bosch LJ/GEG 200/6/2600 L
Regulator .... installed in right-hand wheel housing
Type .... RS/VA 200/6/3
Cut-in speed .... approx. 1820 generator rpm.

Dimensions and Weights

Weights	Delivery Van	Kombi	Micro Bus	Pick-Up without tarpaulin	Pick-Up with tarpaulin
Unladen weight	1050 kg[1] (2314 lbs)	1135 kg[2] (2502 lbs)	1140 kg (2512 lbs)	1080 kg[1] (2380 lbs)	1115 kg[1] (2458 lbs)
Payload	815 kg (1798 lbs)	730 kg (1610 lbs)	725 kg (1600 lbs)	785 kg (1732 lbs)	750 kg (1654 lbs)
Permissible total weight	1865 kg (4112 lbs)	1865 kg (4112 lbs)	1865 kg (4112 lbs)	1865 kg (4112 lbs)	1865 kg (4112 lbs)
Permissible front axle load	950 kg (2094 lbs)	950 kg (2094 lbs)	950 kg (2094 lbs)	950 kg (2094 lbs)	950 kg (2094 lbs)
Permissible rear axle load	1015 kg (2238 lbs)	1015 kg (2238 lbs)	1015 kg (2238 lbs)	1015 kg (2238 lbs)	1015 kg (2238 lbs)

Weights	Double Cab Pick-Up without tarpaulin	Double Cab Pick-Up with tarpaulin	Pick-Up with enlarged platform	Pick-Up with enlarged wooden platform	Ambulance Standard model	Ambulance DIN model
Unladen weight	1125 kg[1] (2480 lbs)	1150 kg[1] (2536 lbs)	1130 kg[1] (2490 lbs)	1150 kg[1] (2536 lbs)	1240 kg (2734 lbs)	1280 kg (2822 lbs)
Payload	740 kg (1632 lbs)	715 kg (1576 lbs)	735 kg (1622 lbs)	715 kg (1576 lbs)	615 kg (1356 lbs)	585 kg (1290 lbs)
Permissible total weight	1865 kg (4112 lbs)	1865 kg (4112 lbs)	1865 kg (4112 lbs)	1865 kg (4112 lbs)	1865 kg (4112 lbs)	1865 kg (4112 lbs)
Permissible front axle load	950 kg (2094 lbs)	950 kg (2094 lbs)	950 kg (2094 lbs)	950 kg (2094 lbs)	950 kg (2094 lbs)	950 kg (2094 lbs)
Permissible rear axle load	1015 kg (2238 lbs)	1015 kg (2238 lbs)	1015 kg (2238 lbs)	1015 kg (2238 lbs)	1015 kg (2238 lbs)	1015 kg (2238 lbs)

Weights	Fire Truck
Unladen weight	1175 kg[1] (2590 lbs)
Payload (with full equipment)	910 kg (2006 lbs)
Permissible total weight	2085 kg (4596 lbs)
Permissible front axle load	1000 kg (2204 lbs)
Permissible rear axle load	1135 kg (2502 lbs)

[1]) with driver   [2]) with driver and seats

Performance

Output .... 42 bhp. at 3800 rpm.
Maximum torque .... 9.7 mkg (70 ft. lbs.) at 2200 rpm.
Maximum speed .... 105 kph. (65 mph.) 3620 rpm.
   Pick Up with tarpaulin,
   Pick Up with enlarged platform
   and with enlarged wooden platform .. 95 kph. (60 mph.) at 3280 rpm.
Mean piston speed at top speed .... 8.32 m/s (1644 ft./min.)
   Pick Up with tarpaulin,
   Pick Up with enlarged platform
   and with enlarged wooden platform .. 7.55 m/s (1486 ft./min.)

Road speeds at 3800 engine rpm.:

		Hill climbing ability on good roads, fully loaded:	
1st gear	24 kph. (15 mph.)	1st gear .....approx. 28 % (16°)	[1 in 3.57]
2nd gear	44 kph. (27 mph.)	2nd gear .....approx. 14.5% (8°)	[1 in 6.90]
3rd gear	74 kph. (46 mph.)	3rd gear .....approx. 7.5% (4°)	[1 in 13.35]
4th gear	110 kph. (68 mph.)	4th gear .....approx. 4 % (24°)	[1 in 25.00]
Reverse gear..............	23 kph. (14 mph.)		
Mean piston speed..........	8.74 m/s (1720 ft/min.)		

Fuel consumption

In accordance with German DIN regulations 9.5 liters per 100 km
                                                  30.0 miles per Imp. gallon
                                                  25.0 miles per U. S. gallon
Pick-Up with tarpaulin.
Pick-Up with enlarged platform
Pick-Up with enlarged wooden platform .. 9.7 liters per 100 km
                                            29.0 miles per Imp. gallon
                                            24.0 miles per U. S. gallon

List of Tolerances and Wear Limits
Type 2 — 1200

General

The term WEAR LIMIT means that parts which approach, or have already reached, the limit given should not be re-used when carrying out an overhaul. When deciding the wear limit of pistons and cylinders, due consideration should also be given to the oil consumption of the respective engine.

Engine 1192 cc (72.74 cu. ins.) — 34 bhp. (40 SAE bhp.)

		Tolerances (new parts)	Wear Limit
1 - Cylinder seating depth in cylinder head		13.90—14.00 mm (.085—.551″)	15.50 mm (.610″)
2 - Cylinder	out of round	0.01 mm (.0004″)	
3 - Piston/cylinder	clearance	0.036—0.054 mm (.0014—.0021″)	0.20 mm (.008″)
4 - a) Upper compression ring	side clearance	0.065—0.092 mm (.0026—.0036″)	0.12 mm (.005″)
b) Lower compression ring	side clearance	0.045—0.072 mm (.0018—.0028″)	0.10 mm (.004″)
5 - Oil scraper ring	side clearance	0.025—0.052 mm (.0010—.0020″)	0.10 mm (.004″)
6 - Compression rings	gap	0.30—0.45 mm (.012—.018″)	0.95 mm (.037″)
Oil scraper ring	gap	0.25—0.40 mm (.010—.016″)	0.95 mm (.037″)
7 - Weight tolerance of pistons in one engine		max. 5 g	max. 10 g*
8 - Weight tolerance of con. rods in one engine		max. 5 g (.18 oz.)	max. 10 g*
9 - Piston pin/con. rod bush	clearance	0.003—0.016 mm (.0001—.0006″)	0.04 mm (.002″)
10 - Connecting rod bearings	clearance	0.018—0.076 mm (.0007—.0030″)	0.15 mm (.006″)
	end play	0.1—0.4 mm (.004—.016″)	0.70 mm (.028″)
11 - Crankshaft main bearing (taking into account the preload by the crankcase) a) Bearings 1 to 3	clearance	0.036—0.098 mm (.0010—.0039″)	0.18 mm (.0072″)
b) Bearing 4	clearance	0.047—0.102 mm (.0019—.0040″)	0.19 mm (.0075″)
c) Steel bearings 1—3 (for cold countries only)	clearance	0.028—0.087 mm (.0011—.0034″)	0.17 mm (.0066″)
12 - Crankshaft at Nos. 2 and 4 main bearing journals (Nos. 1 and 3 bearing journals on V-blocks)	run-out		0.03 mm (.001″)
13 - Crankshaft/main bearing 2	end play	0.065—0.125 mm (.0026—.0049″)	0.15 mm (.006″)
14 - Crankshaft	out of balance	max. 8 cmg (.11 oz. in.)	
15 - Main bearing journals	out of round		0.03 mm (.0012″)

* During repair

		Tolerances (new parts)	Wear Limit
16 - Crank pins	out of round		0.03 mm (.0012'')
17 - Crankcase bore for crankshaft			
a) Bearings 1 to 3	diameter	65.000–65.019 mm (2.5591–2.5598'')	
b) Bearing 4	diameter	50.000–50.025 mm (1.9685–1.9695'')	
c) Seat for crankshaft seal	diameter	90.000–90.045 mm (3.5433–3.5451'')	
18 - Fan pulley	radial run-out	max. 0.8 mm (.031'')	
	lateral run-out	max. 0.3 mm (.012'')	
19 - Crankcase bore for camshaft	diameter	25.020–25.041 mm (.98504–.98587'')	25.070 mm (.98701'')
20 - Camshaft	clearance	0.020–0.054 mm (.0008–.0021'')	0.12 mm (.0047'')
Thrust bearing	end play	0.060–0.114 mm (.0023–.0048'')	0.14 mm (.005'')
Measured at center bearing (between centers)	run-out	0.02 mm (.0008'')	0.04 mm (.0016'')
21 - Camshaft timing gear	backlash	0.000–0.052 mm (.0000–.0020'')	
22 - Flywheel (measured in center of friction surface)	lateral run-out	max. 0.30 mm (.012'')	
	unbalance	max. 5 cmg (.07 oz. in.)	
Shoulder	outer diameter	69.9–70.1 mm (2.75–2.76'')	69.70 mm (2.7441'')
Remachining width of teeth			max. 2.0 mm (.08'')
23 - Valve stem: intake	diameter	7.95–7.94 mm (.3130–.3126'')	7.90 mm (.3110'')
exhaust	diameter	7.92–7.91 mm (.3118–.3114'')	7.87 mm (.3098'')
	out of round	0.01 mm (.0004'')	
24 - Valve head: intake	diameter	31.5 mm (1.24'')	
exhaust	diameter	30.0 mm (1.18'')	
25 - Valve guides: intake	inner diameter	8.000–8.015 mm (.3150–.3156'')	8.060 mm (.3173'')
exhaust	inner diameter	8.000–8.020 mm (.3150–.3157'')	8.060 mm (.3173'')
26 - Valve guide/valve stem: intake	clearance	0.050–0.075 mm (.0020–.0030'')	0.16 mm (.006'')
exhaust	clearance	0.080–0.105 mm (.0031–.0041'')	0.16 mm (.006'')
27 - Valve seating face			
a) intake	width	1.3–1.6 mm (.051–.063'')	
b) exhaust	width	1.7–2.0 mm (.067–.079'')	
c) valve seating face	run-out	0.015 mm (.0006'')	
28 - Valve springs			
loaded length 34.3 mm (1.35'')	load	42.5 ± 3 kg (93.6 ± 6.6 lbs.)	38 kg (84 lbs.)

		Tolerances (new parts)	Wear Limit
29 - Valve clearance (up to maximum oil temperature of 50° C/122° F) intake and exhaust	adjustment	0.20 mm (.008'')	
30 - a) Rocker arm	inner diameter	18.000−18.018 mm (.70866−.70937'')	18.035 mm (.71004'')
b) Rocker arm shaft	diameter	17.984−17.966 mm (.70803−.70732'')	17.955 mm (.70689'')
c) Rocker arm/rocker arm shaft	clearance	0.016−0.052 mm (.0006−.0020'')	0.080 mm (.0031'')
31 - a) Crankcase bore for cam follower	diameter	19.000−19.021 mm (.74803−.74886'')	19.060 mm (.75039'')
b) Cam follower	diameter	18.980−18.959 mm (.74724−.74642'')	18.800 mm (.74015'')
c) Crankcase bore/cam follower	clearance	0.020−0.062 mm (.0008−.0024'')	0.120 mm (.0047'')
32 - Compression pressure (To be checked with the throttle open, engine warm, all spark plugs removed, pressure gauge in spark plug seat and the engine turned over by the starter motor)		7.0−9.0 kg/sq. cm (100−128 psi.)	4.5 kg/sq. cm (64 psi.)
33 - Oil pump: end play of gears/body with gasket (cover removed)		0.066−0.183 mm (.0026−.0072'')	0.20 mm (.008'')
End play of gears/body (gasket removed)			0.10 mm (.004'')
Oil pump gears	backlash	0.03−0.08 mm (.0012−.0031'')	
34 - Oil pressure (only for SAE 10 W-30): at oil temperature of 70° C (158° F) a) at 550 rpm.		min. 0.5 kg/sq. cm (7 psi.)	
b) at 2500 rpm.		min. 2.0 kg/sq. cm (28 psi.)	
35 - Spring for oil pressure relief valve Length compressed: 23.6 mm	load	7.75 kg (16 lbs.)	
36 - Oil pressure contact opens	pressure	0.15−0.45 kg/sq.cm (2.1−6.3 psi.)	
37 - Distance from fan housing to upper edge of throttle ring a) with engine cold	setting	20 mm (.8'')	
b) with engine warm	setting	25−30 mm (1−1.2'')	
38 - Thermostat: after a water bath at 65 to 70° C (149 to 158° F)	length	min. 46 mm (1.81'')	

Clutch (200 mm dia.)

1 - Clutch driven plate	lateral run-out	max. 0.8 mm (.03'')	
2 - Clutch springs	diameter	25.5 mm (1.003'')	
length loaded 29.2 mm (1.148'')	load	44.5−49.5 kg (98−109 lbs.)	
3 - Clutch pedal free-play		10−20 mm (.4−.8'')	
4 - Clutch pressure plate	run-out		0.10 mm (.004'')
5 - Clutch release plate	run-out		0.40 mm (.016'')

		Tolerances (new parts)	Wear Limit
6 - Clutch assy	unbalance	max. 15 cmg (.021 oz. in.)	
7 - Flywheel to release plate	distance	25.8—26.2 mm (1.015—1.030'')	

Front Axle

		Tolerances (new parts)	Wear Limit
1 - Torsion arms	twist	max. 0.2 mm (.0008'')	
2 - Torsion arm/fibre bush (higher limit preferable as bush swells)	clearance	0.20—0.27 mm (.008—.0011'')	0.35 mm (.0138'')
3 - Torsion arm link pin	diameter	19.920—19.910 mm (.7843—.7839'')	
4 - Needle bearing (not installed) inside contact diameter		19.935 +0.010 mm (.7848—.0004'')	
5 - King pin	diameter	23.966—23.953 mm (.9444—.9430'')	
King pin/bush	clearance		0.10 mm (.004'')
6 - King pin/spacer without rubber seals	end play	max. 0.15 mm (.006'')	
7 - Front axle tubes Permissible mis-alignment and lack of parallelism measured 200 mm from the end faces		max. 0.2 mm (.008'')	
8 - Wheel setting (vehicle level horizontally) a) with permissible total weight Toe-in		2—5 mm (.080—.20'')	
Camber (equal value for both wheels)		0°	
King pin inclination		4° 20'	
Caster (axle tubes)		0°	
b) with vehicle unladen (without driver) Toe-in		0 ± 1 mm (0 ± .04'')	
Camber		0° 40' ± 30'	
9 - Swing lever shaft	diameter	23.980—23.967 mm (.9441—.9436'')	
10 - Swing lever shaft bush	reaming dia.	24.000—24.021 mm (.9450—.9458'' dia.)	
11 - Swing lever shaft/bush	clearance	0.020—0.054 mm (.0008—.0021'')	0.12 mm (.0047'')
12 - Steering lever shaft bush	reaming dia.	25.380—25.401 mm (.998—1.000'' dia.)	
Steering lever shaft/bush	clearance	0.027—0.061 mm (.0011—.0024'')	0.10 mm (.004'')
13 - Steering column, installed measured at column tube end	run-out	max. 0.35 mm (.014'')	
14 - Column tube in steering gear housing	depth inserted	45—46 mm (1.71—1.81'')	

Rear Axle and Transmission

		Tolerances (new parts)	Wear Limit
1 - Main drive shaft/needle bearing in gland nut	clearance	0.12—0.19 mm (.0047—.0074'')	0.25 mm (.010'')
2 - Main drive shaft front, bearing surface for 3rd gear needle bearing	run-out	max. 0.015 mm (.0005'')	
3 - Bushes for gearshift housing	inside dia.	min. 15.015 mm (.5911'')	15.250 mm (.6004'')

		Tolerances (new parts)	Wear limit
4 - Inner shift lever	diameter	15.000 – 14.957 mm (.5906 – .5889")	14.750 mm (.5807")
5 - Final drive cover preload on differential bearing		0.10 – 0.18 mm (.004 – .007")	
6 - Rear axle shafts:			
a) Flat end/fulcrum plates/ differential side gear (4 parts)	clearance	0.035 – 0.244 mm (.0013 – .0096")	0.30 mm (.011")
b) Flat end/differential gear (measured at convex ends)	clearance	0.03 – 0.10 mm (.0011 – .004")	0.15 mm (.006")
7 - Plastic packing/housing/rear axle tube/axle cover	clearance	from 0 to 0.2 mm (.008")	0.4 mm (.015")
8 - Starter shaft bush	inside dia.	12.525 – 12.550 mm (.492 – .493")	12.65 mm (.497")
9 - Starter shaft/bush	clearance	0.085 – 0.140 mm (.0033 – .0055")	0.25 mm (.010")
10 - 1st speed gear	end play	0.10 – 0.25 mm (.004 – .010")	
11 - Selector fork/sleeve for 1st—4th gear.	end play	0.10 – 0.30 mm (.004 – .012")	
12 - Synchronizer rings/gears between teeth faces	clearance	1.1 mm (.043")	min. 0.60 mm (.024")

Brakes and Wheels

		Tolerances (new parts)	Wear limit
1 - Master cylinder	diameter	22.2 mm	
Piston push rod, measured from tip to nut	length	61 – 62 mm (2.40 – 2.44")	
2 - Wheel cylinder: front	diameter	25.4 mm (1.00")	
rear	diameter	22.2 mm (.874")	
3 - Brake drums	lateral run-out	max. 0.25 mm (.010")	0.35 mm (.014")
measured at friction surface	front radial run-out	max. 0.25 mm (.010")	0.25 mm (.010")
	rear out-of-round	max. 0.1 mm (.004")	
front	wall thickness	6.4 – 6.0 mm (.257 – .236")	5.4 mm (.21")
rear	wall thickness	6.5 – 6.15 mm (.255 – .240")	5.5 mm (.216')
front	inside diameter	230.2 + 0.3 mm (9.062 + .012")	231.7 mm (9.121")
rear	inside diameter	230.0 + 0.2 mm (9.055 + .008")	231.5 mm (9.114")
	taper	max. 0.1 mm (.004")	
4 - Brake linings	thickness	5.0 – 4.8 mm (.2 – .18")	2.5 mm (.09")
Brake lining, front	width	50 mm (1.96")	
rear	width	40 mm (1.57")	
Oversize	thickness	5.5 – 5.3 mm (.21 – .20")	3.0 mm (.12")
5 - Wheel disc	radial run-out	max. 1.5 mm (.06")	
	lateral run-out	max. 1.5 mm (.06")	
6 - Rear wheel track (with vehicle unloaded)	toe-out	0.5 – 4 mm (.020 – .16")	

List of Tolerances and Wear Limits
Type 2 — 1500

General

The term Wear Limit is used to indicate that parts which are approaching, or have already reached, the value given should not be re-used when carrying out an overhaul. When assessing the wear limit of pistons and cylinders, the oil consumption of the engine concerned should be taken into account.

		Tolerances (new parts)	Wear limit
Engine 1493 cc (91.09 cu. ins.) — 42 bhp. (50 SAE bhp.)			
1 - Cylinder seating depth in cylinder head		11.75—11.85 mm (.462—.466″)	
2 - Cylinder	out of round	0.01 mm (.0004″)	
3 - Piston/Cylinder	clearance	0.035—0.060 mm (.0013—.0023″)	0.20 mm (.008″)
4 - a) Upper compression ring	side clearance	0.08—0.107 mm (.0031—.0041″)	0.12 mm (.0047″)
b) Lower compression ring	side clearance	0.045—0.072 mm (.0017—.0028″)	0.10 mm (.004″)
5 - Oil control ring	side clearance	0.025—0.052 mm (.0009—.0020″)	0.10 mm (.004″)
6 - Compression rings	gap	0.30—0.45 mm (.012—.017″)	0.95 mm (.037″)
Oil control	gap	0.25—0.40 mm (.009—.016″)	0.95 mm (.037″)
7 - Weight tolerance of pistons in one engine		max. 5 g	max. 10 g*
8 - Weight tolerance of connecting rods in one engine		max. 4 g	max. 10 g*
9 - Piston pin/connecting rod bush	clearance	0.003—0.016 mm (.0001—.0006″)	0.04 mm (.0015″)
10 - Crank pin/connecting rod	radial clearance	0.016—0.074 mm (.0006—.0029″)	0.15 mm (.006″)
	side clearance	0.1—0.4 mm (.004—.016″)	0.70 mm (.0275″)
11 - Crankshaft/main bearings (taking housing pre-load into account):			
a) Bearings 1—3	clearance	0.046—0.104 mm (.0018—.004″)	0.18 mm (.007″)
b) Bearing 4	clearance	0.047—0.102 mm (.0018—.0039″)	0.19 mm (.0074″)
c) Steel bearings 1—3 (cold countries only)	clearance	0.043—0.105 mm (.0016—.004″)	0.18 mm (.007″)
12 - Crankshaft at No. 2 and 4 bearings (Nos. 1 and 3 on V-blocks)	run-out		0.02 mm (.0007″)
13 - Crankshaft/No. 1 main bearing	end play	0.065—0.125 mm (.0026—.0049″)	0.15 mm (.006″)
14 - Crankshaft	out of balance	max. 8 cmg (.11 oz. in.)	

* During repair

		Tolerances (new parts)	Wear limit
15 - Main bearing journal	out of round		0.03 mm (.0011")
16 - Crank pins	out of round		0.03 mm (.0011")
17 - Crankshaft bore in crankcase			
a) Bearings 1 to 3	dia.	65.000 – 65.019 mm (2.5590 – 2.5597")	
b) Bearing 4	dia.	50.000 – 50.025 mm (1.9685 – 1.9695")	
c) Oil seal seat	dia.	90.000 – 90.045 mm (3.5433 – 3.5450")	
18 - Belt pulley	radial run-out	max. 0.8 mm (.030")	
	lateral run-out	max. 0.3 mm (.012")	
19 - Camshaft bore in crankcase	dia.	25.020 – 25.041 mm (.9850 – .9858")	25.070 mm (.9870")
20 - Camshaft	clearance	0.020 – 0.054 mm (.0008 – .0021")	0.12 mm (.005")
Thrust bearing	end play	0.060 – 0.114 mm (.0024 – .0044")	0.14 mm (.005")
Center bearing (between centers)	run-out	0.02 mm (0007")	0.04 mm (.0016")
21 - Camshaft gear	backlash	0.000 – 0.052 mm (.0020")	
22 - Flywheel (measured in center of friction surface)	run-out	0.30 mm (.012")	
	out of balance	max. 5 cmg (.07 oz. in.)	
Shoulder	outside dia.	69.9 – 70.1 mm (2.75 – 2.76")	69.70 mm (2.744")
Machining of tooth width			max. 2 mm
23 - Valve stem: inlet	dia.	7.95 – 7.94 mm (.3130 – .3126")	7.90 mm (.3110")
exhaust	dia.	7.92 – 7.91 mm (.3118 – .3114")	7.87 mm (.3098")
	out of round	0.01 mm (.004")	
24 - Valve head: inlet	dia.	31.5 mm (1.239")	
exhaust	dia.	30.0 mm (1.181")	
25 - Valve guides: inlet	internal dia.	8.000 – 8.015 mm (.315 – .3156")	8.060 mm (.3173")
exhaust	internal dia.	8.000 – 8.020 mm (.315 – .3157")	8.080 mm (.318")
26 - Valve guide/valve stem:			
inlet	clearance	0.050 – 0.080 mm (.0020 – .0031")	0.16 mm (.006")
exhaust	clearance	0.080 – 0.110 mm (.0031 – .0043")	0.16 mm (.006")
27 - Valve seats			
a) Inlet	width	1.3 – 1.6 mm (.051 – .063")	
b) Exhaust	width	1.7 – 2.0 mm (.067 – .079")	
c) Valve seating face	run-out	0.015 mm (.0006")	
28 - Valve springs			
Loaded length 33.4 mm (1.314")	load	95 ± 6 lbs (43.5 ± 3 kg)	40.0 kg (88 lbs)

		Tolerances (new parts)	Wear limit
29 - Valve clearance (up to a maximum oil temperature of 50° C (122° F) inlet and exhaust	setting	0.30 mm (.012")	
30 - a) Rocker arms	internal dia.	18.000–18.018 mm (.7086–.7093")	18.035 mm (.7100")
b) Rocker shaft	dia.	17.984–17.966 mm (.7080–.7073")	17.955 mm (.7068")
c) Rocker arm/shaft	clearance	0.016–0.052 mm (.0006–.0020")	0.080 mm (.0031")
31 - a) Cam follower bore in crankcase	dia.	19.000–19.021 mm (.7480–.7489")	19.060 mm (.7504")
b) Cam follower	dia.	18.980–18.959 mm (.7472–.7464")	18.800 mm (.7400")
c) Crankcase bore/cam follower	clearance	0.020–0.062 mm (.0008–.0024")	0.120 mm (.0047")
32 - Compression pressure (with engine warm, throttle open, all plugs out and engine turned by starter)	pressure	9–10 kg/sq. cm (128–142 psi.)	7.0 kg/sq. cm 100 psi.
33 - Oil pump: gears/housing with gasket (measured without pressure)	end play	0.066–0.183 mm (.0026–.0072")	0.20 mm (.008")
Gears/housing, without gasket	end play		0.10 mm (.0039")
Gears	backlash	0.03–0.08 mm (.0012–.0031")	
34 - Oil pressure (SAE 10 W-30 oil only) with an oil temperature of 70° C (158° F) a) At 550 rpm.		min. 0.5 kg/sq. cm (7 psi.)	
b) At 2500 rpm.		min. 2.0 kg/sq. cm (28 lbs/sq. in.)	
35 - Pressure relief valve spring Length loaded: 23.6 mm	load	7.75 kg (17 lbs)	
36 - Oil pressure switch opens at	pressure	0.15–0.45 kg/sq. cm (2.1–6.4 psi.)	
37 - Distance from fan housing to upper edge of throttle ring a) with engine cold	setting	20 mm (.8")	
b) with engine warm	setting	25–30 mm (1–1.2")	
38 - Thermostat: after a water bath at 65—70° C (149—158° F)	pressure unit length	min. 46 mm (1.811")	

Clutch as on 1200 Transporter

Front Axle as on 1200 Transporter

Rear Axle and **Transmission** as on 1200 Transporter

Brakes and Wheels

1 - Master cylinder	dia.	20.64 mm (.812")	
Piston push rod, measured from tip to nut	length	61–62 mm (2.40–2.44")	
2 - Wheel cylinders: front	dia.	25.40 mm (1.00")	
rear	dia.	22.20 mm (.874")	

		Tolerances (new parts)	Wear limit
3 - Brake drums: front and rear	inside dia.	250.0+0.2 mm (9.842+.008'')	251.5 mm (1.043'')
front and rear	wall thickness	6.50—6.15 mm (.255—.246'')	5.5 mm (.216'')
Turning size for oversize brake linings			
front and rear	inside dia.	251+0.2 mm (9.882'')	
	lateral run-out	max. 0.25 mm (0.10'')	max. 0.35 mm (.014'')
	taper		max. 0.1 mm (.004'')
Measured at friction surface	radial run-out	max. 0.1 mm (.004'')	
4 - Brake linings	thickness	5.0—4.8 mm (.18'')	2.5 mm (.09'')
Oversize	thickness	5.5—5.3 mm (.21—.20'')	3.0 mm (.12'')
Front	width	55 mm (2.16'')	
Rear	width	45 mm (1.77'')	
5 - Wheel disc	radial run-out	max. 1.5 mm (.060')	
	lateral run-out	max. 1.5 mm (.060'')	
6 - Rear wheel track (with spring plate settings correct and vehicle unladen)	toe-out	0.5—4.0 mm (.020—.16'')	
7 - Spring plates, unloaded	setting	20° ± 30'	
Model 27	setting	25° ± 20'	
Model 211, M 140	setting	21° 30' ± 20'	

TECHNICAL DATA FOR 1600cc SERIES (1968 & ON)
VOLKSWAGEN TRUCK & STATION WAGON

Engine

Type	Four-cylinder; horizontally opposed, overhead-valve, four-stroke rear engine
Measurements	
Bore	3.36 inches
Stroke	2.72 inches
Displacement	96.66 cubic inches (1,584 cc.)
Compression ratio	7.7 to 1
Maximum SAE hp.	57 at 4,400 r.p.m.
Maximum SAE torque	81.7 lb. ft. at 3,000 r.p.m.
Oil capacity	2.5 quarts
Cooling	Air cooling; belt driven blower
Battery	12 volts

Gearbox

Four forward speeds, one reverse

Four forward speeds synchronized

Gear ratios	1st gear 3.80 : 1
	2nd gear 2.06 : 1
	3rd gear 1.26 : 1
	4th gear 0.82 : 1
	Reverse 3.61 : 1

Final Drive

Power is transmitted through a spiral bevel gear via two double-jointed axles to rear wheels.

Final drive ratio	5.375 : 1

Chassis

Suspension, front	Torsion bars
Suspension, rear	Torsion bars
Shock absorbers	Double acting telescopic type, front and rear
Turn circle diameter	Approximately 40 feet
Tires	Tubeless, 7.00 x 14
Wheelbase	94.5 inches
Track	Front: 54.5 inches
	Rear: 56.1 inches

Dimensions and Weights	Station Wagon	Panel Truck	Pickup Truck	Double Cab Pickup
Length (inches)	174.0	174.0	174.0	174.0
Width (inches)	69.5	69.5	69.5	69.5
Height (inches)	77.0	77.0	77.0	77.0
Ground clearance, loaded (inches)	7.3	7.3	7.3	7.3
Curb weight (pounds)	2,833	2,425	2,425	2,535
Maximum payload (pounds)	1,962	2,370	2,370	2,250
Gas-tank capacity (gallons)	15.9	15.9	15.9	15.9

Performance

Overall fuel consumption   Station Wagon, Panel, Kombi and Pickups (latter without bows and tarpaulin) 22.6 m.p.g.; Pickups with bows and tarpaulin, 22 m.p.g.

Maximum and Cruising Speed   65 m.p.h. (Pickups with bows and tarpaulin, 59 m.p.h.

Brakes

Foot brake   Hydraulic; drum; four-wheel; dual system

Hand brake   Mechanical, operating on rear wheels

www.ingramcontent.com/pod-product-compliance
Lightning Source LLC
Chambersburg PA
CBHW050418170426
43201CB00008B/448